The McGillivray and McIntosh Traders

The McGillivray

and

McIntosh Traders

ON THE OLD SOUTHWEST FRONTIER, 1716-1815

AMOS J. WRIGHT, JR.

Foreword by Vernon J. Knight

NewSouth Books

Montgomery

NewSouth Books

P.O. Box 1588

Montgomery, AL 36102

Design by Randall Williams
Printed in the United States of America

To my dear wife

CAROLYN SHORES WRIGHT

CONTENTS

Preface

This book was some twenty years in the making. Research and data collection is a slow and tedious process since many primary sources are not indexed and one has to just read the old colonial script to find pertinent information. However, in some regards, this can be the most rewarding part of the manuscript development.

The book deals with and expands on the McGillivray family members, including the McIntoshes, who were involved in the Indian trade, and not previously dealt with. The scene is primarily the old southwest, especially present-day Alabama, Mississippi and West Florida.

Many questions have been left hanging and unresolved over the years by previous writers, and many are addressed in this work, but not all are resolved. Was Alexander McGillivray, the Creek Chief, poisoned by the Spanish as rumored in the Creek Nation after his death? What about the identification and fate of the Indian families left behind by the McGillivray traders?

Virtually nothing was known of Jeanette McGillivray, the Creek Indian daughter of Lachlan Lia McGillivray. Now we know that she remained in Alabama after her husband LeClerc Milford deserted her. After his return to France, she soon married Ben Crook, a trader residing at Little Tallasee, the old McGillivray homeplace. The fate of Alexander, Jr., the only son of the Creek chief, who was sent to Scotland in about 1798 to be educated, has been uncovered in the parish records. The Dr.

Wells that treated him for tuberculosis in London has been identified and his biography developed. Lachlan Lia's will of 1767 has been found in the Fraser-Mackintosh Collection of the Inverness Public Library, along with an extract of his last will made in 1795 after his return to Scotland. The children of John McGillivray among the Chickasaw, and the children of James McGillivray among the Choctaw have been identified and reported on. An exhaustive search has been made for the elusive Colonel John Tate, supposedly the husband of Sehoy McGillivray. New information on John McGillivray's plantation in Jamaica has been included.

In developing the manuscript, I frequently quote from my sources trying to avoid paraphrasing the original text. Paraphrasing may lead to erroneous interpretation and mislead the reader. I have let the record "speak" for itself and consequently the text may not be as smooth as desired. I have also included dates and some references in the text in order to avoid the maddening process of continually flipping pages trying to find a date or reference in the endnotes at the back of the book. Also, the manuscript is generally in chronological order.

The reader will note that family names and their relation to other family members are often repeated throughout the text. Due to the same given names among family members, this was necessary in order for the reader to be sure which person is being referred to in the text.

There is also considerable genealogical data that may interest readers, especially the lesser known McGillivrays, along with the identification of their Indian descendants.

A.J.W.

Acknowledgments

During the many years of collecting material for this book, I have become indebted to the many friendly people who have generously assisted me at various libraries, archives, and depositories. Their patience and professional help is greatly appreciated.

Special thanks must go to Dr. Vernon J. Knight of the University of Alabama for his helpful review and comments on the manuscript. My son, A. J. Wright III of the University of Alabama in Birmingham has also been supportive and helpful with his comments.

Also, I wish to thank Dr. William S. Coker of the University of West Florida, now retired, for his most generous offer in allowing me to spend two days browsing through his early collection of the Panton, Leslie & Co. papers. Dr. W. W. Wallace of Mobile has been supportive in furnishing me information on Sophia McGillivray and her descendants.

Special recognition must go to the professional researchers and genealogists that I engaged to search the almost limitless depositories in Scotland and England. Their many hours of poring over the records of Colonial America have brought forth new information of substantial benefit to this work. Graeme M. Mackenzie of Edinburgh searched the archives of the Inverness Public Library, National Library of Scotland, Scottish Public Record Office, and the Public Record Office at Kew. Mackenzie also visited the Mains of Dunmaglass and the McGillivray Cemetery at Dunlichity. Peter B. Ferguson of East Sussex searched the

Society of Genealogists Library, Greater London Record Office, Surrey Record Office at Kingston, and the Public Record Office at Kew attempting to locate some information on Alexander McGillivray Jr. who died in 1802. Thanks to John F. H. Dagger of Kent for his research of the War Office records at the Public Record Office at Kew. His search of muster rolls of the 14th, 16th, 22nd, 34th, 35th and 60th regiments stationed in West Florida at various times, trying to locate the elusive Colonel John Tate. Dagger was also instrumental in locating the burial of Alexander McGillivray Jr. in the parish registers.

I want to thank my dear wife, Carolyn Shores Wright, and my youngest son, Richard A. Wright of Mobile, for their continuous encouragement and support. Without their frequent questions of "How is your book coming?" or "When are you going to finish your book?" this book may never have been completed.

I also want to thank Nan Hall of Huntsville for her enduring patience and advice in converting my handwriting to computer files.

Last I want to thank the following people, and the staff of the following libraries and archives, without whose help I could never have completed this book:

Edwin Bridges and his staff at the Alabama Department of Archives and History, Montgomery; Yvonne Crumpler and her staff at the Linn-Henley Research Library, Birmingham; Shirley L. Hutchens, Samford University Library, Birmingham; Marion G. McGuinn, Reynolds Historical Library, Birmingham; Leora M. Sutton, Pensacola; and Elizabeth Wells, Samford University Library, Birmingham.

Also, Clan Chattan Association, Edinburgh; East Surrey Family History Society, Surrey; Forres Public Library, Forres; Greater London Record Office, London; Highland Family History Society, Inverness; Inverness Public Library, Inverness; Island Record Office, Spanish Town; Jamaica Archives, Spanish Town; Jamaica Library Services, Kingston; Moray District Council Libraries, Moray; National Library of Jamaica, Kingston; National Library of Scotland, Edinburgh; Public Archives of Canada, Ottawa; Public Record Office, Kew; Scots Ancestry Research Society, Edinburgh; Scottish Public Record Office, Edinburgh; Society of Genealogists Library, London; Surrey Local History Council, Surrey; Surrey Record Office, Kingston.

Also, Alabama Land Office, Montgomery; Archives of the Church of Latter Day Saints, Salt Lake City; Archives of the Georgia Surveyor General, Atlanta; Augusta Public Library, Augusta; Bureau of Land Management, Springfield, Virginia; Candler Library of Theology, Atlanta; Charleston County Probate Office, Charleston; Charleston Library Society Library, Charleston; Charlotte Public Library, Charlotte; Emory University Library, Atlanta; Escambia County Archives, Pensacola; Georgia Historical Society, Savannah; Georgia Department of Archives and History, Atlanta; Greenville Public Library, Greenville, South Carolina; Huntsville Public Library, Huntsville; John C. Pace Library, University of West Florida, Pensacola; Library of Congress, Washington; Massachusetts Historical Society, Boston; McClung Library, Knoxville; Mercer University Library, Macon, Georgia; Mobile Public Library, Mobile; Moravian Archives, Winston-Salem; National Archives, Atlanta; National Archives, Washington; National Genealogical Society Library, Arlington, Virginia; Noxubee County Probate Office, Macon, Mississippi; Oklahoma Historical Society, Oklahoma City; Pensacola Historical Society, Pensacola; Pickens County Probate Office, Carrolton, Alabama; Presbyterian Archives, Montreat, North Carolina; Sandor Teszler Library, Wofford University, Spartanburg; Savannah Public Library, Savannah; South Carolina Department of Archives and History, Columbia; South Carolina Historical Society, Charleston; South Carolinian Library, Columbia; Thomas Gilcrease Institute of American History and Arts, Tulsa; University of Alabama Library, Tuscaloosa; Washington Public Library, Macon, Georgia; and William L. Clements Library, Ann Arbor.

A.J.W.

Foreword

During the eighteenth century, much of present-day Alabama and Georgia was a contested frontier, lying just beyond the reach of colonies belonging to England, France, and Spain. As these colonies vied for dominance among each other, the native inhabitants of that frontier, the Creeks, struggled to maintain their independence, while at the same time Creek men increasingly engaged in international commerce. Deer skins, destined for overseas leather goods markets, were procured in massive quantities by the Creeks and exchanged for guns, gunpowder, ammunition, iron hoes and axes, cloth, blankets, kettles, paint, glass beads, scissors, and other necessities and luxuries of European origin. By degrees, as the European and eventually American powers shifted positions around the frontier, Creek ways of life inevitably changed. The eighteenth century had begun with the English colonists prodding the Creeks to take up arms against neighboring tribes, both to procure slaves to work English plantations and to block the efforts of their colonial rivals. The century ended, in contrast, with concerted efforts by American agents to civilize the Creeks, which meant introducing modern plows, cattle and oxen, spinning wheels and looms.

The study of this important phase in the history of the old South by scholars who have sought to understand its events has proven to be a daunting task. The historian is challenged by only barely commensurate sources in French, Spanish, British, and American archives, revealing a multiplicity of perspectives and interests, and this challenge is made more difficult still by the fact that the focus of interest, the frontier, was itself at the feather edge of the literate world. Add to this the clash of New World and Old World cultures, where the anthropologist's sensitivities prove to be of value, and the subject reveals itself to us as one that is reluctant to yield up its secrets, despite the efforts of generations of scholars. This subject is, besides, a moving target, with radically shifting contexts of politics, economics, leadership, war, and peace.

We have some fascinating vignettes. James Adair, an English trader caught up in the middle of these events, wrote a detailed history which shows an unusual interest in, and sensitivity to, the natives' way of life. We are indeed fortunate that anyone with literary interests was there to place these matters on record, in spite of the book's bizarre thesis that the key to Indian origins in America lay in the historical wanderings of the Lost Tribes of Israel. Then there was William Bartram, botanist, writer, and adventurer, the Homer of the eighteenth-century frontier. Bartram left an account of the Creek country which is a wonderfully fresh and almost poetic blend of romantic literature and scientific observation. Somewhat lesser known is the little book by Louis LeClerc de Milford, an amazing autobiography of a young French soldier who came to America, wandered alone into the frontier fearing cannibals. He was befriended by Alexander McGillivray and the Creeks, and rose to the rank of war chief among them. Later he returned to France where he attempted to convince Napoleon of the importance of the Creeks and their Nation. Milford's epic story is remarkably parallel to that of the modern film *Dances with Wolves*, except, of course, that it is true.

But none of these writers were truly pivotal players in the drama that was unfolding around them. The present volume, in contrast, centers on two persons who very much were at the center of events on the eighteenth-century Creek frontier. They are Laughlin McGillivray and his Indian son Alexander McGillivray. To understand the lives and careers of these two men is to focus attention on both sides of the Native American–European equation in its formative years.

As the following pages show, Laughlin Lia McGillivray was a

Scottish-born Indian trader in a family of traders based in colonial South Carolina. With his success in exploiting and expanding the deer skin trade, he was perhaps the prototypical merchant in the deer skin business that so altered native Creek society during the middle years of the eighteenth century. He lived a double life. In the wilderness of the Creek country, he was so well-positioned in the trade that he took as a wife Sehoy, native matriarch of the dominant Wind clan, by whom his son Alexander was born. But in urban South Carolina he was seemingly another person, a successful businessman, who gradually assumed the role of landed gentry, and who consequently abandoned and essentially forgot his progeny in the Indian country. A Loyalist during the American Revolution, he lost much of his property to the Rebel Americans and retired to a family estate in Scotland.

Laughlin's son Alexander became the most important leader the Creeks ever knew. He was educated in Charleston but soon returned to his mother's people, where, after a time, he proved himself a formidable diplomat. As the occasion demanded, he might be seen in British, Spanish, American, or Native dress in order to negotiate agreements favorable to the Creeks. Respected as *Isti Atcagagi Thlocco* (Great Beloved Man), he used his authority to protect the interests of his people, particularly against land encroachment and the threat of foreign invasion. He was, in a sense, born to play this role.

Historians and anthropologists have emphasized that Alexander McGillivray's influence among the Creeks was primarily the product of his unique skills as a "culture broker," equally at ease in the Native and Western worlds. His vision was certainly broader than other, contemporary Creek leaders, and more outward-looking. And it appears to be true that he did not even have a good command of the native languages, and that he frequently made use of an interpreter. Nonetheless, there is no doubt that Alexander identified himself as a Creek Indian, and as the leader and spokesman for the Creek Nation in a time of turmoil and confusion. But there is much more to the picture than that. Prior to McGillivray's time the Creek Confederacy as a political entity was in its infancy, a recent, ephemeral reaction of allied towns to outside aggression. McGillivray did his best to transform this into a real, permanent government. He was personally responsible for making the National Council and its officers a standing institution. In the writer's opinion, the rise to power of Alexander McGillivray, a literate trader's son, among this highly conservative native people is the singular, pivotal fact most in need of understanding in the context of the Creek frontier in the last quarter of the eighteenth century.

In this volume Amos J. Wright Jr. compiles and presents the source materials relating to the lives and careers of Laughlin McGillivray and Alexander McGillivray, plus those documentary materials concerning all of their close relatives and their close associates. The volume represents twenty years of meticulous detective work in the collection of reference material, during which the author has ferreted out details previously unknown, has clarified some of the problems raised by previous research, and has righted several current misconceptions. There is much here that is of genealogical interest, bearing on such matters as the relationship between the McGillivray and McIntosh clans in Scotland, and the fate of Alexander McGillivray's son who was sent to Scotland after the death of his father. It is very revealing that the boy's grandfather, Laughlin, who was still living, neither welcomed nor supported his native-born grandson and would-be heir. Among the many conclusions and carefully weighed opinions offered in these pages, the author has included a consideration of Alexander's cause of death, as he was rumored to have been poisoned by a Spaniard. Mr. Wright has consulted medical specialists on the matter of McGillivray's reported symptoms, and he discusses several possible scenarios that may be compatible with the extant evidence.

Publication of these source materials is sure to further our scholarly understanding of these fascinating individuals who were born into fascinating times.

Vernon James Knight
Department of Anthropology
University of Alabama

The McGillivray and McIntosh Traders

ABBREVIATIONS

ASA	Alabama Department of Archives and History
ASP	American State Papers
BFS	British, French and Spanish Records, Alabama Secretary of State
CCC	Charleston County Courthouse
CCJ	Clan Chattan Journal
ETHS	East Tennessee Historical Society
FMC	Fraser-Mackintosh Collection
GHQ	Georgia Historical Quarterly
GSA	Georgia Department of Archives and History
HR	House of Representatives
HRRS	Highland Roots Research Services
IPL	Inverness Public Library
JA	Jamaica Archives
JCTP	Journals of the Commissioners for Trade and Plantations
MH	Missionary Herald
MMA	Mobile Municipal Archives
MPC	Mobile Probate Court
NA	National Archives
NLS	National Library of Scotland
PAC	Public Archives of Canada
PRO	Public Record Office
SCA	South Carolina Department of Archives and History
SCHGM	South Carolina Historical and Genealogical Magazine
SCHM	South Carolina Historical Magazine
SCHS	South Carolina Historical Society
SRO	Scottish Public Record Office
WLCL	William L. Clements Library

1

McGillivrays of Scotland and Early South Carolina

The Scots are a complicated race being composed of Picts, Gaels, Britons, Angles, Normans, Flemings, and Franks. The original Scots were Gaels being a mixture of Celt and Teuton.

The concept of clanship goes back to the Celtic world particularly from ancient Ireland, where each community was a little kingdom within itself. However, the word "Chief" comes from the Norman-French and was introduced into Scotland by the Normans.

The word "clan" means children and originally each clan was made up only of the descendants. There was little emigration and the chief, being the head of the family and all his clansmen, was obligated to provide a parcel of land to each member of the clan. Generation after generation led to smaller and smaller parcels going to the most distant relative. The chief's influence extended to all branches of his family, including those settled outside of the clan territory. He cared for the sick; both the invalid and widowed received small pensions.

The tradition of tartans and bagpipes has played, and continues to play, a very important role in the Scottish culture. The tartan and bagpipe appear as early as the 16th century. Dancing and music play an important part in their tradition.

After the 1715 uprising, the government felt the power of the Highlanders. Accordingly, forts and blockhouses, properly garrisoned, were built throughout the Highlands. Officially the Highlanders were disarmed, but they concealed their weapons to fight another day.

The Highlanders were crushed at the battle of Culloden and the courts abolished the legal power of the chiefs in 1747. The Scots were banned from wearing the kilt and using the bagpipe. After the suppression of the clans, a population explosion took place bringing on unprecedented hardship. Scotland was originally a forested land, but during this period it was almost denuded. Emigration solved only part of the population problem and the chiefs struggled just to feed their families. At first chiefs discouraged emigration, but eventually many chiefs joined this movement and sometimes the whole family emigrated. Times were so hard that young men were forbidden to marry until they had a house and could support a family.

In relief of these hardships, many Highlanders were recruited into the army where they served throughout the world. Between 1757 and 1762 nine new Highland regiments were raised.

Inter-clan feelings remained alienated and bitter at the end of the 18th century, but Sir Walter Scott changed all that. His writings of the Highlands were poetic and romantic, taking the meanness out of the old feuds. The warring clans turned to fun and games which continue today.

The McGillivrays were a prominent clan family from the Valley of Nairn just southwest of Inverness, the highland capital of Scotland. They were part of Clan Chattan, a confederation of clans in the valley of Loch Ness or Nairn. The original clan members were descendants of a 13th century chief called Gillechattan Mor, and as other clans settled nearby, they too would join the confederation. Clan Chattan eventually consisted of the McIntosh, Farquhaurson, Shaw, McThomas, McPherson, Cattanachs, McGillivray, McLean, McBain, McQueen, Davidson, McPhail, McAndrew, Gow, Clark, McIntyre, Crerar, Gillespie, Gillies, Noble, Ritchie, McHardy, and Mckilligin. The confederation was led by a high chief called the Captain of Clan Chattan, usually a McIntosh.[1]

In 1609 the clan chiefs met and signed a "Bond of Union" putting an end to warfare among themselves and making a stronger clan for resistance to any outside foe.

They met in order to put an end to their quarrels—to sign an agreement whereby they bound themselves to live in friendship, to stand by each other and to maintain and follow the Mackintosh as their captain and chief.[2]

The McGillivrays united very early with the McIntosh. According to the Farr manuscript, "Gilvray the first of this family and of whom the clan McGillivray took protection and shelter from Fargurar the 5th Laird of MacIntosh, in about the year 1263 during the Reign of King Alexander the third." The lands of Dunmaglass were obtained from Calder in 1547 and became the homeplace of the McGillivrays. They were the oldest followers of the McIntoshes and Clan Chattan.[3]

A slightly different account comes from the Gaelic Society[4] where Clan Chattan was originally made up of nine families of Mackintosh. The MacGillivrays were the first and oldest to be incorporated into the clan with a name other than McIntosh. The McGillivrays came from the southwest and settled in the Valley of Nairn long before they appeared in written history. Half of Dummaglass originally belonged to Thanes of Kalder and is first mentioned in 1414. The other half belonged to the Menzies family of Aberdeenshire.

Donald Calder bargained for and won possession for the Menzies half in 1421. The McGillivrays seem to be in possession of Dunmaglass as early as 1547 with the first chief being Farquhar. By 1609, when the bond of union was signed by the members of Clan Chattan, the McGillivrays were already numerous and influential. Dunmaglass had passed from the family of Calder to the McGillivrays for five thousand merks which was equivalent to about 275 pounds. Dunmaglass was the first of many estates belonging to the McGillivrays with some seventeen thousand acres distributed among several estates.[5] The old homeplace was built at Dunmaglass in about 1690 and was located on the eastern side of the River Farigaig some one hundred yards northwest of the Mains of Dunmaglass. The property was sold in 1895 or 1896 to an "English gentleman" who promptly leveled the old house. Today only a few stones can be found on the site. A pen and ink drawing of the house made in about 1850 turned up with the descendants in Canada, but the best description comes from the Ordnance Survey in 1870—"A very large farmhouse two stories high with outbuildings attached. The former entirely thatched and the latter quite new and slated, the whole in good repair."[6]

A large body of McGillivrays from early times lived on the south end of the Isle of Mull near present day Pennyghael which is located at the western entrance to Loch Ness. These McGillivrays never joined Clan Chattan nor followed any of their chiefs, but they may have been the original migrants to the Valley of Nairn.[7]

The McGillivray genealogy we are interested in starts with Farquhar, "Feadhaiche," McGillivray who was the 6th chief. He married Emelia Stewart in 1681 and died in 1714. This union resulted in six children— Farquhar the eldest who became the 7th chief when his father died in 1714; Anna who married Fraser of Farraline; Magdelene who married McIntosh of Holm; David who married Margaret McGillivray; Janet who married Donald McGillivray; and Captain William "Ban" who married Janet McIntosh. The descendants of Farquhar and Captain Ban are the primary concern of this work.[8]

THE STUART rebellion of 1715 found many of the McGillivrays taking part and Captain Ban was a captain in the Clan Chattan regiment. He may have lived at Tomnashangan or Fairy's Hill.[9] A story of his encounter with the fairies has descended into modern times. Captain Ban was also extensively involved in the cattle business in the valley of River Nairn.[10] Fairy's Hill was located at the House of Daviot which is only about five miles southeast of Inverness. Dun Daviot today is just a woodland hill slowly being eaten away by a quarry.[11]

Captain Farquhar McGillivray, the 7th chief and elder brother to Captain Ban, was also a captain in the Clan Chattan regiment during the rebellion. After the Highlanders surrendered at Preston in November 1715, he and some fellow officers were taken to London for trial. He was brought to trial for high treason on 11 June 1716, but due to an error in his indictment he was released. In 1717 he married Elizabeth McIntosh and they had four sons and four daughters. The daughters were Janet,

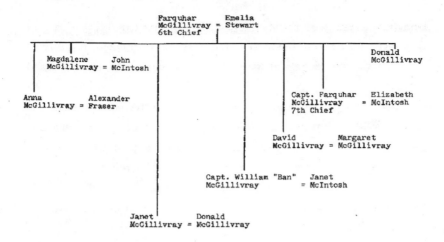

Family of Farquhar McGillivray 6th Chief and Emelia Stewart

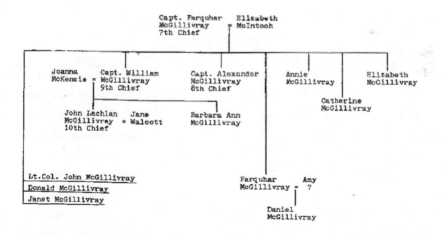

Family of Capt. Farquhar McGillivray 7th Chief and Elizabeth McIntosh

Ann, Catherine, and Elizabeth—all died unmarried. His eldest son Alexander, his heir and the 8th chief, died in 1746 leading the charge of the Clan Chattan regiment at the Battle of Culloden. He possessed several estates including Dunmaglass, but lived at Gask, a house used by his father and grandfather, and located in a more fertile area of the valley.[12] William, the second son, succeeded his brother Alexander as the 9th chief in 1746. He eventually came to America. John, the third son, also came to America where he was a successful merchant and Indian trader. He became a lieutenant colonel in the West Florida militia during the American Revolution. Donald, the youngest son, became a merchant seaman and died unmarried in 1777. [13]

Captain William Ban was the second son of Farquhar and therefore not the first in line to inherit the Clan Chieftainship. He was called Captain "Ban" due to his fair complexion. He married his cousin Janet McIntosh, the daughter of Angus McIntosh of Kyllachy, on 9 February 1714, probably just before his father died in the same year. They had four surviving children—Lachlan Lia, the eldest; William; Jean or Jean Roy; and Lucy. Lucy died in 1734, the same year as Captain Ban.[14]

CAPTAIN BAN was heavily involved with the Dalcromby family of Aberehalder in the cattle business. His inventory and testament at death was mostly a list of debts. He owed a large sum of outstanding rent to Dunmaglass and other sums to the Dalcrombies, plus smaller amounts to others. The original testament was written in 1734, at the time of his death, followed in 1755 by an additional claim on his estate by the Dalcrombies. Farquhar of Dalcromby had taken legal action against Lachlan Lia, as Captain Ban's oldest son, to recover the money owed to his family. The outcome is unknown. Lachlan by this time was a wealthy man and had the means of paying off his father's debts but for some reason seems to have defaulted.[15]

Under Scottish tradition Captain Ban would have named his oldest son Farquhar after his father and the next son Angus, after his wife's father. Lucy was named after his wife's mother and would probably be the eldest daughter; and the second daughter should be named Emilia

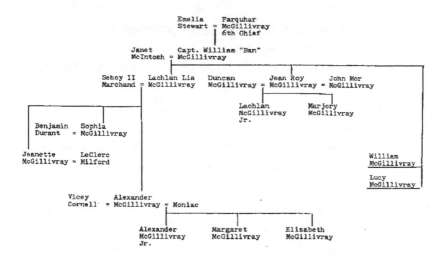

Family of Capt. William "Ban" McGillivray and Janet McIntosh

after his mother; and there should be a Janet named after his wife before other names such as Jean. Most likely there were children with those names that did not survive which was not unusual for that time. The name Lachlan is a family name from his mother's side—the McIntoshes of Kyllachy. Apparently Captain Ban's sons left no "legitimate" issue or they would have been in line to inherit Dunmaglass and the Chieftainship when John Lachlan, the 10th chief, died in 1852.[16]

After Alexander, the 8th chief, was killed in 1746 at the Battle of Culloden, the McGillivray estates were confiscated and the family was in desperate straits for the next decade. By 1750 however, it was safe for the family to take their case to court and try to reclaim their property. Their petition was successful and the estates were restored to the McGillivrays.[17]

The clan spirit and binding of the family were very important, and clan literally means "children." The children of each generation of the clan settled nearby and the clan grew from only the descendants. The clan chief was expected to furnish a parcel of land for each new member of the clan and look after the well being of all the members.[18] However, by the mid-18th century the clan as a recognizable legal entity had disappeared. The judiciary no longer recognized the clan system under the law, but the spiritual link of clanship continued and is thriving among Scots the world over today.[19]

After the rebellion of 1715, the Crown decided to send some of the Highland rebels being held prisoner to America to help settle the colonies.[20] Braden[21] wrote that many Highlanders also voluntarily emigrated to America in 1716 with another wave following in 1735-37. However, Macgillivray[22] wrote that the Scots coming over in 1716 were all prisoners and that the voluntary migration took place in 1722. Also, considerable numbers came after the failed rebellion of 1745-46.

Rebel prisoners sent to South Carolina in 1716 included several McGillivrays. The ship *Savannah* sailed on 7 May, 1716 with 104 prisoners including a Fargus and Donald McGillivray. The ship *Wakefield* sailed on 21 April 1716 with eighty-one prisoners which included "Laughlin, James, Owen, John, William, Alexander, Laughlin, John, John and James."[23] Another ship's list coming to South Carolina in 1716 includes "Fargus, Fargus, James, James, James, John, John, Loughlin, Loughlin, Loughlin, Owen, Owen, William, William and Alexander."[24] Many McGillivrays were in South Carolina by 1716 and with their many offspring and common given names, it is difficult to accurately trace individuals, and later writers have been confused by this problem.

One of the earliest arrivals in America was a John McGillivray who was also a trader out of South Carolina as early as 1716. He traded with the Creeks and should not be confused with the later John McGillivray who was a brother to William, the 9th chief, and a cousin to Lachlan Lia.[25] The early trader, John McGillivray, later appears in the records from a deed dated 20 October 1731, which read—"John Bayly, gentleman of Goose Creek[26] to William Penant and John McGillivray Indian traders of South Carolina, for 407 pounds South Carolina money, 407 acres on west side of Pon Pon River, St. Bartholomews Parish, Colleton County."[27]

On Easter Monday 1734, John McGillivray was chosen one of the vestry men by the parishioners of St. Helen Parish, South Carolina. He was chosen again in 1735.[28] In May 1734 he was granted a tract of land by the South Carolina Council.[29] In April 1736 he advertised for sale five hundred acres and a good house in Port Royal where he was living at the time.[30]

He seemed to have gotten his start as a messenger for the South Carolina Council in 1722.[31] He married Elizabeth Hazzard in April 1736 but he apparently died soon after and his will was probated 12 June 1736 identifying him as a planter in St. Helen Parish, Granville County.[32] He married in April, died in May or June, and his widow married Ephiaim Mekell in June.[33]

Another early McGillivray trader was William who first appears in the records as a packhorseman for Robert Graham in 1717. Graham was a leading trader to the Creeks out of Charleston and was assistant factor in 1718. William was first hired by Graham on 27 December 1717 to accompany John Milborne and two slaves with twenty-three packhorses to the Creek country. Actually only twenty-two packhorses made the trip as one died at pasture before they left. Graham also made the trip and led the party west to the newly established trading post at Tallassee probably on the east bank of the Coosa River in Talladega County, Alabama. The trade goods were valued at 986 pounds.[34]

Packhorsemen were paid from ten to twelve pounds per month and an allowance for expenses while in Charleston.[35] This was good pay for the times, but at fairly high risk. A thrifty person could save enough in a few years to form a partnership and start his own trading business.

The will of William was recorded on 4 July, 1741 indicating he probably died shortly prior to that date. He left all his lands to his sons Robert and Alexander who were still minors at this time. The remainder of his estate was to be divided among all his children—Robert, Alexander, Lucrecia, Elizabeth, Susannah, and Sophia. His wife Elizabeth had maintenance and lifetime residence at his plantation as long as she remained a widow.[36]

William and John McGillivray may have come over as early as 1711. They seem to have some experience before appearing in the records; however, no McGillivrays appeared on the South Carolina list of traders in 1711.[37] Both of these men later married and were successful plantation owners. Thus the pattern was set early—get into the trade, accumulate wealth and live your later years in comfort on a plantation as a landed gentleman.

This early trading post established among the upper Creeks was at Tallassee. When the McGillivrays established a trading post at Wetumpka Old Town on the Lower Coosa River, later known as Little Tallasee, it may have derived its name in this manner.[38]

The author has been unable to link this William and John to the later McGillivrays coming to South Carolina and Georgia, but most likely they were related. William and John, and later Archibald and Alexander, would be instrumental in establishing the family trade dynasty in the 1720s that the colonial agent Edmond Atkin so bitterly complained of some thirty years later. The McGillivrays were to be involved in the Creek trade for some one hundred years—starting with William and John from 1717 to 1735, joined by Archibald and Alexander in about 1725-30, and then Lachlan Lia in 1736. Later cousin John joined Lachlan Lia in about 1750 along with his brother Farquhar and even later cousins James, Lachlan, Finlay, and Daniel. The last of the traders was Daniel, son of Farquhar, who lived in the Creek country most of his life, dying sometime soon after 1812.

Alexander McGillivray was born in 1715 and went to South Carolina about 1730. He was the son of John McGillivray of East Dalcromby and Marjory McIntosh of Kinrara who were married in 1711. His younger half-brother, Archibald of Daviot, came to Georgia in 1736 and was the son of John of East Dalcromby and Janet McIntosh of Daviot who were married in 1719. They were both cousins to Captain Ban and also cousins to Lachlan Lia. Their father John died in 1733. Alexander married Anne Fraser of Balnain after his return to Scotland in 1745 and became the Laird of Knocknagael. He and his half-brother probably returned together. Alexander died in 1753.[39] His son John was a merchant in Guadaloupe and secretary to John Stuart, the Colonial Indian Agent at Pensacola.[40]

Archibald of Daviot came to Georgia with Lachlain and Farquhar arriving in 1736.[41] Some writers[42] have confused young Archibald of Daviot with the Archibald who was a leading trader when Archibald of Daviot arrived in Georgia. They are not one and the same.[43]

Little is known of young Archibald's activities in Georgia, but he returned to Scotland just in time to be caught up in the Jacobite rebellion where he served as a Lieutenant in the Mackintosh Regiment at the Battle of Culloden in 1746. He was one of the few officers to survive the massacre after the battle. His brother Robert was one of those killed. In 1747 he married Lucy McIntosh and they had four children—sons Lachlan, James, Alexander, and a daughter Janet. His son Lachlan was later the manager of John McGillivray's plantation in Jamaica. James was a prominent Indian trader to the Choctaw Country operating out of Mobile and Pensacola. Apparently son Alexander and daughter Janet remained in Scotland. In 1749 he leased the property at Daviot and established himself as a leader in the district. He remained at Daviot where he raised his family and died there about 1789.[44]

Archibald McGillivray came to South Carolina early, probably with the exiles of 1716, and became perhaps the most wealthy and successful trader of his time. Crane [45] gives us some information on Archibald and wrote that Archibald McGillivray and Company employed 103 pack horses between New Windsor, South Carolina, and the Creek country. It took several traders and fifteen packhorsemen to ply his trade to and from the Creek country. By 1750 he owned the largest trading company in Carolina of which he was the sole manager and director. It included the traders Isaac Motte, William Sludders, Jeremiah Knott, and George Cousins. In 1747 another leading Creek trading firm headed by Alexander Wood and Patrick Brown was taken into the company.[46]

Two incidents concerning Wood shows that he was in the trade well before 1747. *The South Carolina Gazette* reported in 1732 that Wood "returning from the Creek Nation found Peter Shaw, a trader, and his servant on the path dead." Shaw was scalped and his servant's "head cut off."[47] Just four months later Wood "found on the trail between Coosas and Chickasaw Simon Leach, his packhorseman Robert Johnson, Lewis, and a half-breed brother to James Welch." All were dead with their heads cut off. These murders were believed to have been the work of the Choctaw at the urging of the French.[48]

Archibald may have arrived in 1716 as an exile but no later than 1722. We first pick him up in the Colonial records when Patrick McKay, General Oglethorpe's representative in the Creek nation, sent a message to Archibald in the summer of 1735 ordering him to gather all the traders and meet McKay at Halfway House to escort him into the Creek country. The traders conducted McKay to Tallassee on the Tallapoosa River where he told the twelve traders present that the Indian trade belonged to Georgia, and any Carolina trader caught without a Georgia license would have his trade goods confiscated. Jeremiah Knott, one of the traders, was ordered by McKay to leave the Nation which Knott proceeded to do, but in the process lost three hundred pounds of deerskins.[49]

The fact that McKay directed his message to Archibald indicates that he was the lead trader, or a representative of South Carolina, or probably both. Leading traders served as semi-official representatives of the government. They kept colonial officials informed of activities in the nation, and from time to time traveled to Charlestown to report in person and attend to business. In any case this event indicates Archibald had been in Carolina and the trade for some number of years prior to 1735. Archibald ran an ad in January 1737 offering to sell his "Indian trading boat" at New Windsor.[50] No doubt the boat was used to transport goods between Savannah and New Windsor. Just six months later an entry in the journal of Thomas Causton, first bailiff of Savannah, on 4 July 1737 states that the license of "Archibald McGilbury" a trader to the Creek Nation, was renewed on that date.[51]

Archibald was co-executor of the will of one John Johnston of New Windsor who died on 27 January 1739. New Windsor was the headquarters of the South Carolina traders and was located on the Savannah River, in South Carolina, a few miles below Augusta.[52]

McGillivray and Company placed an ad in the South Carolina Gazette[53] announcing that Isaac Motte of New Windsor had voluntarily left the company and was no longer connected with it. The members of the company were now "Archibald McGilivray, William Sludders, Jeremiah Knott, and George Cussings."

A few months later he ran the following ads:

Archibald McGillivray intends to depart this Province the first of May next, he therefore desires all persons that have any demands on the said McGillivray either on his own account or as McGillivray and Company, to bring their accounts by the 5th of January next, to Mr. James Osmond, who has a power to discharge the same. And all persons indebted to the said McGillivray and Company, are desired to pay the same the first of January next, or else their Bonds, Notes, and Book debts will be put in the hands of James Graeme Esq. Footnote: the Co. partnership of the said Co. will be expired the 24th June next.[54]

Whereas a co-partnership hath for sometime past subsisted between Archibald McGillivray, William Sludders, George Cussings and Jeremiah Knott; and as they had lately agreed to be concerned with Alexander Wood and Patrick Brown in the said co-partnership, this is to give notice to all persons concerned, that the late co-partnership with the said Wood and Brown is entirely disolved, and that the co-partnership continues (as formely) in the name of Archibald McGillivray & Comp.[55]

Whereas the co-partnership between Alexander Wood, Patrick Brown, Archibald McGillivray, William Sludders, Jeremiah Knott and George Cussings still continues. This is therefore to forewarn any person or persons whatever not to trust or credit any of the said company accounts, except Archibald McGillivray, who is appointed sole manager and Director of the said Company. In witness thereof we have here unto set our Hands this 11th day of September 1741.

The above was signed by William Sludders, Patrick Brown, and George Cussings.[56] Why Archibald did not sign this ad is a mystery; the whole series of advertisements concerning the partnership is confusing.

Augusta, a frontier town and fort, located on the Savannah River at the fall line, was fast becoming the trading center. Trade goods could be brought upstream from Savannah and skins floated down to Savannah for trans-shipment via Charleston to markets in London and beyond. An Augusta trader, John Gardner, on 14 July 1741 prepared a list of traders coming through Augusta from "other parts." This reference no doubt meant South Carolina. As we saw from the McKay episode, friction was developing over the trade between South Carolina and her new neighbor to the south. This survey[57] was probably made for Georgia officials and included the following:

Trader	Men	Pack Horses
Wood & Brown	8	60
Archibald McGillivray	3	18
Daniel Clark	4	20
George Cousins	4	30
Jermiah Knott	4	30
William Sludders	4	25
George Galphin	4	25

Braund[58] writes that Archibald probably had the largest trading company in South Carolina. By 1741 he had several partners but remained the sole manager of the company. Braund writes that Archibald and Alexander Wood had retired from the trade by 1743. However, this was not the case for Archibald.

In August 1743 Wood advertised for a runaway slave from his plantation [59] He announced in August 1744 for everyone to pay their debts [60] This type of ad usually indicated that someone was preparing to leave the province. Wood advertised his plantation on Goose Creek for sale in 1747.[61] He also advertised for runaway slaves, a man and woman, from his plantation, Point Comfort, some twenty miles from New Windsor on the Savannah River.[62]

In July 1744 Archibald ran the following ad in the *South Carolina Gazette*:[63]

·Whereas Archibald McGillivray intends to depart this Province in

November next, he therefore desires all those who have any Demands on him, or McGillivray and Company, to bring in their accounts that they may be discharged (their co-partnership being now expired). He likewise desires all persons who are any ways indebted either to the said McGillivray, or McGillivray and Company, to pay the same before the said time or else they must expect to be sued without further notice.

This ad was repeated on 13, 20, and 27 of August.
In December 1744 he ran the following: [64]

All persons indebted to Archibald McGillivray, either on his own accompt, or accompt of the estate of John Johnson, deceased, are once more desired to pay off their Respective Debts by the 20th of December instant, as he preposes to leave this Province sometime in January following.

On 25 January 1745, an entry in the Commons House Journals records that Archibald McGillivray "Indian trader" petitioned the South Carolina House of Commons for payment of trade goods delivered to the Creek Indians in the amount of eleven pounds, plus the cost of transporting the goods at two shillings and sixpence per pound. Apparently the goods the traders were authorized to deliver were not what the Creeks wanted, so the traders furnished from their own stock what the Indians wanted, and were petitioning for reimbursement.

On the date of this Journal entry, a petition was read into the records from Lachlan Lia McGillivray, "Indian Trader in the upper Creek nation" reporting that there was an opportunity to open the trade with the Choctaw. The last Journal entry concerning Archibald came on 18 January 1746 where he was payed 827 pounds.[65]

Robert Pringle writing to his brother Andrew Pringle in London on 2 February 1745:

There is one Archibald McIlvray who has been here for these twelve or fifteen years in the Indian trade, and got by his Industry (with a good

character in said Trade) two or three thousand pounds Sterling who
went Passenger for London about a fortnight ago in the ship Triton,
Capt. Mcfarland, and am informed intends out here again after he has
seen his Relations in the North of Scotland. It is likely that he may want
a correspondent in London & may be worth your while to get acquainted with him. . . . He is a Good Plain sort of a man & always kept
his Credit exceeding well here. I believe he is Recommended to Messrs.
Samuel & William Baker to whom all his Deer Skins Go Consigned of
which he has shipped a Good Quantity.[66]

Apparently Archibald was back in South Carolina a year later and
remained there since he appears on the jury roles of Charleston in
1757.[67]

2

Lachlan Lia Comes to America

There have been various views as to when Lachlan Lia came to America and how he started in the Indian trade. From Lachlan we have an affidavit dated 21 May 1784[1] which states that he came to America in 1737, and that he was "now sixty-five years old." This would place his birth in 1719; therefore, he was eighteen years old when he arrived in Georgia.

A search of the records in Scotland failed to turn up any record of his birth nor baptism. The testament records in the Commissariot of Inverness prior to 1800 reveal no Lachlan McGillivray. Baptismal records in the old parochial registers of the County of Inverness record only one Lachlan McGillivray being baptized and the date is 7 October 1724—some five years too late for Lachlan Lia.[2] Parish registers did not start in Daviot until 1774 and we really don't know where Lachlan Lia was born.[3] It seems likely however that Captain Ban would have preferred one of the more fertile estates in the valley instead of Dunmaglass which was located up in the hills.[4]

Captain Ban in 1715 was living "at Tomnashangan or Fairies Hill" which is also known as Dun Daviot and was located some twelve miles from Dunmaglass.[5] In 1717 Captain Ban was given a tenancy in Petty which was probably the small estate his father Farquhar had once owned.[6] After 1717 Captain Ban seems more connected with Dunmaglass, but since other family members were living there, he could have been born at Druim-a-Ghadha, a farm on the Dunmaglass estates.[7] So we have three possibilities of where Lachlan Lia was born—Fairy Hill or Dun Daviot; Petty; or Druim-a-Ghadha.

Albert J. Pickett, author of the first history of Alabama, performed an outstanding service in recording many early Alabama events. Pickett gathered much of his information firsthand from interviews with the participants of the historical events. Pickett was born in North Carolina and came to Alabama with his parents in 1818. He was well educated and studied law, but preferring to write, he became a regular contributor to the *Alabama Journal* and *The Planter's Gazette*. He came from a wealthy family and had the time to pursue his scholarly work. He lived in Montgomery but owned several plantations in the area. He was aide-de-camp to Governor C. C. Clay during the Creek War of 1836. During that conflict he made many contacts with the Indians that he later utilized in gathering information. He took three years in writing his history, but a lifetime in gathering the material, much of it firsthand. His history was published in 1851 and he died 28 October 1858.[8]

Pickett's version of Lachlan Lia's arrival has been repeated over the years by many writers.[9] Since the story has been repeated so often, it is worth repeating one more time for reference purposes. A search of the Pickett files in the Alabama Department of Archives and History failed to reveal his source for Lachlan's arrival and start in the Indian trade. Most likely his source was a proud Indian descendant of Lachlan. Pickett's version has Lachlan arriving in America at age sixteen, penniless and a runaway from his home in Scotland. He arrived at Charleston and almost immediately became acquainted with the Indian traders where he was taken in and was soon on his way to Indian country. Lachlan arrived on the Chattahoochee River where he was given a "jack knife" by his employer and he soon traded the knife for skins. Thus was launched one of the most successful trading careers in Colonial America.

Part of the story may be true since Lachlan joined his cousins Alexander and Archibald's trading house out of Charleston. However, the record hardly supports such a penniless beginning. When Lachlan arrived, Archibald and Alexander already had a thriving Indian trading business among the Creeks located at Little Tallasee near present day Wetumpka, Alabama. There is little doubt due to the closeness of clan members, that Lachlan was welcomed and probably recruited into the largest trading house in South Carolina. Some of the confusion has arisen from a ship's passenger list that has a Lachlan McGillivray arriving in Georgia in January 1736 at age sixteen along with, supposedly, his cousin Farquhar, age thirty, and Archibald McGillivray, age fifteen.[10] Scores of McGillivrays, including many named Lachlan, arrived between 1716 and 1750.

In 1725 a petition was presented to the South Carolina Commons House of Assembly to compensate one "Lockland McGilivray" for the loss of clothes and thirty pounds in bills that he lost in an unfortunate accident carrying express messages to the "Savanna Garrison." The petition was denied.[11] However, in November 1725 "Lockland" was paid four pounds from the Indian fund for "going express."[12]

George Cousins, who was a trading partner to Archibald McGillivray, in 1735 describes a confrontation with the Lower Creeks while he was trading on "behalf of the Estate of Lauchlane McGillivrey deceased."[13] The will of "Lauthlan MacGiloray" was probated on 19 June 1734 leaving two-thirds of his estate to his father Daniel McGillivray and one-third to his cousin Archibald McGillivray.[14] In all likelihood this Lachlan was a trading partner with Archibald and Alexander. While Archibald was carrying on the trade at Little Tallassee among the upper Creeks, his cousin Lachlan was trading among the Lower Creeks on the Chattahoochee River.

McGillivrays could well have been in South Carolina prior to 1715. The trade was flourishing and by 1690 the Chiefs of Coweta and Cusseta had visited Charleston. One Carolina trader, George Smith, returned from the Chattahoochee River in the spring of 1690 with 2800 skins.[15]

The Council to the Lords Proprietors dated 11 September 1670 said that Dr. Henry Woodward had been among the Indians "some considerable time." He was taken prisoner by the Spanish and taken to St. Augustine and then transported to the Leeward Islands where he became a surgeon on a privateer. He had recently been fourteen days "westward" as far as Chufytachyque and the Casseea and Kaiamah. He had become important to the Colony in dealing with the Indians and could not be dispensed with. His value was "his familiar acquaintaince amongst the natives, and his knowledge of their language."[16]

Woodward was on the Chattahoochee trading with the Creeks by 1685 or earlier,[17] and by 1688 he had sent two of his traders west as emissaries where they offered friendship and trade to the Chickasaw.[18] This visit to the Chickasaw established and opened the trade, especially in Indian slaves, with the English. This trip also created a loyalty from the Chickasaw that lasted until the British evacuated America nearly a century later. Woodward as early as 1671 had made his will—"due to the hazards he was taking on a journey northward of Ashley River."[19] During this early period he was also establishing the trade with the Alibama at the forks of the Alabama River sometime around 1690.[20]

Probably many journeys west by these adventurous early colonists go unrecorded. They were probing the interior at an early date and New England traders may have traveled as far west as New Mexico in 1678.[21] A South Carolina directive dated 10 April 1677 forbade trading with the Westoes and Cusseta without a license.[22] B.F. French wrote that Colonel Abraham Wood of Virginia had probably been on the Mississippi River as early as 1654.[23] By 1640 the Virginians knew the "land beyond the mountains."[24]

James Sutherland who had arrived back in Charleston in 1722 wrote that he had traveled thirteen hundred miles "up the country NW from Charlestown."[25] In 1621 the Virginia Company made plans to set up a factory to produce glass and glass beads,[26] no doubt to be used for the Indian trade.

A letter from John Stewart to William Dunlop of London, dated 23 June 1690, said that he was outfitting a pack train for a trading trip to the "Chikesas" and that he would be the first "Briton" to do so. There were to be three caravans, with one probably belonging to Thomas Welch. Stewart wrote "when God sends me back I am to cross the mountains to go a trading to the Chekesas." This observation means that he had been there before, and probably he was one of the two men sent by Woodward to the Chickasaw in 1688 to establish the trade.[27]

In 1698 South Carolina shipped 64,448 deerskins to Great Britain with the trade reaching its peak in 1706 when 121,355 skins were shipped.[28] So, by the time Lachlan Lia arrived, the Indian trade was well established and flourishing.

More recent biographical writings about Lachlan come from Neeley [29] She suggests that Lachlan arrived in Georgia in 1736 as an indentured servant along with Cousin Farquhar and young Archibald. They were among a group of 163 Highlanders recruited in the Inverness area. Cashin[30] also follows Neeley.

General Oglethorpe ordered Hugh Mckay and George Dunbar to sail for Scotland and recruit "one hundred men free or servants" from the Highlands. They were allowed free passage for ten servants over the one hundred and also fifty women and children. They recruited this number in the "immediate vicinity of Inverness." The Presbyterian minister John McLeod was selected as their pastor to be paid fifty pounds annually. Many of the recruits were gentlemen unused to labor and were allowed to bring servants along. Others were former officers in the Army.[31] Captain Dunbar arrived at Savannah on 10 January 1736 with two hundred passengers from Scotland on the *Prince of Wales*.[32] Oglethorpe arrived one month later with one hundred and thirty passengers.[33] When they arrived at Tybee Road, they were immediately sent to their destination at New Inverness, later known as Darian. "All who so desired at their own expense," were permitted to go up to Savannah and Josephstown.[34]

Although times were hard in Scotland, and it is possible that Lachlan was a recruit of General Oglethorpe, the likelihood that he was an indentured servant is very small. Servants that came with Mackay were indentured from four to fourteen years and their passage was five pounds.[35] He came from a prominent family, was well-educated, and joined his wealthy relations Archibald and Alexander, the leading traders in South Carolina. The McGillivrays in America reached out and recruited their kin back in Scotland to work in the trading business, which benefited the whole clan.

We know nothing of Lachlan's activities from his arrival until his first appearance in the records in 1742. The South Carolina House journals record on 27 January 1742 that Lachlan made a claim of 244 pounds for acting as interpreter to the Indian Agent James Bullock in the Creek nation. The claim covered 122 days from 12 June 1741 to 13 October 1741.[36] This claim and another for twenty-eight pounds for Sludders, McGillivray and Company were allowed by the committee on petitions and accounts on 24 February 1742.[37] They were paid another

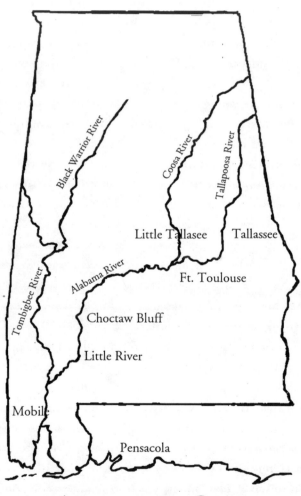

ALABAMA — 18TH CENTURY

seventy-eight pounds on order of the Agent James Bullock for various goods delivered to the Indians.[38]

Lachlan, in just four short years, had learned the Muskogee tongue and was fluent enough to be an official interpreter for South Carolina. He had also formed his own trading company in partnership with Sludders and at age twenty-two was well on his way to becoming one of the most successful traders in Colonial South Carolina and Georgia.

Some writers[39] would have us believe that young Lachlan toiled for four years as a servant on the farms of Darian and soldiered for Oglethorpe on his expedition to St. Augustine in the summer of 1740 and then suddenly appeared one year later in Charleston as a fluent Creek interpreter for the government and already having his own trading company. The time and dates are just not possible. Lachlan was well-educated and private education in Scotland was costly—much more than the five pounds fare to America. His condition may have been poor, but he was not destitute.

Probably young Lachlan was one of the Highlanders that went to Savannah and on to Charleston soon after landing. He joined Archibald's trading caravans to the Creek country and spent many months or even years[40] at the McGillivray trading post located at Little Tallasee on the Coosa River just north of Fort Toulouse. Here he learned the Muskogee language which could only be learned fluently when conversing with the natives on a daily basis over a long period of time. He gained valuable experience and saved enough money to form a trading partnership with Sludders in 1741. This is why we hear nothing about him until he returned to Charleston from the Creek Nation in 1741. There was no way he could learn the language fluently, gain trader experience, and form a trading partnership while farming and soldiering at Darian.

We know that another ship arrived at Savannah from Scotland in November 1737.[41] A Duncan McGillivray embarked on 24 June 1737 and arrived in Georgia on 20 November.[42] Also, Oglethorpe arrived at Frederica on 17 July 1738 with six hundred men, women, and children aboard a man-o-war.[43] The passage was only five pounds.[44] Alexander and Archibald, as we shall see later, were already planning their retirement from the trade and needed a reliable relative to learn and take over the trade in a few years especially since Alexander planned to return to Scotland permanently.

Another first cousin to Lachlan Lia, John McGillivray, became an important part of Lachlan's life in Georgia and later on their final return to Scotland. John was the son of Farquhar, the 7th chief, and brother to William, the 9th chief, who also later came to Georgia to enter into the plantation and land enterprises with Lachlan. John came to Georgia in 1755 and then moved on to West Florida in about 1764.

John McGillivray first appears in a letter he wrote to Governor Ellis of Georgia on 20 December 1757 and posted at Augusta. He reported that some Choctaws had arrived in the Creek Nation and wanted to establish a trade with the English. John thought this development was an opportunity to break up the monopoly the French enjoyed with the Choctaw.[45] Another letter dated 28 December 1758 from John McGillivray, James McQune, and George Cornell, traders at "Abacoochees, Oakfuskees, and Tuccabatches," to Lieutenant White Outerbridge, the Commander at Fort Augusta, informs him that some fifty Choctaw had come to the Creeks wanting to buy goods for their families as they were in "great want" and were willing to "quit the French."[46]

Edmond Atkin became the first Colonial Superintendent for Indian Affairs for the Southern District in 1757. From various contemporary descriptions, Atkin approached the Indians with a haughty and arrogant attitude. Alden[47] and Cashin[48] wrote that Atkin was visiting the Creeks and giving a "talk" at Tuckabatchee on the Tallapoosa River on 28 September 1759 when a Creek warrior became enraged and attacked Atkin with a hatchet. These historians also noted that only with the intervention of John McGillivray, a Creek named Molton, and Waggonfield, Atkin's secretary, prevented Atkin from being hacked to death.

On 22 April, 1758 a Creek council was held at "Macklasses," on the Tallapoosa River, which had been called by Colonial officials in Georgia to negotiate the cession of the coastal islands of "Ussabaw, St. Catherine, and Sapala." The Georgia representatives won their case and a deed was signed by the Creeks granting the islands forever to Georgia. John McGillivray was present and signed the deed as a witness.[49]

We only get a glimpse of John here and there in the records until the Revolution. We read of him again in 1761 when on 3 July the Georgia Council passed trade regulations to control the trade and traders. The Indians had been complaining for years about the unfair treatment they received from some of the traders. However, the trader-merchant influence in Charleston and Savannah had prevented any meaningful legislation since many of the Council members were either in the trade, were merchants or both. The new rules were to bring some organization out of near chaos by assigning specific traders to specific towns and hopefully making them more accountable. The town of "Abbecoochee," located near the Coosa River in Talladega County, was assigned to John McGillivray.[50]

A most unusual letter comes from Henry Laurens[51] dated 29 August 1763 and addressed to the London trading firm of Cowles & Harford. Laurens was probably the leading merchant-broker in Charleston prior to the Revolution. During the Revolution he took up the patriot cause and went on to become President of the Continental Congress. Laurens' letter reads:

> Neither Mr. Appleby nor I can conceive on what foundation John McGillivray, whose name we never heard of before, could be shipping goods to London for Austin, Laurens & Appleby—from Guadaloup especially as we know of no effects that we had any right to in that Island. Therefore we request you to make some further inquiry into this matter; perhaps some person may have made free with our names to secure their own property on one hand and save a premium on the other.

Another letter from Governor Johnstone of West Florida to Montault de Monberant, a deputy to John Stuart, dated 26 June 1765, mentions John McGillivray in West Florida who "has been much among the Creoles of Guadaloupe, he is at present sick and delerious."[52] This John

McGillivray was the son of Alexander McGillivray and Anne Fraser and a second cousin to Lachlan Lia, Alexander being the cousin that assisted Lachlan Lia in getting started in the trade. John was a merchant in Guadaloupe and later became secretary to John Stuart at Pensacola. Through this office and his connections with the McGillivray family, he learned the trade at an early age. We know he died while a young man and his death may have come from the sickness mentioned above by Governor Johnstone. We do not know the outcome of the inquiry that Laurens asked for, but there is little doubt this John was misusing the good name of the firm Austin, Laurens & Appleby.[53]

John McGillivray, the first cousin to Lachlan Lia and our main subject here, probably came to West Florida shortly after the cession of Florida by the French to the British in 1763. Some writers have been confused as to the relationship of John and Lachlan Lia. This confusion was caused by an affidavit Lachlan made when he returned to England after the Revolution. Coldham[54] wrote that John is Lachlan's nephew; Wright in Coker[55] said Lachlan sent his nephew John to Mobile to supervise the western branch of the trade. John was not the nephew of Lachlan, but was his first cousin. The confusion comes from Lachlan's own affidavit dated 21 May 1784, and written in behalf of John's claim of compensation from the Crown for his losses suffered during the Revolution.[56] The affidavit was written in the third person; therefore, making it more likely to have been written by someone other than Lachlan. The pertinent phrase here is "he [Lachlan] made overtures to his nephew John McGillivray who he considered as his heir . . ." This characterization is an error; John repeatedly refers to Lachlan as his cousin. John in an affidavit[57] dated 18 October 1783 in support of his brother William's claim against the Crown, writes there was a "convey-ance" from his brother to his cousin for a plantation, which was a sham, hoping to keep the rebels from confiscating it.

William, the Clan Chief, in his claim for compensation in 1783, wrote that he owned two plantations in Georgia. One was called Wester Gask which was a gift from his cousin Lachlan McGillivray in 1773.[58] In the same claim William stated:

... when he was coming away [leaving Georgia] his cousin Lachlan McGillivray being likely to stay, claimant [William] sold his plantation to him for between nine and ten thousand pounds sterling—made a conveyance of it and took his bond for the money. The sale was only a sham one to protect the Estate from forfeiture. This cousin paid part and his brother [John] the other part of his debts.

William in a memorial directly to Lord George Germain, the British Secretary of State for America, petitioned for his claim of compensation and described how his cousin Lachlan promised to make him his heir if he would come to Georgia and help run his enterprises. This William did in 1773.[59] The will of William McGillivray probated 25 January 1784 records that he willed Gask [Estate in Scotland] "to John McGillivray" and names "John his brother; Lachlan his cousin" as his executors and his sister Anne McGillivray as Executria.[60]

The will of John McGillivray dated 25 February 1788 in London, reads that after his debts and funeral expenses are paid he bequeathed to—"Cousin Lachlan McGillivray" a lifetime annual annuity of five hundred pounds in consideration of slaves and other personal property "delivered over" to John in the Province of Georgia.[61] Lachlan made a will in Savannah in 1767, and no later will could be found, but from the papers of his young cousin, John Lachlan, who was the son of William and succeeded him becoming the 10th Chief upon William's death, there was found in 1852 an extract of Lachlan's will.[62] It reads—"General Disposition and Deed of settlement in favour of John Lachlan McGillivray, his cousin of Dunmaglass." John Lachlan being the son of William was a second cousin to Lachlan.

We cannot account for the mistake made in Lachlan's affidavit in 1784. John and William were the sons of Captain Farquhar McGillivray and Elizabeth McIntosh. Captain Farquhar was a brother to Lachlan's father, Captain William Ban, both being sons of the 6th Chief, Farquhar and Emilia Stewart.[63] In any case, this is ample evidence, which will be elaborated on later, that John, William, and Lachlan were first cousins.

John's later career in West Florida and William coming to America in 1773 will be covered in later chapters.

We next hear of Lachlan Lia from a letter to William Pinckney, South Carolina Commissioner for Indian Affairs, dated 2 May 1749, wherein he gives a report on Creek Indian affairs in the Nation.[64] Lachlan, just over a short decade, became a large landholder in Georgia. His first grant of land consisted of one hundred acres on "Kynions" Creek near Augusta and was made by the Georgia Council on 6 November 1749. He was to build a grist mill on the Creek and was identified to the Council as an "Augusta Indian Trader."[65] The next year Lachlan claimed 120 pounds for "Indian expenses as Linguist which ought to be paid."[66] The South Carolina Commons House of Assembly three months later authorized the payment for his services.[67] Again on 30 May 1753 at a Creek Council held with Governor Glen at Charleston, Lachlan was sworn in as the interpreter.[68]

Lachlan, writing to William Pinckney on 18 December 1751, informed him that the French at the Alibamas had completed their fort [the fort was rebuilt] "which is a pretty strong one." A boat had recently come up the Alabama River from Mobile bringing a "priest, popery, and Brandy." He said that the priest has come as a missionary for the fort.[69] Lachlan was living just a few miles north of the fort at Little Tallasee and could readily receive reports from the Indians as to what was taking place at and around the fort. Lachlan, a leading English trader, could reside and run his trading post for many years only a few miles from the French at Fort Toulouse. There was probably some unwritten agreement that the French would not molest Lachlan—for the occasional exchange of trade goods that the French were unable to obtain even from their own government. Indeed at Mobile the French garrison sometimes went hungry due to their dependence on being supplied from outside sources. Governor Glen confirmed this to Lyttelton on 10 August 1756 when he writes that the French obtain their goods at St. Augustine where New York merchants send large quantities of goods. These were in turn used in the trade at the Alabama fort.[70]

Lachlan wrote a report from New Windsor, South Carolina, to

Governor Glen on 8 September 1754 giving him the latest accounts from the Creek Nation. He was acting as a semi-official agent for Glen among the Creeks. He apologized for the dirty and "incorrect paper" and asked that it be sent back to him in the Creek Nation where he will have time to correct it. He wrote "that I am so hurried since my arrival here about settling our Company affairs that I can hardly spare time to eat Dinner."[71]

For some unknown reason, in 1754, the South Carolina Commissioner for Indian Affairs awarded the trading license for the upper towns of "Pukantallahasee, Woccukay and Weetomkee Old Town, alias Little Talassee" to trader John Baxter. These were the towns held by Lachlan and he petitioned the Council to reclaim his trade. He complained that he had been a licensed trader since 1744 and "he knew not" why Baxter was awarded the towns when his license had not expired, and there had been no complaints against him. Baxter had obtained the "license of William Sludders deceased last October to the great Detriment and loss of your Petitioner, which is a great grievance." The Governor and Council found in favor of Lachlan and revoked Baxter's license declaring it null and void.[72] Apparently some conflict arose between the Commissioner and Lachlan which caused him to so flagrantly override Lachlan's license and give it to Baxter.

The trade of Georgia and South Carolina was dominated by a few men who were also merchants in Augusta, Savannah, and Charleston. Until about 1750 the trade was concentrated with the South Carolina Traders at New Windsor, their headquarters just across the Savannah River from Augusta.

Old Savannah Town was up the Savannah River just below the falls and grew around Fort Moore which was built by South Carolina in 1712. By 1736 it was renamed New Windsor.[73] At this location the Creek and Cherokee trails merged to cross the river at the fall line. Charleston merchants maintained warehouses there for the Indian trade and it was the rendezvous for the English traders.

New Windsor was the center of the Indian trade until Augusta was built by General Oglethorpe. On 14 June 1736 Oglethorpe ordered

Noble Jones to lay out a town of forty lots at Kenyon Bluff. This was the location recommended by the Charleston merchant Samual Eveleigh, who wanted to move his warehouses from New Windsor Bluff. Oglethorpe at the same time started building Fort Augusta at the same location adjacent to the fall line. The inhabitants of New Windsor were alarmed that Georgia would take over the trade. It was predicted that the merchants and traders would simply move across the river and set up business, which they did, and in a short time New Windsor was almost a deserted town.[74]

When adequate docking facilities were built at Savannah in 1752, the trade started shifting to Georgia with Augusta the central collection point for the traders.[75] Savannah had been at a competitive disadvantage with Charleston due to the lack of adequate port facilities. As early as 1737 complaints were made to the trustees that it took three times as long to unload a ship as one with dock and crane facilities.[76] Apparently the cargo had to be off-loaded onto smaller boats.

At Augusta, located at the fall line, the traders held their spring gathering, because the warehouses that stored the Indian trade goods were located there. After proper preparation they were shipped downriver on flatboats to Savannah and the British markets. From there the horse caravans, usually consisting of forty horses, were launched; these expeditions traveled across the mountains and rivers into Creek, Choctaw, Chickasaw, and Cherokee lands. Some of the traders resided in Augusta and the Indian country, moving back and forth between colonial life and Indian life. Most that resided in the Nation, even part time, had taken Indian wives, fathered children, became members of the tribe, and maintained "homes" there. They were known as Indian Countrymen.

Despite the traders' presence, Augusta grew slowly. In June 1765 it had only 138 white males, 402 women and children, 501 black slaves, and 90 Chickasaw Indians.[77]

Governor James Glen writing to Edward Fenwick on 1 June 1756, says the six principal traders to the Creeks were—McQueen, McCartan & Campbell, McGillivray, Douglass, Clark, and Galphin. The Creeks wanted the same trade prices as those given to the Cherokee, even though the Creeks were further away, but Glen says the trade prices must be settled by these six principal traders.[78] This response indicates the power and influence the men of Augusta had over the trade.

By September 1754 Lachlan had formed another trading company.[79] On 12 February 1756 a bill was submitted by Clark & McGillivray for food and supplies furnished the Creeks from 14 October 1755 to 12 February 1756. The bill was inclosed in a letter from Lachlan to Governor Glen and the South Carolina Council dated 17 February 1756.[80]

Lieutenant White Outerbridge, Commander at Fort Augusta and Fort Moore, writing to Governor Lyttelton on 17 July 1756 says Daniel Clark was a partner with Lachlan McGillivray. Also Rae & Barksdale were partners with them.[81]

Hamer[82] writes that in 1754 there were six partners in Brown, Rae & Company—Patrick Brown, John Rae, George Galphin, Lachlan McGillivray, Isaac Barksdale, and Daniel Clark. Traders were often involved in more than one firm, and this is apparently the case with Lachlan. Henry Laurens writing to Richard Oswald & Company on 19 July 1756, states that Clark & McGillivray were owed five hundred pounds by Thomas Rock of Bristol, probably for goods shipped to Bristol by the Company.[83]

In 1755 Lachlan found himself in a dilemma. He wrote Governor Glen of South Carolina on 1 February informing him that the Governor of Georgia was planning a council with the Creek Indians and has notified Lachlan and George Galphin of the council. Lachlan expected that they would be the intepreters, but he felt that since "being engaged to your Excellency there may be a problem of conflict." Lachlan asked for guidance in the matter.[84] We do not know what advice the Governor gave him, but this is an indication that Lachlan's loyalties were in transition from South Carolina to Georgia.

Daniel Pepper, the South Carolina Indian Agent, made several trips to the Creek country and in a report to the Governor dated 30 March, 1757, he complained that "Clark, McGillivray, Rae, Barksdale, and Spencer" have not been in the Creek Nation since his arrival there. He reminded the Governor that these traders were obligated to reside in the Nation six months of each year.[85] Their license could be revoked for this violation, but it was rarely used against the traders—especially those that were influential in the colonial government.

A document[86] appearing in the South Carolina Indian Affairs records and titled only "Journal of an Indian Trader" with the first entry dated 11 January, 1755 and the last on 25 May, 1755, has some fifteen pages and is a rambling account or report of events taking place in the upper and lower Creek country. The account covers meetings with the French and the Spanish; councils quoting the chiefs at length; ball games and many other events taking place in the Nation. The writer goes unidentified, but it is almost certain that it was written by Lachlan McGillivray. He wrote about the chiefs visiting his house on their way home from visiting the French at Fort Toulouse which was located at the junction of the Coosa and Tallapoosa Rivers. Lachlan's house and trading store were located at Little Tallasee only about five miles from the Fort. He mentioned acting as interpreter for the Creeks on many occasions, and that he moved freely among the Indians, knowing the chiefs well. He also attended ball games only one-half mile from the Fort.

On 1 February, 1755 Lachlan wrote to Governor Glen that the Commandant at Fort Toulouse had delivered a letter to him from the French Governor in New Orleans to Governor Glen. Lachlan again raised the question with Glen about serving Governor Reynolds of Georgia and requested guidance from Glen.[87] This incident brings into sharp focus the relationship between the French at Fort Toulouse and the English traders almost surrounding the fort, often only a few miles away, but still remaining unmolested by the French. The traders were protected by the Indians and the French were dependent, to some degree, on English trade goods. This situation also reveals the recognition by the French of Lachlan's position in British colonial affairs.

Lachlan, again writing to Glen on 13 May 1755, informed him that a new French Captain had arrived at Fort Toulouse bringing with him trade goods. He had informed the Creeks that the French would trade at lower prices than the English.[88] Lachlan watched and reported on activities of the French at the Fort.

Patrick Brown, head of the Company, and considered the leading trader-merchant of the Indian trade, died on 2 July 1755. Henry Laurens, writing to James Cowles on 4 July 1755. said:

> Patrick Brown who was at the head of that Company that consigns to Mr. Rock was buried the night before last. The rest of the Company we are told are about to separate which will very probably carry the bulk of the Creek trade to Georgia as none of our people who have ability to carry on that trade think it worth the trouble and risque. This late Company, two or three of them were always in the Nation to make the most of their affairs & by it they must have made money which is not to be done by sending people abroad to trade for you unless better men could be found for the purpose than at present.[89]

On the same date Laurens wrote to Devonsheir, Reene & Loyd, "Two days ago died Patrick Brown who was at the head of that Company that consign skins to Mr. Rock. We hear the others are going to separate which may possibly give us a chance of buying more skins than we have been able to do lately, as they monopolized three-fourths of all that were taken in the Creek and Chicasaw Nations."[90] These two letters are contradictory. In the first, Laurens said that the trade would probably move to Georgia. In the second, he wrote that they may be able to buy more skins. What he describes in the first was what was taking place. Why he said the opposite in the second remains a mystery unless he was talking about a onetime deal.

Edmond Atkin, the Indian agent, writing to Governor Lyttelton on 20 May 1756 said that Mr. Glen's favorite interpreter was McGillivray.[91] Glen reaffirms his confidence in Lachlan in a letter to Lyttelton dated 23 January 1758 after Lyttelton had succeeded Glen as Governor of South Carolina. He wrote "If McGillivray be in town he is a man of sense and substance, and may be trusted, and he knows centimes more of their affairs than any other trader."[92]

Lachlan writing to Lyttelton on 13 July 1758 from Augusta enclosed a report from James Adair, a Chickasaw trader and later author of the well-known work *History of the American Indian*, in regard to "the situation at Mobile." Lachlan said that it would be to great advantage if the British possessed Mobile and New Orleans. He reported that the Shawnee had come to the upper Creeks bearing scalps which angered the Creek chiefs. The Creeks had proposed an expedition against the "new French fort on the Mississippi." Lachlan, according to instructions from Mr. Bull, Lieutenant Governor of South Carolina, had forwarded powder and ball to the Creeks for that purpose. Lachlan concluded his letter with:

> Mr. Adair is the bearer of this therefore Your Excellency I presume
> will have an opportunity to ask him all the necessary questions on that
> head, and submit to your superior judgement, if Your Excellency should
> think such a person necessary he may be usefull in his way, he is a person
> I have no connection with. I pity his misfortunes.[93]

A long, twelve-page, and strange letter purported to have been written and signed by "Laughlin McGilvery" dated 14 July 1758, and posted from Augusta, reveals a personality completely uncharacteristic of Lachlan Lia. Lachlan Lia never signed his name in this manner, always as "Lachlan McGillivray." The handwriting was poor, the spelling and construction only fair, and the whimsical and poetic tone is unlike Lachlan Lia. For example—

> I cheerfully proceed to Your Excellencys command. The Indian
> Traders liken the Indians to the Swallows. They charm us in the summer
> of our prosperity with their pleasant notes, whilst everything is smiling
> around us. But, when the winter of adversity overtakes us they are fled
> far off in search of a warmer sun.

He reported on the French activity among the Choctaw and Creeks, and what the Spaniards were up to. He included in some detail what it would take for the Colonies to send a land army of six thousand men to capture Fort Toulouse and Mobile. As he rambled, he discussed the Greeks and the wooden horse.[94]

This long letter is an informed report written by someone well acquainted with the Creek, Choctaw, and Chickasaw Indians. The letter, even if written by some third person on behalf of Lachlan Lia, is so uncharacteristic of him that serious doubt remains as to his being the author. However, the report was probably written by James Adair as it comes closer to his style of writing, but would he sign it Lachlan McGillivray?

Lachlan, to Lyttelton on 14 August 1758, informed him that the Chickasaw, now living on two five hundred acre tracts near Fort Moore which belonged to Lachlan, wanted to swap their land within the township of New Windsor for the two tracts. The exchange was agreeable if the Governor approved.[95] The Governor approved the land exchange.

Edmond Atkin, the new and first Superintendent of Indian Affairs, arrived at Augusta and wrote to Lyttelton on 24 November 1758. He stated that the principal traders were located at Augusta and were mostly concerned with furnishing trade goods to others for transport to the Nation. They had not visited the Nation in a long time. The traders did not want anyone looking into "the true state of the trade." Atkin called a meeting of all the traders to be held "near" the Creek Nation, but he was having trouble finding a "horse escort" to accompany him. He wrote "that Mr. McGilivray's conduct throughout hath been very exceptionable."[96]

Enclosed in Atkin's letter was one from the surveyor, Ellrich Tobler, who wrote that Lachlan had sent him a warrant to survey 1000 acres for Daniel Clark in April 1757. Also another warrant to survey 1500 acres that had been swapped to Lachlan by the Chickasaw.[97]

"John Pettycrow" [Pettigrew] acted as interpreter at a meeting between Atkin and the Chickasaw probing into the land transactions with Lachlan. The Governor of South Carolina had originally given them a large tract opposite Augusta, but they had slowly abandoned this land because of their "enemies," and that their young men went to

Augusta to get drunk and would drown trying to swim back across the river. They had left this land in about 1748 and now lived on the Augusta side. They traded and signed an agreement with Lachlan for the land they now lived on. He planted on their old land opposite Augusta and also used it for a large herd of cattle. It was located opposite John Rae's house. They traded with Lachlan even though their tract was much larger than the one they received, but he was "white people" and they were "red people," not knowing better. Their land now suited them even though it was small. Atkin chastised the Indians and said that the Governor gave them the right to live on the land—he did not sell it to them. They had no right to trade it to Mr. McGillivray. They were "wrong" in signing a paper with McGillivray because the land belonged to the King. Atkin continued to chastise the Indians. They remained silent. They had signed a document giving their land to Lachlan, but they had no paper from him for their land. The tract Lachlan had received was twenty thousand acres.[98]

If Lachlan had not committed fraud on the Indians, he had bordered on it, and at best certainly took advantage of the Savannah River Chickasaw. We can also empathize with the Indians as they had to sit silent while Atkin berated and humiliated them.

Robert Pringle, writing on 21 January 1743, said of Atkin "our Gentlemen of the Council are of such profound judgement and parts (and particularly that conceited Gentleman Mr. Atkin) that they do not think it worth their while to advise with or have the opinion of the merchants in anything Relating to the welfare of the Province."[99] Atkin was serving on the South Carolina Council at this time.

Atkin on 26 October 1758 issued a call, arrogant and haughty in tone, to all the traders to meet him near the Creek Nation. They were to inform all the headmen of the Upper and Lower Creeks.[100]

Atkin issued a proclamation on 16 November 1758 that he would prosecute any trader caught taking whiskey into the Nation. Just a few days before, on 2 November, the Justices of the Peace in Augusta proclaimed that laws against transporting whiskey into the Nation would be enforced.[101]

Atkin again to Lyttelton on 10 December 1758 wrote "Mr. McGillivray having given me notice of a Resolution he hath taken suddenly (at least as far as I know) to go to Charlestown tomorrow morning. On account of the Danger his Brother is supposed to be in his life. I think it improper to miss the opportunity of writing to you by him." Atkin informed the Governor that he had obtained twelve light horsemen to escort him and he was having his meat cured and his luggage packed. He stated that the "resident traders" at Augusta do not plan to go to the meeting with him. He is "well-informed that John Rae has sold his license to Wm. Fraser and McGillivray his Ga. license to Wm. Struthers. Neither had been in the Nation for two or three years." He said that the traders would swap licenses around and even have fictitious towns. The Georgia Assembly was considering a tax on skins not shipped from Savannah and the traders were in such a "ferment" they were threatening to move across the river to South Carolina. They were already clearing the woods opposite Augusta and John Spencer had erected some buildings there.[102]

This is the first indication we have had that Lachlan had a brother in Charleston. The manuscript of the McGillivray family in the National Library of Scotland[103] indicates Lachlan had an older brother named William.

The will of Daniel Clark, a trading partner with Lachlan Lia, who died in April 1757, included as benefactors Lachlan McGillivray, Alexander McGillivray and his wife, John McGillivray, William McGillivray, and William Sluthers.[104] This Alexander was probably the mariner; John was probably Lachlan's cousin John who came over about 1755; and William may have been Lachlan's brother. Clark left his books to William McGillivray and William Sluthers.

Alexander McGillivray was a ship captain that sailed in and out of Charleston to other parts along the east coast and the Carribean Islands. He first appears in the records in 1745 when his ship *Eleanor* was cleared for entering Charleston from Montserrat and return thereto. Montserrat is a tiny island of thirty-two square miles and part of the Leeward Islands in the West Indies about 160 miles north of Martinique.[105] In 1755 he was listed as carrying a cargo of slaves into Charleston.[106] In 1757 he was master of the ship *Adventure* owned by Samuel Brailsford and Thomas Middleton.[107] On 27 June 1761 he arrived in Charleston from Providence, master of the sloop *King of Prussia*. On 16 June 1763 he arrived from Georgia, master of the sloop *Dolphin*[108] This was probably his last voyage since he died in December 1763.

He was buried in the St. Michaels Churchyard in Charleston. His gravestone reads—"Here lieth the Body of Capt. Alexr. McGillivray who departed this life December the 24th 1763, aged 43 years."[109] His will was probated on 7 January 1764. His wife's name was Elizabeth and in his will he bequeathed to his "brother Lachlan McGillivray" a mourning suit of clothes and a mourning ring.[110]

From this will several writers have assumed that Alexander was the brother to Lachlan Lia.[111] Captain Alexander may have been the brother of Lachlan Lia, but it is problematical, and there is no direct evidence that ties this Lachlan with Lachlan Lia.[112]

A Dr. William McGillivray appears in the records in 1731 as owning land on Wadmalaw Island in Colleton County, South Carolina.[113] In 1734 he gave "loving gifts" of land and slaves to his wife Elizabeth, daughters Mary and Elizabeth, and sons Robert and Alexander.[114] Dr. William died in 1739. His will was probated on 4 July 1741 and recognized his wife Elizabeth, sons Robert and Alexander, and daughters Lucrecia, Elizabeth, Susannah, and Sosiahe. Probably daughter Mary had died between 1734 and 1739, and three new daughters had been added to the family.[115] His son Alexander married three times between 1749 and 1756.[116] At his death in 1756, he left his estate to his wife Elizabeth and son William. He was a planter in Colleton County which adjoins Charleston County. His will was probated on 7 January 1757.[117] This William, the grandson of Dr. William, became a Captain of the Dorchester Militia of Colleton County in 1782. He was married to Ann Hinckley and they had a son named William Christopher Hinckley McGillivray.[118] He was a loyalist and appeared on the rebel enemies list of South Carolina in 1779.[119] Capt. William died or was killed sometime in 1782 as his widow Ann married William Russell on 14 June 1783.[120]

Returning to Lachlan Lia, he wrote to Lyttelton on 2 April 1759 that he did not accompany Atkin to the Creek Nation for the traders council because Atkin did not ask him; therefore, he felt "he was not acceptable."[121] Atkin took his time about going to the Nation claiming he was having a hard time hiring and organizing his escort. He finally called for the meeting to be held at Tallassee on the Tallapoosa River on 24 June 1759. The Lower Creeks were concerned about his safety and also planned to escort him from the Chattahoochee to Tallassee on the Tallapoosa.[122]

Atkin, to Lyttelton on 2 October 1759, posted from Tuckabatchee, wrote that while he was in Council on 28 September with the Creek headmen at Tuckabatchee:

> . . . a head warrior of Cussehta seized with a fit of madness, suddenly started upon the cabbin behind me, and with a pipe hatchet fell on me & by repeated blows brought me to the ground, before I saw him, or anyone red or white did the least thing to prevent it. So soon as I recovered my feet, seeing great numbers rushing out of the cabbins on each side of the square, & imagining as most other did at first, that it must be a premeditated action & the effect of a conspiracy, Bleeding as I was immensely, & not knowing at first but that my skull was split, I called aloud to all the white people, to take up arms.[123]

A deposition by John Reed, who was present, said that Atkin was attacked by a Cusseta Indian named Tobacco Eater and Atkin was saved only by his suddenly turning and was wounded on the head and arm.[124] Governor Ellis, writing to Lyttelton on 16 October 1759, reported that he had an account from an Indian present at the meeting—"the blow was occassioned by Mr. Atkin threatening to deprive the Cussetas of its trade, as he had done some other towns, in very uncommon and prevoking language; and that had not a half-breed fellow, whom he had recently affronted, generously interposed to save him, as no one else would, so much were they displeased with his talk."[125] Nowhere in the documents relating to the attack on Atkin is John McGillivray mentioned and there is no evidence that he was even present.[126]

Atkin to Lyttelton, 30 November, 1759, wrote among other things that:

> Estates have been got in succession for a great number of years in two Births by engrossing the whole trade of 450 Albahma Indians & dealing with them & others his Majesty's Enemies; to wit Lachlan McGilivray's store at Little Talsey, & Spencer's more infamous one, not as I myself had always thought in Mocalussa, but a mile & half from it in the woods, for greater privacy.
>
> I went from thence to Mocalussah, where I expected to find Spencer according to his license & from whence he used to date his letters; but I was conducted to his house a mile & half further, alone in the woods, and nearer to the French fort. There I reconnoitied well the political ground around that neighborhood and first put a stop to the nearest stores giving credit as before to the Albahma Indians, & to any further dealing in particular with those of Taskegy & Couessality, some of the Headmen whereof had distinguished themselves against me. This Spencer approved of, while he only thought it would be the means of bringing more grist to his own mill; that is those who used to deal at Little Talsey Store, to his own store. But when he smelt something like gunpowder, a mine springing, he started & went off for Augusta, after such contemptuous, insolent & audacious behavior in sight of the Indians, & leaving such orders with Germany his storekeeper that either he must be no longer a licensed trader, or I no Superintendent. I removed to the Wolf's own house in Mocalussah (it being judged no longer safe where I was); and from thence I found it necessary to issue an injunction on the 7th of September to all the Traders on the Upper Towns, for the Reasons set forth, to have no dealings whatever with those Albahma Indians, none of whom had approached me, tho they had been advised to do it by the Wolf. The Albahma Indians threatened not to pay their debts, without fresh credit to fit themselves out for hunting. The two nearest stores no longer thought safe, Struthers (who acted positively till June on acct of Lach. McGilivray but whither on his

or his own since, he pretends he knows not) removed the effects from Little Talsey for better security, as did Germany Spencers, according to his orders in such case, to Fushatchey, passing by Mocalussah." Atkin says Germany is going to "quit Spencer's Employ."[127]

Atkin accused Lachlan of trading with the enemy at Fort Toulouse and the "French Indians," which lived in several towns around the Fort and known as the Alibama, which was a serious accusation. His wrath at Spencer, Lachlan's trading partner, took on a threatening tone to the Governor, that either Spencer must go or the Indian Superintendent. William Struthers, another partner of Lachlan's, apparently ran the trading house at Little Tallasee. There is little or no doubt that Lachlan knew of this trade and condoned it for the sake of making large profits.

Atkin said that the presents given by the French to the Oakchoy were English goods. He had seen the cloth and blankets. The Tuskegee and Coosada were the worst offenders in trading English goods to the French.[128] No doubt the Tuskegee and Coosada were getting their English trade goods from the Little Tallasee and Mucclusa stores operated by Lachlan Lia and John Spencer.

The trader Jerome Courtonne in 1758 made a list of the Upper or Lower Creek towns and their headmen. In his footnotes he said Little Tallasee was in the "Abican district" and the Chief was Second Man who often visited the French fort only five miles away.[129]

Atkin was not finished with his accusations in his thirty-three page letter to Lyttelton. He continued:

> I have many heavy accusations to make against Lach. McGilivray, besides what concerns his illegal Dealings at his store at Little Talsey. To him I impute the first Disregard paid to my instructions; and the refusal made at Augusta in fact, tho not in words, to give me information I wanted in Relation to the goods carried to the Creek Nation. He countenanced Nathlettoby the Chickasaw under his misbehavior to me, and also Tahgulky the Twins son lately & others of Coweta, by entertaining & handing them to Savannah. As well as by privately

inviting the Mortar & Gun down thither, at a time when they all ought to have been held in contempt by every Subject & everyone should have rather helped to cause them to make a submission to me.[130] He also promoted a private trade with the Choctaws independent of the Company, than which nothing could be more prejudical to the King's service, and to him I must impute it, that I have been hatcheted worse in Wells Gazette by letters dated at Augusta than by the Tobacco Eater—shall this man transmit by sale to William Struthers, or any other man, the infamous trade at Little Talsey by which his family have been getting Estates in succession already above thirty years.[131]

This is a significant revelation by Atkin—that the McGillivray "family" had possessed the trading house at Little Tallasee since the late 1720's. This being the case, it must have been founded by William and John McGillivray and owned a few years later by Archibald and Alexander McGillivray and the other Lachlan who was dead by 1735. Most likely Lachlan Lia came to America for the express purpose of learning the trade at Little Tallasee, and as Atkin said, they all became wealthy from the trade albeit was illegal.[132]

In a report dated 29 January 1719, the French were accused of instigating the Alibama Indians in 1715 to attack and murder the English traders at their "factory" in the forks of the Alabama River. By 1717 the French had built Fort Toulouse on the factory site. The English lost the trade of the Chickasaw, Alibama, and Tallapoosa worth about six thousand pounds annually. This amount represented a large trade at this early date. The report also stated that the English factory had been there "above thirty years" placing its establishment somewhere around 1690.[133] No doubt this was the trading house established by Henry Woodward and carried on the trade there until attacked and disbursed in 1715 by the French and their Indian allies. The French had taken advantage of the Yamassee war of 1715, which devastated the struggling colony in South Carolina, and knew the English, being in a weakened condition, could not retaliate nor keep them from building Fort Toulouse. With Fort Toulouse established and garrisoned by French troops, the English did the next best thing and promoted the establishment of the trading house at Little Tallasee only a few miles away founded by McGillivrays. The establishment of their trading house came within a few years of this report of 1719.

On 17 September 1759 Atkin issued an injunction to all the Upper Creek traders forbidding them to trade with the Alibama Indians. He says the French are giving out more presents than they had in the last five years. Many of the presents were English goods—cloth and blankets that Atkin said he had seen for himself.[134]

A meeting held between Atkin and the Upper Creek chiefs on 28 September 1759 was attended by most of the traders, including John Rae and Lachlan McGillivray. Atkin was rapidly stirring the pot and apparently Lachlan felt it was in his best interest to attend this meeting and make his own evaluation of Atkin's actions.[135]

This was the last time Lachlan would appear in the Creek Nation. He also attended a meeting on 9 July at Tuckabatchee Square. The 28 September meeting was probably one of the largest ever held among the Creeks. Most all of the traders and interpreters were there along with the headmen of the Upper and Lower towns.[136] Atkin's arrogant attitude and rude treatment of the Indians most likely led to the Creek uprising against the traders in 1760. In late 1759 the Indians were making threats against Atkin's life. Also contributing to the turmoil was the Mortar's Conspiracy fostered among the Cherokee and Creeks.[137] Mortar was a leading Creek chief in the French interest.

All the French activity was intended to stir up the Creeks and Cherokee against the English. They somewhat succeeded since the Cherokee later attacked and destroyed Fort Loudon and the Creeks murdered several English traders.

Atkin recorded a talk he had with the Gun Merchant on 10 November 1759 when he repeatedly tried to get the Gun Merchant to tell why Atkin's talk at the "great" meeting at Tuckabatchee was not answered by the Indians. The Gun Merchant professed not to know why the Chiefs lost their "wits," but said he had never known of a talk not being answered.[138]

The traders not only were drawing fire from the Indian Superintendent but now began to receive it from Governor Ellis of Georgia. Ellis,
writing to Lyttelton on 7 December 1759, enclosed a letter he had
written to "John Rae, Francis McCartan, Lachlan McGillivray Esq's, and
the other merchants and storekeepers of the town and district of Augusta." Ellis noted that there were unlicensed traders on the river above
Augusta supplying goods, arms, and ammo to the Cherokee. They were
receiving these goods from merchants in Augusta and he enjoined them
from dealing or furnishing goods to any unlicensed trader at risk—"and
I must likewise acquaint you that any person who shall hereafter be
detected in offending against this notification and Injunction will be
disqualified from ever obtaining or enjoying any Indian license either by
themselves, their substitutes, or dependants."[139]

Atkin to Lyttelton on 9 January 1760 accused Lachlan of getting the
Chickasaw Chief drunk on his arrival at Augusta. He thought Spencer's
license should be taken from him—"He remains incorrigibly impudent
& obstinate, declaring that he expects & will hold a license so long as he
pleases to go abroad. He & Lachlan McGillivray went the tour of
Savannah & Charleston together. Besides one of them was scarce one day
sober while in the Creek Nation, and the other had not been in it for
years." He cautioned the Governor not to believe the lies and poison pen
about him in Charlestown. The two had ruined Atkin's reputation
through "lies." He called Spencer a "Madman & Fool."[140]

Atkin to John Cleland 23 December 1759 said that he had recently
learned that John Spencer's license had been renewed, unless the license
was revoked he would lose all his credibility among the Indians and
traders.

> With respect to Spencer, no words scarce can describe the badness
> of his case, whether with Regard to his abusive ill usage of the Wolf &
> degrading him with his own people, or his contemptuous & audacious
> Behavior towards me or his entire Breach of the Instructions given with
> his license, or his illegal trade with his Majesty's enemies. . . . Whereas
> Spencer has not for many years settled either one of seven Towns named

to his license; and not more than one sixth part of the leather traded for by him in a year, is taken from all those towns. It is not enough to revoke his license. The penalty of his Bond must be sued for and the King's Attorney General ought to prosecute him for his trading with the Kings enemies; whereupon I have sufficient proof upon oath.[141]

An order by Atkin dated 18 September 1759 empowered James Germany to take over the trade from Spencer, including his goods. Spencer threatened Germany, but Atkin ordered him to move the goods to Muccalussa. An affidavit by Germany supported Atkins's account of his confrontation with Spencer. He said that Spencer threw a tantrum when Atkin ordered his goods removed from the woods. He cursed Atkin and threw his hat on the ground and said that no Commissioner could tell him what to do. All he could do was take his license and then he would still trade under his Son's name. The affidavit was witnessed by traders George Mackenzie and Joseph Wright. Wright notes that he was so ashamed of the behavior that he left the room.[142]

An affidavit dated 23 November 1759 by Thomas Perriman—

> that the said Mr. Spencer, most commonly came up in the winter from Augusta to his said store, & returned in the summer; spending about half his time at the store, & leaving him the said Perriman there the rest of the year, to sell his goods for him that the orders which he received from the said Spencer were, to buy all the skins that came, let them come from where they might. By which he understood, that he was to deal not only with the Indians of any Town named in his license for trading, but with any of the French Indians of the Albahma Towns, and with the French themselves. And he did accordingly so deal with all alike, where of he did from time to time acquaint the said Spencer, who approved of his so doing. The French came every year bringing deerskins and trade for Blankets, stripped flannel, calico & other things. Spencer sometime did go to the French fort. After Capt Pepper of S.C. came to the Nation, Spencer has rarely gone to the fort and the French do not come as often.[143]

Atkin had a better case against Spencer since Spencer was active in the Nation and resided there part-time. The case against Lachlan was more difficult since Atkin had said himself that Lachlan had not been in the Nation for "years." Even with Spencer he had little success and none against Lachlan. Atkin did become agitated at Lyttelton's inaction over Spencer's case. Atkin to Lyttelton 1 February 1760 writes that Spencer "had almost closed a bargin with John Browne for the sale of his Trade according to license; But Browne insisted on his warranting another Spring Trade."[144]

Lyttelton finally moved to have Spencer investigated. He was ordered not to go to the Creek Nation until the Attorney General had completed his investigation of Atkin's charges. However, the Attorney General decided there was not enough evidence to prosecute.[145]

Lieutenant White Outerbridge to Lyttelton on 6 February 1760:

> Mr. McGillivray sett of yesterday for Little River twenty-five miles above this place under the escort of fifty men—who goes to the assistance of John Vann. Mr. McGillivray's intent of going to Little River is to find a party of Creek Indians now there and if possible to get them to go against the Cherokees. He is empowered by the magistrates of this place to offer them to the amount of a piece of strouds a scalp.[146]

Lieutenant Outerbridge to Lyttelton on 16 February 1760 wrote that Lachlan's people were bringing corn across the river from his plantation to Augusta when they were fired on by a party of Cherokee. They killed one horse and wounded another. Lachlan collected the white people about him plus two or three Chickasaw and several Creeks that were visiting at his house. They crossed the river and chased the Cherokee away and found nothing but a few of their blankets.[147]

Poor Atkin received no respect, and complained to Lyttelton that Spencer was "readying to return to the Creek Nation," and that "the Commissioner is the fast friend, I believe, of him & his friend [Lachlan]."[148] Apparently nothing ever came of Atkin's charges against Spencer nor

Lachlan.[149]

The illegal trade was widespread where an easy dollar was to be made. A letter from William Pitt Chatham to Lyttelton dated 23 August 1760 states—"there is an illegal trade carried on by English subjects of North America and West Indies to the French Islands as well as French settlements at Mobile and Mississippi Rivers. Large sums of Bullion are also sent to these places in return for goods." He directed Lyttelton to aggressively pursue these criminals and do everything in his power to apprehend and punish "all such heinous, offenders."[150] The illegal trade had reached such dimensions that even the Crown had taken notice and steps were taken to curtail, if not to eliminate it.

The arrogance of the traders may go back as far as 1752 when Georgia moved from a private corporation to a royal province. The new governor, John Reynolds, did not arrive in Georgia until two years later. During this period the province was virtually leaderless and the traders did much as they liked. Once this influence was established, they would be reluctant to give it up and it set the stage for later conflicts with the authorities.[151] The Province depended also on the tax and tariffs collected from the lucrative Indian trade.

In closing this chapter and since we have discussed Lachlan Lia's character, it is befitting to include the description left by James Adair in his *History of the American Indian* first published in 1775. Adair was a trader to the Cherokee and Chickasaw and as Lachlan stated above, he had no connection with Adair.

Adair described Lachlan as "humane and intelligent." Lachlan was instrumental in bringing peace between the Cherokee and Creek and Adair said it was due to the Indians having "their favourable opinion of his steady, honest principals."

Adair recommended George Galphin or Lachlan McGillivray as the Superintendent of Indian Affairs [which went to John Stuart].

> Every Indian trader knows from long experience, that both these gentlemen have a greater influence over the dangerous Muskohge, than any others besides. And the security of Georgia requires one or other of

them speedily to superintend our Indian affairs. It was chiefly, the skilful management of these worthy patriots, which prevented the Muskohge from joining the Cheerake, according to treaty, against us in the year 1760 and 1761—to their great expence and hazard of life, as they allowed those savages to eat, drink, and sleep at Silver Bluff below New Windsor garrison, and at Augusta fifteen miles apart.[152]

3

The Trading Partners

The Colonial powers used the Indian trade for political purposes in addition to its economic contribution to England. It very quickly dominated the Indian way of life and when they became dependent on the trade by the middle of the 18th century, their ultimate fate was cast. Trade brought on debts by the Indians who could only pay those debts with the commodity most wanted by the settlers—land. With the trade brought traders who lived in the Creek country, married Indian women and fathered many half-bloods. These half-bloods went on to become the leaders and chiefs as their destiny more and more intertwined with the colonial nations.

The early trade out of Augusta was virtually monopolized by Brown, Rae and Company who became powerful players not only with the Creeks but with colonial authorities. However, when the Spanish captured Mobile and Pensacola in 1780-81, the monopoly began to unwind when Panton, Leslie Company was established at Pensacola and Mobile under a royal charter from Spain giving them the monopoly of the Creek and Choctaw trade. Panton, Leslie Company became a lively competitor for the Augusta traders, but never fully replaced them.

As the Creek Indians became more dependent on the trade goods of the "white man," their winter hunts also became less productive as game became more scarce. The devastating Creek Wars of 1813-14 and 1836 left the Creeks almost destitute. The trade was almost dead; they could not remain in one place long enough to raise a crop; land speculators, settlers, and the militia continually harrassed them, until the frantic Indians, under severe duress and threat, finally agreed to emigrate in 1838 to Indian Territory.

Lachlan Lia McGillivray was an astute businessman and well understood the Indian culture and language. He formed many partnerships with fellow businessmen and traders out of Augusta. He had a warehouse in Augusta and a trading post at Little Tallasee which made for a lucrative enterprise. By 1760 he was a landed gentleman of Savannah and spent his time there. The history and interrelationships of these men make for interesting study.

Patrick Brown came from southern Ireland and was a licensed trader in South Carolina by 1737.[1] In 1741 he moved to Augusta to become a partner to Archibald McGillivray & Co. He became the senior partner after Archibald retired in 1744 and this company dominated the trade for years to come.[2] In 1741 Alexander Wood and Brown were allowed 185 pounds for goods furnished to the Creeks on Bullock's expedition to the Creek Country.[3] This would indicate that they were partners and probably joined Archibald at this time.

By 1750 Brown was expanding his trade and had taken in several partners. A letter from Brown, Rae & Co. to the trustees dated 13 February 1750 says they were formerly of three houses, but were now joined in one company. They had seven partners in the company, some licensed to trade "long before Georgia was settled." The Assembly was debating taking their license at this time which he wrote would do the company great harm. Over the years they had contributed considerably to the good relations between the Indians and the Colony. They also planned to soon bring shipping to Savannah so they could import-export from Savannah instead of Charleston.[4] The company retained its license.

One of the most notable of the partners was John Rae and the business became Brown, Rae and Company. Brown ran the business in Augusta; Rae managed the transportation of skins from Augusta to Charleston; John Pettigrew was a trader to the Chickasaw; Isaac Barksdale, Daniel Clark and Lachlan McGillivray were the traders to the Upper

Creeks; George Galphin was the trader to the Lower Creeks. Galphin and McGillivray emerged as the two leading traders among the Creeks. They seem to have been close friends, but they ended up on opposite sides of the American Revolution.[5]

Brown formed two companies—Brown, Rae & Co. and Patrick Brown Co. Brown was active in the business and left the trading post at Augusta for occasional travel to the Creek Country. In 1747 on his return from the Creek Nation to Augusta, he reported to the Governor that "Malatchee," a principal chief among the Lower Creeks, had informed him that if the Governor sent troops to attack the French fort[6] he would meet him "in the woods and tell him to return" or he must "take what followed."[7] In this same year he was named administrator of the estate of his brother, Thomas Brown, who also was an Indian trader and had a plantation on the Congaree River.[8]

Brown also served as a South Carolina licensed trader and in 1750 was assigned to the Upper Creek towns of "Kileegees, Hillebees, Refallys [Eufaula], Muchlases, Chowasees, and Tasawsa, or the Village, and Chulacogee or Black Drink Old Town."[9]

On 13 February 1750, Patrick Brown, William Sludders, Daniel Clark, and Lachlan McGillivray purchased a lease on five hundred acres in the "Township of Augusta" bordering the Savannah River. For some reason the deed was not recorded until 19 June 1752. The deed was witnessed by Isaac Barksdale and John Rae and brought to Savannah by Brown.[10] This acquisition was an important step in moving the business from New Windsor to Augusta. They were in business there by 1751 or earlier.[11]

Brown and Barksdale tended the store and business in Augusta while Rae, using slaves he owned, employed them in transporting goods and skins to Savannah and Charleston. Galphin, Pettigrew, Clark, and McGillivray were traders to the Creeks where there was always two or three of them resident in the Nation looking after the Company business.[12] This combination of skills and attention to affairs contributed substantially to the success of the company, although with success came resentment from the competition. This resentment grew as the company reached almost monopolistic control over the Creek trade.

Complaints against the Company reached such a high level that in 1752 the South Carolina Council President recommended that none of the licenses of the "Augusta Company" be renewed. The traders also created resentment among the Savannah merchants by moving most of their skins to Charleston for shipment. However, it appears the Company continued to enjoy its virtual monopoly, and the complaints came to nothing.[13]

The Committee on Indian Affairs for the South Carolina Commons House held a hearing on 14 June 1751 concerning problems in the Cherokee Nation. A party of Cherokees had killed a settler and wounded another on the Oconee River and the Committee was seeking ways and means to punish the Cherokee. Patrick Brown "a trader to the Creek Nation" was called to testify. Brown related that the Cherokee and Creek warriors held the colonists in low esteem and thought that instead of revenging the murders, South Carolina would likely send presents instead. Brown said that to stop the murders, stop the trade and the Indians would soon deliver up the guilty.[14]

Brown died on 28 June 1755 and his will was probated on 15 August. He appears to have been from Dublin since he named as heirs a brother and sister living there. He also included a brother living in Londonderry. His partners "Daniel Clarke" and "Laughlin McGillivray" were named two of the four executors of the will.[15]

John Rae came from northern Ireland and arrived in South Carolina in 1730. He became a boatman and moved trade goods between Augusta and Charleston.[16] Flatboats plying the Savannah River during this period were about ten tons loaded. They had a crew of six hands and a steersman. It took fifteen days to go upstream from Savannah to Augusta and four to five days to float downriver.[17]

An entry in the Commons House Journal of South Carolina on 29 November 1749 reports that Rae had recently arrived at Charleston from Augusta bringing news that the smallpox was among the Creeks and Chickasaw. The journal also noted a party of visiting Chickasaw on their way to Charleston and the Assembly in a motion of panic requested that the Governor dispatch a messenger express and turn them back before reaching Charleston.[18]

In 1750 Rae is listed as a licensed South Carolina trader to the "Creeks, Cowetas and Weetomkees."[19] In 1759 Rae owned 550 acres, had a wife, two children, thirty-six slaves and requested a grant for another eight hundred acres near Augusta.[20] He was also a Justice of the Peace in Augusta in 1758.[21]

The Georgia Act regulating the trade assigned traders to a specific town or towns in order to make the traders more responsible and less abusive to the Indians. In July 1761 Rae was assigned to Cusseta of the Lower Creeks and also to the "Oakchoys opposite the said fort [Fort Toulouse]." The towns of "Soogaspoogas, Oakfuskees, Wichagoes, and the Illahatchie" were assigned to "Rae and Mackintosh."[22]

Frontier settlers frequently fortified their houses for protection against Indian raids. Two of the strongest private forts in the Augusta area belonged to John Rae and Francis McCartan. Rae's house was located about 3.5 miles north of Augusta. In 1764 a detachment from Fort Augusta garrisoned Rae's fort, but by 1766 they were back in Augusta.[23]

Rae sided with the Americans in the Revolution and Lt. Colonel Thomas Brown of the Kings Rangers writing to Governor Patrick Tonyn of East Florida in February 1776 said that Rae was a member of the Georgia Provincial Congress and a "colleague" of George Galphin. He reports that Rae, Elbert, and Graham had five to six thousand cattle ranging between the Savannah and "Hogechie" Rivers south of Augusta.[24]

We hear more of Rae in a letter from John Stuart, the British Superintendent of Indian Affairs for the Southern District, to General Clinton on 15 March 1776. Stuart wrote:

> Rae was many years a trader from Augusta to the Creek Nation, licensed by Sir James Wright. He and his partner Graham were now employed by the Congress of Georgia to distribute ammunition to the Creek Indians. They undertook to seize and deliver Mr. Taitt, my agent,

to the Congress and carried up handcuffs for the purpose but found his influence with the Indians superior to theirs.[25]

John Rae's will was probated in August 1778. The document mentioned many friends and relatives, but strangely does not mention his long time partner Lachlan Lia.[26]

A Robert, James, and William Rae were all involved in the trade and were related to John. We do know that Robert was a brother to and in the trade with John and probably James and William were also his brothers.[27] Little is known about these three except a glimpse here and there. David Taitt, Creek Agent for John Stuart, visited Robert and James at the Chehaw Town on the Chattahoochee River in April 1772. Robert acted as an escort for Taitt and they spent several days visiting the towns in the area and attending to Taitt's business.[28] Robert was appointed a commissioner in 1775 to the Southern Indian tribes by the fledgling Confederation of American States.[29] This same year he was at the Uchee Town among the Lower Creeks attending a Council.[30]

Robert died some time in 1779 and his will was probated on 13 October. He was a partner in Rae, Whitfield & Company; Rae, Elbert & Company; and Rae, Elbert & Graham.[31]

All we know of William Rae was a report by Robert French who in May 1760 brought the news to Savannah that the Upper Creeks had attacked and killed several resident traders. He gave a deposition that he saw William Rae lying dead on the ground in front of his trading house at the Oakfuskees. He also saw William Robertson, a pack horseman, dead.[32]

John Pettigrew appeared in the record for only a short period. He was the trader to the Chickasaw and sometimes to the Choctaw. He spoke the Chickasaw language[33] and lived at the Chickasaw Village named Breedcamp[34] which was located among the Upper Creeks near the Coosa River. In 1750 he transported ammunition to the Choctaw and requested fifty pounds for his "trouble."[35] He maintained a trading house among the Chickasaw and in October 1752 a party of Choctaw raided his trading house located about twenty miles from the Chickasaw.

They killed the five Chickasaw who were guarding the house.[36]

We hear of Pettigrew again in 1759, when he owned three hundred acres, had a wife, two children, and twenty slaves. He was requesting a grant for an additional five hundred acres.[37] We know that he was dead by 1764 even though his estate was not settled until 1773.[38]

We first hear of Isaac Barksdale when the South Carolina Assembly allowed him seventy-eight pounds for goods he furnished to the Creeks during James Bullock's visit to the Nation in 1741.[39] He was a licensed trader by 1750 and was assigned to the "Oakfuskee" and "Soocaupogas" of the Upper Creeks.[40]

The journal of Thomas Bosomworth was written in 1752 in the Creek Nation during his travels as the Georgia Agent. An entry on 8 January reads that James Germany was the storekeeper for Barksdale.[41] Germany was a respected trader and lived on the Lower Tallapoosa River in later times and was still there in 1796 when Benjamin Hawkins made his first visit to the Creeks. He was also an interpreter for both the Creeks and Colonial officials.

Barksdale's will, dated 8 November, 1757, freed two female slaves— Nanney and Nancy—along with Nancy's two mulatto children named Johnny and Salley. Jane Rae, daughter of his partner John Rae, received six of his slaves.[42] Most likely Johnny and Salley were his children.

Our first account of William Sludders comes from Captain Patrick McKay, the Georgia Agent, writing on 12 July, 1735 to Lieutenant Governor Broughton, reported how he had "turned out" several of the Carolina traders for not having Georgia licenses. He removed Sludders from the Upper Creeks to the Chickasaw.[43] In July 1741 Sludders was listed as passing through Augusta from South Carolina with four packhorsemen and twenty-five horses.[44]

Sludders, writing on 2 May, 1749 to Governor Glen of South Carolina, posted at the "Oakchoys," reported on the results of a Creek Council where Sludders had read a "talk" from the Governor which he said was well received. Efforts were being made to make peace between the Cherokees and Creeks. The Creek Chiefs asked the Governor to meet them at Ft. Moore or Savannah Bluffs due to the sickness they caught when visiting Charleston and often resulted in deaths among the Chiefs.[45]We know that Sludders was at Breed Camp in 1752 and died in October 1753.[46]

Daniel Clark was also on the list of traders moving trade goods through Augusta to the Creeks in 1741. He had four packhorsemen and twenty pack horses.[47] In 1750 Clark was assigned to the "Coosaws, Abecoos, and Shawanoes on the Key Mulgoe Creek between the Cassaws and Breed."[48] In October Clark sent a report, while at the Cowetas, to the Georgia Commission of Indian Affairs describing the arrival at Coweta of a French officer and several soldiers from Fort Toulouse. They were well received by the Lower Creeks and stayed three days.[49] Clark maintained a trading house and lived in the village of Abecoochee just east of the Coosa River in Talladega County.[50] He was one of the executors of Patrick Brown's will in 1755. He died on 19 April 1757 and his will was probated on 18 May 1757. He apparently came from Inverness, Scotland, where he still had a brother. He mentioned a number of people in his will including Alexander McGillivray [the mariner] and his wife; John McGillivray and William "Sluthers." He left twenty-five pounds to the Charleston Library Society. Lachlan McGillivray was also one of the executors of his will.[51]

Some writers have located Clark in West Florida in later years. Starr[52] wrote that he was a member of the Council and friend of Governor Johnstone where he led a group called "Scotch Party." Braund[53] wrote that Clark attempted to establish a trading business in West Florida with several other traders.

There was a Daniel Clark appearing in West Florida as early as 1765 where he was a prominent member of the West Florida Commons House and served many years in a number of positions with the Council. He was elected from the Mobile District where he was also Customs Collector. He was also an American during the coming Revolution.[54]

Another record on Clark comes from the account book of Major Robert Farmer, the British Commandant at Mobile, where an entry dated 15 February 1765 shows payment to Clark of fifty-seven pounds and six shillings for presents given to the Indians on his passage to the

Illinois Country.[55] Clark wrote, on 18 July 1766, to General Taylor, the military commander of West Florida, asking Taylor to pay a debt of eighty-eight pounds to a John Bradley and deduct that from the amount owed to him for wood delivered in Mobile.[56]

Clark became a large landowner in West Florida, being granted over six thousand acres in 1768, 69, and 70.[57] He was a "reduced Captain of the Pennsylvania troops" and remained in West Florida after the Revolution. In 1795 he was in New Orleans and was a partner in Clark & Rees Co.[58] He was married and had a son Daniel Jr.[59] Various land claims between 1800 and 1804 refer to him as "Colonel."[60] Apparently he later moved to New Orleans to gain the protection of the Spanish government and conducted his business as a Spanish "citizen." There was some similarity between the Clark of West Florida and Clark the partner in Brown, Rae & Co., but the probated will supports his death in 1757 and they were two different people.

George Galphin, along with Lachlan McGillivray, became the leading trader of his day among the Creeks. Galphin traded with the Lower Creeks whereas Lachlan Lia traded among the Upper Creeks. They were never rivals and even though they took opposite sides in the Revolution, they remained stout friends.

Galphin was born in northern Ireland in 1710 and reached America in 1737. He was the son of Thomas and Barbara Galphin. On 28 December 1736 he married Catherine Sanderson, but in less than a year he sailed to America never to return to Ireland. His wife lay claim to his estate when he died in 1780.[61] This forty-four year marriage remains a mystery and apparently Galphin never spoke of it.

He first appeared as a trader in 1741 when he passed through Augusta from Carolina with four packhorsemen and twenty-five horses.[62] Hamer[63] writes that he first appeared as a trader in 1746, but as we see from the above, he was in the trade sometime before 1741. Hamer[64] writes that he had four hundred pack horses by 1750 and during the years 1752 to 1774 he received land grants from South Carolina totaling 7247 acres. He lived at and maintained his trading house at Silver Bluff on the Savannah River near Augusta.

Notes furnished to Albert J. Pickett by Dr. Thomas B. Holmes, states that Galphin arrived at Georgetown, South Carolina, in 1745, where a friend trusted him with an outfit and he made a successful trading trip into Indian Country and got his start.[65] This account seems doubtful as it would be contrary to good business practices for a novice, just arrived, to be given an expensive outfit to plunge into the hostile wilderness. Also, this story is almost the same that Pickett uses for Lachlan Lia.

A speech made by Malatchi, the principal Lower Creek Chief, on 7 December 1747, at a Council with Georgia authorities, revealed that Galphin was asked to interpret a paper left by General Oglethorpe when he visited the Creeks at Coweta. Maltachi said Galphin "told us the contents of that paper was that we had given away all our lands to the King, which made us very uneasy, to think that he should impose upon us so, and give us a paper to take away our lands and not let us know anything of it."[66]

In a letter to the Governor of South Carolina dated 22 March 1755, Galphin informed the Governor that a French officer with three cadets had been among the Lower Creeks to escort the Chief named "Twin" on a trip to New Orleans. They had given Twin a suit of clothes "that is all covered with gold lace." A Spanish captain with ten men had also arrived to take Twin and other headmen to St. Marks for a council with Spanish officials. Galphin reports he persuaded Twin not to go with either the French or Spanish officer.[67]

The Act by the Georgia Council to regulate the Indian trade, passed in July 1761, assigned Galphin to Coweta among the Lower Creeks on the Chattahoochee River.[68] Romans[69] writes that Rae and Galphin had driven cattle through the Creek Country to Pensacola in fulfillment of a contract in 1764-5. This was strictly contrary to Creek policy and had never before been allowed. The Creeks protested the intrusion into their Country to South Carolina officials, but to no avail.

In 1765 John Bartram, the naturalist and father of William Bartram, traveled through the Atlantic Coast colonies and in September visited Galphin at his plantation on the Savannah River. Bartram wrote that

Galphin received large grants from South Carolina and built his house and trading post near Silver Bluff. He used four hundred packhorses in the Indian trade. Bartram stayed two days and Galphin took him a mile downriver from his house to Silver Bluff. The silver lay below the water line and in earlier years the Spanish had attempted to mine the silver by diverting the river. When they abandoned the project, they had dug several feet deep and had uncovered petrified trees, as hard as "flint." Bartram wrote caustically that "ye Scotch highlanders is very lazy & careless, making poor improvements where setted."[70]

Henry Laurens, probably the most prominent merchant and broker in South Carolina, and later President of the Continental Congress, wrote to Galphin in 1770. "After thanking you very heartily for your politeness & civilities when I was lately at your Hospitable castle on the banks of the Savanna I must request you to send the 400 buchels of corn which I purchased of you."[71]

Emistisiguo, a principal Chief of the Upper Creeks, speaking at a Council with Governor Peter Chester of West Florida on 31 October 1771, protested that "Besides Mr. Galphin who was the first that drove cattle, thro our nation, there are many others driving cattle and settling cowpens on our land without our consent."[72] This was the very thing that had alarmed the Indians about Galphin—when it is done one time, there was no end to it. These cowpens were probably some of the earliest settlers on the lower Alabama River in Spanish territory.

Hamer[73] wrote that Galphin retired from the Indian trade in 1774 to spend more time in operating his plantation at Silver Bluff. His nephew David Holmes took over active management of the trading business.

Traders commonly extended credit to the Indians until they could bring in their skins from the winter hunt. Usually this indebtedness grew over a period of time until there was no way the Indians could pay off their debts. Colonial officials would threaten to cut off the trade unless the Indians ceded more land to pay for their debts. The unfortunate Indians had little choice since land was the only asset they could use to pay the debt. Of course debt was extended liberally in order to entrap the

Indians who little understood these business transactions. In 1775 the Indians were indebted to Galphin in the amount of 9,791 pounds or about $35,000. A treaty was made and ratified in 1775 whereas the Creek and Cherokee would cede sufficient lands to pay for all the traders' debts. The Revolution delayed the sale of the lands and they were confiscated by the new state of Georgia. A provision was provided however whereby claimants could petition for restitution at a later date after the war. The heirs of Galphin petitioned for redress in 1793. The case dragged through the courts until finally settled in 1848. The U.S. Treasury paid off the claim plus interest in the amount of $234,871.[74]

During this stormy period of the early rebellion, each person had to choose between the rebels or the King. In 1775 Galphin made his choice openly by accepting an appointment as one of the Georgia Commissioners to the Southern Indians.[75]

John Stuart, writing to General Henry Clinton on 15 March 1776, stated that Galphin:

> for many years a trader in the Lower Creek Nation, by which he has acquired a considerable fortune and become unavoidably acquainted with many of the Chiefs, but this sort of acquaintance would not have give much weight had he not upon every occasion been employed by Sir James Wright and Lieut-Governor Bull to interfere in Indian Affairs and to carry whatever point they had in view: the influence derived from his being so employed he now exerts in behalf of the rebels whose Commisioner he is.[76]

Galphin having lived in the Nation for many years had substantial influence with the Lower Creeks and through his persistent efforts the Indians were effectively neutralized during the Revolution, notwithstanding the strenuous efforts by John Stuart and his deputies to enlist the Creeks to his Majesty's cause. We can see some of Stuart's frustration in the tone of his letter above.

A letter from the Creek Agent, David Taitt, to Lord George Germain dated 6 August 1779, stated that Galphin was "the rebel agent" and "a most infamous man, had by large presents and promises formed a Party among the Indians in two towns in the Upper Creeks to kill Mr. Cameron [the Cherokee Agent], myself and interpreters." Galphin and his Indian party got as close as four miles when Taitt was warned by friendly Creeks. They told him of the high price Galphin had placed on his scalp.[77]

Lieutenant Colonel Thomas Brown, the famous Commander of the Kings Rangers, on or about 1 June 1780 arrived at Galphin's home at Silver Bluff, arrested and charged him with treason, but before the case could be tried, Galphin died on 1 December 1780.[78]

The Colonial Georgia Council, after reoccupying Savannah in 1780, passed a "Disqualifying Act" on 6 July, which forever banished from the Province a long list of "rebels." George Galphin the "rebel Supt. of Indian Affairs" was on the list.[79]

Galphin had made his will in 1776. The eight page will distributed all his worldly goods to his children and scores of friends and relatives in Georgia and Ireland. The most notable item was granting the freedom of his mulatto daughters and half-blooded Indian daughter. He included his sons John and George whose mother was a Creek woman named Metawney. These two half-blooded sons were later renegades on the Georgia frontier and became outcasts of the Lower Creeks. His estate was very substantial including cash funds, land, houses, slaves, cattle, horses, and other assets. But as a matter of interest into the personality of George Galphin, he left nothing to his wife in Ireland, nor to his four mistresses in South Carolina—Sapho, a mulatto; Nitshukey, a Creek; Rachel Dupee, a white; and Metawney, a Creek.[80] His will was probated in 1782;[81] however, his wife Catherine Sanderson came to America, apparently after his death, to lay claim to his fortune. She may have succeeded as she died in November 1795 at Placentia just outside Savannah.[82]

Of the seven partners, three—Brown, Barksdale, and Clark—were dead by 1757. The fate of Pettigrew is unknown although we know that he was dead by 1764.[83] Rae and Galphin took up the Rebel cause during the Revolution, whereas Lachlan Lia remained a staunch loyalist. The partnership appears to have fractured sometime during the 1760's.

Sentiments of rebellion were stirring by 1765 and people began taking sides. It was most probably this difference that caused the partners to go their own way.

John Spencer, at one time a partner with Lachlan, first appears on the list of traders compiled in July 1741 and having three packhorsemen and sixteen horses.[84] On 11 November 1750 Spencer wrote from the Oakchoy to William Pinckney of South Carolina reporting on various rumors in the Creek Country—one being that the French were going to build a fort on the Choctaw Path at a place called "Cawhambo," and it would be garrisoned by two hundred men. In 1752 he was the assigned trader to Mucclassa on the Lower Tallapoosa River.[85]

In 1755 the South Carolina Council, investigating the Indian trade, took testimony from Spencer. The Council reported that Lachlan had greatly exaggerated the Creek requests for lower trade prices in order to drive their poorer competitors out of business.[86] We do not know if Spencer's testimony was damaging to Lachlan or not; however, in November 1754 the Council records describe him as a "creditable trader in the Creek Nation."[87] In January 1756 Lachlan purchased all the goods, credits, etc. of "John Spencer deceased" for three hundred pounds.[88]

Notwithstanding the above "deceased" account, a Spencer in November 1759 carried a talk from the head chiefs of the Choctaw Nation to Governor Ellis of Georgia. The talk was given by the Choctaw at Mucclassa.[89] This may have been John Spencer's son which he mentioned earlier.

In January 1760, Edmund Atkin, the first Superintendent for Indian Affairs, filed a complaint against Spencer for "trading in the woods, and with his majesty's enemies and not having settled a Trading House in the town for which he had obtained a license to trade."[90] Usually a trader trading "in the woods" was doing so without a license or dealing in illegal goods such as whiskey. In trading whiskey, the trader frequently managed to get the Indians drunk and then fleece them of their skins, with the Indians finding out later that all they had left was a hangover. Large profits could be made in this manner. Alden[91] wrote that

Spencer's license was revoked on 7 February 1760 by Governor Lyttleton of South Carolina.

In May 1760 a large party of Cherokee, accompanied by a Creek Chief, carried an important talk to the French at Fort Toulouse. The Cherokee had with them two English prisoners and many scalps. The Creek Chief was a brother to the important Chief Mortar, who had a close relationship with the Cherokee. The Creeks were offended that the Cherokee would bring two English prisoners into the Nation. The Creek Chiefs threatened to "knock them on the Head," but the French Commandant at the Fort promised to take the prisoners and send them back to the traders. But when the Creek Chiefs arrived at the fort to take custody of the prisoners, they found that Spencer had already purchased them from the Cherokee. The Creeks were enraged that they had to reimburse Spencer for the prisoners. This situation was the same to them as having paid their enemies, the Cherokee, instead of receiving them without cost from the Commandant.[92]

In 1761 Spencer was licensed by South Carolina as a trader to Little Savannah [Shawnee] House opposite to the Mucclassa on the Lower Tallapoosa River.[93] Spencer was killed in 1763 by the Upper Creeks. Carolina authorities demanded that the murderers be turned over, but Mortar influenced the Creeks to refuse.[94]

The Spencer we find in the trading records after 1756 appears to be of a totally different personality than the one "deceased" in 1756. No reference can be found after 1756 that indicates this John Spencer was a partner to Lachlan Lia.

The last of Lachlan Lia's partners was John Graham who came to Georgia in 1753 from Scotland. He became a prominent merchant at Savannah having an import-export trade in addition to being a planter and plantation owner. He was a member of the Georgia Council and Lieutenant Governor from 1776 until 1782. After the evacuation by the British of Savannah he went to East Florida.[95]

John Graham was appointed Superintendent of Indian Affairs for the Western District in 1782. He was at Savannah in July 1782 with two hundred Choctaws, but since they had arrived in January and were not used, they returned by way of East Florida. Graham asked for direction to employ the Chickasaw and Choctaw on the Mississippi River to harass the Spanish.[96]

Graham was in St. Augustine by October 1782 and wrote Carlton about his Chickasaw harassing the Spanish on the Mississippi River. They had just captured the wife of the Illinois Commandant —who was promptly released. He laments that he always tries to have one of his officers present on these raids to prevent "Acts of Barbarity."[97]

Lachlan and Graham were partners in the trade as early as 1768.[98] They also jointly owned land together.[99] Lachlan Lia did not die until 1799 and he long outlived his old friends and partners he was so long associated with in the Indian trade.

4

The Landed Gentleman

The turmoil among the traders created by his majesty's Superintendent of Indian Affairs, Edmond Atkin, no doubt had an effect on Lachlan Lia and his outlook on the trade. Atkin's serious accusations of his being involved in the illegal trade was apparently never pursued by South Carolina or Georgia officials. However, this confrontation with Atkin must have been an embarrassment, and a major factor in his decision to give up the trade and become a "gentleman farmer." He likely had been planning such a move for some time and followed through at this time.

By 1761, or earlier, he had given up the trade as a direct participant. The Georgia Act for Regulating the Trade, passed in July 1761, did not list him among the licensed traders.[1] He seems to have continued as a merchant in the trade until 1769 when his cousin William McGillivray noted in a letter that Lachlan Lia had "disengaged" from the trade.[2]

During the late 1750's and early 1760's Lachlan Lia was already in transition from the trading business to plantation life in Savannah. He had been busy using his accumulated wealth and influence to gain thousands of acres of rich farmland and virgin timber tracts—all in or near Augusta and Savannah. He was involved in many land transactions, especially obtaining land grants from the Colonial government.

He had served in the General Assembly and was re-elected in 1760 representing Augusta. As a member he made many good contacts that served him well in later years.[3]

His most important land acquisition came on 3 February 1762 when he purchased Vale Royal from Pickering Robinson for 1335 pounds. This was a pre-arranged deal since Robinson had received the grant from Georgia only two days previously. Lachlan made his home on this plantation which was located on the south bank of the Savannah River bordering the town of Savannah to the northwest.[4]

The plantation consisted of one thousand acres and by 1764 he had built a barn, a "good" overseer's house, and a rice-pounding machine operated by water. He planted rice on Vale Royal and also on Hutchinson Island which he had acquired. The island was large and located just opposite Savannah. He also owned another tract called Springfield consisting of 445 acres and adjoining Vale Royal. Springfield was higher ground and was used to raise horses. The Augusta Road ran parallel to the River and alongside Vale Royal toward the northwest.[5]

Lieutenant John Mackay's Chart of the Savannah River as late as 1833 identified Vale Royal just upstream from Musgrove Creek with rice fields just beyond. Hutchinson's Island is shown almost entirely in rice fields, but by 1849, Lieutenant M.L. Smith's Chart shows the island in corn and cotton fields.[6] The island was described by the earlier traveler, Francis Moore, in 1735—"the great part of which is open ground, where they mow hay for the Trustee's horses and cattle."[7] It was known as Hutchinson's Island as early as November 1734. It was described as "excellent land for the feeding of cattle."[8]

Before buying Vale Royal and moving to Savannah, Lachlan lived in Augusta where he owned the White House Tract which he and Daniel Clark purchased in 1756. Here they lived and had their trading house. It was on the main road and just northwest of Augusta and below where the road forked—one path following the Savannah River to the Cherokee Country, and the other branching westerly to the Creeks. The tract consisted of five hundred acres and it was put up for sale in 1764 and in 1765 it was owned by a partnership of John Brown, William Struthers, John McGillivray, and William Trevin. Robert Mackay owned the tract in 1770 and during the Revolution he fortified the house making it a stockade.[9] In 1780 Lieutenant Colonel Thomas Brown, Commander of the Kings Rangers, occupied Mackay's house where it was described as a store building near the river. Brown and his Indian allies were attacked by Colonel Elijah Clark and the Georgia militia. Brown was saved by the timely arrival of British regulars from Ninety-Six under the command of Lieutenant Colonel John H. Cruger.[10]

Being a good loyalist and a leading citizen of Georgia, Governor James Wright had bestowed on Lachlan a commission of "Captain of militia." When the Governor met with a Creek Indian delegation in December 1762, the clerk recorded that "his Excellency addressed himself to them by Captain McGillivray."[11] That same year he and his troop escorted Wright to Augusta where he attended a large council with the Indians.[12]

Henry Laurens, the prominent Charleston merchant, writing on 12 October 1762, discussed a business matter concerning "Messrs. McGillivray & Co." He wrote that Lachlan was a "safe" man and that he resided "chiefly around Augusta & Georgia, say Savanna. When he comes this way if I have proper opening I will speak to him."[13] In the spring of 1763 the following appeared in the *Savannah Gazette*.:

> The Gentlemen belonging to the first troop of horse militia, commanded by Lachlan McGillivray Esq. are ordered to appear, compleatly accounted, at the Captain's house on Saturday the 4th of June next, at eight of the clock in the morning, it being a general muster. No frivolous excuses will exempt absentees from being mustered. By order of the Captain, James Muter clk.[14]

A later article on 9 June indicates Lachlan and his horse troop participated in a review on 4th of June celebrating the King's birthday.

Lachlan took his place among the elite society of Savannah and became the owner of thousands of fertile acres in the Colony. He not only received large grants over the years, but he was also purchasing land. Land grants had to be improved or risk forfeiture. The recipient also had to have sufficient family members, indentures, hired help, or at a later date slaves, in order to work the land and make it productive. Lachlan, being a bachelor, apparently met these requirements with hired help, slaves and indentures. Over a twenty-one year period he received the following grants:

5 June 1754	500 acres on Little Ogechee River
15 May 1756	500 acres on Little Ogechee River
15 May 1756	Town Lot in Hardwick
8 September 1756	500 acres near Augusta to Lachlan and Daniel Clark
8 September 1756	Town Lot in Augusta to Lachlan & Daniel Clark
1 February 1757	50 acres to Lachlan & Clark
July 1757	300 acres about 17 miles below Augusta
July 1757	Town Lot in Augusta
November 1757	100 acres at New Savannah
6 December 1757	400 acres on Savannah River
7 February 1758	500 acres in Augusta district to Lachlan and John Spencer
18 May 1758	50 acres in St. George Parish
4 September 1759	100 acres for Alexander McGillivray – infant
November 1759	1000 acres in Halifax district
3 December 1760	100 acres St. Paul Parish
January 1761	1000 acres on Altamaha River
7 July 1761	1000 acres in St. George Parish
27 November 1761	Town Lot in Savannah
3 February 1762	100 acres in St. George Parish
3 February 1762	Town Lot in Augusta
7 February 1762	100 acres in Savannah Township
7 September 1762	Town Lot in Savannah
3 December 1762	Town Lot in Augusta
3 January 1764	Town Lot in Augusta
6 March 1764	392 acres in St. Andrews Parish

6 March 1764	Town Lot in Savannah
6 March 1764	Farm Lot (45 acres) in Savannah
6 March 1764	Town Lot in Augusta
3 April 1764	500 acres in St. Paul Parish to Lachlan, John Rae and George Galphin
5 April 1764	500 acres St. Paul Parish to Lachlan, John Rae & George Galphin (surviving partners of Brown, Rae & Co.)
7 May 1765	45 acres in Christ Church Parish
4 November 1766	100 acres in St. Matthew Parish
1 September 1767	10 acres in Savannah
6 September 1768	500 acres in St. George Parish
1 November 1768	5 acres in Savannah
3 October 1769	750 acres in St. Andrews Parish
3 October 1769	750 acres in St. Daniel Parish
3 April 1770	1000 acres in St. David Parish
3 April 1770	600 acres in St. Marys Parish
1 November 1775	300 acres St. Paul Parish
1 November 1775	400 acres St. Paul Parish[15]

Notices began appearing in the fall of 1763 indicating Lachlan was leaving the Province. He asked speedy payment of all debts and advertised property for sale.[16] Again on 27 October[17] Lachlan advertised that he was leaving the Province in a few months and asked payment of all debts. He advertised for sale three lots in Savannah; and surprisingly, Vale Royal consisting of 1000 acres with 220 acres of "good rice land;" a large new barn; rice pounding machine by water; good overseer's house one and one-half miles from Savannah; 800 acres known as Sabine Fields two and one-half miles from Savannah well timbered in white and red oak; 200 acres of good rice land including new barn and dwelling house; 350 acres two miles from Savannah on Ogechee Road with dwelling house and barn; 500 acres on Little Ogechee River; 1000 acres in Halifax fronting on the Savannah River; and 450 acres in Halifax with house and other improvements.

During this period he continued to advertise and also made some sales—on 21 February 1764 he sold one hundred acres for ten pounds to Henry Bell;[18] 7 April he sold five hundred acres on Little Ogechee River for one hundred pounds to James Habersham;[19] 23 February 1764 he advertised for sale several horses, cows, and calves;[20] 1 March he advertised five hundred acres for sale by John Rae, George Galphin, and Lachlan McGillivray with the notation that they are the "surviving partners of Brown, Rae and Company;"[21] and on 27 September he advertised for sale horses of Chickasaw blood and steers that are "plow broken." The sale was to be at Vale Royal plantation with the notation that "his plantation is entirely free of the smallpox."[22]

Lachlan Lia had made his fortune in the New World and was ready to return to his homeland and live the gentleman's life in the Valley of Nairn. Something, which we have been unable to uncover, changed his mind and he remained in Georgia with later visits to Scotland, until he sailed for England in 1782. Lachlan Lia probably foresaw the coming storm clouds of the Revolution and wanted to sell out and take his fortune back to Scotland. Most likely he changed his mind because he could not sell the bulk of his land holdings at a reasonable price and he was not about to walk away at this point.

A series of letters written by Henry Laurens to Lachlan Lia and James Cowles in Bristol reveals his mediation efforts in a dispute between the two. His letter to Lachlan on 2 January 1764:

> This covers a letter from our good friend Mr. James Cowles of Bristol which he requests me to forward & also to use my interest with you to comply with the request therein which as I learn from him is for 92.19 pounds sterling due to him for interest on your account. I know him for many years experience to be so reasonable a man & so fair a dealer that I am persuaded he would make no charge but what was strictly consistant with justice & the custom of trade & indeed as he represents he will be rather a looser by your correspondence if this sum

is not paid to him. On the other hand I know you for many years experience too, to be a man of so much honour & punctuality that I am sure you will not withhold a doit [small Dutch coin] from Mr. Cowles or any other man that he has a just right to claim from you. Therefore, I make no doubt your giving orders for payment of the above mentioned sum or assigning such reasons for not paying it as will be satisfactory to him.[23]

Laurens to James Cowles on 24 January 1764—

By the first good opportunity after the receipt of your favour of 4th November I conveyed your letter to Lachlan McGillivray in Georgia under cover of one from myself as per annexed copy which I hope will produce a good effect. I believe he will not be offended at my freedom & I shall in due time communicate what he may say in reply.[24]

Laurens to Cowles & Hartford, 8 May 1764—

I wrote you per Higgins & Chisman the 5th Instant to which please be referred. This addition is first to inform Mr. Cowles that Mr. Lachlan McGillivray is going to London in the ship *Polly*, Capt Ratsey, to sail some day in this week. Therefore tis needless for me to urge him, Mr. McGillivray, further to a compliance with Mr. Cowles just demand as he will probably have a much better opportunity of doing it in Bristol & I am in hopes there will no obsticle to success, for if I am not much mistaken in that Gentleman he will not refuse to do what he ought to do both as an honest man & as a generous merchant.

The *Polly* cleared for sailing on 10 May but we cannot confirm that Lachlan was aboard; in fact, it appears that he changed his plans for some reason, and postponed the trip.

At about the same time Laurens was having trouble collecting interest from Lachlan, he was in court defending himself from a complaint brought by Richard Collis and his daughter Elizabeth. On 14 May

1764 Lachlan was required to post a four thousand pound bond in the South Carolina Court of Chancery. From the record it cannot be ascertained what the complaint was, but a four thousand pound bond in 1764 was enormous and the complaint must have been serious. Lachlan's attorney filed an answer to the complaint on 28 May 1764 and for a year Collis made no further responses in court. Consequently on 6 June 1765 the court dismissed the complaint, but Lachlan had to pay court costs.[25]

On 7 February 1765 Lachlan sold five hundred acres in St. Pauls Parish for four hundred pounds to Telhero Rouantre. This land was originally granted to Lachlan and John Spencer, but passed to Lachlan when Spencer died.[26]

Lachlan, John Rae, and George Galphin petitioned the Governor and Georgia Council in January 1765 for fifty thousand acres to lay out a township for new settlers from Ireland. John Rae and George Galphin came from Ireland. Rae came to America in 1730 and arrived in Georgia in 1734. For some years he had a trading boat carrying deerskins from Augusta to Charleston. By 1750 he was a partner of Patrick Brown. Rae purchased a plantation four miles from Savannah in 1760 and named it Rae's Hall. Two years later in 1768 they still had not brought over any immigrants and they asked for a three-year extension. However, the Board of Trade had disallowed the Act granting the land, but it never arrived to Governor Wright until March 1768. The Board was afraid that the immigrants coming from Ireland were weavers and persons of skill who would set up manufacturing to compete with England. Also they wanted the Protestants to remain in Ireland.

Rae and Galphin, unaware of the disallowance of the Act, went ahead and recruited 107 people who departed Belfast in September 1768 and arrived at Savannah on 2 December. The Georgia Council granted a sum of money to pay their passage as promised. Wright had to explain to the Board that the disallowance arrived too late to prevent the immigration and the cost was 560 pounds. Governor Wright named the new settlement Queensborough. It was on Lamberts Creek about three miles from present Louisville.

The recruiting in Ireland was continued by Rae's cousin Matthew

Rae and the *Hopewell* cleared Belfast on 5 October 1769 with 166 immigrants and arrived at Savannah 6 December. A sum of two hundred pounds was appropriated for their care and given to John Rae to disperse. Emigrants continued to come over and on 4 February 1771 John Rae petitioned for and received another 25,000 acres.[27]

Queensborough hardly survived the Revolution. Many were loyalist and had their lands confiscated, and the war devastated the area. After the Revolution the town of Louisville was laid out only three miles away and by 1800 Queensborough was only a memory.

Lachlan again ran an ad[28] saying he planned to sail for England in the Spring and wished to settle all issues before he left, and if his debts had not been paid up, they can rest assured of being sued. On 29 August 1765[29] Lachlan advertised for "two runaway negro slaves" from his plantation and offered a reward of ten shillings sterling for their return. He also warned people against trespassing on his land and "cutting timber and marsh grass."

On 10 October 1765[30] Captain Lachlan McGillivray summoned his horse troop for muster at his house on Vale Royal. Again on 4 June 1766[31] Captain McGillivray ordered his troop to muster. These were routine milita training exercises.

A most interesting deed written on 12 March 1764, but not recorded until 1767, reveals considerable insight into the private life of Lachlan, but also leaves us with unanswered questions. The deed deals with a child—James F. Barnard—whose father was Edward Barnard and mother was Abigal Minis, both indentured servants. It is unclear if they were indentured to Lachlan, but it would seem likely that they were. The deed in part reads—

> Whereas Lachlan McGillivray of Vale Royal in Christ Church Parish in said Province of Georgia, esquire, by his hand and deed of gift duly executed and dated the twelfth day of March in the year of our Lord one thousand seven hundred and sixty four did give and grant out of the affection he had for the above James Frazer Barnard, his Godson and for his better advancement unto the said James Frazer Barnard his heirs and

assigns all that tract of land containing three hundred and fifty acres situate and being in the township of Savannah aforesaid and consisting of several farm lotts contigious to each other to have and to hold the said tract of land and other the—thereby given and granted with the apportionment to him the said James Frazer Barnard his heirs and assigns forever agin and by the said deed of gift duly recorded in the Secretary's Office of the said Province.[32]

Abigal Minis is referred to as a "gentlewoman" which under the circumstances probably means "a woman of refined manners and good breeding."[33] The Minis were a prominent family in later times.

Edward Barnard became a prominent citizen of Georgia and was later a Justice of the Peace.[34] James Frazer was an early trader and associate of Lachlan Lia in the trade. Edward Barnard was his son-in-law and continued Frazer's business after he retired.[35]

Barnard was married to the daughter of James Frazer; he has a son out of wedlock by an indentured servant. The child was named for his grandfather James Frazer and given the surname of his father; Lachlan Lia was the Godfather and gave a substantial gift to the child. One can only imagine what is the relationship of all these people.[36]

In 1761 he gave a slave to Bellamy Roche, the daughter of Matthew Roche,[37] and in May 1767 he deeded two slaves "for love" to Miss Temar Oates, the daughter of John Oates, his manager and overseer of Vale Royal. If Temar died before age twenty-one, one slave was to go to "my natural son" Alexander McGillivray and the other to Fanny Oates, sister to Temar. The deed was witnessed by John Oates and Alexander McGillivray.[38]

John Oates on 30 January 1780 made a deed or bond to trustees James Robertson, Georgia Attorney General, and Alexander McGillivray, Commissary of the Creek Indians, which gave "one-half lot and four slaves for the use of the Black woman Rose, property of Lachlan McGillivray of Vale Royal. On Rose's death, the property was to go to Oates daughter, Temar Oates.[39]

John Oates' will was probated on 17 June 1789 and it mentions his children and grandchildren. The will seems to have been drawn before 1781. He mentions his daughter Temar Waters, wife of Sinclair Waters, who was one of the executors.[40]

Lachlan returned to Georgia sometime between 30 January and 8 June 1780. During his forced absence he made the Attorney General and his son Alexander McGillivray the trustees of his estates between the time Governor James Wright returned in July 1779 and Lachlan arrived sometime between January and June 1780.

Lachlan had involved his half-blooded Indian son in his affairs and given him a position of trust at a very early age. Most likely if Alexander had remained in Savannah with his father he would have been a major heir to his estates. But the young man gave up the white man's world and went home to Little Tallasee on the Coosa River to be with his mother and his sisters. After reverting to the Indian lifestyle, Alexander became little more than a footnote in Lachlan's life.

Lachlan was busy and involved in other things besides land acquisitions. Alden[41] writes that Lachlan was appointed in 1767 by John Stuart to serve as his representative on the survey party that was to determine the line between Georgia and the Creek Nation.

Lachlan was sued in the summer of 1767 because of a survey error that overlapped his 188 acres with 1495 acres belonging to George Galphin.[42] The suit was brought by the Reverend Joachim Zubly when the Governor of South Carolina refused to issue him a new grant.[43]

Zubly also had a serious dispute with Lachlan over ownership of some 1800 acres in Georgia. Zubly was born in Switzerland in 1724 and ordained in 1744. Soon after coming to South Carolina he moved to Savannah and was a Presbyterian minister there by 1760. Zubly sympathized with the rebels during the Revolution and was elected to the Continental Congress in 1775 where he energetically participated in the work of that body. However, he became disenchanted with the cause when it became obvious that ultimate independence was the goal of Congress. He returned to Georgia in 1777 and came under the suspicion of the Council of Safety which arrested him in late 1777. He was banished from Georgia and half his estates were confiscated. He fled to

South Carolina but returned to Savannah when the royal government was re-established in 1779. He died in July 1781.[44] Lachlan and Galphin ran ads in the early spring of 1768 warning people that Zubly was trying to sell the land in question, but he did not have title.[45]

On 12 June 1767 Lachlan made his will and his cousin John also made his first will a few months later in December 1767.[46] Lachlan left his estate to his cousins John and William McGillivray. Only in case the intent of the will "cannot, by rules of law, go in a manner as I have herein before given and bequeathed it," the estate would be divided among his many relations in America and Scotland.[47] His son Alexander was only one of the many relations mentioned. His Indian wife Sehoy was not mentioned, nor his two daughters Sophia and Jeanette.

The *Savannah Gazette*[48] on 8 July 1767 reported that Lachlan sailed on the schooner *Nocturnal*, Captain Tufts being the master, for Charleston and "from whence he is to go to the northward." He likely was going to Philadelphia or New York on business. He was back by 15 January 1768 when Henry Laurens writing to Smith and Bailles says he tried to sell Lachlan a cargo of slaves, but they could not come to terms on the deal. He wrote that Lachlan was with the House of Mr. Graham & Co. and was in Charleston with Mr. Hall of the house of Inglis and Hall. Laurens sent the cargo of slaves to Savannah where they were taken by Graham and Co. who in turn sold 80 slaves to Penman & Co. of St. Augustine.[49] Apparently Lachlan and Laurens closed the deal before he left Charleston. This places Graham & Co., and Lachlan, squarely in the slave trade which was a very lucrative enterprise.

He was appointed Justice of the Peace for Christ Church Parish on 10 February 1768.[50] On 8 May he was chosen as a representative in the General Assembly for St. George Parish.[51] Then on 3 September he acted as the official interpreter for Governor Wright at a council with the Creek Indians in Savannah. For the first time, the clerk records Lachlan with the sub-title "Esquire."[52] Lachlan was now a landed gentleman of means.

Laurens again wrote to James Cowles on 24 May 1768 saying he is still trying to get Lachlan to pay the bill of interest claimed by Cowles.

The letter in part reads—"I shall probably see Mr. McGillivray within ten days at Savanna & in such case shall stir him up to do you justice, otherwise shall do it by a letter. . . ."[53] This letter also seems to indicate that Lachlan never made his trip to England where he was expected to meet with Cowles and settle the account. With the winds of rebellion stirring he may have been unable to sell his plantations. He had made his fortune and if he could sell out, he could return to Scotland and live in comfort the remainder of his life.

Laurens, writing to Lachlan McIntosh on 5 December 1768, mentioned a bill drawn on "McGillivray, Graham & Clark."[54] This partnership included John Graham and John Clark. It is unknown if John Clark was related to Lachlan's earlier partner Daniel Clark, but it seems plausible that he was.

Lachlan ended up the year of 1768 by being engaged as surveyor, along with James Mackay, to mark the "Indian line" above Augusta.[55] Lachlan appeared very busy in 1769. He advertised for sale some seven hundred to eight hundred head of cattle.[56] On 3 May[57] he subscribed to the building fund for a new "Presbyterian Meeting House" where he was a trustee. On 31 May[58] he ran an ad warning that a tract of land had been properly surveyed and warned anyone against trespassing. The land in question was jointly owned by John Graham, John Rae, and Lachlan. On 19 June Lachlan took one William Handley to court for debts unpaid and owed to him. Handley was a merchant in Savannah and owed Lachlan 1376 pounds—a sizeable sum.[59] On 12 July he served on the Grand Jury.[60] Deeds dated 8 and 9 August conveyed 450 acres on the Savannah River from one Adrain Loyer, a gunsmith in Savannah, to John Graham, James Graham, John Clark and Lachlan for the sum of 485 pounds.[61] On 4 October[62] he advertised for a good overseer for "one of Mr. McGillivray's plantations." He also had a house for rent with garden and pasture. He ended up the year being chosen president of the St. Andrews Club of Savannah. Present at this "joyous" meeting was the Governor and Chief Justice of Georgia.[63]

Lachlan's cousin William McGillivray, Chief of the Clan, wrote to him on 23 August 1769 from Dunmaglass. He said that his brother

Donald, the sea captain, had been visiting him and he understood that Lachlan Lia and John McGillivray were going to buy him a vessel. He went on to say that the family estate "is but small" and he cannot afford to marry as he must care for his mother and sister.[64] This letter gives us some insight into the family—Lachlan had wanted William to marry so there could be heirs to the Clan Chieftanship. Due to William's economic condition, Lachlan later went to Scotland and recruited William to come to America where he would make him his heir and he could make his fortune. This would allow him to return to Scotland, marry, create heirs, and live comfortably at Dunmaglass.

Early in 1770[65] Lachlan served notice in an ad that he planned "to leave the province" in early summer and he includes the usual notice about everyone paying their debts owed to him. On 21 February[66] Lachlan is again appointed Justice of the Peace for Christ Church Parish. On 25 April[67] an ad appears for two runaway slaves from Lachlan's plantation on Hutchinson's Island. A reward would be given if they were returned to Vale Royal.

Sir James Wright, Governor of Georgia, writing to the Earl of Hillsborough on 28 May 1770, said that the packet of papers being

> delivered by Mr. Lauchlan McGillivray a gentleman of very considerable property and one on whose information in every respect relative to the affairs of this Province your Lordship may entirely confide, and I think myself more particularly happy in having the opportunity, as Mr. McGillivray resided the greatest part of his time for upwards of 20 years in the Creek Nation, understands the Indian language better than they themselves, and is perfectly well acquainted with their strength and the nature and Policy of the Trade with them, and will be able to give your Lordship the fullest and clearest satisfaction with respect to any inquires you may think proper to make, and I must not omit to mention that he is also a firm friend to Government.

Sir James continued, "My Lord there are now two vacancys in the Council for filling up which, I begg leave to recommend Anthony Stokes

Esqr. His majesties Chief Justice and the Bearer Mr. McGillivray." Wright continued that there may be another vacancy and in that case he would recommend Mr. Pryce the Attorney General.[68] Lachlan was now moving in the upper circle of Georgia politics and society.

A "talk" given by the Creek chiefs to Sir. James Wright at Augusta on 1 May 1771 referred to Lachlan, saying "he came very young to our nation and knew well how we lived and that the white people was oblidged to be satisfied with the same coarse food that we used."[69] We are not sure if Lachlan was present at this meeting, but it seems likely that he was since the Chiefs referred to him. He may have been acting as interpreter. We know that he was in England by January 1772.

Before Lachlan went to England he prepared a document that gave power of attorney to three men—John Graham, James Habersham, and Nathanial Hall. The document was written 2 May 1770, just before Wright wrote to Hillsborough that Lachlan was hand carrying his letter dated 28 May 1770, but it was not executed until 1 January 1772. The power of attorney would not have been activated until Lachlan left the country. Notwithstanding Wright's letter, Lachlan delayed his journey until probably December 1771.[70] He was back in Georgia by 17 April 1773.[71] Research in Scotland and England has turned up only a few letters written by Lachlan while he was there in 1772, but they are revealing and give us insight into family affairs, and also give us a time when he returned to Georgia.

Henry Laurens confirmed Lachlan being in Scotland, writing to William Cowles 29 May 1772, "Mr. McGillivray resides in Scotland, but I know not in what part. I do expect to see him before my return to America."[72] Laurens again writing to Cowles on 25 September says, "Be pleased to present my respects to him [Cowles' uncle] & let him know that the Mr. McGillivray of whom he sometime since spoke & wrote by you to me, is now in London."[73] Laurens was in England at this time and planned to be there for some time.

His sister Jean Roy[74] married one Duncan McGillivray, a tenant on one of the McGillivray estates. Duncan died in 1781. From this union came two children—Lachlan Jr. who came to Georgia and managed the plantations for Lachlan and William; and a daughter Marjorie. Marjorie died in 1842 leaving no descendants. Apparently she never married. Her will records her total estate of only forty-eight pounds, which she left to her nieces and a set of silver spoons to one William McGillivray.[75]

Lachlan, writing to his sister Jean from Inverness on 16 August 1772, said that he was furnishing her one milch cow four years old, young cows, one young work horse, twenty-four young breeding sheep, a ram, and young bull. He hoped it was sufficient to stock her farm at least temporarily.

Now Sister Jean if you and your worthy husband consider the expense and concern I take for you & family, you will certainly allow that I have a right to expect your utmost diligence and care of what I put into your hands and that you will improve it to the best advantage. Be assured that I have no pleasure in throwing more money to no purpose, and when that is the case I will be tired and induced to slack my hand, on the contrary, when you convince me and the world that you manage your farm & cattle to the best advantage, It will be an encouragement to me to do the more for you. I am told your worthy husband thinks himself too much of a gentleman to put the sheep when you are not at home, and that once in particular when you stay at the house of Dunmaglass one evening Duncan & his man would not put up the sheep but oblidged you after running home to go to the hill for them, what can I think of such a dispicable worthless wretch as that; it is truely provoking; I wish I could speak to him, but you may tell him from me, if he does not use his utmost industry and care, in managing the stocking; I will certainly turn him out of the place and let him get bread where he will. As to the farm I think he has no business to meddle with it. And it is my desire that he shall not desert nor interfere with the man who may be intrusted with the mangement of it. But if he continues in his obstinancy and will not act the part he is desired to be directed, he will have cause to repent it, when it will be too late to mend. He may assure himself that I will be as good as my word. I wish you health & I am your affectionate Brother. Lachlan McGillivray

P.S. I shall keep the task of Ballanayacek in my own hands untill I see matters managed in some degree to satisfaction. for I find that you are so weak & silly to let that husband of yours do what he will as it shows you want of spirit, or you would—.[76]

Jean Roy was first married to Duncan McGillivray, but was later married to one John Mor McGillivray by 1797.[77] William ,writing from Dunmaglass, had reported to Lachlan as early as 1769 that he had established sister Jean and her husband on a farm, had bought cattle for them, paid their debts and placed their two oldest boys in school at a total cost of fifty-five pounds.[78]

Another letter from Lachlan to Baille John McIntosh at Inverness dated 16 October 1772 concerned his accounts and Lachlan mentioned that he was sailing for Georgia in "six or seven days."[79] Lachlan wrote again to McIntosh and said "Dunie" is returning with him to Georgia on the Georgia Packett.[80] "Dunie" was Captain William McGillivray, the 9th Chief and laird of Dunmaglass. The laird was traditionally called after the homeplace, in this case Dunmaglass.[81]

Captain William McGillivray, the 9th Chief, succeeding his older brother Alexander in 1746 after Alexander was killed at the Battle of Cullodon, came to America with Lachlan late in 1772 later writing "at the desire of a cousin."[82] He was persuaded because the cousin—Lachlan Lia—was worth 38,000 pounds and promised to make William his heir. William, as the Clan Chief, was having difficulty holding the family estates together, and this was an attractive offer that would restore the financial well being of the McGillivray estates. Lachlan followed through on his promise. On 8 July 1773 he decided to sell William part of his plantations and slaves for the negligible sum of ten shillings.[83]

John, cousin to Lachlan Lia and brother to William, was a witness to the deed. He came from West Florida to meet his brother William whom he probably had not seen since leaving Scotland in about 1755 or earlier. Fitzpatrick writing to John Miller on 7 July 1773 confirms that John and his partner William Struthers "were out of the Province of West Fla."[84]

William succeeded to the Chieftainship as a very young man at a difficult time. The McGillivray estates had been confiscated after the Battle of Cullodon, and William and his three brothers had to fare for themselves. John, of course, came to Georgia and became successful in the trade. Farquhar came to South Carolina and may have acted as an agent for the McGillivrays in Charleston. He later joined John in Pensacola and worked in the Indian trade. He was reported to have been a Presbyterian minister, but there seems to be little evidence to support this. Donald was the youngest and had a career in the merchant fleet and died unmarried in 1777.[85] Back in 1769 William had written to Lachlan Lia that Donald had spent the summer with him and he was pleased to note that John and Lachlan Lia had promised to buy a ship for him.[86]

William traveled a great deal and frequently lived in the south of England. William raised, and was Captain of, a company in the 89th Regiment of Foot in 1759 and served in India until 1765. There were fifteen John McGillivrays in the Regiment. When his company was returned home and disbanded, he involved himself in community affairs, and in 1768 he served as Master of the Freemason's Lodge. The financial affairs of the family were still relatively poor and William now in his forties, and still a bachelor, was urged by Lachlan Lia to marry and continue the family line, but William replied that "the family estate is but small, it devolved on me deeply burdened, in which situation it still remains." However, his position improved and he married Johanna Mackenzie, daughter of Alexander Mackenzie, and they had two children—Barbara Anne and John Lachlan. William's three sisters—Anne, Catherine, and Elizabeth—did not marry and remained at Dunmaglass. Anne raised John Lachlan in his early years with the loving help of Lachlan Lia who had returned to Scotland by this time. She also helped manage the family affairs.[87] John Lachlan was born on 6 October 1781. William's daughter Barbara Anne, died at Inverness, age seventeen, on 29 June 1800.[88]

William traveled to Georgia with Lachlan Lia on his return and John was there to welcome them home. William traveled with John back to Mobile and probably through the Creek country, giving William his first look at the American wilderness. William's training for the Indian trade was short and he returned to Savannah to manage his plantation by 1774. Fitzpatrick writing to McGillivray & Struthers Co. on 13 September 1773 mentioned that he had the "leather" ready "& your Brother will take charge of it in town & let you know the price for Both which articles you'll please credit my account."[89] William also invested in land on the Tensaw River north of Mobile and owned a plantation there called Grog Hall. However, it was abandoned by 1780.[90]

Lachlan busied himself tending to the affairs of his plantations and also began to take part as a loyalist in the simmering rebellion. On 5 January 1774 he advertised[91] for rent a house, large new barn, negro houses and sixty acres of cleared land about two miles from town. Also, a pasture all under fence located one mile from town. He also advertised on 26 January, 23 February and 1 March 1774[92] to lease a house and land. In addition his plantation called Springfield was for rent. On 2 November 1774 he advertised[93] for a lost pacing sorrel offering a reward of twenty shillings.

An incident of mystery occurred on the McGillivray plantation at this time when a man was found dead. A coroner's inquest, held 11 February 1774, returned a finding that the man was murdered by persons unknown.[94]

The patriots of Georgia were stirring, and Tondee's Tavern in Savannah was their gathering place. The business was located at the corner of today's Broughton and Whitaker Streets and only a short walk from the riverfront. The tavern was built in 1766 or 1767 by young Peter Tondee, and became a popular meeting place. Here on 27 July 1774, the Sons of Liberty held their first meeting after the news from Boston arrived. The first Provinicial Congress of Georgia was held here after the news of Lexington arrived in May 1775. This meeting erupted into a march on the King's powder magazine where the powder was sent to Boston along with rice and some funds. On 5 June a liberty pole was erected in front of the tavern, no doubt with the owner's blessing. On 21 June the famous-infamous Council on Safety was organized. However, the final break with the mother country came when the second Provincial Congress met at the tavern from 4 through 17 July where all manner of business was transacted which launched Georgia irrevocably into the American Revolution.[95]

An interesting anecdote to the above comes from the letter written by Governor Ellis to Governor Lyttelton 6 June 1757. He discusses the case of a man on trial in Georgia and says "these folks would give up the greatest priviledge of Englishmen for the sake of opposition. 'Tis amazing to what a length that spirit will carry men."[96] The Governor did not realize how prophetic his statement was some twenty years before the Revolution.

No doubt Lachlan along with his fellow loyalists was alarmed at these events, especially since none of the rebels were challenged or arrested by the authorities. The action of the rebels was promptly condemned, and a petition containing nearly five hundred signatures, including Lachlan's, was circulated protesting this blatant disrespect for the Crown.[97] In September he also signed a loyalist notice supporting the King which appeared in the *Savannah Gazette*.[98] These petitions eventually were used by the rebels to blacklist and banish the loyalists.

Lachlan's nephew, Lachlan McGillivray Jr., son of his sister Jean Roy, was in Georgia by the spring of 1775. Most likely he came to America when Lachlan returned from Scotland with William in 1772. Lachlan Jr. was appointed a commissioner of the work house[99] and was elected to the "Parochial Committee" for the town and district of Savannah on 18 September.[100]

Another Lachlan McGillivray, "carpenter," was fined for not appearing in court after being summoned.[101] A deposition given by Thomas Corn on 7 August 1775, concerning the escape of some "rebels," mentions that it was believed that "Lachlan McGillivray of Savannah, carpenter" delivered the keys enabling the rebel prisoners to escape.[102] This Lachlan was not Lachlan Lia, but it illustrates some of the problems of sorting out the many McGillivrays in Georgia and South Carolina.

A strange notice appearing in the *Savannah Gazette*[103] reports that "Lachlan McGillivray Esq" was chosen a member of the Provincial Congress to replace a member who declined to serve. This most surely was an effort by the rebels to "smoke" Lachlan Lia out into the open and make him declare for or against. Obviously the appointment was rejected by Lachlan and he cast his lot solidly behind the Crown. During the early days of the coming Revolution, many loyalists were appointed to various positions by the Provincial Congress. Those sympathetic to their cause served, those who were not refused, and the Congress knew where each stood.[104]

An advertisement and reward for the return of "a bright bay horse" strayed from the plantation of Lachlan Mcgillivray Esq. appeared in the local newspaper. The horse was branded with the initials WMG, and the ad was signed by William McGillvray.[105] Lachlan advertised[106] earlier for three runaway "negro men" from his plantation at Vale Royal. They were to be delivered to the overseer Mr. Durant for a reward of ten shillings and all reasonable expenses. The overseer was Benjamin Durant, married to Lachlan's Creek Indian daughter Sophia.

The Rebellion was now in full swing and Lachlan felt the full force of it on 19 April 1775 when Georgia laid claim to Vale Royal. This action must have been a crushing blow to Lachlan as Vale Royal was his home and the heart of his land holdings in Georgia.[107] However, Lachlan continued to join the protest and he signed a loyalist petition which protested the "unlawful acts" of the Council of Safety and Parochial Committees of the Provincial congress.[108]

Sir James Wright, writing to Lord Dartmouth on 1 November 1775, recounted how he doubted he would have the ability to "hold" on much longer. However, to fill vacancies on the Council he recommended Josiah Tattnall, Lachlan McGillivray and Charles William MacKinen. "These are Gentlemen who I think are all proper persons to be of the Council."[109]

Coleman[110] wrote that in early 1776 Governor Wright, his council and other royal officials were arrested by the Council of Safety. After being held two days they were released on parole. British ships arrived in port seeking provisions. Wright escaped and boarded *HMS Scarborough*. In early March the British troops landed on Hutchinson's Island to secure provisions. After an encounter with the rebels, they escaped with

1600 barrels of rice. The rice probably came from the plantation warehouses of Lachlan and William McGillivray.

The ship *Inverness* was burned by the rebels in the Savannah River near Hutchinson's Island on the night of 3 March 1776, along with several other ships. The *Inverness* was half owned by John McGillivray, one fourth by Lachlan and one fourth by the London merchants John Clarke and David Milligan. The ship was valued at 2000 pounds and total loss including the cargo of rice and deerskins came to 13,709 pounds. Most of the loss was covered by insurance.[111]

A letter from Sir James Wright to the Secretary of State more likely reflects what really happened. The letter dated 26 March 1776 reports that some British vessels anchored at Savannah had captured four rebels, including Raymond Demerie, the Commander of Fort Loudon, hoping to obtain some intelligence. When this became known to the rebel forces in Georgia, they immediately siezed three of the Council along with Lachlan and William McGillivray. The rebels threatened to send all the prisoners to Cambridge, Massachusetts, if the four rebels were not freed. An agreement was reached to exchange the prisoners. The loyalists were allowed to return to their homes on parole, not to have any connections with the King's ships nor troops in Georgia. The safety of their person and property would be secured. They also were free to take any possessions on board the ships and leave the Province.[112] At this time Lachlan and William probably sailed back to England with Sir James Wright.

An expedition to retake Georgia from the rebels was assembled by the British in New York, consisting of about three thousand troops under the command of Lieutenant Colonel Archibald Campbell of the 71st Scottish Regiment. General Prevost was to march his troops from St. Augustine and cooperate with Campbell. Campbell landed his troops unopposed just below Savannah on 29 December 1778 and quickly recaptured the town for the Crown. The rebels did a poor job of defending the city and many were killed. In just a few days Savannah was under British control.[113]

The assault by the British pushed the rebel militia back through the city in the direction of Vale Royal. The Americans tried to retreat across

Musgrove Creek, the northern boundary of Lachlan's Vale Royal. Only a portion succeeded in escaping while others were cornered between the Savannah River and the mouth of Musgrove Creek. The creek was at high tide and the plantation rice fields were flooded. Thirty Americans drowned in the fields trying to escape.[114]

On 24 January 1779 Campbell set out for Augusta with one thousand troops and arrived on 31 January with little opposition. As rebel opposition grew and General John Ashe with twelve hundred North Carolina troops arrived opposite Augusta, Campbell saw his loyalist support melt away, and decided to evacuate Augusta and move down the river toward Savannah. On 4 March royal civilian government was restored with Campbell acting as Governor. A Council and slate of officials were appointed. Governor Wright and other officials were ordered back to Georgia. Governor Wright, Lieutenant Governor John Graham, and Chief Justice Anthony Stokes arrived at Savannah in July 1779. Throughout this period of British possession, they controlled only a radius of twenty-five to forty miles from Savannah while the rebels controlled the back country. General Lincoln mustered some five thousand American troops and marched toward Georgia where he planned to confine the British to Savannah and stop their raiding the back country. Campbell decided to make a false advance toward Charleston and this so alarmed Lincoln that he rushed back to Charleston. The French minister was asked to assist the Americans but refused, saying the French fleet was occupied in the West Indies. However, an appeal was made directly to Count d'Estaing, Commander of the French fleet and troops in the American waters, for help in retaking Savannah.

To the surprise of everyone d'Estaing appeared off the Georgia coast on 1 September 1779 with twenty-two ships of war and four thousand troops. Governor Wright sounded the alarm and the British rushed to improve their defenses. The French landed and confronted General Prevost with a surrender ultimatum. They negotiated for two days giving the British time to improve their defenses—then Prevost refused to surrender. On 23 September the French commenced a siege of the town. Heavy artillery began bombardment on the night of 4 October and continued through 8 October, causing considerable damage to Savannah. The siege did not work, so d'Estaing personally led a frontal assault of French and American forces against the British lines on 9 October. They were thrown back with considerable loss of life and d'Estaing himself was wounded. They withdrew on 18 October and the French sailed away on 20 October. The American troops returned to South Carolina leaving Savannah in British hands.[115]

With Lachlan Lia still in England, on the afternoon of 16 October 1779

> there was a good deal of skirminshing on Mr. McGillivray's plantation between some negroes and a party of rebels, and the latter were several times driven from buildings on the plantation into the woods. Want of ammunition, however, obliged the blacks to retreat in the evening with the loss of one killed and three or four wounded.[116]

Savannah at this time had swamps on each side reaching back from the river. The town consisted of about 430 houses and the only "public" building of any consequence was a church—probably Christ Church.

Contemporary maps of the siege in 1779 made by French officers clearly show the "McGillivray plantation" just upriver from Savannah and bordered by a stream that drains the nearby swamps and rice fields. A road leads to a house in the center of the plantation—apparently the residence of Lachlan Lia. A large plantation is shown on Hutchinson's Island with a loading dock and road leading from the river to a house at the edge of the plantation. Several other buildings are shown—probably for storage.[117]

Sir James Wright compiled a list dated February 1779 of attorneys that had been banished from Georgia by the rebels. William McGillivray was identified on the list as a Captain in the Army on half pay, and was now located in London.[118]

Lachlan and William were in England during the rebel occupation of Savannah, but we know little of their activities. William wrote to Campbell Mackintosh from London on 16 February 1779 and congratulated him on his marriage to William's cousin. He planned to soon return to Georgia where he hopes to recover his property. He stated he is under threat of death from the Georgians.[119] William again wrote to Mackintosh on 28 April 1779, discussing some business, and said, "Lachlan is much recovered after a severe illness which he in a great measure imparts to his anxiety to save as much as possible of my property."[120]

Governor James Wright returned to Georgia in July 1779. Lachlan and William arrived sometime between February and May of 1780. They waited to see when and if Governor Wright could restore law and order.[121]

The years of 1780 and 1781 left few records to tell us what happened to Lachlan during this period. In 1780 Lieutenant Colonel Thomas Brown and his famous King's Rangers occupied Augusta. Brown made his headquarters in the trading house of Robert Mackay which was a stone building on the Savannah River and was once the "white house" belonging to Lachlan. Brown's rangers and Indian allies dug an earthwork around the house, but Colonel Elijah Clark, the rebel commander, dug another earthwork around Brown's cutting them off from the river. Brown was saved by the arrival of British regulars under Lieutenant Colonel John H. Cruger from the fort at Ninety-Six.[122]

Thomas Brown became the most effective loyalist fighter in the province, where he led his King's Rangers on lightning raids into Georgia from his base of operations in loyalist East Florida. Brown's aggressive and sometimes harsh treatment of Georgians came from a personal experience in their hands. By 1775 loyalists were being tarred and feathered by the rebels. One of the more famous of these was against Brown who was taken from his home in Augusta on 2 August 1775. He was tarred and feathered and ridden from town in a cart. It took him six months to recover.[123] This incident made Brown an intractable enemy of the rebels who for years raided and plundered the Georgians.

A journal entry of the Georgia Commons House dated 8 June 1780 reads:

A memorial from Lachlan McGillivray, with his name subscribed thereto, was presented to the House, setting forth that being informed George Galphin Esqr. is to be attained of high treason, he begs leave to represent him as a man universally esteemed by all that knew him, and who has faithfully served his King and country, under the British Government, and that at the commencement of the Rebellion, he declared he would never take any part therein, further than to prevent the merciless savages from murdering the helpless women and children which he happily effected, he therefore hopes this House will be pleased to extend their mercy and forgiveness to him.

The House ordered that the memorial lie on the table for all to peruse.[124]

It is notewrothy that Lachlan, a staunch loyalist, would come to the defense of his old friend and partner, since Galphin did more than anyone else to keep the Creek Indians neutral in the conflict. However, Lachlan's plea had no effect on the Assembly since they passed an act on 6 July 1780 banishing forever from the Province a long list of rebels. George Galphin, "rebel Supt. of Indian Affairs," was on the list.[125] Both actions were for naught as Galphin died in late 1780.

Lachlan was still trying to carry on some semblance of business. He submitted a claim to the British for provisions furnished to the Indians in June 1780. The account was approved by Alexander Cameron, the Indian Agent.[126] As late as May 1782, McGillivray, Graham and Clark Co. were making claims against the Crown where in 1770 the Cherokee had ceded land to pay their debts to the traders, but they had never received any payment or settlement of those debts.[127]

An ad was placed in the *Royal Georgia Gazette* on 1 May 1781[128] for the return of a runaway slave named Edinburgh—his Guinea name being Sula. He was missing from one of Captain William McGillivray's plantations on Hutchinson's Island. He was branded on the chest with the initials WMG. If delivered to Lachlan McGillivray a reward of one guinea would be given for his return. This person was Lachlan McGillivray Junior, the son of Lachlan Lia's sister Jean Roy. Lachlan

Junior was the manager of William's plantations.

On 24 January 1782 Lachlan ran an ad[129] saying "that he intends to be absent from this province for sometime" and wants debts owed to him paid promptly or the accounts will be turned over to an attorney. Lachlan realized the British were losing the war and he was "cutting his losses" and preparing to return to Scotland.

On 4 May 1782 an act of the Georgia General Assembly lists the names of those loyalists whose property had been confiscated. The act provided that "whereas the aforesaid treasons and other atrocious crimes justly merit a forfeiture of protection and property." Lachlan Lia was fourth on the list along with Governor James Wright, William Panton, and Charles Weatherford.[130]

Although Cornwallis surrendered at Yorktown on 19 October 1781, the war continued in the south for several more months. Rebel forces surrounded Charleston, but the British held on and it became the last city to give way. In January 1782, Colonel Wade Hampton crossed the Savannah River to secure Georgia. He successfully repelled Creek Indian reinforcements and surrounded Savannah. On 11 July 1782, the British evacuated the town.[131]

At this time Governor James Wright appealed to General Alexander Leslie, Commander of the Southern Dept, for ships to send the slaves directly from Georgia to Jamaica. Leslie in turn requested the ships from the North American Commander Sir Guy Carlton on 19 July 1782. His request was for "Sir James Wright and the principal inhabitants" of Savannah along with some two thousand slaves. A six-ship convoy was made available and was led by the *Zebra*, a sloop of war.[132]

Colonel John traveled with this convoy taking some sixty-six slaves for his plantation in Jamaica. He had earlier purchased a ship in Jamaica to take the slaves from Georgia. Arriving in Jamaica, the slaves and other goods were unloaded and a new cargo loaded that was bound for England. However, the ship sank enroute, but Colonel John's losses were covered by insurance.[133] Some 2420 whites—men, women, and children—and 3609 slaves escaped from Georgia to East Florida.[134]

Lachlan Jr. who was the manager of Captain William McGillivray's plantation near Savannah, traveled to London with Lachlan Lia and William, where they spent the next two years preparing and submitting a claim for losses sustained by William and John. Lachlan Lia never made a claim since he had deeded all his property to his cousin John hoping to prevent confiscation by the Georgia authorities. John traveled from West Florida to Savannah sometime late 1781 or early 1782. No doubt he had to hurry the closing out of his business affairs after the Spanish captured Pensacola in 1781. We know that John was back in Savannah in May of 1782. John sailed with the fleet to Jamaica in order to protect the many slaves they had on board. The slaves would be used on the plantation John had established there at least by 1778. He had placed his cousin Lachlan McGillivray, the son of Archibald, in charge of his plantation at an early date. John remained in Jamaica for nearly a year looking after his business affairs. He was back in London by July 1783 where he assisted Lachlan Lia, William, and Lachlan Jr. in their claims against the Crown.[135]

The war in the south had ended when the British sailed from Charleston on 14 December 1782.[136] Lachlan Lia McGillivray had foreseen this event by January 1782, had made preparations to leave America and return to London, and then later to Scotland. A notice appearing in the *Royal Georgia Gazette* on 23 May 1782, reads that Lachlan McGillivray Esquire sailed for Falmouth, England on his majesty's packet boat *Halifax* with Captain John Boulders the master. Sailing date had been 18 May. He sailed away leaving a fortune in land and other property that he would never recover. He also sailed away leaving an Indian wife and three children in the Creek Nation to provide for themselves as best they could.

5

McGillivrays in West Florida

The French ceded Florida to England in 1763 and by 1764 John McGillivray, brother to the clan chief William and cousin to Lachlan Lia, had arrived in West Florida. John set up a partnership with William Struthers, who probably came to West Florida at the same time, and quickly established their business out of Pensacola and Mobile—principally Mobile. Lachlan Lia may have had a financial interest in the partnership, but no evidence has been found to support this idea.[1] The McGillivrays, Struthers, and McIntoshes plied their trade with the Choctaw and Chickasaw and to a lesser extent with the Creeks.

John soon became embroiled with the military authorities—primarily the West Florida Commandant at Mobile, Major Robert Farmer. Robert Rea,[2] Major Farmer's biographer, describes an incident that occurred on the Pensacola streets in 1764 which involved some of the traders working for John McGillivray. Rea wrote that the "bullies" insulted a French lady, the guard was called out, but all the "ruffians" had escaped except one Richard Jones. Rea also alleged that John McGillivray was "insolent" toward the military court. Using the same sources as Rea, a very different version can be presented. In a letter from John to Governor Johnstone,[3] he outlines what happened and protests the mistreatment of civilian inhabitants by the military. John continued that John McBean, having just arrived from the Indian country, was drunk and accidentally fell against the lady knocking her down, but meaning no harm. The military guard later appeared at McGillivray's house and arrested Richard Jones, Joseph Cornell, John Proctor, Henry Golding, and John Oares in addition to McBean. During this encounter, Jones said something about McBean going off or escaping. Jones was immediately taken off and thrown into the "Black hole." The other traders were not even involved or present when the lady incident occurred.

A court-martial ordered by Major Farmer was convened in just three days and no evidence was presented against any of the prisoners except Jones. The only evidence presented against Jones was that he remarked to McBean that he should run off and escape, and for this he was given 250 lashes and a two dollar fine. The court had taken no oaths nor made any record. McGillivray contended that as civilians their rights were violated and the court martial was illegal since only the commander of forces (General Gage) could authorize a court-martial; also McGillivray was denied the opportunity to even testify before the court.

McGillivray also reported that the soldiers searched his house at a later time where there happened to be one William James. The soldiers fired on James luckily missing him, but he was still brought before Farmer who acknowledged his innocence and released him. The traders involved immediately left Pensacola for the Indian country where they felt safer with the "savages."

This type of arrogant and arbitrary behavior later brought many complaints against Farmer. Finally General Gage ordered that he be court-martialed on several counts. Farmer was acquitted by his fellow officers, but his career was ruined and he soon left the army and became a "gentleman farmer" near present day Stockton, Alabama, on the Mobile River.

John McGillivray soon became a respected and leading merchant in West Florida. He seems to have lived at Mobile most of the time and represented that district in the West Florida Commons House of Assembly during the first session from November 1766 to January 1767, and again during the sixth session in 1772; however, Governor Chester never convened the 1772 assembly.[4] John may have been absent during the 1766 session. On 5 November he sent a letter to the Assembly "begging leave of absense for some time." He later requested a leave on 24 December, and in both cases his request was granted.[5]

John continued to have problems. In 1765, in Mobile, Richard Painter was indicted for stealing some clothing from the "warehouse of John McGillivray."[6] By 1768 John had formed a partnership with William Struthers under the name of McGillivray & Struthers Co. On 31 January, the Company bought a house and lot in Mobile for $240. The deed was witnessed by "Farqd [Farquhar] McGillivray."[7] Farquhar was a brother to John and William. On 28 November 1767 the Company was paid $11.06 for transporting provisions to the garrison at Fort Tombechbe on the Tombigbee River.[8]

As early as 1766 John was an important figure in West Florida Indian affairs where he brought about peace between the Creeks, Choctaw, and Chickasaw. He also accused the powerful Colberts of the Chickasaw of stirring up trouble.[9]

The letterbook of John Fitzpatrick is an important source of information on John McGillivray and his business. Fitzpatrick for many years resided at Manchac on the Mississippi River, an important trading post or town upstream from New Orleans and near present day Baton Rouge. It is remarkable that his letterbooks survived and he faithfully kept it updated until Florida was ceded to Spain. Many of Fitzpatrick's letters are to McGillivray & Struthers, but these disappear from the letterbooks by August 1778. Fitzpatrick was a middle man obtaining deerskins as far away as the Illinois country and trading them to McGillivray & Struthers. The traders came down in February of each year to Manchac bringing their skins.[10] Fitzpatrick alone shipped thousands of skins to McGillivray & Struthers each year making them one of the larger trading firms in West Florida.[11] The company asked Fitzpatrick not to reveal what they paid him for the skins, as it would "upset the traders."[12] He also charged a five percent fee for "storage and commission."[13]

The first letter appears 30 June 1768 and was posted from New Orleans. Fitzpatrick said that John McGillivray was then in New Orleans, but Fitzpatrick was having difficulty collecting on some skins and was unable to pay a debt to John in the amount of 881 reales.[14]

John traveled frequently to the Chickasaw Nation and was there in April 1769 and returned by way of Natchez.[15] On 2 September Fitzpatrick writes to McGillivray & Struthers from New Orleans and reports how he had saved their flour which had gone bad. The Spanish authorities were confiscating all bad flour to "throw it in the Mississippi," but through a "stratagum" he had managed to trade it for peltry. He was able to do this only because of the scarcity of flour in New Orleans.[16] McGillivray & Struthers traded in many products including skins, tobacco, flour, musket balls, powder, guns, and also sold slaves to merchants and planters in the "up country."[17]

The military Spanish Governor, Alexander O'Reilly, arrived in New Orleans in August 1769, and he closed the port and River to English trade. McGillivray & Struthers had to close their New Orleans branch in only a few days.[18] However, the trade traffic continued illegally almost unabated and the Spanish eventually opened the River again.

McGillivray & Struthers publicly acknowledged the sale of a house and lot in Mobile to one John Favre. It seems that Favre had lost his bill of sale dated 10 April 1770. They also owned a tract of land on the Tombigbee River called Sunflowers, but it was abandoned by 1780.[19]

John was sometimes caught up in a controversy and although he had a full-time business, he still was involved in Indian affairs. At a general Council between the Creeks and British officials held at Pensacola on 29 October 1771, John Stuart denied receiving a message from governor James Wright supposedly hand delivered by John McGillivray.[20]

McGillivray & Struthers were busy in 1771 planning the expansion of their business. They planned on purchasing a ship to ply the waters between Mobile and New Orleans, and up the Mississippi River to Manchac. This would provide a larger profit and more security in moving goods back and forth. By 1772 the Company had purchased a sloop for this purpose.[21]

Bernard Romans, the British topographical engineer for the Southern District, recorded in his journal on 18 January 1772, as he traveled down the Tombigbee and Mobile Rivers, that he had passed "Campbells, Stuart, Ardrys and McGillivrays."[22] The locations seems to be somewhere between the forks of the Mobile and twenty-seven Mile Bluff which places it on the upper Mobile River. Alexander McGillivray, the Creek chief and the son of Lachlan Lia, later owned a plantation on the Alabama River near the mouth of Little River in extreme northern Baldwin County; however, the plantation mentioned by Romans most likely belonged to John or even James McGillivray.

Further evidence of John's investment in lands comes from the Spanish period of Florida when in 1787 a petition by one Simon Landry reads, "who resides within the jurisdiction of Mobile with all due respect represents to your Excellency that there is a tract of land containing forty arpens,[23] situated on this river, which was abandoned eight years ago by a certain Mr. McGillivray. . . ."[24]

One Pedro Oliver in 1796, probably the Spanish Creek Indian Agent stationed at Little Tallasee until Alexander McGillivray died in 1793, appeals for a grant of twenty arpens of land on the Mobile River. He says the plot

> constitutes a part of the land occupied by a man named John McGillivray and his associates in trade before the surrender of the province to the arms of his majesty, since which time the said lands have been abandoned and never reclaimed by any person.[25]

William McGillivray, Chief of the Clan and brother to John, owned a plantation on the Mobile River called Grog Hall. It was located on both sides of the river and bordered on Bayou Cedera, known today as Cedar Creek, or about twenty-five miles north of Mobile. Grog Hall Creek, just south of Cedar Creek, today continues the name.[26] Peter Juzan in 1787 petitioned for fourteen arpens at this location saying it was abandoned in 1780 by McGillivray. He described the land as being north of Cedar Creek which places it near Mount Vernon.[27]

In 1796 one John Baptiste Alexander petitioned for twenty arpens on Mobile Bay at a place called Lausemaville which had belonged to "John McGillivray and Associates of Mobile."[28] This is later called the Mandeville Tract and was located about three miles below Mobile on the bay. Camp Mandeville was a large staging area for Andrew Jackson's troops in 1812-1815.[29] It was a sickly climate and many Tennessee volunteers died there. Desertion was high and seven soldiers were executed on 21 February 1815.[30]

John also owned land on the lower Tombigbee River. In 1787 Thomas Wheat petitioned for eight arpents of land abandoned by McGillivray in 1780 called Sunflowers. The same year James Danley and Daniel Johnston petitioned for ten arpents and five arpents respectively at a place called Sunflowers on the Tombigbee River abandoned in 1780 by McGillivray.[31]

John's Sunflower plantation was located at or near Sunflower Bend which today is a cut-off of the Tenn-Tom Waterway and located at mile 78.6 on the Tombigbee River. Just a few miles west of Sunflower Bend is Little Sunflower Church, Sunflower Church, and Sunflower Community on U.S. 43. There was also a Sunflower stop on the Southern Railroad at Sunflower Community. There is also a Sunflower Church a few miles east in Monroe County, but the name may not be related to McGillvray's plantation.[32]

Hamilton said that the Bend was named from the "Englishman Sunflower" and another place he said Mr. Sunflower lived below McIntosh Bluff which was some twenty miles down river from the Bend.[33] He was here referring to a petition by Daniel Ward in 1787 for fifty arpents on the Tombigbee previously owned by James McIntosh. "The north side is vacant and the south is bordered by lands called Sunflowers."[34] In all these petitions it was referred to in the plural meaning more than one Sunflower plantation. Much of this land was used as "cowpens" to run cattle on and it could have been in two tracts or one large tract. The author believes this area is the namesake of John McGillivray's plantation. His plantation in Jamaica was also called Sunflower.

John owned 250 acres 105 miles upriver from Mobile on the Tombigbee, just below the Spanish line (32°28') in Choctaw County, below the mouth of Tuckabum Creek. The land was being claimed in 1809 by Edward Lloyd Wailes.[35] John had received several large grants—2375 acres in 1770, 1000 acres in 1776 and 500 acres in 1777.[36] In 1808 the heirs of John McGillivray were trying to obtain title to some of John's land in West Florida. They were represented in this effort by Peter Swanson.[37]

John was a small slave trader and frequently loaned money taking slaves as collateral.[38] McGillivray and Struthers bought two slaves in 1770, nine in 1772, seven in 1773 and two in 1774.[39] John owned some twenty to thirty slaves in 1777.[40] In 1779 the Company of Struthers, Swanson, Miller & McGillivray bought two slaves.[41] McGillivray, Struthers, Swanson, Mackintosh & Company bought fourteen slaves in 1775.[42] It was not unusual for a wealthy trader to be connected to several partnerships with a frequent turnover of partners. John worked these partnerships out of both Mobile and Pensacola.

We know that John owned a plantation in Jamaica after the Revolutionary War, and some evidence exists that he owned it as early as 1778. He was importing rum, sugar, and coffee into West Florida by this date and it is reasonable to assume some of these goods were coming from his plantation in Jamaica.

John in partnership with Peter Swanson signed a receipt for $2162 for trade goods to the Indians.[43] Swanson and McGillivray Company submitted a bill for $259 for "rewards and presents to the Indian parties employed for the defense of Mobile and Pensacola."[44]

Miller and Swanson was an important trading house located in Pensacola and John Miller was also a partner to John McGillivray. Fitzpatrick, writing to McGillivray and Struthers on 13 September 1773, says "By this opportunity have sent what goods was in my hands of Mr. Stuarts addressed to your John Miller; with an account of there being disposed of." Fitzpatrick writing again on 26 December referred to "your Mr. Miller."[45]

J. Leitch Wright in Coker[46] gives a good summary of John Miller's career in West Florida and later in the Bahamas. This Miller was a well-to-do merchant in Pensacola, a member of the West Florida Assembly, and later a supporter of William Augustus Bowles. However, there was another John Miller that Wright fails to address. This John Miller first appears as a signer of a letter from the Creek traders to Governor

Lyttelton of South Carolina dated 31 July 1756.[47] In 1758 he was a witness, along with John McGillivray and others, to the cession of Ussabaw, St. Catherine, and Sapalo Islands to Georgia by the Creeks.[48] He is mentioned again in 1764 as an Indian trader.[49] In 1770 he was an interpreter at a Creek Council held at "Palaachicola" on the Chattahoochee River.[50] David Taitt, the Creek agent, writing in his journal, records on 30 April 1772 that John Miller, "a trader to the Eutchee," came to see him and read a letter from George Galphin.[51] This same year he was identified in Council Minutes as being a trader from Georgia.[52]

Taitt to John Stuart on 7 July 1776 again identifies John Miller as a trader to the "Eutchees."[53] Panton, writing to Carondelet on 17 March 1799, says "one of my traders who resides on the other side of the Scambia named John Miller."[54] Benjamin Hawkins, writing to David Mitchell on 17 August 1813, accuses the Governor of Pensacola of delivering arms and ammunition to the Creeks, since they could not come to Pensacola. "He would deliver it to them at Miller's place."[55] Big Escambia Creek merges with the Conecuh River to form the Escambia River just below the Alabama-Florida line. It was here in Spanish territory that Miller lived. If this John Miller were in the Creek Country from 1756 to 1813, fifty-seven years, he lived a long life indeed, but some of the old "Indian countrymen" did live a long time.

Neither Coker nor Wright enlighten us as to what happened to John Miller after he finally lost his fight to replace Panton Leslie Company. The John Miller identified as being on the Escambia-Conecuh River in 1799 and again in 1813 may have been the Miller of Pensacola and Bahamas.

Peter Swanson also had business dealings with John McGillivray. They jointly owned several lots in Mobile that were used and cultivated by one C. McCurtin.[56] Swanson and Miller received a grant of 2250 acres in West Florida in 1770[57] and Swanson was a witness to the published bans in Mobile on 8 June 1778.[58]

Captain James Logan Colbert, a trader among the Chickasaw, also appeared to work for McGillivray. He submitted a bill of thirty-nine pounds to Swanson and McGillivray for "rations, wages and supplies" from 25 January to 31 May 1780. The bill was paid by the Company.[59]

By March 1782 Swanson was in London pursuing his business interests. Fitzpatrick used Swanson to settle many accounts that were left open when the British evacuated West Florida. As the loyalists abandoned their property and holdings, there were many unpaid accounts and unfinished business.[60] He represented himself and John McGillivray or his heirs in protesting United States restrictions on their claims to land granted them by the British Government. Their lands were about to be forfeited in 1804. James McGillivray, cousin to John and Lachlan Lia, also signed the protest.[61]

Charles Stuart, cousin and deputy to John Stuart, was in Savannah with John McGillivray where Charles was about to sail for England. John Stuart writing to General Haldimand on 3 February 1774, says that because of new conflicts between the Creeks and Choctaws he could not let Charles go to England. He was ordering Charles and John back to West Florida.[62]

By June 1774 John was back in Mobile where he seems to have been having some business problems. In August he was in Natchez and planned to return through Manchac.[63] His troubles may have been with John Miller who by 1776 was in business with Alexander McIntosh at Pensacola. McIntosh was a cousin to John and Lachlan Lia McGillivray.[64] Fitzpatrick in a business transaction had paid Miller a sum of money and instructed Miller to pass an additional $2700 on to McGillvray, but Miller for some unknown reason kept the money. Later John writes Fitzpatrick that he expects to be paid, and Fitzpatrick replied that he understood that the debt would be taken care of through Miller and that Miller should have kept John informed. This seems to indicate that Miller had pocketed the money. It was about this time that Miller went to the Bahamas and later to London. By December Fitzpatrick complained that he had 5500 pounds of "fine Illinois scraped skins" for which he could not find a buyer.[65] Apparently, because of hard feelings, John had not purchased the skins from Fitzpatrick.

William Bartram, writing in his journal for July 1777, while in Mobile, said:

Messrs. Swanson and 'Gillivray, who have the management of the Indian trade carried on with the Chicasaws, choctaws, upper and lower Creeks, etc. have made here very extra ordinary improvements in building." Bartram also visited the settlements of Manchac on the Mississippi where he noted the improvements made by the English, "particularly the warehouses of Messrs. Swanson & Co. Indian traders and merchants.[66]

William Struthers, the longtime partner of John McGillivray at Mobile, had been a trader in the Creek Country for many years. He seems to first appear in the records in 1755 when a letter, dated 20 September, was written to Governor Glen of South Carolina from the Shawnee titled "King and Headmen assembled at Shalapheagyee."[67] The Shawnee had taken some white captives on one of their raids near the Ohio River where many of their relatives lived. One of these captives, a white girl, was in the hands of the Sylacauga Shawnee, but they turned her over to "Wm. Struthers who lives as a trader in our town."[68]

Struthers, on one of his return trips to Augusta wrote a report to Governor Wright of Georgia which was read into the Council minutes on 21 July 1761. His report included several talks he had received from the Creek Indians, and about other activities taking place in the Nation.[69]

In July of the same year, the Georgia Council, because of the many complaints from the Indians, decided to assign the traders to specific towns. Struthers was assigned to Little Tallasee including "Hutchee Chubba" and he would also share the towns of Wewoka and Newtown with trader J. Morgan.[70]

Lachlan Lia had his Indian home and trading post at Little Tallasee. Lachlan would have already known Struthers from Augusta, but when Struthers was assigned to Little Tallasee, Lachlan had the opportunity to become better acquainted. They developed a lasting friendship which likely carried over to his becoming a partner with John McGillivray in the West Florida trade. Although there is no direct evidence that Lachlan was involved in the West Florida trade, it seems likely that he had at least a financial investment in McGillivray & Struthers Co. On 10 April 1764, a Creek Council was held at Little Tallasee, and was attended by several traders, including Struthers.[71]

A letter from Struthers to Governor Johnstone of West Florida, dated 10 April 1766 and written from Mobile, informs the Governor of the activities in the Creek Nation. He closed the letter by saying that his "Partner" was dangerously ill in Augusta and he must rush back to the Creek country.[72] Struthers's partner was likely Lachlan Lia who was residing in Augusta at this time. Struthers, writing from Mobile, appeared to already have been in transition from Georgia to the West Florida trade, and we know he was established there by 1768. He was appointed temporary Creek Agent by John Stuart in 1766, but he served only a short time.[73]

Struthers acted as a carrier of peace talks and mediator between the Creeks and Choctaw in 1770 on behalf of Superintendent John Stuart. He also served in the West Florida Assembly, representing Mobile, during the 5th and 6th Assembly which convened in 1771 and 1772.[74]

In 1776 Struthers was accused of being a rebel, probably because on 13 June 1775 he joined many others in signing a petition to the Provincial Congress in Savannah calling for it to join all other colonies "to secure and restore the liberties of all America, and for healing the unhappy divisions now subsisting between Great Britain and her colonies." This was not what the hot-headed loyalist wanted to hear. Struthers protested the accusations and declared he was a loyal British subject. The West Florida Council held a hearing and after an investigation Struthers was acquitted. However, he was made to take an oath of loyalty and post a one thousand pound bond. Also he could not leave the Province without the Governor's permission.[75]

It appears that McGillivray & Struthers survived until at least August 1778. Fitzpatrick wrote:

> [I] therefore am endeavouring to settle all my affairs as soon as possible in these parts being allmost assured there will be troublesome

times this way ere long, for which should be happy if all the Gentlemen that I have connections with was paid. I have paid the House of McGillivray & Struthers. . . .[76]

Struthers apparently went to Georgia in late 1781 or early 1782. There he was paid 276 pounds for rice by Governor James Wright just before the British evacuation in July 1782.[77]

Struthers was in London by March 1784 where he made a deposition for loyalist claims by one Isaac Bailou. Struthers was also an attorney and seems to have been representing Bailou in his claim.[78] Struthers returned to America and again appears in the records in 1793 where it is reported he was insane. His estate was represented by James Mather, a leading merchant of New Orleans.[79] This is the last we hear of Struthers.

John Stuart, writing to George Germain on 13 April 1778, claimed he had offered the position to the John McGillivray Agency of the Choctaw and Chickasaw.

Mr. John Mcgillivray, a gentleman of fortune intimately acquainted with the Choctaw and Chickasaw Indians, their language and customs, I considered as the fittest person to be employed in managing the Indians of said two nations; and being convinced that he would be a valuable acquisition I used all my influence to induce him to undertake the service, and in order to ensure success promised to apply to the governor to give him command of a provincial corps to be raised by him, in which he has been successful.[80]

John refused the appointment.

There were a number of McGillivrays in West Florida besides John, and most or all were related to John and Lachlan Lia. They were also involved in the trade and some worked for McGillivray & Struthers.

There was another John McGillivray in West Florida at this time who was a cousin to John, William the Clan Chief, and Lachlan Lia. He was the son of Alexander McGillvray and Anne Fraser. This is Alexander, the Creek trader, who came to South Carolina early and was in the trade with Archibald McGillivray. Alexander returned to Scotland to become the Laird of Knocknagael.[81] Young John had earlier been a merchant in Guadaloupe and had caused some trouble to Henry Laurens of South Carolina.[82] Young John became secretary to John Stuart, the Superintendent of Indian Affairs, and hand carried messages and letters from Stuart to various officials.[83] In 1765 a heated disagreement arose between young John and Stuart's deputy at Pensacola, the Montault de Monberant, a Frenchman who Stuart thought would be useful since he had served in similar positions under the French at Pensacola. It seems that Monberant's son had received news from Forneret, the interpreter at Mobile, that he heard a rumor from young John McGillvray to the effect that Monberant was about to be fired. Monberant was incensed and on 20 June wrote a letter to Stuart and Governor Johnstone demanding that John be punished for his "malice' and disgraceful behavior".[84] Nothing came of the incident as young John became ill and died shortly afterwards.[85] He was about twenty-four years old at the time of his death.[86]

Then there was Finlay McGillvray who was in business with Senior Don Hendry of New Orleans.[87] In 1774 he traveled up the Mississippi River to Manchac where Fitzpatrick sent some goods by him to be delivered to Peter Swanson.[88] Fitzpatrick wrote to Peter Swanson on 26 March 1782 and said that "Findley" had a small account with him that had been paid.[89] Finlay was in Georgia by 1767 where he was at the time overseer of Vale Royal outside Savannah. John McGillivray in his 1767 will left Finlay twenty pounds.[90] Finlay died in 1769.[91]

James McGillivray was the son of Archibald McGillivray who came to South Carolina in 1735 and later returned to Scotland where he became the landed gentleman of Daviot. James's mother was Jane or Lucy McIntosh and he also had a brother, John, in Georgia, and a brother, Lachlan, in Jamaica who was the overseer of John McGillivray's estate near Bath. James, John, and young Lachlan, all brothers, were cousins to John of West Florida, Lachlan Lia, and William the Clan Chief.[92]

James first showed up in 1778.[93] On 24 November he signed wedding bans in Mobile and was mentioned in the record as a "Scottish

Merchant" on the Tombigbee River.[94] James was prominent in the Mobile community and was chosen by Governor Chester on 1 February 1780 to inventory the goods and property for the late Major Robert Farmer.[95] He was granted eight hundred acres six miles southeast of Natchez on 12 February 1788.[96] James stayed on after the Revolution when on 15 March 1784, he sold a slave to one Don Miguel Eslana for three hundred dollars. He was also in the trade with Captain James Colbert, a leading trader among the Chickasaw and father of several half-blood sons who ruled the Chickasaw Nation for many years.[97]

Alexander Cameron, the Creek Agent, was burdened after the death of Stuart with the expenses that John Stuart had entailed and apparently Cameron was adding to this by continuing the "lavish" spending for Indian presents. General Campbell became upset at the Indian expense account and informed Cameron that he would no longer approve Indian expense bills. He also ordered Cameron to dismiss his assistants in the field. Cameron replied on 30 June 1780, reacting in a distraught manner telling Campbell it was a mistake to dismiss James McGillivray, Frazier, and Welch, on whom he depended so much, and that they could not be brought back so readily at a later date.[98]

After the Revolution, the United States required all residents that had English or Spanish land grants, or otherwise owned land in the former provinces, to register for certification from the United States government. If the lands were not registered by the specified date, they were subject to forfeiture. James and Peter Swanson protested in 1804 that they were not given enough time to make their claim.

A letter from Timothy Barnard to Governor Edward Telfair of Georgia said that James McGillivray was hand carrying letters from "Mr. McGillivray." "Mr. McGillivray" is Alexander McGillivray, the Creek Indian Chief. James had brought one hundred horseloads of ammunition from New Orleans and it was now at Pensacola where the Upper Creeks were going down to get it. Each town would get ten to twelve horseloads.[99] James was still in America in 1789 when Alexander McGillivray writing to Governor Miro on 24 June mentioned "his friend James McGillivray had arrived from south Georgia where he had been in pursuit of some runaway Negroes."[100]

James may have remained in America as late as 1804, but the following notice appeared in the *Columbian Museum* and *Savannah Advertiser* on 11 June 1806—"James McGillivray late of Savannah died January 29, 1806 at Daviot near Inverness."[101] In 1808 heirs of James were still trying to obtain title to land in West Florida granted to him by the British.[102]

The legacy of James McGillivray is not finished with his death in 1806. Choctaws wanting to become American citizens under the provisions of the Dancing Rabbit Creek Treaty in 1830[103] had to become duly registered with the American Agent. In the register the following is listed:

> 13 June 1831, Robert McGilvery, 2 children, half breed man
> 23 August 1831, John McGilvery, 5 children, half breed man
> 23 August 1831, Turner McGilvery, 2 children, half breed man[104]

Gabriel Felder, the land agent, wrote from Pickensville, Alabama, on 15 May 1833, inquiring whether "John, Turner and Gordon McGilbry" had their "names duly registered."[105]

Another agent, Thomas Wooldridge, on 12 October 1833, writing from Lowndes County, Mississippi, said that "John Mcgilbry" and "Taner McGilbry" have taken citizenship as Choctaws under the treaty of 1830, and had made a claim to some land divided by the Alabama-Mississippi line.[106] The only land claimed in Alabama was Section 33 which is described in the surveyor's field notes as "3rd rate swampy level land, growth oak, ash and hickory" with a creek running through the section. This section lays between Pickensville and the Tombigbee River.[107]

"John McGilbry Indian" cultivated ten acres with a family of eight—three males over sixteen and three females under ten. He had 640 acres granted to him under the Choctaw treaty of 1830 on the Tombigbee River near "Tongue's Bluff." However, his daughter Lucy was old enough to have a child of her own.[108] Gordon, Turner, and John McGillivray claimed several sections of land along the Alabama-Mississipi line in Pickens County, Alabama, and Noxubee County, Mississippi.[109]

John received a United States Government grant in 1834 of 1936 acres for himself and children in Noxubee County, Mississippi.[110] He received a patent signed by President Martin Van Buren dated 21 June 1839 for:

> 640 acres T16 R19 Section 33
>
> 320 acres W1/2 T16 R19 Section 34
>
> 320 acres E1/2 T16 R19 Section 28
>
> 320 acres W1/2 T15 R19 Section 3

Also he received Section 35 T16 R19, patent dated 18 November 1851 signed by Millard Fillmore.[111] United States land records also show that he received the W1/2 of Section 28 T16 R 19 on 29 May 1845.[112]

John had sold his land on 2 March 1836 to Rueben H. Grant and Jefferson Clements for $2200. The deed was recorded on 5 July 1836 with John signing his mark.[113] His daughter Lucy was denied a claim to Section 3 T15 R19 in Noxubee County on 14 November 1844, even though it had been reserved for her on 14 February 1841. It was noted in the tract book that she had a child in 1845 named Susie.[114] She was granted the SE 1/4 of Section 34 T16 R19 on 19 March 1845.[115] Lucy sold her 320 acres to Thomas D. Wooldridge for two hundred dollars with the stipulation that the money would not be paid until she received legal title, which she did, and the deed was recorded on 2 March 1838. There is no explanation of the discrepancy of 1/4 section and 320 acres. Lucy also could not write. She signed the deed with her mark. Part of Lucy's problem comes to light in the deposition made on 22 November 1834 by her father John McGillivray. She had been registered as one of his four children under the Treaty of Dancing Rabbit Creek, but the agent failed to record her as his child or head of household. He had registered four children over ten years old. At the time of the treaty, Lucy had one child under ten years old and still had this child and lived on her land. The deposition was taken in Lowndes County, Mississippi, and John signed with his mark.[116]

Alabama records show that only Turner McGillivray received a grant in Alabama. In 1845 he was granted 281 acres of Section 33, R17W T21S in Pickens County along the Alabama-Mississipi line. The state line splits section 33 and he received that part of the section in Alabama.[117] Turner also received 317 acres in 1834 located in Noxubee County.[118] He also received part of section 2 T15N R19E which was approved 29 March 1845.[119] He sold his land to Grant and Clements for one thousand dollars on 2 March 1836. The deed was recorded on 5 December 1838 with Turner signing his mark.[120] It is unknown why it took thirteen to fourteen years for Turner to receive his grant in Alabama. The above is verified by an entry in the Alabama Tract Books where Section 33, R17W T21S in Pickens County is "Reserved for Turner McGilbry under Choctaw Treaty of 1830."[121]

Gordon McGillivray was granted 937 acres in 1834 in Noxubee County.[122] He also received NE 1/4, Section 34 T16 R 19, after it was "held under advisement," on 4 November 1851 and finally approved by the President on 5 July 1921. He received all of Section 35 T16 R19 on 28 October 1851.[123] It just cannot be explained from the records why these grants were held so long—the one case nearly one hundred years and then going to second or third generation descendants. There was no record of Gordon selling his land; however, it must have been sold by his heirs as the land today is broken up into many smaller plots.

No further record was found on Robert McGillivray and he could hardly have been the Robert employed by Swanson and McGillivray in 1779 since he would be too old in 1831—but not impossible.

One interesting footnote to the McGillivrays of Noxubee County reveals a Nicolas McGillivray who sued John Dent and Burwell Brewer on 10 May 1847. The suit was continued several times by the court until 12 May 1849, when the attorney for Nicolas moved for dismissal which was granted, although he had to pay the defendant's court costs. It is not clear from the sketchy records what the suit was about. Because Nicolas was "unknown and an Indian" he had to post a bond.[124]

The 1831 Choctaw census contains the following information—

John McGilbry (Indian), 8 in family, lives near Tombecbe Tongue's
Bluff. Good hickory land. 640 acres.

Turner McGilbry, 3 in family, adjoins Tombecbe, good hickory
land. 640 acres.

Gordon McGilbry, 4 in family, adjoins Tombecbe, 640 acres.[125]

These McGillivrays, half-blood Choctaw living on the Tombigbee
River, are very likely to have been the sons of James McGillivray who was
a trader and resident among the Choctaw on the Tombigbee River. All
the dates are compatible.

A Robert McGillivray was a Choctaw interpreter in West Florida
where he and Charles Stuart certified a statement furnishing provisions
to the Choctaw visiting at Mobile from 24 November to 31 December
1779.[126] On 26 December 1779, he witnessed the will of one Charles
Walker who was a planter in the Mobile District.[127]

On 26 March 1782 Robert had drawn a draft on Peter Swanson to
pay for some horses bought for his majesty's service and a bill was
submitted by Swanson and McGillivray to British officials for supplies
furnished to the Chickasaw in 1780.[128] Robert and "Colbert's Indians"
had taken the supplies out to the Chickasaw Country. With Robert
authorized to write drafts on the company, it would appear he held a
responsible position and most likely a relative although he has not been
identified. In order to be proficient in the Choctaw language and act as
interpreter, Robert had been in the Indian country for several years
spending most of that time among the Choctaw. There was a Robert
McGillivray who signed as a witness to a letter dated 9 April 1816 at the
Chickasaw Agency.[129] There is no way of knowing if this was the same
Robert McGillivray.

In 1772 an Alexander McGillivray was considered one of the
principal inhabitants of Mobile where he served in the West Florida
Assembly.[130] This Alexander seems to disappear from the records early
and his relationship to the other McGillivrays cannot be established.

Farquhar McGillivray was the brother to John and William the Clan
Chief, and was reported to have come to Georgia in 1736 along with

Lachlan.[131] In 1742 he signed a petition of complaint about the hardships at Darian where the Scottish immigrants were settled by General Oglethorpe. The petition was carried to England and presented to Parliament—all to no avail.[132] He served on the Charleston jury in 1751 and 1767.[133] In 1767 he was in Mobile working with his brother John in the Indian trade.[134] He was a witness for McGillivray and Struthers on a business transaction in 1770.[135]

Whyte[136] wrote that the Reverend Farquhar McGillivray returned to Scotland in 1780. His wife's name was Amy and he had a son named Daniel who remained in America. This is the same Farquhar who supposedly tutored young Alexander McGillivray, the son of Lachlan Lia, and later the famous Creek Indian Chief. It is only from secondary sources that we have the claim that Farquhar was a Presbyterian minister and also the tutor of young Alexander, although it is plausible that this was the case. We do know that Farquhar was married by 1769.[137]

There were two Farquhars in Charleston and they are sometimes confused[138]—Farquhar, the cousin to Lachlan Lia, and another Farquhar, a cabinetmaker. Farquhar, the cousin, was in West Florida by 1767, married by 1769, and back in Scotland by 1780; whereas the cabinetmaker was dead by 18 January 1771. His testament was to be read at St. Michaels church and his "nearest of kin," George Gray, was appointed to administer the estate.[139]

Peter Hamilton, the early Alabama historian, wrote that one of the first Spanish land grants in the Mobile district was a tract one league in length on both sides of the Mobile River at 21 Mile Bluff. It was granted on 18 December 1781 to Pierre Juzan, the Commissary for Indians at Mobile. The tract had formerly been owned, in British times, by Henry Lizard and Thomas McGillivray. Lizard was murdered and John McGillivray bought the land at auction.[140] This Thomas McGillivray is another mystery and no further reference to him could be found.

A Lachlan McGillivray signed for John McGillivray a receipt in Mobile in March 1780 for various trade goods. The amount was $15.9 1/2.[141] This Lachlan was probably Lachlan Junior who was the overseer of Vale Royal. He was the son of Lachlan Lia's sister Jean Roy. He submitted a bill of $211 dated 9 June 1780 for the cost of corn, beef, and bacon furnished to the Choctaw and Chickasaw "on their return home from Pensacola." He caustically noted at the bottom of the receipt "for which I have signed five receipts of this tenor and date."[142] Most likely Lachlan Junior fled to West Florida when the rebels captured Savannah. He later returned to Savannah and returned to London with Lachlan Lia. He assisted in compiling the necessary evidence to file claims for losses in Georgia.

Daniel McGillivray was probably as well known in West Florida as his Uncle John. He first appears in the records in 1773 when he was given a grant of five hundred acres in West Florida.[143] By 1775 he was already a member of the trading house of Miller and Swanson of Pensacola.[144]

From the Daniel McGillivray papers we learn that Charles Stuart, the deputy Indian Agent, employed Daniel as an interpreter in July 1778. A paper dated only 1779 and appearing to be an invoice from Daniel to "John McGillivray Esquire" for services rendered on "the Natchez expedition" which included:

*Ten head of horses at $50 each—$500.
*Two years as manager and keeper of John's "Cowpen"—$428.
*Salary while at Natchez and Manchac—$214.
*Other miscellaneous items.

The total was $1527.[145] By this time John was the Commander of the West Florida Militia with a commission of Lieutenant Colonel. He was ranging up and down the Mississippi River trying to keep the Americans at bay. Daniel had been working in the Natchez district assisting John.

Daniel received another grant of three hundred acres fourteen miles northeast of Natchez in May 1779.[146] Daniel McGillivray, who was John's nephew, remained in the Creek Nation under the protection of his kin, the famous Creek Indian Chief Alexander McGillivray. Alexander, writing on 25 December 1784, mentions that Daniel and another relative, Moniac, had arrived at Little Tallasee with Daniel almost dead but that he had recovered.[147]

Alexander was using Daniel to carry important messages and to be his representative at meetings among the Indians.[148] Daniel was also used in Alexander's trading business. Alexander writing to Panton in September 1788 says "I have instructed Daniel McGillivray concerning the skins he carries down, of the Wewocoe store. . . ."[149]

After the Revolution Daniel also worked for Panton Leslie Co. in Pensacola who now had a virtual monopoly of the Creek and Choctaw trade with a royal charter from the Spanish government. During this period Daniel also worked with John McDonald, the Cherokee Agent for Panton Leslie Co., and was the carrier of messages between McDonald and the Company.[150]

A letter dated 19 November 1794, from the Creek Chief Mad Dog to the Governor of Georgia, complained about the "disturbances" created by the traders among the Creeks. He named several traders, including Daniel, and says they are bribed by Panton and the Spanish government.[151] Many of the traders were notorious for spreading rumors and lies among the Indians, often causing turmoil and confusion. The Indians often hardly knew who or what to believe.

After Alexander died in 1793, Daniel became more involved with Panton and continued to keep him informed on activities in the Creek Nation, not only the Indians, but also the traders and Spanish agents in the nation.[152] In 1795 he was a magistrate in the Creek country and any "criminals" were brought before him.[153]

Daniel in turn had complaints against the Indians. Writing to Panton on 23 October 1796 from Little Tallasee, which was his residence, he complained of the Indians stealing his riding horse and leaving him "afoot." He also included a list of goods that was needed by his storekeeper at Oakfuskee.[154]

Benjamin Hawkins, after being appointed in 1796 as the Creek Indian Agent for the newly founded United States, decided to travel through the Creek country on his way to the Creek Agency located on the Flint River near present day Macon, Georgia. Arriving at the fork of the Alabama River, he visited Daniel, who lived one-half mile from the "old Tallasee Town," now deserted since all the residents had removed a few miles down the Coosa to Hickory Ground. He wrote that Daniel is:

> a trader, a native of Scotland, formerly a trader among the Choctaws, but for 12 years a resident and trader among the Creeks, he has a Creek woman and a son 6 years old. He has been a meddling, troublesome man, talkative and capable of misrepresentation among the Indians. His woman was very attentive and did everything she could to render my situation comfortable. Mr. McGillivray cultivates a small field with the plow, lying on the river.

His house was three hundred yards from the river. The falls were one-half to three-fourths of a mile below his house. At Hickory Ground Hawkins met the principal chief, "McFassion, a cousin of Gen. McGillivray."[155] McFassion is probably Malcolm McPherson who will be covered in a later chapter.

Hawkins, in one of his journal entries dated 11 February 1797, wrote that a Colonel Kirkland was killed traveling through the Creek Nation. An Indian named Catt was accused of the murder. Catt was captured and taken first to Hickory Ground where he was then taken to within fifteen miles of Pensacola and held there. His captors went to see Daniel McGillivray who was then in Pensacola. Daniel sent for the Spanish Governor and advised him of the murder and the circumstances. Governor White told McGillivray that the deed was done outside Spanish territory and there was nothing he could do. Daniel decided to "sleep on it." The next day he decided Catt must die and ordered John Forbes and Lewis Milford to go with Robert Walton, hear the prisoner's case, and if guilty, execute him. Panton wanted him to wait so Catt could have a fair trial, but Daniel said no. The men examined Catt and of course found him guilty. They then took him ten miles inside the Spanish border where Catt begged that they not hang him, but if he must die, shoot him instead. He begged that his clothes be removed since they belonged to the murdered man, but they refused his request. They hanged him from a limb reaching over the path, and he hung there for six or seven days, finally being cut down by some passerby who stripped him of his clothes. He lay for three or four months without anyone touching him.[156] This episode reveals the influential position that Daniel held with the Creeks and consequently with the Spanish authorities.

Daniel was still keeping Panton informed in 1799 and was living at Little Tallasee. He mentions Alexander's sisters Sophia and Sehoy, and his nephew David Tate. Daniel said that he had been ill but was recovering.[157]

William Panton, writing to Governor Gayoso in New Orleans on 24 July 1800, referred to Daniel as "an old trader in the Creek Nation."[158] Daniel may have been an "old trader," but he was still interested in world affairs and was to live several more years. He asked Panton, in a letter dated 6 May 1800, if he could send him some newspapers to read.[159] In 1803 Daniel assisted General James Wilkinson, as interpreter, on a survey of the United States boundary line near the Alabama-Tombigbee River junction.[160] Daniel also acted as guide and interpreter for Benjamin Hawkins in 1802 when he and General Pickens were appointed to run the line between the Choctaw and Natchez district.[161]

Daniel remained in West Florida after the Revolution and tried to reclaim his land grants. He had to get the grants certified by the U.S. Government. Adam Bingaman, who later married the widow of Alexander McIntosh, a cousin to Daniel, acted as his attorney on these claims in 1804.[162]

On 13 June 1807, he signed a document authorizing the Creek Chief, Big Warrior, to act as "attorney" for himself and John Forbes Co. in collecting all debts owed to them in the Creek Nation.[163] John Forbes had been the branch manager and partner in Mobile for Panton Leslie Co.

When John Innerarity visited the Upper Creeks in 1812 trying to collect debts owed to Panton Leslie Co. and now the John Forbes Co., he made a list of the traders and the amount each owed the Company. Daniel was listed as owing $1927, a large amount for that time.[164] This was the last we hear of Daniel in the records.

General Thomas Woodward, the perennial Indian fighter and

Major General of the Alabama Militia, wrote extensively of his experiences and contacts with the Creek Indians—especially of the Creek Wars of 1813-14 and 1836. Woodward says Daniel came to America with Lachlan Lia and John Tate. He says his name was Daniel McDonald and after Alexander McGillivray died in 1793, he took the McGillivray name and consequently benefited from Alexander's estate. Also, that he was the father of Bit-Nose Billy McGillivray. Professor Wyman also says "Bit Nose Billy" was William McGillivray, the half-blood son of Daniel.[165] Some recent writers[166] have continued Woodward's story about his name being McDonald; however, Daniel could hardly have come over with Lachlan Lia as this would have placed him in the Creek Country for some seventy-five years plus, with an age close to one hundred in 1812. We know he was not a McDonald since we pick him up in the records in 1773 as a McGillivray long before Alexander's death in 1793. In fact, Daniel was the son of Farquhar McGillivray of South Carolina and later West Florida, who in turn was the brother to John and Clan Chief William McGillivray, and consequently a cousin to Lachlan Lia. If Daniel had a "recognized" heir that was living in 1852 when John Lachlan McGillivray, the 10th Chief, died, he would have been the next in line to inherit the Chieftainship and the estates in Scotland.[167]

All indications are that Daniel was a loyalist during the Revolution and elected to stay and live in the Indian Country after the Revolution, where he lived comfortably and with considerable influence. He also spent much of his time in Pensacola and the Spanish territory. Like many Tories of the time, he had a safe haven in both and was out of reach of the Georgia authorities—protected by the Creeks in Indian country and the Spanish in West Florida. The six-year-old son mentioned by Hawkins grew up to be William McGillivray, the Chief of Hickory Ground at a later time. William, when twenty-three years old, was a chief by the time the Creek War of 1813-14 erupted. He was hostile toward the United States and worked closely with William Weatherford in trying to defeat the American forces. He was one of four Indian leaders in the Battle of Calabee on 27 January 1814 where the Creeks defeated the Georgia Militia under General John Floyd.[168]

The Creek Chiefs, meeting with the U.S. Commissioners in 1824 at Broken Arrow on the Chattahoochee River, refused to cede more land to the United States. The Chiefs signing the document included "Wm. McGilvery."[169]

A Congressional Committee in 1825 inquired into the possible misuse of an appropriation to the Creek Indians. They were concerned that equal distribution of the funds was not being made among the Indians. They had reason for concern. Chief William had traveled to Washington in 1825, along with other Creek Chiefs, to sign a treaty. The Indian delegations usually stayed several months in Washington living off the expense of the government. The Chiefs were paid handsomely. Part of the agreement, based on a list signed by Thomas L. McKenney on 25 April 1826, lists some twenty-five Chiefs to be paid $153,500. Chief William was to receive four thousand dollars.[170]

William, with several other chiefs, returned to Washington in 1832 where they signed the removal treaty. William could not write and he signed the treaty with an X mark.[171] He is also listed in the Creek census of the same year as the principal chief of "Hickory Ground Town" with two males and one female in the household. He also owned twenty-five slaves.[172]

A document in the National Archives, dated only 1833, and titled "Names of Chiefs of the Creek Nation & the Township & Range in Which each town is located," has William McGillivray listed as Chief of "Pocheshatchie or Alabama" and located at T20 R17.[173] This is difficult to reconcile and may be in error. This was a turbulent time for the Creeks and there was considerable movement within the Nation. Pocheshatchie was located on the upper reaches of Hatchet Creek in Clay County some fifty miles to the north of Hickory Ground. The quadrangle map places the town on the Coosa River above Jordan Dam. There was an Alabama town located at the forks during early and late times. The Spanish explorer Delgado visited the forks in 1685 and mentions "Aymamu" or Alabama town.[174] Bartram visited the town in 1777.[175] It would appear that the "Alabama town" had moved upstream and joined the Pocheshatchie.

Enoch Parsons, a removal agent, writing to the Secretary of War on 21 January 1833, said:

> William McGilvery one of the Creek Chiefs" is entitled to a section of land. "He has two parcels of land he has made improvements on but which cannot be included in his section unless he can have it in two parts. He has two children and wishes them to have a part of the reserve and requests that such be approved.[176]

Alexander Sommerville, another removal agent, writing to Colonel John B. Hogan, Superintendent of Creek Emigration, on 10 July 1835, said he was leaving for Hickory Ground where "McGilvery" was chief. He was told that McGillivray was in favor of removing in the fall and would likely take "a great many more with him."[177]

Chief William McGillivray led a removal party of 3022 Creek Indians that left Wetumpka on 6 August 1836. The party reached Memphis six weeks later and from there traveled by water to Little Rock where they arrived on 20 November. By the time they reached Little Rock only 2000 remained.[178]

John McGillivray of West Florida also left descendants in the Chickasaw Nation. Accounts are sketchy and tracing their genealogy leaves a lot to be desired.

James Logan Colbert, the long time Scot trader and loyalist living with the Chickasaw, raided up and down the Mississippi River during and after the Revolution. His Indian raiding parties were used primarily against the Spanish boats plying up and down the river between New Orleans and St. Louis. These raids were little more than outlaw pillaging and plundering with a cloak of legitimacy. In May 1783, a Spanish convoy making its way upstream to St. Louis was followed and attacked by Colbert and his mixed band of loyalists and Chickasaw Indians. He captured several Spaniards, but the battle cost him his second in command, "McGillivray," who was killed in the action.[179] Since Colbert had Chickasaw warriors in his party, they would have had a native leader or chief and it is logical he would be second in command. This was Samuel

McGillivray, son of John McGillivray.[180]

The other McGillivray appearing among the Chickasaw comes later and a little more is known of him and his activities in the nation. He was also the son of John McGillivray.[181] This son was named William McGillivray and called Captain with the spelling consistently "McGilvery." The Captain has no particular military significance as the Indians and whites of this period frequently called some chiefs "Captain" merely to designate a leader or chief. He seems to first appear in the records in 1814. The Chickasaw Chiefs had met in Council on 27 September 1814 and "agreed unanimously" to join Jackson's army. "Wm McGilvreay" was paid $40.50 by the United States disbursing officer at New Orleans for "lost rifle, shot pouch, powder horn, mold, knife, tomehawk, scabard & belt" on the night of 23 December 1814, during the battle with the "enemy" at the plantation of M. LaCoste.[182]

He was later a Chickasaw representative, along with Levi Colbert, the son of James Logan Colbert, to observe the survey of the line being run between the Nation and the United States. The United States surveyor was General John Coffee who started the survey in December 1816.[183] In order to fill this important assignment for the Nation, he would have been a high ranking and trusted chief.

In 1818 General Andrew Jackson was one of the Commissioners sent to the Chickasaw Nation to obtain, by treaty, their lands west of the Tennessee River in the states of Kentucky and Tennessee. After receiving threats and then bribes from these "reputable commissioners" it was finally agreed to by the Chickasaw. As part of the settlement a secret bribe of twenty thousand dollars was given to the five ranking chiefs, "Captain McGilvery" received $666, whereas George and Levi Colbert each received $8500.[184] Moser wrote that McGillivray lived between 1754-1844. He served as a Lieutenant of a Chickasaw detachment in the Creek War.[185]

Three Cumberland Presbyterian ministers, Samuel King, Robert Bell, and James Stewart, on 11 September 1820, signed an agreement with the Chickasaw Chiefs to open a school at Charity Hall only three miles from the Cotton Gin Port on the Tombigbee River. Among the

Chiefs signing was "William McGelbra." The school opened in November 1820.[186]

In 1821, when the missionary Thomas C. Stewart came to the Chickasaw Nation, it was divided into three districts. The Chiefs of these districts were Tishomingo, Samuel Sealy, and "William McGilvery."[187]

In July 1829 Mr. Holmes, the missionary to the Chickasaw, convened a "religious council" near Tokshish, Mississippi, for the Choctaw and Chickasaw. The meeting was in reality a camp meeting held under an arbor and able to seat one thousand people, not unlike the very successful Methodist camp meetings among the Indians. The Indians would come from far and wide and stay two or three days at these meetings. The principal chiefs attending included "Capt. McGilvery."[188]

In 1830 a meeting was held between the United States Commissioners and four Chickasaw Chiefs. The Commissioners were seeking a treaty for removal of the Chickasaw to Indian territory west of the Mississippi River. The chiefs wanted to look at the land in the western country before agreeing to swap their homeland. This agreement was signed by "Major Levi Colbert, Col. G. Colbert, Major Jas. Colbert and Captain Wm McGilvery" in that order.[189]

Williams[190] wrote that this Captain McGilvery was a "descendant of Lachlan;" however Lachlan was little associated with the Chickasaw and seems to have never returned to the Creek country after 1760. Captain McGillivray along with Samuel was of mixed blood and the sons of John McGillivray who spent much of his time in the Chickasaw Nation during and before the Revolution.[191] He died near Doaksville in Indian Territory at age ninety.

A "William McGilbery" appears as head of household on the Chickasaw muster rolls taken in 1839. His family consisted of one male between ten and twenty, one male between twenty and fifty, one male over fifty, one female under ten, two females between ten and twenty, one female between twenty and fifty, and one female over fifty. There were also seven slaves.

There was also a "John McGilberry" among the Chickasaw in the same 1839 muster roll. His family consisted of one male under ten, one male between ten and twenty, one male between twenty and fifty, one female under ten, two females between ten and twenty, one female between twenty and fifty, and one female over fifty. He also owned seven slaves.[192]

There was also a "James McGilivary" listed in the Creek Census of 1832. He had one male and two females in his family and no slaves. He lived at Tuskegee Town which at this date was located in Macon County, Alabama, and was formerly located adjacent to old Fort Toulouse and near the McGillivray family at Little Tallasee and Hickory Ground.[193] This James could very well be the son of trader James McGillivray who died in Scotland in 1806 and was the father of the Choctaw McGillivrays. Over the years he lived and traded in both the Choctaw and Creek Nations.

No McGillivrays appeared on the 1847 Chickasaw census taken in Indian Territory after removal. This would seem to indicate they remained in Mississippi or were dead by this time.[194]

Returning to John McGillivray and his activities in West Florida—James Willing and his small troop of continentals arrived unexpectedly at Natchez and terrorized the settlers along the river. Willing had moved to Natchez in 1772 and attempted to be a contractor for the Army at Pensacola, but his business enterprises failed and he soon squandered his fortune. As the Revolution progressed, he became more outspoken on behalf of the rebels and consequently lost many former friends. He became bitter at his situation and returned to Pennsylvania in 1776. Being the brother of Thomas Willing, who was a partner with Robert Morris, a powerful figure of the Continental Congress, he was tapped by the Commerce Committee for a secret mission. Being in Natchez for four years made him a natural for the expedition the Committee had in mind.

He was commissioned a Captain in the Navy and given a "volunteer crew" of twenty-seven men and the riverboat USS Rattletrap. The Army outfitted the boat and crew at Fort Pitt and he sailed (floated) down the Ohio on 11 January 1778. His mission was to cause "disturbances" and confusion among the loyalist settled on the lower Mississippi, and to establish friendly relations with the Spanish authorities at New Orleans. By the time he reached the mouth of the Yazoo he had about one hundred men. John Stuart had stationed a party of Choctaw at Walnut Hills as a lookout for any Americans coming down the river, but they had left their post and returned home when Willing floated by.

Willing surprised the settlers and landed at Natchez on 19 February raising the American flag over Fort Panmure. The intimidated settlers signed an agreement to remain neutral and not take up arms against the United States. He raided and plundered plantations and settlements along the river taking slaves and property. By the time he reached Baton Rouge his motley army was then about two hundred. Willing was allowed by Governor Galvez to auction his plunder in New Orleans including some 680 slaves. His gross came to about $75,000. Willing lingered during the summer at the expense of Galvez who became impatient with his procrastination.[195]

Willing finally sailed from New Orleans on 15 November 1778, but he was pursued at sea by the British and his sloop was captured. He was sent to New York where he escaped, was recaptured, and placed in irons to languish in prison for the next two years finally being exchanged.[196]

Governor Peter Chester of West Florida writing to the military commander, Major General Augustine Prevost, on 21 March 1778 said that he was trying to raise a Provincial Corps under command of John McGillivray Esq., "who has greater influence about Mobile, and with the Traders in the Indian Country, than any other Person in the Province." However, he doubted that more than one hundred men could be raised and they will only agree to enlist for the expedition to Natchez.[197]

Strained relations existed between the civilian militia and the regular British troops. John's Loyal Refugees of the West Florida Militia were paid forty shillings a month, had to furnish their own horse, saddle, and clothing because the regional commander General Campbell would not grant an allowance for them. Whereas the Loyal Forresters under Campbell were paid one shilling five pence per day and were furnished a horse, saddle, clothing, and equipment. They also received bounty money and their officers nearly double the pay of same rank in the Loyal

Refugees. The Regulars jealously guarded their prerogatives and stand-ing with the Crown. They were not subject to the Colonial Governors and refused to let their men serve under militia officers even though it was clearly in the best interests of the Crown to do so. This continual bickering and non-cooperation between military and civilian authorities contributed substantially to the British defeat on the American Fron-tier.[198]

Lieutenant Colonel John McGillivray marched his horse troop to Manchac on the Mississippi and there took command from Captain William Barker in late June 1778. Barker was commander of a troop of British Regulars that had arrived earlier.[199] On 6 July John was informed of the arrival of a Captain Conner and twenty-three Americans from Fort Pitt to reinforce Captain Willing.[200] Captain Willing did not linger. After wreaking havoc on the British settlers, he moved on to New Orleans. He remained there for several months with the permission of Galvez. John and his troop had arrived at Manchac too late, and Willing had slipped away into Spanish territory where they could not pursue him.[201]

Captain Barker, writing to John McGillivray on 12 September 1778, said that a United States Colonel with reinforcements arrived at Manchac on 11 September by boat and there were rumors that a large troop was descending the River from Fort Pitt. Barker had captured a boat on the river that had papers on board proving that Galvez was not neutral as he claimed. Barker felt that Galvez, in assisting the Americans, gave him justification to attack Spanish boats on the River.[20] John, on 7 October 1778, wrote a strong letter to Galvez accusing him of protecting "robbers" such as Captain Willing's band of Americans, and insinuated he may be inviting war between Spain and Britain.[203]

A motion made and passed by the West Florida Assembly on 3 November 1778 reads:

> Mr. Speaker, I move that the thanks of this House be presented to
> Lieutenant Colonel Commandant John McGillivray for the zeal he has
> always shown to his Majesty's service; for his having, upon the very first

alarm of the Rebels intending to make an attack upon this Province, cheerfully offered to put himself at the head of such forces as could be raised to repel his Majesty's enemies; for his having, to the evident detriment of his own private affairs, employed his whole time in using his influence to get a sufficient number of men embodied for that purpose, and for his activity in endeavoring to put the Natchez in the best state of defense that their present circumstances could admit of.

The motion passed unanimously. The Speaker was ordered to communicate the same to Colonel McGillivray. The motion was made by Mr. Gould.[204]

In 1779 Governor Peter Chester refused to call the General Assembly into session. He felt the composition of the assembly would make it unproductive. The populace petitioned for the call and James McGillivray, cousin to Lachlan and John, signed the petition. John became one of the leaders in trying to get Governor Chester removed from office. Their protests brought results from the Secretary of State who in 1780 rebuked Chester for not calling the assembly into session and passing the necessary laws to provide for a militia.[205]

The turbulent situation in West Florida was fast closing in on the loyalists. The King of Spain, on 29 August 1779, secretly authorized the Governor at Havana to assist Governor Galvez in the attack and capture of Mobile and Pensacola. Galvez was specifically instructed to lead the expedition and had been promoted to Brigadier for that purpose. Galvez was to be furnished with the necessary troops, supplies, and ships for the expedition.[206]

Galvez thought the Natchez settlement should be captured first, which he proceeded to do in September 1779. It was soon after this event that John left Pensacola. He boarded a ship which was captured by the Spanish and he was taken prisoner to Havana where he languished in prison for ten months before he was exchanged and made his way to Savannah in late 1780 or early 1781.[207]

Galvez could now turn his attention to Mobile without worrying about an attack from the back country. He moved decisively to take

Mobile in 1780 and Pensacola in 1781.[208]

Before leaving Pensacola, John had left his affairs in the hands of attorney David Ross.[209] Apparently his partner William Struthers also left Pensacola at this time, although he returned to West Florida at a later date. John, back in Savannah making ready to sail for Jamaica, had collected from Governor James Wright in May and June of 1782 some forty-eight pounds for supplying provisions to house the militia and ninety-two pounds for rice.[210]

Daniel McGillivray went back to the Creek Nation living out his life there. James McGillivray went to South Carolina, but remained in the employment of Alexander McGillivray, the Creek Chief, and we have one last account of him in America. Alexander wrote to John Habersham of South Carolina on 18 September 1786, expressing regret that nothing had been done about the white settlers on Creek hunting grounds, and that this had been expressed to the Governors by "Mr. James McGillivray," but the Governors "had taken no notice of it."[211] The last we hear of James is a death notice appearing in the newspaper *Columbia Museum & Savannah Advertiser* dated 11 June 1806, reporting that James McGillivray died at Daviot in Scotland on 29 January 1806. Sometime between 1804 and 1806 James had returned to Scotland.

6

McIntoshes in West Florida

Alexander McIntosh was the son of John McIntosh of Holm and Janet Baillie. His grandfather was Angus McIntosh of Holm. His father was first married to Anne McGillivray which produced his half brother William McIntosh of Holm who never came to America. His brother, John McIntosh, did come to America as did Alexander. Alexander's aunt, Catherine McIntosh, married Lieutenant Benjamin McIntosh, son of the "old Brigadier of Borlum" who came to America in 1736 and whose descendants played a large role in Colonial Georgia and the Revolution.[1]

Alexander's father came to Georgia in 1736.[2] It is not clear whether Alexander came to Georgia with his father or was born in Georgia. Since his father married Janet Baillie in 1724, it is most likely he was born in Scotland and the family came with John in 1736 or followed at some later date. Alexander McIntosh was a cousin to Lachlan Lia McGillivray on his mother's side.[3]

The McIntoshes, like the McGillivrays, had long been in Georgia and the Carolinas and involved in the Indian trade. Perhaps the earliest account comes in 1726 when a Carolina trader named McIntosh, bound for the Creek Country, was attacked and killed on the trail by a Cherokee war party.[4]

Alexander first appears in the record in 1767 where he is an elected member of the West Florida Commons House of Assembly representing the Mobile district.[5] To have been elected to the Assembly this early, he probably arrived soon after the British took possession of Florida in 1764. He served in every session from 1767 through 1772. Darlymple[6] writes that he began his career in West Florida as a Captain of Provincial troops about the time Major Farmer arrived as military commander.

In 1768 Alexander McIntosh and John McGillivray were appointed to a commission to hear and adjudicate disputes that may arise on the duties imposed on slaves imported into the colony.[7] By 1769 he was in the trading business under the name of Alexander McIntosh & Co. and was located in Natchez on the Mississippi River. He may have had some difficulty getting started, since John Fitzpatrick, the merchant broker at Manchac, would not accept his draft until it was confirmed by McGillivray & Struthers.[8] Apparently there was a business relationship between John McGillivray and Alexander.

He was also at this time acting as an interpreter which indicates he had spent considerable time in the Indian country. Interpreters had to be fluent in the Indian language and acceptable to both sides, although sometimes each side had their own interpreter. They developed their credibility over many years by truthfully interpreting for both sides. Alexander was later doing business under the name of Miller McIntosh Co.[9]

Alexander in 1770 was granted five hundred acres near Natchez and another five hundred acres in 1772 near Point Coupee just upriver from Baton Rouge. He was married to Anne Shell or Shield and they lived on their plantation near Point Coupee. They lived there for a few years before moving to Natchez and settling on a plantation there. They were living there when the Spanish captured the town in 1779.[10]

Charles Stuart, deputy agent to his cousin John Stuart, wrote to John on 12 June 1770, complaining of not having an agent among the Chickasaw and Choctaw. John had been forced to furlough his deputy agents due to tight budget constraints. Charles continued that he was unable to enforce the regulations and could not "prevent transiet persons from going without leave into the Indian nations and holding meetings or propagating reports among them. There is now in the nation two of them Mr. Alexander McIntosh and Mr. Strothers who were taking advantage of the times." He felt compelled to give Alexander a "nominal commission as Commissionary" and had given him strict orders at Mobile not to call meetings or hold talks with the Indians.[11] This is indicative of the independence enjoyed by the traders. They were the source of the lucrative Indian trade that brought skins to England for manufacture of all the end products that contributed to the English economy. For this reason the Crown was very tolerant toward the traders.

Earlier McIntosh had been in trouble with the British authorities and James Adair, a long-time trader among the Chickasaw and the first historian of the southern Indians, gives us the only account of this event that could be located. Adair aided the authorities in preventing the "debauchery" of the Chickasaw by the sale of rum to them by the traders. He supported the arrest and prosecution in 1766 of John Buckles and Alexander McIntosh.

> [McIntosh] debauched the Indians with rum to the uneasiness and disgust of orderly traders, the loss of their numerous outstanding debts and every chance of fair trade...in his Arabian like methods of plunder-ing the Indians. . . . He would make a new Hell of this place, and it is hoped that he may go thru Purgatory properly.[12]

Some prominent and wealthy traders got their start by trading rum "in the woods," and no doubt Adair was resentful of these young upstarts invading his trading domain.

Alexander was affiliated with McGillivray, Struthers, Swanson, Mackintosh and Company. He was responsible for escorting the skins to New Orleans and Mobile and returning with merchandise and Indian trade goods. He would transport the skins downriver to the point of high tide and there they were placed aboard waiting schooners. In May 1770, he boarded a schooner under command of Captain Gerome. Fitzpatrick, wrote to John McGillivray, and said that Alexander, on his return from Mobile, became stranded on Cat Island for fourteen days due to the "carelessness" of the ship's captain. After running short of food, he made his way inland with the help of two "hired hands." He employed eight Indians and some others to help transport his trade goods from the stranded ship to a landing place where they could be picked up by boat. He planned to sue the ship's captain for all his costs and damages.[13]

Perhaps earlier, but by 1773 McIntosh & Co. was in partnership with McGillivray & Struthers. Fitzpatrick reported to McGillivray that Alexander was busy selling his skins for cash so he could settle his accounts.[14]

Alexander owned some 3950 acres on the Tombigbee and Mississippi Rivers by 1773 and was to acquire much more over the next few years. By 1779 he owned an additional 6850 acres.[15]

Alexander also attended to his social and civic duties by being a witness to published banns in Mobile on 10 August 1770 where he is identified as an Indian trader.[16] He was also in the slave trade where he loaned money taking slaves as collateral.[17]

In May 1773, Alexander was having to move his trade goods upriver to Manchac by horse-drawn carts due to the river being too low to go by boat. He also visited with Daniel McIntosh on his way upriver.[18] Daniel was probably his cousin.

His wife, Anne McIntosh, was very much involved in the trade business where she bought and sold various trade goods through Fitzpatrick. Alexander was away from home for long periods and his wife, ahead of her time, ran the business. However, Fitzpatrick was having his problems with Alexander. He wrote in August 1774 complaining in a long letter to Alexander that he can and does account for all transactions and Alexander is welcome to examine the books. He said, "I am in hopes you will come down with Mr. McGillivray when he returns from the Natchez so that all may be settled in his presence to our satisfaction as I really look upon it that I have already lost time enough in the affair." In June, Fitzpatrick had managed to sell some of his skins and was able to send him four hundred dollars in gold. Alexander was now a partner with John Miller under Miller & McIntosh, but he also retained his McIntosh & Co. and his relations with McGillivray &

Struthers.[19] Fitzpatrick in 1777 was still having trouble with Alexander, and wrote Donald McPherson that their disagreement may end up in court.[20]

Captain James Willing, in command of a small party of Americans, slipped down the Ohio and Mississippi Rivers and arrived at Natchez in 1778 and caused a panic among the English settlers. Willing was a resident of Natchez before the war and knew the territory and many of the settlers personally.[21] When Willing arrived at Natchez he apparently had specific objectives in mind—to settle old scores of hard feelings. Willing ordered Lt. McIntire to slip past Natchez and go directly to Colonel Anthony Hutchins and Alexander McIntosh's plantations. McIntosh had moved from Point Coupee sometime in 1777 or 1778. McIntire killed cattle, hogs, and other farm animals on McIntosh's plantation. He ransacked and plundered the house and took six of his slaves. Willing had earlier captured Alexander along with William Eason and William Williams. They were released later when Willing drifted on down river.[22]

Willing's presence on the Mississippi caused alarm throughout British West Florida. The West Florida Assembly quickly authorized the raising of a regiment of five companies. John McGillivray was commissioned Lieutenant Colonel in Command and Alexander was made "first captain." He was an experienced officer and was sent to Natchez to assist Lieutenant Colonel Anthony Hutchins in retaking control of Natchez.[23]

During this period Captain Alexander McIntosh remained at Natchez in command of Fort Panmure. Later, in 1780, this duty caused him some problems. James Jellison, a contractor, presented a claim against Alexander to the Natchez Court for $438 due him for work performed on the fort some two years earlier. Jellison lost his case and had to pay court costs.[24]

In 1781 a group of American sympathizers headed by John and Phillip Alston concocted a plan to capture Natchez in the name of the Crown, but hold it for annexation later to the United States. Alexander got wind of the plan and warned the Spanish authorities. When a force of some two hundred American sympathizers marched on Fort Panmure, the Spanish were prepared; but after a siege of two weeks, the Fort surrendered and the Spanish prisoners were transported downriver to Point Coupee.[25]

The compassion of Alexander is revealed when he accepted the guardianship in 1781 of six children who had been deserted by their rebel father while fleeing to the Choctaw Country. Their mother, Elizabeth Alston, wife of Phillip, had recently died. The estate deserted by Alston was sizeable and included slaves and land. Alexander had to sell off some of the cattle and slaves to provide for the children.[26]

In August 1781 Alexander and his wife Anne were involved in a lawsuit.[27] This may have been another problem with John Fitzpatrick, since he wrote Peter Swanson on 26 March 1782 that he and Alexander were going to "arbitration."[28] Alexander purchased some cattle in October 1781.[29] On 29 March 1782 Anne, his widow, was held accountable for the cash received from the sale of part of the Alston estate.[30] This means that Alexander died sometime between 15 October 1781 and 29 March 1782. Less than a year later, in November 1782, Anne was married to Adam Bingaman, an attorney.[31] Just another year later in November 1783, Bingaman was considered by the Natchez Courts to be Alexander's "heir."[32] Over the next decade Bingaman obtained several grants of land from the Spanish and continued to expand his holdings and wealth. By 24 March 1804, Anne was dead and her will left everything to Bingaman. No mention was made of children from either marriage.[33]

When in 1804 the United States Government required a certification of all Spanish land grants, Bingaman laid claim to some 5850 acres as "Alexander's heir" and was certified in 1804-5. Bingaman had profited greatly by marrying the widow of Alexander.

James McIntosh first appears in the 1767 will of Lachlan Lia McGillivray.[34] He, at that time, was in West Florida and Lachlan bequeathed him five hundred pounds in his will.

His parents were James McIntosh of Kyllachy and Marjory McIntosh. His father died in 1778 and his brother, Captain Angus McIntosh of Kyllachy, died in South Carolina in 1779. His sister Jane married Archibald McGillivray in 1747, soon after his return to Scotland from

Georgia, where he became the owner of Daviot in 1749. Jane died in 1764 and Archibald in 1789. James's father was a brother to Janet McIntosh, the mother of Lachlan Lia McGillivray. This made James and Lachlan Lia first cousins.[35]

James lived an active life in West Florida being a trader, interpreter, plantation owner, trader in slaves and businessman. He had likely emigrated to Georgia or South Carolina and moved to West Florida with his cousins John and James McGillivray soon after the British occupation in 1764. James McIntosh also had a brother William in West Florida and they appear in the Natchez records together. Little is known of William other than these sketchy appearances.[36] He was not the Captain William McIntosh who was the father of the Lower Creek Chief William McIntosh.

James started receiving Spanish land grants in 1787. He was granted 2847 acres on the Homochitta River some twenty to thirty miles below Natchez. In 1788, he was granted another eight hundred acres about six miles southeast of Natchez. He purchased eight hundred arpents on Bayou Sara in the Natchez district in 1791.[37]

James also owned land on the Tombigbee River under English grants. Daniel Ward petitioned Govenor Miro in 1787 for fifty arpents formerly owned by James McIntosh "now deceased" and abandoned in 1781.[38] In 1787 George Walton petitioned for twenty arpents on land "which formerly belonged to Mr.McIntosh commonly known by the name McIntosh Bluff which said land was abandoned by the aforesaid McIntosh in the year 1780."[39] Hamilton also recognized that McIntosh Bluff was named for James.[40] It is unknown why James never reclaimed this land under the Spanish. Ward's claim that James was dead was probably used to enhance his chances of receiving the grant.

In 1790 James successfully bid for the plantation of one thousand acres owned by the heirs of William Hiorn. The land was sold for $1625 to satisfy Hiorn's debts. James had trouble determining the boundaries and asked for a survey which was completed in 1791 by William Dunbar, the deputy surveyor for the Natchez district.[41]

From 1804 to 1807, James made several claims to the United States

Commission to have his earlier grants certified. His claims for some 2600 acres in three tracts, including his "Belmont" plantation, were approved, but claims for several hundred more acres were rejected.[42]

There was a Eunice McIntosh, "widow," that James seems to have some relation to as they owned adjoining land in two tracts. She made claims for 1366 acres in two tracts and a lot in Natchez.[43] She also owned some slaves.[44] James also witnessed a power of attorney for a Mary McIntosh, "widow," in May 1793.[45] We do not know who Mary and Eunice were, but Eunice was probably the widow of his brother William.

In 1809 James was recommended to open the trade route down the Coosa River to connect with the Tombigbee settlements and Mobile.[46] He undertook this trade but had problems with the Creeks. In an affidavit 24 January 1810, sworn before the Justice of the Peace for Blount County, Tennessee (probably at Maryville), he states that Pathkiller, Chief of the Cherokees, had told him he could safely store his trade goods at Turkeytown, located near Centre, Alabama, in Cherokee County and the home of Pathkiller, until the Creeks gave their approval to move the goods on down the Coosa River. However, about one hundred Creek warriors suddenly appeared and forceably took the trade goods.[47]

The Creek Chiefs had sent a threatening letter to Pathkiller about his letting whites come down the Coosa River and settle on his lands. Chief Ridge of the Cherokee sent a reply in May 1809 chastising the Creeks for stealing the trade goods at Turkeytown—which was whiskey and other property belonging to James McIntosh.[48]

The James under discussion here should not be confused with another James McIntosh who was in West Florida at a later date. The later James was the son of Captain William McIntosh of Revolutionary War fame, who is best known as the father of the famous Lower Creek Chief William McIntosh.

A Daniel McIntosh was also a trader in West Florida, but virtually nothing is known of him. He was a trader out of Pensacola in 1772. He conducted his business with John Fitzpatrick at Manchac.[49] Fitzpatrick writing to Peter Swanson on 7 June 1775 laments the death of "Mr.

McIntosh" and especially the circumstances of his death. We hear no more about Daniel after this event, and since he seems to have worked for Swanson & Co. it probably applies to the death of Daniel.[50]

Later there was a John McIntosh that appears as head of household in the 1831 Choctaw census. His family consisted of six with one being white, assumed to be John. There were also five slaves. He had 480 acres near the Tombigbee in Noxubee County, Mississippi, which was "good land, with good water."[51]

The McIntoshes, like the McGillivrays, were Indian traders and landed gentlemen. But, unlike the McGillivrays, they were not loyalists and were able to adapt and flourish under the Spanish and the Americans.

7

Return to England

Before Savannah was evacuated by the British in 1782, Lachlan Lia had sailed for London in May. John, after some delay, sailed for Jamaica where he already owned some property and a plantation. John stayed a short time and was back in London by July 1783.

In the meantime, Georgia authorities lost no time in offering for sale confiscated properties seized from the loyalists. Apparently Georgia officials never knew that Lachlan Lia had deeded all his properties in Georgia to John McGillivray because all these properties were confiscated and sold as belonging to Lachlan. This seems strange since Lachlan and John later admit in affidavits to the Crown that their purpose in doing this was a hoax and only to try and save their properties from confiscation by Georgia authorities. This being the case, they would have made it known to Georgia authorities; otherwise it would indeed be an empty gesture.

In June 1782, only one month before the British left Savannah, Vale Royal, the home of Lachlan Lia and consisting of one thousand acres, was sold to Joseph Clay who was Paymaster General of the Southern Department for the Continental Army, and a prominent Savannah merchant. Clay was also a member of the Continental Congress.

Returning to his home in Savannah after the British evacuation and reviewing the ruin and devastation the war had wrought, Clay writes on 5 February 1783:

A return to our own country was the utmost of our wishes &
though twas to a desolated & ruined one yet the idea of having so far
prevailed against the enemy that had been by every means in her power
trying to crush us overbalances every other consideration—a country
like ours will very soon recover & far exceed her former situation, her
natural advantages with respect to agriculture & commerce are so great
that her increase & rise will be rapid.[1]

The confiscated lands were auctioned by a Board of Commissioners
and Clay bid on Vale Royal and Springfield, plus sixty adjoining acres.
Vale Royal sold for 6200 pounds and Springfield for 1352 pounds. All
this land subsequently came to be called Vale Royal. On the sixty acres
of high ground, east of Musgrove Creek, Clay constructed his mansion.
The house was three stories with a basement.[2] Clay continued to
purchase adjoining land and lots and ended up owning a substantial
stretch along the Savannah River. Clay used Springfield to raise cotton
and in 1793 he borrowed $32,000 to purchase slaves. He mortgaged
Vale Royal and other assets to secure the loan. Clay did well and the loan
was paid off in only a few years. Clay died in 1804 without a will. His
estate, valued at $276,000, went to his wife and children. Vale Royal was
valued at $60,000.

In order to make an equitable distribution among the many heirs,
the estate was sold. A description for the sale read—"the very valuable
plantation and tract of land called Vale Royal containing about 1000
acres of which 400 were tide and inland swamp, the remainder prime
cotton land." Vale Royal sold to the highest bidder, Benjamin Maurice,
a Savannah merchant, for $31,500. A few months later Springfield,
described as 623 acres, was sold to Ralph Clay, one of the heirs, for
$14,000. Apparently the sale was a cover for Joseph Stiles, one of the
estate administrators and Clay's son-in-law. Stiles soon possessed Vale
Royal and Springfield. He continued making improvements including a
brick factory. Seventy-one of his 124 slaves were employed on Vale
Royal. He operated both plantations until his death in 1838 leaving a

widow and 10 children. In 1839 various inherited tracts began to be sold off and by the Civil War the plantation was fragmented. The area had become an industrial area containing a railroad and other commercial waterfront property. Springfield, now consisting of 960 acres, was purchased by the City of Savannah for $27,840 and resold in lots and small acreages.[3] The plantations were now unrecognizable from the days when Lachlan Lia grew rice on Vale Royal and used Springfield for his horse stables and pasture.

The official record shows the confiscated estates of Lachlan McGillivray as being sold quickly after the evacuation. They included the following:

13 June 1782—Chatham County (Savannah)

200 acres	Hutchinson's Island	2700 pounds
200 acres	Hutchinson's Island	2800 pounds
445 acres	Springfield	1357 pounds
1000 acres	Vale Royal	6200 pounds
Family of Negroes		290 pounds
Fellow & Wench		200 pounds

2 September 1782—Burke County

1000 acres	Mathews Bluff	4050 pounds

10 September 1782—Burke County

Town lot	Augusta	310 pounds

18 November 1782—Wilkes County

100 acres	Reeds Mill Creek	300 pounds

13 June 1782—Slaves belonging to Lachlan Lia:

Doctor	60 pounds
Sepio	60 pounds
Frences	65 pounds
Barrock	50 pounds
George	25 pounds
Forterno	50 pounds
Sibbey	35 pounds
Tenah	50 pounds

Sappo	28 pounds
Samson	45 pounds
Cumbo	40 pounds
Pompey	70 pounds
Sarah	50 pounds
Charles	60 pounds

Total value was 18,895 pounds.[4] A slightly different version, but not significantly so, resides in the Public Record Office.[5]

Soon after their arrival in England, William's health began to fail and in the summer of 1783 he went to Wales on medical advice to avail himself of the famed goat's milk found there. John tried to get him to return to Inverness, but William sailed for Portugal hoping a summer climate would help his recovery, but he died there that same year.[6]

When William died, the Clan leadership passed to John Lachlan, his son, who became the 10th Chief, while scarecely a year old. He was raised by Anne, William's sister, until her death in 1790. Lachlan Lia carefully watched over him and also managed the family affairs.[7]

The will of William was made while he was in London and was probated on 25 January 1784. He left an annuity of fifty pounds to his daughter Barbara Anne until she reached age twenty-one or married. Thereafter, she was to share in the profits of the estate. He willed Gask to his brother John while naming John and Lachlan as executors, and his sister Anne as executria. They were also to act as guardians to his children's estates. His "beloved son John Lachlan" also shared in the estates, plus any settlement he received on his claims against the Crown.[8]

During peace treaty negotiations, the Americans were instructed to give no concessions to the loyalists. Britain broke the impasse by abandoning its support of the loyalist issues. The final agreement contained a weak clause where the Congress would "recommend" to the states that loyalists who had not borne arms could place a claim for return of their property, and others who fought for the Crown or who had gone into exile would have one year to purchase back their property from the new owners. The states ignored the Congressional recommendations and the loyalist refugees were afraid to try and reclaim or purchase their properties. A few loyalists returning to their homes in Connecticut in 1783 were mobbed and beaten. Disappointed by the treaty provisions, the exiles in London redoubled their efforts to secure some kind of restitution from the Crown.

Parliament passed the Compensation Act establishing a five-member commission to hear and judge the loyalist claims for their losses in America. Claims for uncultivated land, uncollectable debt, and currency depreciation were all excluded from claims. The tenure of the commission lasted from 1783 to 1789. The commission heard 3225 claims while compensation was granted to only 2291 claimants. The Crown paid out three million pounds which accounted for only 37% of the total amount claimed. The wealthy loyalists who could file well documented claims received the most reward. Of the sixty to eighty thousand loyalists, only seven thousand went back to England. Most fled to Canada, Florida, Jamaica, and the Bahamas.[9]

Lachlan and John spent virtually all their time in London preparing their claims on behalf of John and William for their losses in Georgia. William's claim is summarized as follows.

*He was a Captain in the 89th Regiment of Foot.

*In the rebellion of 1776 he was imprisoned twenty-two days for his loyalist sentiments.

*In 1777 he was banished and his estates confiscated because he refused to take an oath of allegiance to Georgia.

*The claim was dated 18 October 1783 and William was dead by this date.

*He was delayed in Charleston for twelve months in 1778 and was unable to gain passage due to his loyalist sentiments. He was able to bring away only two body servants.

*He owned two plantations on Hutchinson's Island.[10] One was called Wester Gask having 140 acres which was a gift from his cousin Lachlan McGillivray in 1773. The other contained 925 acres and was purchased from Lachlan in 1774.

*The two plantations were contiguous and at the time of purchase no "apprehension of danger from the commotion and that did not enter into the consideration of the purchase."

*He had the plantations appraised in 1776 and their valuation was 2700 pounds, but he felt this was low.

*In 1775 the rebels took from him seventy negro slaves plus their children.

*About forty of his slaves died and his brother John took sixty-six to Jamaica.

*His brother stayed until the evacuation of Georgia and "none of his relatives engaged in the rebellion."

*When he was about to leave the province, his cousin Lachlan McGillivray being likely to stay, William sold his plantation to him for between nine and ten thousand pounds sterling. A conveyance was made and he took Lachlan's bond for the money. The sale was only a sham and hopefully would protect the estate from seizure. Lachlan and his brother John also paid his debts.[11]

John McGillivray filed an affidavit in support of William's claim and also dated 18 October 1783. It is summarized as follows:

*John went to America in 1755. After a stay in Charleston, he moved on to West Florida.

*He is brother to William, the claimant.

*He was well acquainted with William's property since he acted as his brother's attorney in 1781-82.

*Lachlan gave William part of the plantation and sold him the other part. He thinks the land was worth fifteen pounds per acre in 1774.

*There was nothing of any value remaining on the plantations except the buildings. They had had the "moveables" and rough rice thrown into the hold of a ship, but it had spoiled.

*Lachlan McGillivray Jr., a nephew of Lachlan Lia, relocated to Georgia when West Florida was captured by the Spanish. He lived with his uncle and kept John's books.

*John paid William's debts of approximately 1400 pounds, whereas Lachlan paid 300 pounds of his debts.

*John bought a vessel in Jamaica in 1782 for 1800 pounds to be used for transporting his negro slaves to Jamaica. He sailed to Jamaica and landed the slaves and from there sailed with a convoy to England. His ship carried freight on his brother's account, but the ship foundered on the way to England. John believed he would fully recover his loss from his insurance.

*He believes the plantation in Georgia was sold, before he left Charleston, to John Kean for thirteen pounds per acre.[12]

William had also made a deposition in early 1783 soon after his return to England and before his death. This was in support of his claim before the Commissioners. He attached a list of losses which totaled 11,098 pounds.[13] In addition to the claim, he wrote directly to Lord George Germain, the Secretary of State for America, requesting a commission of Lieutenant Colonel in the Army. The deposition is written in the third person.

To the right honourable Lord George Germain his Majesty's principal Secretary of State for America. The memorial of Capt. William Mackgillivray, Humbly Showeth—

That your memorialist who was a Captain in the Army so early as 1759 & is now on half pay, went in 1773 at the desire of a cousin supposed then worth upward of 38,000 pounds sterling, of who had persuaded to make him his heir, to Georgia in America; and unhappily for him to the almost ruin of his property in Great Britain became a purchaser of lands & negroes then—that for his attachment to his most gracious Soverign & Country, and uniformly holding forth his detestation & abhorrence of the treasonable & rebellious measures, which were some time afterwards adopted in America, he was committed to prison & severely treated, that as soon as he was enlarged, his first object was to dispose of his property in Georgia, & return to Britain to offer his service

to his country. In pursuance of which Plan, not being able to procure
any money for his estate, which would be of use to him in this country,
he determined to risk it with his cousin on the success of his Majesty's
arms, and accordingly conveyed it to a person in Georgia and took his
Bond for near 10,000 pounds sterling being its value—that the usurped
Legislature of Georgia, after various means for the distress of Loyalists,
passed a law confiscating all the property, which such of them as refused
to swear allegiance to the States of America, & abjure their Sovereign &
possessed at any time since the Battle of Lexington in April 1775, which
effectually defeated your memorialist arrangement. That your memorialist, after leaving Georgia, was at Charlestown South Carolina in the
most disagreeable situation imaginable, oblidged to wait for a passage to
Europe for near 12 months, which was frequently refused him on
account of his difference in sentiment, at the same time that it was often
signified to him, how offensive & even dangerous his appearance was,
and that sometimes he met with insult & ill treatment — that having
been thus mistreated & striped of his property for his attachment to his
country, your memorialist humbly conceives he has some title to its
notice, and therefore wishes to recommend himself to your Lordship's
good offices.

He is informed that were he in the Army again the date of his
Commission would entitle him to the rank of Lieut Colonel — he has
an estate in the Highlands of Scotland, where he is likewise the head of
a Clan and his — —, he has no doubt of being able to rise men for his
Majesty's Service, if it were his pleasure to confer a Command on him,
which he would endeavour by every means to merit — He humbly begs
leave to submit his case to the consideration of your Lordship and as in
duty bound will ever pray.

Will McGillivray[14]

William had claimed 11,098 pounds, but was paid only 2890
pounds, less than the 1/3 average paid by the Crown.[15]

They were also busy helping their friends by making depositions for
support of their claims. Lachlan signed a deposition in support of

William Harding in about 1784 for his claim of 1465 pounds for lost property confiscated by Georgia and South Carolina in 1781. Lachlan stated that he knew Harding to be a very trustworthy and sober man and had been employed by Lachlan in 1768 to construct rice cleaning machines. Also John Graham signed an addendum confirming what Lachlan had said—not having first hand knowledge "but being well acquainted with Mr. McGillivray who signs the above certificate & knowing him to be a man of worth and credit—I have not a doubt but what he sets forth with said certificate is strictly true and just." 25 March 1784.[16] John McGillivray also gave a deposition 7 May 1784 in favor of Harding—saying he knew him when constructing rice cleaning machines on Vale Royal.[17] Lachlan and John signed an affidavit with others on the appraisal price of rice in Savannah at the request of Samuel Douglas, a merchant of Savannah.[18]

On 28 July 1783, John wrote to Farquhar McGillivray of Dalcrombie, a cousin, informing him that he had just recently arrived in London from Jamaica. Subsequent to his arrival in England, he went to see his brother William and "Mr. Lachlan." He visited Lachlan, and his sister with the two children, at Tanies Stock fourteen miles from Plymouth. His brother having gone to Bristol, he visited him there for two days. His brother, William, had been ill, but seemed to be recovering with the help of his travel by sea and the Dunmaglass goat's milk. Their presence in London was "absolutely necessary" for the support of their claims. He would pay off all of William's debts and was committed to pay "Mr. Lachlan" five hundred pounds per year. It seems that Farquhar had purchased some land for John adjoining Dunmaglass and the rent therefrom would be sixty pounds yearly. John goes ahead to say that "Mr. L McG is with me now fat & hearty."[19]

Lachlan also made an affidavit in William's behalf—

Lachlan McGillivray formerly of the Province of Georgia in North America but at present of the Parish of Saint Martin in the Fields in the County of Middlesex being duly sworn on the Holy Evangelist of Almighty God maketh oath that he was an inhabitant of Georgia and

South Carolina from the year of our Lord one thousand seven hundred
& thirty seven until the year one thousand seven hundred and eighty
two and that he was well acquainted with the nature and the value of
lands in those Provinces that in particular he very well knew a plantation
containing two hundred and thirty two acres and upwards situated on
Hutchinson's Island near Savannah—which belonged to Captain William McGillivray and had formerly been the property of the deponent.
That the said plantation fineTide Rice Swamp under high cultivation
and at the most moderate computation Lands of such quality were
valued at Twelve Pounds Sterling money of Great Britain per acre and
that he the deponent had lands of the same quality upon the same Island
belonging to him for which he would not have taken twelve pounds per
acre before the commencement of hostility between Great Britain and
America. The said Lachlan McGillivray further maketh oath that he is
sixty five years of age and hath taken his passage for Inverness in North
Britain.

> Lachlan McGillivray
> Sworn before the Commissioners of
> American claims at their office in
> Lincolns Inn Fields the 21st day
> of May 1784
> Charles Monroe, Asst. Sec.[20]

Another affidavit made by Lachlan Jr.:

Lachlan McGillivray the younger formerly of Christ Church Parish
in the Province of Georgia but at present of the Parish of Saint James in
the liberty of Westminister being duly sworn on the Holy Evangelist of
Almighty God maketh oath that in the year on thousand seven hundred
and eighty two he resided in the said Parish of Christ Church in Georgia
and was at that time principal manager of the Plantation and estates of
William McGillivray Esquire and thereby he acquired a particular
knowledge of the nature and value of the crops thereon growing and
which were abandoned and left to the Americans when his majesty's

troops were withdrawn from that country in the month of June in that year and the deponent maketh oath that on the Plantation called Gask on Hutchinson's Island in the said Province and which belonged to the said William McGillivray there was at that time planted and growing and in excellent order and condition two hundred and twelve acres of rice and which the deponent is convinced would have yielded at least two hundred and thirty barrels worth at a moderate estimation upwards of thirteen hundred pounds sterling money of Great Britain and the deponent also maketh oath that some short time before the Troops evacuated the Province, a party of the Rebel forces carried from the plantation of Lieutenant Colonel John McGillivray a valuable negroe carpenter the property of the said William McGillivray who was worth at least estimation seventy pounds sterling and that the said property belonging to the said William McGillivray thus take away and abandoned was worth fourteen hundred pounds sterling or thereabouts and the deponent further maketh oath that he is to embark in a few days for Jamaica on board the Justina—bound to that island the damage done by the late huricane to the property of the said William McGillivray and other persons for whom he is manager having rendered his presence there absolutely necessary.

Lachlan McGillivray Jr. Esquire
Sworn before the Commissioners of
American claims at their Office
Lincoln Inn Fields
November 5, 1784
Charles Monroe, Asst. Secretary.[21]

Lachlan Junior was the nephew of Lachlan Lia being the son of his sister Jean Roy. He had come to America to join his kin in the administration of the McGillivray plantations and also to seek his own fortune.[22]

John McGillivray prepared his memorial to the Commission on 17 March 1784 in which he asked for compensation for his losses. The memorial is lengthy and the following is an extract of the highlights:

*He was a Lieutenant Colonel commanding a corps of volunteers in West Florida.

*For many years before the war he was engaged in the trade from Georgia and West Florida with the Creeks, Chickasaw and Choctaw. He amassed a "very considerable fortune for himself, a great part of which he invested in lands, slaves and other usual subjects of property in those countries."

*In 1778 a Mr. Willing from Pennsylvania came and "plundered" on the Mississippi River and reported he would be followed by three hundred men.

*He obtained an appropriation from West Florida of five thousand pounds and proceeded to the Chickasaw and Choctaw to prevail on them to repel the American forces.

*Having received a commission from Governor Chester of West Florida to raise a corps for the defense of the province and "ample powers from Colonel Stuart" to employ the Indians, he proceeded to the Natchez and obtained their support.

*From the Natchez he proceeded to Manchac where he found Captain Barker and a contingent from the 16th and 60th regiments who expected an attack from Willing who was in New Orleans. He stayed for two months until danger had passed. He moved back to the Natchez when he heard American forces were on the Illinois under Colonel Clarke and Linn.

*Willing came upriver from New Orleans and engaged John and lost some thirty killed and prisoners.

*In 1779 he learned that Savannah had been retaken by Colonel Campbell and he made ready to leave Pensacola and go to Georgia. On his passage he was captured by a Spanish man-of-War, "stript of his shirt and carried to the Havanna where he was closely confined in the common prison." He attributed this to Don Galvez who was offended when John accused him of protecting Willing and his men in New Orleans.

*After ten months imprisonment he was exchanged and went from

Savannah to New Providence, Charleston, Augusta and through the Creek Nation to Pensacola. During the Spanish seige of Pensacola he had several opportunities to distinguish himself "in the face of the enemy."

*At his own expense he helped many distressed British subjects and helped several deserters, negroes and others to make their way through the Creek Nation.

*He made his way back to Savannah but found that the Georgia legislature, meeting at Augusta on 4 May 1782, had declared his whole estate, both real and personal, to be confiscated.

*When Georgia was evacuated by the British, he went to Jamaica, but left behind his estate which is detailed below:

A. 1000 acres adjoining Savannah called Vale Royal. 165 acres were under cultivation. It had a good dwelling house with kitchen, stable, hospital house, negro houses, large gardens well laid out with vegetables, fruit trees for table use and to supply the town. Also a large barn, corn and peas house with about 40 negro houses. A frame for cattle machine house with plank. 6000 pounds value.

B. 150 acres on Hutchinson Island nearly opposite the "Savannah property." Improved and cross fenced, large barn, machine house, store house, corn house, overseer's house, hospital house, and negro housing to accomodate 50-60 negroes. 1800 pounds value.

C. 48 1/2 acres on Hutchinson Island. Marsh land used as pasture for horses and cattle. 194 pounds value.

D. 540 acres west and within a mile of Savannah laid out as a farm and garden lots by the name of Springfield. 200 acres cleared, partly fenced, overseer's house nearly finished, negro houses for 100 slaves. Lachlan had it resurveyed and found 630 acres, whereas Georgia sold it as 700 acres. 2160 pounds value.

E. 750 acres in St. Andrews Parish on Altamaha River. Mostly planted in rice. 1125 pounds value.

F. 1000 acres in St. Davids Parish on the Altamaha. 1500 pounds value.

G. 750 acres in St. Davids Parish — 2/3 swamp. 1150 pounds

value.

H. 600 acres in St. Marys Parish on Great Satilla River. 600 pounds value.

I. 500 acres in St. George's Parish about half swamp. 250 pounds value.

J. 100 acres in St. Mathews Parish mostly pine. 37 pounds value.

K. 350 acres in St. Thomas Parish mostly cypress swamp. 262 pounds value.

L. 550 acres in St. Davids Parish on Little Satilla River. 550 pounds value.

M. 2500 acres with two tracts joining each other on Great Satilla River. 1250 pounds value.

N. 100 acres in St. Pauls Parish on the Savannah River. 50 pounds value.

O. Lot and house in Savannah. 150 pounds value.

P. Lot in Savannah—no improvement. 50 pounds value.

Q. 300 acres joining the common of Augusta town in the Parish of St. Paul. Mostly oak land. 450 pounds value.

R. 950 acres with two tracts on the Great Ogeechee River mostly swamp and pine land. 1425 pounds value.

S. Three lots adjoining each other in Savannah. 200 pounds value.

T. A mortgage on a lot in Savannah with two dwelling houses, stable and kitchen. 300 pounds value.

U. Lot in town of Hardwick. 5 pounds value.

V. Lot on Tybee Island. 20 pounds value.

W. 1000 acres on Savannah River in Halifax district. 2000 pounds value.

X. 500 acres on Wilmington Island. 320 pounds value.

Y. One half of an undivided tract on Great Satilla River containing 1400 acres. 420 pounds value.

Z. Loss of crops and personal property:

54 acres of rice at Vale Royal. 337 pounds

60 acres of corn at Vale Royal. 225 pounds

35 acres of potatoes at Vale Royal. 350 pounds

150 acres of rice on Hutchinson's Island. 937 pounds

70 acres of corn and 5 acres potatoes at Wilmington Island. 225 pounds

24 negroes, 23 taken from Vale Royal. 1200 pounds

Large boat, 20 canoes and other goods. 100 pounds

50 head of horses. 400 pounds

Transporting 254 negroes to Jamaica. 1075 pounds

Expenses in Charlestown. 300 pounds.

Total loss for John McGillivray — 27,462 pounds.[23]

John was actually paid 9048 pounds for his loss. This equates to the average of one third paid by the Crown.[24]

Lachlan also made an affidavit to support the claim of John McGillivray and was dated the same date as his affidavit for William— 21 May 1784. The highlights are as follows:

*Accumulated a considerable fortune and invested in land.

*At the beginning of the Revolution he was in possession of the property on the attached schedule. The whole of 11,190 acres. "That in the Year of our Lord one thousand seven hundred and eighty one the said Lachlan McGillivray having by reason of his years and infirmities become less capable to manage and take care of his affairs in America which required a good deal of care and attention and having during the Rebellion in America suffered much persecution and vexation for his attachment to his Majesty's Government and being therefore desirous to extract himself from the distress and perplexity he had laboured under in consequence of the troubles he made overtures to his nephew[25] John McGillivray who he considered as his heir as he the Deponent was never married to give up to the said John McGillivray immediately what the deponent intended the said John McGillivray should receive at his death to wit, all the land, houses and real estate in Georgia belonging to the Deponent upon the said John McGillivray securing to the Deponent an annuity competent to support him during the term of his natural life and the Deponent further maketh oath that the said John McGillivray

in consequence of the said proposition, having desired the Deponent to name for what sum he would have an annuity for his life secured to him the Deponent mentioned that three hundred pounds sterling per annum would be as much as he would have occasion for upon which the said John McGillivray said that three hundred pounds per annum was not sufficient and that the said Lachlan McGillivray might have occasion for five hundred pounds per annum and said he would have a settlement for an annuity to that amount made out which was accordingly done and executed to the said John McGillivray in consideration whereof the said Lachlan McGillivray by Indentures of lease and Release dated the tenth and eleventh days of September in the year of our Lord one thousand seven hundred and eighty one sold and conveyed unto the said John McGillivray and to his heirs and assigns forever all those several plantations mentioned in the schedule—hereunto annexed and herein before referred to and the said Lachlan McGillivray further maketh oath that his title to the said several tracts of land containing in the whole eleven thousand one hundred and ninety acres and a half as aforesaid was clear perfect and indisputable and free from every incumbrance whatever and that the valuation stated against the several tracts in the said schedule is to the best of the Deponent's knowledge and belief fair just and moderate and that if the Deponent had been inclinable to have sold the same before the Rebellion he verily believes he could have got more for the said lands than they are estimated at in the said schedule and that he the Deponent would not have sold the said lands to any indifferent person for the sum of twenty one thousand five hundred and four pounds. . . .

Lachlan McGillivray[26]

The schedule that Lachlan attached is almost identical to the one that was attached to John McGillivray's memorial.

The accounts of Lachlan reveal that he paid John specific amounts during the two to three year period they spent in London preparing their claims. In May 1784 John was paid for his lodging in London plus several cash payments. He gave John 600 pounds to send to his nieces. The total paid out to John was 2857 pounds.[27] This large sum paid to John indicates that Lachlan had been able to take large sums of money out of Georgia for deposit in Great Britain.

The index for loyalist claims includes John and William, but not Lachlan. This of course indicates Lachlan never made a claim since he had deeded all his property to John near the close of the Revolution for an annuity of five hundred pounds. It is not clear why John would agree to this since it must have been obvious that the war was lost and most of the property had already been confiscated earlier. John would have no way of securing the property in Georgia.[28]

The state of Georgia went about the business of selling confiscated estates. Over the years several advertisements appeared in local newspapers announcing the sale of such property. Apparently Georgia authorities never knew that Lachlan had deeded his property to John since the sale notices indicated the property formerly belonged to Lachlan. An example was in the *Gazette, State of Georgia*, 30 June 1785:[29] 750 acres in St. Andrews Parish, 750 acres in St. Davids Parish, 1900 acres in St. Davids Parishs, 1000 acres on Altamaha River, 2500 acres in St. Marys Parish, and 500 acres in St. Marys Parish. Some of these acreages fail to agree with the schedule attached to John and Lachlan's affidavit. The sale of Lachlan's property was still going on as late as 1792.[30]

John writes to his cousin Farquhar McGillivray of Dalcrombie, dated 1 January 1786, posted London, and informs him that he recently received letters informing him of the loss of forty Negroes in Jamaica due to a hurricane. He had decided to stay in London until he was examined by the Commission concerning his claims. If he was not there, all would be lost.[31]

Charles Graham of London in an accounting on 27 July 1786, recorded that he paid Lachlan the following sums according to John McGillivray's instructions:

> 16 July 1784 paid Lachlan McGillivray 100 pounds
> 25 April 1785 paid Lachlan McGillivray 100 pounds
> 12 August 1785 paid Lachlan McGillivray 100 pounds

12 December 1785 paid William Struthers 100 pounds
21 December 1785 paid William Struthers 88 pounds
4 January 1786 paid Lachlan McGillivray 100 pounds
6 April 1786 paid Lachlan McGillivray 100 pounds
21 April 1786 paid Lachlan McGillivray 100 pounds.

John deposited funds with Graham "from time to time" to pay Lachlan the annuity.[32]

John writing to Farquhar of Dalcrombie on 30 November 1786 said that he was sailing for Jamaica in a few days.[33] John arrived in Jamaica in early 1787 to inspect his plantation and look after his investments there. He stayed for nearly a year and embarked for England in late 1787 aboard the ship *Minerva*. John became ill and died just one day out and presumably was buried at sea. We have no evidence as to what happened to him so soon after embarking.

Jamaica was an unhealthy place, especially for Europeans. John probably died of yellow fever. The symptoms and conditions are well described by John Hunter, M.D., a British medical officer in the Army and Superintendent of the military hospital in Jamaica from 1781 to 1783. He wrote that fevers and fluxes, often combined together, were violent in their attack and often fatal. It became worse in the rainy season, even in the normally dry regions. Mosquitoes were very bad in the swampy low country, but the mountains were healthy. Newcomers were especially susceptible to the fever with symptoms of "chills, hot flashes, headache, loss of strength, sick of stomach and violent vomiting, spit is green-yellow bile, pulse is quick, back pain, soreness in arms and other parts, laboured breathing, and called by the Spaniards black vomit." The symptoms may last for only six or seven hours, but more commonly fifteen to twenty-four hours.

Four British regiments were sent to Jamaica in 1780 and landed on 1 August. By 31 January, just six months later, half the regiment was dead and most of the other half unfit for duty. In less than four years 5250 soldiers died on Jamaica due to the fever.[34]

John's plantation was called Sunflower and was located near Bath only a few miles from the coast on the extreme east end of the island. This is only about thirty miles from Kingston, the capital. It is unlikely John boarded the ship in ill health. He probably became ill in the short fifteen to twenty-four hours mentioned before he died the first day out.

Lachlan Lia's second cousin, Lachlan McGillivray, the son of Archibald McGillivray of Daviot, was in Jamaica as the manager of John's plantation.[35] We find from the following correspondence that others had an unsavory view of Lachlan of Jamaica.

A letter dated 10 February 1788 from attorney Ralph Fisher of Jamaica, to Charles Graham, the McGillivray attorney in London, informed Graham that John McGillivray was dead—"the day after he embarked at Port Royal on board the ship Minerva for Lancaster." He continued by saying that Lachlan was the manager of John's estate in Jamaica and had joint power of attorney with Fisher. Lachlan has brought suit for balance of pay he claims is owed to him in the amount of three thousand pounds. He charged two hundred pounds "for his trouble in looking after the Negroes that remain & a few acres of the land planted in coffee." Fisher planned to defend against the suit. He expected a power of attorney to be sent over by the Executors in order to sell the land and Negroes. John had been in the process of building a new house at Bath. Lumber and labor furnished so far had amounted to seventy pounds.[36]

Fisher wrote again to Graham on 1 March 1788 reporting that he would see to the sale of the land and Negroes, but there had "been a very great loss of Negroes," which he said he had no accounting of from Lachlan. He continued that he and Lachlan were not on good terms— "the behaviour of the namesake, the instant the old gentleman turned his back gave me a bad opinion of him & we have not since been upon any terms of acquaintance."[37]

Lachlan writing to Graham on 5 March 1788 and posted Bath, Jamaica, informed Graham that he was disappointed in the legacy left to him—although "he was thankful for it." He was due for ten years labour under the "Equator suns." John had acknowledged the debt as just and had paid him for his cash disbursements made for him in West Florida.

His health was better since he used the "Bath waters" and had removed his "Rheumatic complaint." Also, three more negroes had died.[38]

Young Lachlan acquired the plantations from the estate of John McGillivray that were near Bath, named Sunflower and New Gardens, from which in 1813 he shipped large quantities of coffee and timber. This same year he also sold thirty-one breeding stock for 296 pounds.[39]

On 10 June 1797, he sponsored the baptism of a "mulatto" man named James McGillivray, probably his son. He continued over a long period (1797-1810) to sponsor the baptism of his slaves.[40] Lachlan died in Jamaica in 1816 and at that time had 112 slaves valued at 12,410 pounds.[41]

There were other McGillivrays in Jamaica—a John died there in 1770.[42] Another John died in 1737 with his estate valued at 7408 pounds.[43]

To clear up any confusion, this Lachlan was manager of John McGillivray's plantation; whereas Lachlan Jr, mentioned earlier, was manager of William McGillivray's plantations, both in Jamaica.

The will of Lieutenant Colonel John McGillivray was dated 22 November 1786, and made in London before he sailed for Jamaica. It was probated on 8 February 1788. The will stipulated that after payment of his just debts and funeral expenses, his remaining estate is bequeathed to:

> *Cousin Lachlan McGillivray to be paid 500 pounds yearly until his death in consideration of slaves and other personal property "delivered over" to John in the Province of Georgia.
> *Sister Anne McGillivray — 100 pounds yearly
> *Cousin Alexander McGillivray — 10 pounds yearly.
> *Nephew John Lachlan McGillivray — 2000 pounds.
> *Sister Barbara McGillivray — 2000 pounds.
> *Cousin Farquhar McGillivray — 1000 pounds.
> *John McGillivray (son of Farquhar) — 100 pounds.
> *Jannet McGillivray (daughter of Farquhar) — 100 pounds.
> *Cousin John McGillivray (son of Alexander) — 200 pounds.

*Lachlan McGillivray (son of Archibald) — 400 pounds.

*Daughters of Charles Graham — 100 pounds.

*Charles Shaw (son of Alexander Shaw) — 100 pounds

*Eleanor Hughes (sister of Bailey Wm. Hughes) — 100 pounds.

*Lachlan McGillivray (son of Muran McGillivray) — 200 pounds.

*David McGillivray (son of Alexander McGillivray) — two good field slaves, one man and woman.

*Anne McGillivray could continue on the farm, as she now resided there, for the rest of her natural life.

*The remainder of his estate in Jamaica he willed to his nephew John Lachlan McGillivray and in the event he died without heirs the estate went to his sister Barbara McGillivray.

*If interest was not sufficient to pay the three annuities above, they are to be paid in proportion to the sum bequeathed.[44]

An appendix to the will of John McGillivray deals with his estates in "North Britain" which he leaves to his nephew and Chief of the Clan, John Lachlan McGillivray. John's primary concern in his will is that the annuity of five hundred pounds be paid promptly to Lachlan Lia. His will read:

> . . . by my said will given and bequeathed unto the said Lachlan McGillivray and it being my principal desire and intention that the said annuity to Lachlan McGillivray should be most punctually satisfied and paid I therefore desire it to be my will that if it should so happen that my Executors should at anytime not have sufficient assets in their hands to satisfy the same, it should be satisfied from the estate and payment made.[45]

An accounting by the executors of John's will (nd), sometime shortly before Lachlan Lia died, in 1799, says that due to the five hundred pound annuity to Lachlan, the interest from the rent of the estate does not exceed that amount, making it impossible to pay the other legacies named in John's will until Lachlan dies.[46] The five hundred pound annuity John had willed Lachlan Lia was a heavy burden on the estate and caused hardship to others in the will. Lachlan Lia was a wealthy man—an example being his ability to pay John nearly three thousand pounds after they returned from Georgia to London. Lachlan was too shrewd a businessman not to have sent and carried large sums of money back to Scotland before the Revolution. Why he would continue to burden John's legacy by accepting the annuity each year remains a mystery.

John appointed his cousin Lachlan Lia and his sister Anne as guardians of John Lachlan and his sister Barbara Anne. They were also trustees of the estate until the children came of age. They in turn appointed Campbell McIntosh as the attorney for the estate. Mr. McIntosh was an old and reliable friend to the McGillivrays who resided at Inverness, where also, Lachlan Lia was spending most of his time.[47] The guardianship fell solely to Lachlan Lia in a short time as Anne was dead by 3 February 1791.[48]

After John died, the record contains fewer documents of the McGillivray family. However, a few letters from Lachlan Lia reveal some of the mundane chores of managing Dunmaglass and his fondness for his young cousin John Lachlan, the 10th Chief.

Lachlan Lia writing to Campbell McIntosh, his attorney in Inverness, on 12 August 1790, discusses a disagreement he has had with some tenants living on the estate. There was some problem on defining the boundaries of Dunmaglass.[49] Lachlan Lia wrote again on 23 November to McIntosh concerning problems with the affairs of "his late cousin— Miss Amy," also known as Anne. She had remained unmarried and lived at Dunmaglass to help raise John Lachlan.[50]

Campbell McIntosh was an attorney in Inverness that handled the McGillivray affairs for a long time and was also a trusted friend. He also was probably related to Lachlan's mother, Janet McIntosh. He was appointed custodian for the estate of William McGillivray which went to his children John Lachlan and Barbara Anne. With William's death, John Lachlan became the 10th Chief of the Clan. Lachlan Lia became very fond of John Lachlan and looked after him closely. He probably became the substitute son that Lachlan Lia had never really known. The lands of the estate were vast and consisted of Dunmaglass, Aberchalder, Gask, Taillie, half of Invirerney and some other lands, making John Lachlan a very wealthy heir. The document making McIntosh custodian of the estate was dated 3 February 1791. It was signed by the three trustees—Lachlan McGillivray, William McIntosh, and Baille William Inglis.[51]

Lachlan, writing to McIntosh again on 16 August 1791, expressed how happy he was "to hear that my Johnny is out of danger & in a fair way of recovery; blessed be God for his mercys."[52] The boy apparently had been sick but was recovering. He was now nine years old and Lachlan had sent him to Inverness to be educated in the care of McIntosh.

Another letter, in a shaky hand, to McIntosh dated 8 September reads:

> I wish to see Johny here with me if it should be but for a week or ten days for that purpose I send his own mare for home by the bearer; this providing he is not put to any school at Inverness; but if he is at any school I dispense with his coming to see me at present. I bless God that I find myself much better than I have been for some months past, I got out of bed and can walk a little in my room & I hope in the course of next week to walk without doors. I have gone & professed heather Thachor to examine the thatch of the house here & it appears that the whole back part must be new thatched, because the old does not cover the top of the wall, being much decayed.[53]

The old homeplace at Dunmaglass was built in 1690 and torn down in 1895 by its new English owner. The house was located one hundred yards northwest of the Mains of Dunmaglass. A search of the site in 1985 uncovered some loose stones and evidence of a foundation.[54]

Lachlan foresaw the end coming and in 1795 he wrote his will. Unfortunately the record book containing the will in Inverness is now lost; however, from a document titled "Inventory of Miscellaneous Deeds and Papers not included in former Inventories" found in the

Repositories of John Lachlan McGillivray Esquire of Dunmaglass, there resides an extract of Lachlan Lia's will. This extract is dated February 1852, the year of John Lachlan's death:

> Extract General Dispostion & Deed of Settlement by Lachlan MacGillivray Esquire late of Georgia now residing at Inverness in favor of John Lachlan MacGillivray Esquire of Dunmaglass (designed now of Dunmaglass and my cousin) and the heirs of his body whom failing to Barbara Ann MacGillivray his sister German and heirs and assignees whatsomever of all and sundry Debts and sums of money, and in general his whole heritable and moveable Estates and especially the Balance of annuity and other sums due to him under the last will and testament of Colonel John MacGillivray and relative Bonds and 300 pounds and interest due to him by the heritable Bond granted to him by Farquar MacGillivray of Dalcromby and indebtment thereon: and he thereby named and appointed the said John Lachlan MacGillivray whom failing his said Sister to be his sole Executor or Executrix appointing them to pay his debts and funeral expenses and any legacies he might leave and especially to pay to Miss Marjory MacGillivray,[55] my niece and living in family with me the sum of 200 pounds previously settled by him upon her and if not paid by me during my life.

The will was dated 4 July 1795 and recorded in the Burgh Court Books of Inverness on 20 July 1799.[56] An interesting annotation in the margin of the extract reads "This was a wealthy old Bachlor who was personally well known to General John Mackenzie of Balivil."

It is unfortunate that there was no inventory of his estate attached to the extract, which would have established a value of his estate. The penned annotation in the margin—"Wealthy old Bachlor" says a lot.

Lachlan Lia McGillivray died on 16 November 1799 at Inverness, age eighty, and was buried in the family cemetery at Dunlichity. The cemetery is located about halfway between Dunmaglass and Inverness near the northeast end of Loch Duntelchaig.[57] A search of the cemetery in the fall of 1991 found no identifiable grave marker for Lachlan.[58]

Lachlan Lia's death notice appeared in the *Edinburg Advertiser* 26-29 November 1799 and simply reads "Died at Inverness, upon the 16th curt. Lachlan McGillivray Esq. late of Ga."[59]

Although the obituary says he died at Inverness, for an Edinburgh newspaper this would have included Dunmaglass. The family had a town house in Inverness where Miss Anne McGillivray died in 1790. John Lachlan later had a town house on Margaret Street in Inverness and it may have been the same one used by Lachlan on his frequent visits there. By 1750 only Wade's military roads were worthy of the name. There were few bridges over the rivers and systematic road building in the Highlands did not commence until about 1803, when they were subsidized by the government. The seventeen miles from Dunmaglass to Inverness would have been trying for an old man such as Lachlan. With the roads being almost impassable in the winter months, he probably spent the summer at Dunmaglass and the winter in Inverness.[60]

The notice of his death appearing in the *Georgia Gazette* on 21 August 1800 was short and without comment—"Lachlan McGillivray formerly of Georgia died November 16, 1799 at Inverness."[61]

By the time John Lachlan came of age in 1803, he was the owner of a great amount of property and money. He inherited his father's estates, his Uncle John's substantial fortune, and the legacy of Lachlan Lia. In addition he also inherited the holdings of his sister Barbara Ann who died in 1800. No McGillivray chief had ever held such a large part of the Strathnairn Valley. He was educated at the College of St. Andrews where he was in trouble several times while a student. He purchased an officer's commission in the army and served until 1805. He was a Lieutenant in the 10th Regiment of Dragoons and fought in the Irish Rebellion. He married Jane Walcott, daughter of Captain Thomas Walcott of Inverness. They lived in Inverness, but he traveled frequently. Jane died childless at Edinburgh on 10 October 1843. John Lachlan died on 6 February 1852 at Inverness. He was buried in the family cemetery at Dunlichity. Unexplained, most of his fortune of forty thousand pounds and vast estates were willed to his tenants.[62]

A contest over the will began immediately by the McGillivray heirs for possession of the estate, which continued in the courts from 1852 to 1859. The succession to Dunmaglass and the chieftainship could only go to the "nearest heir male," which was between John McGillivray of the Dalcromby line, and later after his death his son Neil John, and the Reverend Lachlan McGillivray of Lairgs line. The question between them revolved around which of the two brothers of Alexander, 5th Chief of Dunmaglass,[63] was the elder—Donald the tutor of Wester Dalcromby or William of Lairgs and Easter Dalcromby. Since Donald was the tutor[64] to his young nephew Farquhar, following Alexander's early death, and now the 6th Chief,[65] he was obviously the oldest since the post of tutor always went, by Highland tradition, to the senior uncle. So the succession to Dunmaglass went to Neil John McGillivray, who became the 12th Chief.

John Lachlan's other estates however were to go to "nearest heir GENERAL," which may include women or descendants through the female line. The contest was between the descendants of Captain William Ban McGillivray[66] and his brother David McGillivray. Captain William Ban was declared the eldest therefore his descendants would inherit the remaining estates. His only children having descendants at this time were Jean Roy and Lucy, both the sisters of Lachlan Lia. Jean Roy's descendants were accepted as the only lawful heirs. Lachlan Lia's descendants, through his Indian family, were the rightful heirs, but they were never considered legitimate under Clan tradition nor Scottish law.[67]

John Lachlan in his will had left some six thousand pounds to his faithful servant of twenty-nine years, Miss Charlotte Clark. When she died in 1859 at age fifty-three, she left a trust for the establishment of two schools—one at Nairnside and another near Dunmaglass. The schools operated until the 1940's and are now converted to private residence. John Lachlan and his wife Jane were buried in the family cemetery at Dunlichity as was their servant Charlotte Clark—a most unusual occurrence.[68]

Today the old homeplace at Dunmaglass is gone and the lands dispersed. Many of the McGillivrays migrated to America, Canada, the West Indies, and Australia where their many descendants reside today.

8

The Indian Legacy

No discussion of the McGillivray family is complete without including what is known about their Indian families that were left in Alabama and Mississippi—at that time part of Georgia and West Florida.

Albert J. Pickett, the early Alabama historian, is cited by many modern writers as their source of information on Lachlan Lia's Indian family. Pickett collected much of his data for his *History of Alabama* through oral history. Pickett's romanticized description of Lachlan's departure from Georgia in 1782 would seem to reflect the wishful thinking of Lachlan's descendants. "His plantation and negroes he abandoned in the hope that his son Alexander, his two daughters, and his Indian wife, then living upon the Coosa, might be suffered to inherit them."[1] As we have seen in earlier chapters, Lachlan had no intentions of leaving his estates to his Indian family. His Scottish clan kinship was much stronger in his decisions on what to do with his wealth. Lachlan had deeded his lands and most of his property to his cousin John just before leaving Georgia for the last time in 1782. However, as early as 1767, Lachlan included only a pittance in his will for his son Alexander, with the vast bulk of his wealth going to Cousin John and nothing to his Indian wife and daughters.[2]

It appears that Lachlan never returned to the Creek country after 1760, some twenty-two years before his final departure for England. He spent those years living a life of comfort and prestige on his plantation near Savannah, hardly the picture of a loving father and husband as depicted by Pickett. There is no mention in Alexander's correspondence that he ever visited his father in Savannah after returning to the Indian Nation.

There has been much discussion as to when his son Alexander, who became the famous Creek chief, was born. Probably one of the earliest accounts we have is a petition for a land grant presented to the Georgia Council on 4 September 1759.

> Read a Petition of Lachlan McGillivray for Alexander McGillivray
> an infant setting forth that the said Alexander McGillivray is part owner
> of a cowpen on Boggy Gut in the Province whereon were five hundred
> head of cattle and also of six negroes. Therefore praying for one hundred
> acres to be granted the said Alexander McGillivray on the upper large
> spring the north side of the Beaver Dams in the Range of Cattle
> belonging to the said cowpen.[3]

The question is: How old is an infant? Webster merely says it is an early period of life; however, the Alabama Supreme Court in 1925 says, "a person is an infant until he arrives at his majority as fixed by law."[4] This writer's humble opinion is being unable to walk. However, the land grant of one hundred acres petitioned by Lachlan was granted to Alexander on 3 February 1762. He was approximately twelve years old at this time. The grant was in St. George Parish "bounded on all sides by vacant lands."[5] It was not unusual for heads of households to request grants for each of their children, and sometimes justifying it on the number of slaves or indentures, in order to obtain as much land as possible.

John Pope[6] in his journal of travels through the Creek Country in 1791, and while visiting Alexander at Little Tallasee, writes that Alexander was thirty-two years old but looked forty-five. Some writers believe Pickett subtracted the forty-five from 1791 instead of thirty-two—hence Pickett gives Alexander a birth date of 1746.[7] Caughey[8] followed by many writers says Alexander was born in 1759, using Pope as the source.

Coker[9] writes that Alexander was born on 15 December 1750 based on information furnished by James Doster. Cashin also writes that Alexander was born on this date. He references a copy of the will he received from Professor W. W. Wallace.

Alexander was born on 15 December 1750 according to a will made by Lachlan on 12 June 1767.[10] The proper reference for Lachlan's will of 12 June 1767 is Copies of Various Deeds, Document #1, Section 16, Fraser-Mackintosh Collection #3429, Inverness Public Library.

One Edward Mease writing to the Earl of Hillsborough on 26 November 1771 enclosed a copy of his journal that was kept while traveling from Pensacola to Natchez through the Choctaw Country. Somewhere in southern Mississippi he made this entry.

> At this place we met with a party of thirteen Creeks or Talapouses, headed by one McGillivray a half bred man, they were curiously painted according to their custom in war and said (to use the leaders own expression who spoke broken English) that they were hunting Chactas. They had their prisoners who I believe were women as I understood they were not to be sacrificed, but I did not see them, being on the other side of the Creek.[11]

It is unlikely this was Alexander since he spoke English fluently. Pickett continues with his story of young Lachlan.

> At Hickory Ground, a few miles above the fort, he found a beautiful girl, by the name of Sehoy Marchand, whose father once commanded at Fort Toulouse, and was there killed in 1722, by his own soldiers, as we have already seen. Her mother was a full blooded Creek woman, of the tribe of the Wind, the most aristocratic and powerful family in the Creek nation. Sehoy was an Indian name which had attached to many persons of the family, time out of mind.
>
> Sehoy Marchand, when first seen by young Lachlan McGillivray, was a maiden of sixteen Cheerful of countenance, bewitching in looks, and graceful in form. Her unfortunate father, Captain Marchand was a

Frenchman, of dark complexion and consequently, this beautiful girl scarcely looked light enough for a half blood; but then her slightly curled hair, her vivacity and peculiar gesticulation, unmistakenly exposed her origin. It was not long before Lachlan and Sehoy joined their destinies in marriage, according to the custom of the Indian Country. The husband had established a trading house at Little Tallasee, four miles above Wetumpka on the east bank of the Coosa, and there took home his beautiful wife.

Pickett goes on to say that Alexander was the firstborn and at age fourteen Lachlan took him to Charleston to be educated. After a few years he worked in a "counting house" in Savannah, but was shortly returned to Charleston where he was placed under the tutelage of Lachlan's cousin, the Reverend Farquhar McGillivray.[12] Several writers over the years have used Pickett and repeated his version of the McGillivray story.[13]

Alexander spent some time in Charleston with his father's cousin, Farquhar McGillivray, who was his tutor. In 1753 Farquhar lived on the south side of Broad Street;[14] however, in 1765 he lived on Elliot Street.[15] Farquhar moved to West Florida and became involved in the trade with his brother John. Alexander may have spent most of his time in Savannah where he clerked as an apprentice in the Merchant house of Inglis and Hall; however, Jones[16] writes in 1887 that he clerked in the commercial house of Samuel Elbert. It was at about this time that Alexander returned to the Creek Country at age seventeen.

Pickett drew much of his information from people still living in his time that were participants in the history that Pickett wrote about in 1851. During an extensive interview he had with "Abram Mordicai, 92 years of age, who had lived sixty years among the Creek Indians;" Mordicai told Pickett that Alexander was born at Hickory Ground, educated in Scotland, slim, five feet ten inches tall and died at Pensacola by poison.[17]

LeClerc Milford, the longtime friend and companion to Alexander, writes in his memoir that Alexander was the son of a Creek woman and a Scotch trader. His mother was the daughter of a French officer who had commanded at Fort Toulouse.[18] J. D. Dreisbach, married to the great granddaughter of Alexander's mother, writes that Alexander's mother, Sehoy, was a full blood Tuskegee and a member of the Wind Clan.[19]

General Thomas S. Woodward also wrote that Alexander's mother was a full blood Tuskegee and not the daughter of a French officer; however, Zespedes, writing to Galvez on 16 August 1784, referred to Alexander McGillivray "as a quarter Indian Englishman"[20] which indicates that his mother was a half blood. The Spanish were very class conscious and kept up with these matters.

Governor O'Neill, Spanish Commandant at Pensacola, wrote on 19 October 1783 that Alexander was the half-breed son of a Scotchman and an Indian woman of the Wind Clan, who also was the sister to the Creek Chief Red Shoes.[21]

Alexander wrote on 22 June 1788, confirming this. "The Bearer is Red Shoes, brother to one of my uncles[22]. This is an odd way for Alexander to describe Red Shoes since he also would be his uncle. This indicates there was at least one other uncle to Alexander.

O'Neill writing to Miro on 28 July 1788 says the "Talapuche Chief" was Alexander's uncle. He had gotten drunk in Pensacola and had said the British were sending troops and ammunition to overthrow the Spanish and take St. Augustine. He further says that Alexander had told him these things.[23]

Alexander writing to Governor O'Neill on 3 January 1784, mentions his "relation" Chief Red Shoes, who was always a faithful friend and leader. He had tried to cure his "fondness for strong waters," but he was never able to overcome it. Red Shoes, in trying to retrieve some stolen horses, had been killed. Alexander describes him as an old man—"the brothers and nephews of the deceased in short the whole family are the crossest and most mischievous on the Tallapousie River."[24]

There has been considerable confusion over Red Shoes[25] since there were several chiefs named Red Shoes. One was Chief of the Coosada who was still alive in 1793.[26] He was so opposed to the Chickasaw War that he led a band of Coosada and Alibama Indians west where they settled on the Red River. A few years later they removed to the Trinity River in Texas.[27] Today their descendants still live in Texas and Louisiana.

In 1793, the uncle of Alexander, Chief Red Shoes lived at Tuskegee town in the forks of the Alabama River.[28] To complicate things further, there was a Choctaw Chief Red Shoes in the 1730's and 1740's.[29] He was called the "Great Red Shoes" and was killed by the French for trading with the English in 1748. His Indian name was "Shulashumimashtabe" and his town was Quansheto.[30]

In 1792 there was another Choctaw Chief named "Sulushastabe or Red Shoes." Lieutenant Stephen Minor of the Spanish Army, traveling over the "path to the Choctaw Nation," later known as the Natchez Trace, encountered Red Shoes on the trail and on 21 March stayed overnight at Red Shoes' house somewhere in the Choctaw Nation.[31] Governor Gayoso's soldiers shot and wounded the son of this Choctaw Chief in 1791. Gayoso ordered him treated at the Natchez military hospital where he recovered.[32]

Peter Brannon, past Director of the Alabama Department of Archives and History, wrote that Lachlan's wife Sehoy was buried "on the river bluff there near the Indian Mound" in present day Montgomery.[33]

Mary Ann Neeley wrote that it was doubtful Alexander's mother, Sehoy, was part French as Marchand never commanded Fort Toulouse.[34] There is little doubt about the existence of a Captain Marchand, but there are questions about dates pertaining to him. As noted above, Pickett says he was killed in 1722, but the evidence indicates otherwise. He is mentioned in May 1724 in connection with a soldier of the Alabama garrison, and again in January 1725 concerning members of his company at Mobile.[35] There is a letter from him dated 15 September 1732 while commanding at the Natchez. Galloway says he is probably Francois Marchand de Courtel. In December 1723 he appears as a Captain in the Mobile baptismal records; as Commandant at Fort Toulouse in 1727; and a Captain of the Mobile garrison in 1730.[36]

The most definitive work and authority on Fort Toulouse to date is Waselkov. His research places Captain Marchand as Commandant at Fort Toulouse in 1720-1723 and again in 1727-1729. There was a mutiny at the fort on 23 August 1721 where the officers were taken prisoner, but were later released.[37]

An account of the mutimy written by Bienville on 25 September 1721 is included in his letter dated 6 April 1722.

> I have the honor to inform the Council by my letter of the twenty-fifth of September that three sergeants and five soldiers of the Companies of Lamothe's regiment had deserted from Mobile and had gone to Fort Toulouse where they corrupted two-thirds of the garrison who rose in revolt, seized the officers whom they bound and set off for Carolina. The officers, whom they had unbound as they left, went and asked the Alabama Indians for assistance which they gave them with such briskness that in less than two hours there were two hundred and fifty men who pursued them and overtook them at a distance of ten leagues. They attacked them, killed eighteen of them on the spot and took the rest alive whom the officers of that garrison tried before a court martial and condemned the sergeant who remained to be tomahawked immediately and all the others to be convicts for life.[38]

Obviously, there was a mutiny where eighteen of the enlisted personnel were killed. The officers, although temporarily taken prisoner, were released. If Commandant Marchand had been killed, Bienville would have mentioned it. Also, all the mutineers would have been put to death.

Cashin, Lachlan's biographer, also writes that Marchand was never Commander at Toulouse, but he is in error.[39] Captain Marchand was not killed as reported by Pickett and others. It makes better reading if the brave father is killed instead of deserting his family when his tour of duty is over. No doubt Pickett obtained this story from family descendants.

Marchand was a witness to the published banns of the church in Mobile in 1726 and again in 1732.[40] Andrews also confirms "Francis Marchand DeCourtel" as being at Fort Toulouse in 1717 and Commandant in 1720-23 and again in 1727-29. He adds that according to legend Sehoy married him in 1722.[41]

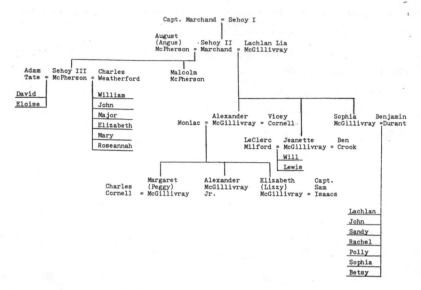

Family of Capt. Marchand and Sehoy I

There are also differences on how many children Lachlan had. Brannon[42] writes that there were four—Alexander, Sophia, Sehoy III, and Jeanette. "A Brief History of the McGillivray Family," by one of the family, Major J. D. Dreisbach, writing in 1884, and who gained most of his information from David Tate's wife who was his mother-in-law. He also obtained information from William Weatherford's older sister, and from Jonah the body servant of Alexander. Driesbach was born on 24 May 1816 at Circleville, Ohio, and died in 1896. He came to Alabama in about 1843. In 1844 he married Josephine Bonaparte Tate, daughter of David Tate and Margaret Dyer. He was a Captain in the home guard during the Civil War, a state senator, and Baldwin County Superintendent of Education. Driesbach says Lachlan had five children—Sehoy III, Alexander, Elizabeth, Sophia, and Jennie.[43] It appears that Driesbach, in error, included Elizabeth the daughter of Alexander.

A short history of the family by Dr. Marion E. Tarvin, writing from Galveston, Texas, in 1893 to Professor W. S. Wyman of the University of Alabama, says Lachlan had five children—Sehoy III, Alexander,

Sophia, Jeannet, and Elizabeth. Tarvin was the grandson of David Tate and great grand nephew of Alexander McGillivray.[44]

A. B. Meek, writing in 1857, says Lachlan's wife was a "half breed" who had been married to a Tuckabatchee Chief by whom she had a daughter named Sehoy. The daughter married Colonel John Tate, a British officer at Fort Toulouse. Sehoy Marchand married Lachlan in 1740.[45]

A paper on the McGillivrays, no date, on file at the Gilcrease Institute, by Thomas F. Meagher Jr., says Lachlan had four children—Sophia, Jeanet, Sehoy III, and Alexander.[46] LeClerc Milford, the Frenchman who married Jeanette, the daughter of Lachlan, writes that Lachlan had five children—two boys and three girls. He lost one son and two daughters in early life. He sent Alexander to Charleston to be educated.[47]

Pickett writes that Lachlan had three children—Alexander, Sophia, and Jeanett.[48] Benjamin Hawkins writing in 1809 says "Mrs. Durand and Mrs. Weatherford, the first a sister and the other a maternal sister only" of Alexander.[49] Mrs. Durant was Sophia and Mrs. Weatherford was Sehoy III.

Pickett records that Colonel John Tate lived during the Revolutionary War at Red Ground, which was near Little Tallasee, and was the British Agent. He married Sehoy Robinson, half-breed and half sister to Alexander McGillivray.[50] Abram Mordecai informed Pickett in 1848 that, during the Revolutionary War, an Indian town existed on the site of the "Alabama Town, where Colonel Tate drilled squads of Tories."[51]

Woodward writes that Sehoy III was a McPherson and lived part time with Lachlan Lia and part time with Daniel McGillivray. Her first husband was John Tate, by whom she had "Davy Tate." Charles Weatherford was her last husband by whom she had four children.[52]

Captain Pedro Olivier, the Spanish agent to the Creeks, lived at Little Tallasee with Alexander and writing to Governor Carondelet on 14 June 1793, mentions that Alexander had a half-breed relative that he called "brother."[53] Alexander wrote on 1 February 1789 complaining of the mistreatment of his sister Sophia by the trader Timothy Lane in Pensacola. He wrote: "my Relation MacPherson had already resolved to kill him, he abused my sister and others in Mr. Panton's yard."[54]

Earlier, O'Neill had written to Miro on 10 September 1788 that Alexander had decreed that Lane must die because of his carrying news to Pensacola of Bowles landing in Florida with a load of ammunition. Also, trader O'Keefe had written to O'Neill informing him of Bowles landing, but he had to flee the Nation under threat of his life.[55]

Lane was an unsavory character that Spanish officials in Pensacola used as an informant of activities in the Creek Country. In 1788 Alexander complained to O'Neill that Lane was conspiring to have him killed.[56] His complaints went unheeded by the Spanish and Miro writes to Alexander that Lane was a Spanish citizen and he cannot discipline him.[57] Alexander complains to Panton that he will not visit Pensacola until Lane is punished[58] and in the summer of 1789 complains to Cruzat that Lane continues to insult the Indians and that something will happen to him since he no longer can restrain his warriors.[59] Hawkins in 1797 writes that Lane was called Paddy Lane and was trader to Tuckabatchee.[60] Lane survived all the controversy and was still a trader in 1812—owing Panton Leslie Co. some $708.[61]

There was an August McPherson who was a Creek trader out of Savannah who had his license renewed on 29 August 1737.[62] An Angus McPherson, who was a Jacobite exile from Scotland, was transported from Liverpool to South Carolina arriving on 7 May 1716.[63] It is very likely that these are one and the same person—August probably being a corruption of Angus since there is no tradition in Scotland of the given name August.

There were several McPhersons in the southern colonies and Indian country during this time period. There was a Donald who was "Commisary of Indian Provisions" at Natchez in 1778.[64] He was still in Pensacola as late as 1781.[65] There was an Alexander McPherson that received a thousand acre grant in 1772 and a William who received six hundred acres in 1772—both in West Florida.[66] A Captain James McPherson, under General Oglethorpe, commanded the rangers on the Savannah River.[67] There was also a John McPherson, Indian trader, living on Goose Creek, near Charleston, in 1743.[68] Most of these appear on the scene too late to be Sehoy's husband except John and August who were both Indian traders, but we know that August was a trader to the Creek Indians.

Another footnote to the McPhersons—in 1812 John Innerarity, successor to Panton Leslie, and John Forbes Co., entered in his journal that a Creek named "Tingyhaby" or "McPherson's son" owed the Company $508. He was a trader operating out of Pensacola.[69] This is most likely Malcolm McPherson's son.

It appears likely that Angus (August) was married to Sehoy Marchand which produced a son named Malcolm McPherson and a daughter named Sehoy. As we saw earlier, Captain Pedro Olivier mentions that Alexander had a half-breed relative he called "brother;" also, Alexander mentioned "My Relation MacPherson;" and Hawkins wrote in December 1796 that "I arrived at the Hickory Ground and spent one hour with the principal chief of the town McFasshion, a cousin of Gen. McGillivray."[70] Depending on who Hawkins' informant was may indicate whether it was MacPherson or MacFassion, since the two were used interchangeably.[71] Hawkins may have been told MacFassion, also spelled Mackfation, and only that he was a relative.

A letter from the Creek Chief Singer to William Panton 28 September 1799 clears up much of the confusion over Malcolm McPherson and Jeanette McGillivray. Singer was a prominent chief of Little Tallasee and accompanied Alexander to New York in 1790 and signed the treaty with Washington.[72] Alexander appointed him second in command of the Creek Nation, but Mad Dog, the powerful chief of Tuckabatchee, became the head chief on Alexander's death in 1793.[73] McPherson had just died in 1799 and had been married to Singer's sister. Singer wanted to care for the children and wanted the eldest son to take over McPherson's affairs. Creek tradition gave the worldly goods of the deceased to his nearest female relatives, not to the wife and children. Singer had to get his nearest relatives to agree, but Jeanette would not agree until Singer "and the other sister Mrs. Durant" gave her a straight talk." The nearest relatives to McPherson was Sehoy, his sister, and Jeanette and Sophia, his half sisters, and they had taken control of his affairs.[74]

This Creek tradition is again reported by William Panton in a letter to John Leslie on 28 August 1793. When Alexander died, his sisters, especially Sophia and Sehoy, seized control of his cattle and other worldly goods. The children were "naked," using the Indian description for poor, and Panton visited the Creek country and persuaded the sisters to share and divide up the cattle and slaves for the children. It took the persuasive influence of Panton to change their minds. Panton placed the cattle and slaves under a white man of his choosing.[75]

There was a "McPherson" listed as a Chief of "Little Talleseys" in 1794 who had been invited by the Spanish to a council at Pensacola. [76] This was Malcolm McPherson. Stiggins, in his history of the Creeks, mentions that at the Battle of Holy Ground in 1814 William Weatherford and "McPherson a half-breed of Scotch and Indian" had heard a few days earlier that the Army of General Claiborne was about to attack.[77] This is likely the son of Malcolm McPherson since Malcolm had died in 1799.

Cockran[78] writes that McPherson was a half blood cousin to Alexander—probably using Hawkins. He adds that McPherson operated out of Coweta. He raised a large party of Indians to go to Charleston and Savannah during the Revolution, but they were threatened by the Cussetas and nothing came of the affair. This story is very similar to the aborted expedition David Taitt led in 1779. Also, John Stuart would never have permitted a war party, led by an Indian, to go to Savannah. He always insisted on a British subject to lead any war party. One of his greatest fears was that the Indians would get out of control and massacre numerous settlers and British subjects. The McPherson Cockran refers to is likely Donald McPherson who was the British Commissary of Indian Provisions in 1778.

We should note that Hickory Ground was a second home for Alexander McGillivray and became the unofficial capital of the Creek Nation. Although he lived at Little Tallasee, only four miles away, he conducted much of the Nation's business at Hickory Ground. Between his death in 1793 and Indian removal in 1838, Hickory Ground became more and more the seat of power. The Creeks living at Little Tallasee slowly drifted away after Alexander died and it was almost deserted by Hawkins's time.

After Alexander died, Panton writing to Governor Carondelet in March 1793, says the Spanish should confer titles and small pensions on members of the Nation "and if you appoint Mr. McGillivray's Brother with their approbation, Chief over all until His nephew, McGillivray's son, comes of age. . . ."[79] Some writers think Panton was probably referring here to Alexander's brother-in-law Milford, but it seems unlikely that Panton would have made two mistakes in the same sentence— "brother and nephew." The brother referred to here is Malcolm McPherson.

Sehoy McPherson, later Mrs. Weatherford, was in fact a half sister to Alexander on the maternal side based on the clear statement of Hawkins and Woodward. Woodward says her name was MacPherson. Pickett says Robinson, but in any case Lachlan's wife, Sehoy Marchand, had been married before he knew her, making Pickett's story about her being sweet sixteen when Lachlan found her very doubtful, but romantic when Pickett was writing in the 1850's.

It appears that we can confidently establish that Sehoy III McPherson was a half sister to Alexander on his mother's side and Malcolm McPherson was a half brother to Alexander and brother to Sehoy III. This would also account for Panton recommending that "Mr McGillivray's Brother" be appointed to replace Alexander until Alexander's son, Alexander Junior, came of age. Panton did not mean "brother-in-law" as some historians have stated. We will cover Milford in more depth later, but we know he was in serious disagreement with the Spanish authorities at Pensacola to the extent that they were actually hostile towards him. Also, it is known that the Creek Chiefs would not accept him as a replacement for Alexander. Panton was well informed of all these sentiments; it was his business to know, and he would not have jeopardized his business monopoly by recommending someone that he knew would not be accepted by the Spanish nor the Creek Chiefs. Malcom McPherson would have been acceptable by his position as Chief of Hickory Ground, one of the most important towns in the Nation and being Alexander's half-brother from the Wind Clan.

Pedro Olivier wrote to Carondelet 11 June 1793 saying a relative of McGillivray was "Chief of the warriors of the town of Hickory Ground, a half-breed who accompanied him on his last journey to New Orleans, whom he called brother and who is a favorite of his."[80] William McGillivray, the half-blood son of Daniel, later succeeded Malcolm McPherson as Chief of Hickory Ground.

Daniel McGillivray, Lachlan Lia's cousin, writing to Panton on 28 September 1799 and 27 July 1800 reports that McPherson died 1 July 1799 and that he left a son. This of course was Malcolm McPherson, Chief of Hickory Ground. This corresponds to the letter, as mentioned above, written by Singer on the same date trying to straighten out the children's affairs. Singer was trying to get McPherson's son in charge of the children's affairs instead of McPherson's sister Sehoy III and half sisters Sophia and Jeanette. This is the same son mentioned by Stiggins as being at the Battle of Holy Ground in 1814.[81]

Back to the number of children that Lachlan Lia and Sehoy II produced—the two family descendants, Driesbach and Tarvin both say five children; Milford says five; Woodward says three; Pickett says three and Owen[82] says three. The key to this disagreement is Milford's statement that a son and two daughters were lost early. However, we can account for five if Sehoy III and Malcolm McPherson are included, plus Alexander, Jeanette and Sophia McGillivray. Due to the high death rate many families had half brothers and sisters. In this case, Lachlan Lia would have been looked upon as "father" of all five children with Sehoy II as the maternal mother of all five.

Tarvin writes that Sehoy III, Alexander's half-sister, first married Colonel John Tate in about 1768.[83] By Tate she had one son, David Tate, and a daughter, Eloise. David was born at Little Tallasee in 1778.[84] David was sent by Panton as a companion to Alexander Junior to Scotland in 1798 to be educated. David got into trouble with his schoolmaster at Banff and was sent home to America. He was twenty at that time and in 1800 he married Mary Randon of Baldwin County.[85] David and Mary had four daughters—one of them, Eloise, was Driesbach's wife.[86] David lost his wife and her mother and father at Fort Mims in 1813. He died in 1829 and is buried near his homeplace at old Montpelier in Baldwin County.[87]

Under the Creek treaty of 1814, David was given a land reserve from fractions of Sections 17, 18, 19, and 20 at T4 R3E. The claim was certified 12 April 1820.[88] He was also given part of Section 29 which was divided by the Alabama River and just south of Little River in Baldwin and Monroe Counties.[89] David's cowpens were located twelve miles below Little River at a fine spring which is the source of the Perdido River. Although his principal residence was not located here, it was the original cowpens of Alexander McGillivray.[90] All these reserves were in and around the mouth of Little River in Baldwin County.

Colonel John Tate is reported as a British officer stationed at old Fort Toulouse during the Revolutionary War.[91] Brannon[92] writes that he was the Indian Agent stationed at Hickory Ground near Fort Toulouse. This seems doubtful since David Taitt was serving at this time as the Creek Agent living at Little Tallasee when in the Creek Country.

The case for Colonel John Tate being the husband of Sehoy and father of David Tate warrants further exploration. Cashin[93] following Cotterill[94] wrote that it was the Creek Agent David Taitt that was married to Sehoy. However, Cashin wrote just a year earlier following the Woodward version that Colonel Tate led a party across the Chattahoochee where he "became violently ill and was said to be deranged. Their devotion to him was so great that most of the Indians returned with Tate to Coweta town where he died and was buried."[95] David Taitt apparently came to West Florida in 1764 as a land surveyor soon after the British took control.[96]

John Stuart in February 1772 decided to send Taitt on a trip to the Upper and Lower Creeks to observe and gather information about their roads, villages, chiefs and about the conduct of the traders. Stuart wrote:

> [Taitt is a] good surveyor and a person of prudence, he will answer
> the purposes of observing the disposition of the Indians and obtaining
> some knowledge of their intrigues with the Spaniards and the western

tribes as well as of giving a more perfect idea of the geography of the country in which all the printed maps are shamefully defective.[97]

He wrote to Taitt on 20 January informing him that he was being sent to the Creek Country to observe and map the country.[98]

Taitt did such a good job of recording his trip and making a map of the Creek Country that Stuart recommended him to the Georgia Council to be a Justice of the Peace in the Creek Nation "to prevent disorder among the Traders and report those without license." His appointment came in June 1773.[99]

Stuart wrote to Lord George Germain on 23 January 1778 saying Alexander McGillivray had visited with him in December 1777 and expressed his hopes that everything could be mended. McGillivray said he had no objection to their sending an agent back to the Creek Country, but the Chiefs objected to Taitt who they found "obnoxious." The agents, Cameron, Taitt, and McIntosh, had all fled to Pensacola when they learned of a conspiracy to kill them.[100] Governor Tonyn of East Florida had warned Taitt as early as April 1776 that the Georgia Council had appointed six traders to enlist the Indians to capture Taitt and bring him in irons to Savannah.[101] Taitt may have been obnoxious to the Creeks, but he was back at Little Tallasee by April 1778.[102]

Taitt on 6 August 1779 wrote a long letter to Lord George Germain explaining his activities. He had orders from Stuart in 1777 to collect a party of Creeks and march to Georgia. Taitt wrote to John Stuart on 13 August 1777 that he was having trouble collecting enough Indians to attack the rebels. He set out on 21 September, and was soon informed that George Galphin had given large presents to two of the towns among the Upper Creeks to kill Cameron, Taitt, and the interpreters. This caused confusion among his war party and the threat on his life caused the friendly Indians to urge him to go to Pensacola. He claimed he was "entirely ruined by the Treasury refusing to pay the late Colonel Stuart's bills." The practice was for the agents to bill Stuart who in turn billed the Treasury.[103]

Governor Peter Chester wrote to Germain on 24 August 1778

saying that John Stuart had notified him that a body of hostile Creeks had set out to commit attacks against West Florida, and Taitt "has lately been obliged to quit his residence in the Indian Country through fear of being massacred by the disaffected part of the nation, is now here" in Pensacola.[104]

In early 1779 Stuart ordered Taitt to gather and lead a Creek war party to Savannah to help relieve the city then under siege. He set out on 4 March, but after crossing the Chattahoochee River, he ran into stiff opposition from the Georgia rebels. The party split up and Taitt made his way through the lines to Savannah.[105]

John Stuart died on 21 February 1779 and the Indian Department was thrown into confusion. Governor Chester appointed Indian Commissioners for West Florida until a new Superintendent could be appointed.[106] Robert Taitt was one of the Commissioners appointed by Chester. He may have been a brother to David Taitt.[107]

Taitt was surely disappointed that he was not chosen to replace Stuart as Superintendent but the Crown decided to split the Southern District. On 25 June 1779, Lord Germain appointed Lt. Colonel Thomas Brown as Superintendent of the Eastern District which included the Creeks, Cherokees, and some smaller tribes. He appointed Alexander Cameron Superintendent of the Western District that included the Choctaw, Chickasaw and some smaller tribes.[108]

By early 1780 Taitt was back in West Florida where he was captured at Mobile by the Spaniards and later paroled on 29 July 1780. At Pensacola, Taitt spent his time trying to collect for his expenses on the expedition to Savannah in May 1779. He was broke and could get no one to honor his bills. Merchants were threatening to sue him as they had already done against Cameron.[109] Taitt made his way to Savannah and arrived on or about 15 Decmber 1781 and reported to Governor James Wright. He remained there until he sailed from Charleston to England in January 1782.[110] A number of memorials on Taitt's behalf were made to the Crown—Taitt's own memorial, dated 24 September 1783, stated he was Deputy Superintendent of Indian Affairs for the Creek Nation from 1772 to 1780. He was taken prisoner by the Spanish at Mobile in

1780 and held for two months until paroled. Galvez accused him of breaking his parole and threatened to execute him. He had received no pay since 1779 and had become destitute.

Governor Chester, late of West Florida, stated that Taitt was confined by Galvez and held prisoner on a ship where he was ill-treated and his property seized. He later made his escape from Pensacola. William Johnstone, Lieutenant Colonel of Artillery, said Taitt was mistreated by Galvez because of his influence with the Indians. He escaped from Pensacola. Johnstone gave him high praise for his conduct.

Sir James Wright stated that Taitt often resided in Savannah bringing in parties of Indians to visit and council with the Georgia officials. He was at Savannah when D'Estaing lay siege to Savannah in 1779. David Taitt held five thousand acres within the area ceded to the Americans, but he had no way to dispose of the land north of the 31st parallel since the treaty with America failed to recognize such ownership in West Florida.[111]

Taitt lived out his last years in London trying desperately to get the Crown to recognize his claims along with thousands of other loyal subjects who had lost all during the Revolution and resulting treaty provisions. The last time he appears in the records he was living in England in 1793.[112]

Richard Taitt, probably David's brother, representing David and himself, protested to the U.S. Government over the pending forfeiture of their lands because they were not given enough time to file their claim in 1804. The new American Government required all land grants and purchases under the Spanish and British governments to be re-certified. If the deadline was not met, the lands were forfeited to the United States.[113]

There was a Robert Taitt who left Grenada for economic reasons and settled on 550 acres located on the Escambia River north of Pensacola. He was a slave dealer and claimed Oliver Pollock of New Orleans had taken his vessel containing nearly two hundred slaves.[114] Nothing further is known of this Taitt.

There are some parallels between Colonel John Tate and David

Taitt—the spelling of the name is just a variation. They both were portrayed as "British Agents." They lived during the same period in the Creek Country; they both lived near Little Tallasee; and both supposedly led a Creek war party to the Savannah River in 1779. Here the story parts with Taitt surviving the war, but Colonel Tate becoming ill, dying in 1779, and being buried near the Chattahoochee River where a monument stands at his grave near the gate to Fort Benning, Georgia.

Alabama's early historians—Pickett, Meek, Owen, Woodward, and Halbert—all say it was Colonel John Tate. Woodward wrote that he had seen the grave of Colonel Tate many times which would be pointed out to him by different Indians, including the renowned Chief Little Prince. Tate was buried on a hill just east of Cusseta. Woodward obtained this information from various Indians and Little Prince, who accompanied Colonel Tate on the expedition to the Savannah River.[115] Brannon, a more recent Alabama historian, also believed it was Colonel Tate.[116] Brannon wrote that Colonel John Tate established his headquarters at Econchati, present-day Montgomery, and drilled American Tories on present day Commerce Street. The Colonel is buried on Woolfolk's Hill at Fort Benning, Georgia.[117] If there was no Colonel Tate, as implied by Cashin and Cotterill, then who is buried at the gravesite near old Cusseta?

Driesbach says Sehoy was married to Colonel John Tate, and Driesbach was married to the granddaughter of Colonel Tate. Driesbach obtained his information from his mother-in-law, the wife of David Tate, Colonel Tate's son; the oldest sister and oldest son of William Weatherford; and from old Jonah the servant of Alexander McGillivray.[118] Jonah was a participant and the others only one generation removed. It is difficult to believe that all these people were wrong—especially the daughter-in-law of Colonel Tate. Surely she knew the name of her husband's father! Also, Cashin and Cotterill offer no evidence to support their assertion that it was David Taitt who married Sehoy III.

Supposedly Colonel Tate died in 1779 and Sehoy married Charles Weatherford in 1780. David Taitt, the Creek Agent, had sailed from Charleston to England in January 1782, which would mean that

Weatherford married Sehoy III while her other husband, David Taitt, was still in the territory. This is unlikely and not in keeping with traditions of the Indians.

The Creek Chiefs had objected to David Taitt returning as their agent. No less than Alexander McGillivray himself visited John Stuart in 1778 to protest for the Chiefs that Taitt was unacceptable and "obnoxious."[119] In 1778 Taitt had to flee the Creek Country to Pensacola to avoid "being massacred" by the Creeks.[120] There is no way Alexander would have treated his brother-in-law in this manner. Also, the Creek Chiefs held high regard for anyone of the Wind Clan and would have reluctantly accepted him as they did the other notorious and "obnoxious" brother-in-law, Charles Weatherford who married Sehoy III. Alexander mentions David Taitt only once in a letter to John Linder in 1788 and casually writes that "the then British Agent Mr. Taitt" had seen a bill of sale for the slave that Linder and Alexander were in dispute over.[121]

David Taitt did not leave West Florida and the Creek Country until 1781 and for many years he had been involved in numerous exploits and expeditions in and around the Creek Country. If David Taitt was married to Sehoy III, some of these deeds would have been passed down to his descendants and historians. None of these exploits have attached themselves to Colonel John Tate except the ill-fated expedition to Savannah where he lost his life. Also, David Taitt owned thousands of acres of land in West Florida and his heirs (not of the Indian Country) were still trying to recover this land as late as 1804. At best, it is a very weak case for David Taitt being married to Sehoy III.

Still, it is very troubling that not one reference could be found of Colonel John Tate in the official correspondence, reports, journals, and other documents by the thousands that the author has reviewed.

An exhaustive search was made in the Public Record Office looking for Tate. The Army Muster Rolls of the 16th, 22nd, 34th, and 60th Regiments, which served in West Florida during the Revolution, were searched. Also, Commission books, Army lists, musters and pay lists, List of Officers in Provincial Regiments, Loyalist Compensation Claims, and

Lists of Royal Artillery Pensioners were searched.

A John Tate entered the Army Register as an Ensign in 1756 and served in the 24th, 69th, and 84th Regiments until 1765. He was serving in India as a Captain when the 84th was disbanded. None of his regiments ever served in America.[122] This was the only John Tate found who was a Commissioned officer. A John Tate, who was a gunner in the Royal Artillery served from 1769 to 1772, but his service was in England, Scotland, and Gibralter.[123]

There is one more significant footnote to the disagreement over Tate vs. Taitt. One Adam Tate was an Indian trader out of West Florida as early as 1773 and probably from several years earlier. He was returning to his native North Carolina when he was detained in Savannah by American authorities thinking he was David Taitt, the British Agent. He had left West Florida in 1773 and remained in North Carolina until 1775 "at which time his concerns not being altogether settled in West Florida, he went there and returned last August [1779] to this place and from thence to North Carolina to become a citizen of that State, but was rejected. . . ." He was released when several gentlemen, including Martin Weatherford, signed affidavits that he was not David Taitt. He was given a pass to continue to North Carolina where it was noted that he "is a true friend to the American cause."[124] Note that Adam's name is spelled Tate whereas David's is Taitt. He left West Florida in late 1779 after being a trader up to 1773 and again from 1775 to 1779. 1779 was the year before Sehoy married Charles Weatherford. Was this Adam the contender for Sehoy III's love and the father of David Tate?

C. H. Driesbach, the great grandson of Sehoy III and Tate, writes that Alexander's sister Sehoy III married a Scotchman named Adam Tate and by him she had one child, a son named David Tate. Adam Tate died and left a will with Alexander McGillivray leaving his property to his son David.[125] The Driesbach family deeded Sehoy's and William Weatherford's burial plot to Baldwin County in 1972.[126]

David Tate, probably the son of Adam Tate, was a prominent citizen in south Alabama and appears frequently in the records. It is distressing that he never mentioned his father's name for the record. Until further information surfaces on this matter, it appears that Adam Tate was the father of David and married to Sehoy III.

Faust wrote that Lachlan had three children, Alexander, Sophia, and Jeanette. Alexander had a half sister on his mother's side named Sehoy McPherson. She married a Colonel Tate by whom she had Eloise in 1775 and David in 1776. She was widowed in 1778 and married Charles Weatherford that same year. They had six children.[127]

J.D. Driesbach wrote in 1874 that soon after Colonel Tate died in 1780, Sehoy married the Creek trader Charles Weatherford by whom she had six children, William, John, Elizabeth, Major, Mary, and Roseannah. William became the famous Creek Chief known as Red Eagle and led the attack on Fort Mims during the Creek War of 1813-14.[128]

Among the Pickett papers is a note furnished by Col. Robert James which describes William as 6' tall and 165 pounds. In the fall of 1826 he died from fatigue and exposure as the result of a "desperate bear hunt."[129]

Driesbach wrote later in 1884 saying Charles Weatherford and his brother John came to Georgia in 1750 from England.[130] The first time Charles appears in the record is in a letter from James Beamer, a Cherokee trader, to Governor Lyttelton, the Governor of South Carolina, dated 25 February 1759. He reported that Charles and others living around Ninety-Six in South Carolina and the Broad River in Georgia, were trading with the Cherokee "in the woods."[131] Trading in the woods was the term used for illegal trade, usually involving the sale of whiskey to the Indians, or Tafia, a cheap rum made from sugar cane juice and molasses.

Charles was branded a loyalist during the Revolution and appeared on the famous list of loyalists compiled by the Georgia General Assembly, whereas all property was confiscated due to their "treasonous conduct."[132]

Charles fled Georgia, like many Tories, for the safety of the Indian country in present-day Alabama. Many tories elected to settle on the Alabama-Tombigbee Rivers below the 32nd parallel within the safety net of Spanish territory, or some preferred the Indian country where they also were untouchable by the Americans. He was in the Creek Country as early as 1777 and engaged as a messenger for Alexander McGillivray.[133]

Charles, already an experienced trader and familiar with the Creeks, adapted well by marrying into the powerful McGillivray family and the Wind Clan. However, by nature Charles always seemed to be in trouble. In a letter written by Governor O'Neill at Pensacola to his superior, Governor Miro of Louisiana, dated 24 March 1787—

I have your answer to the petition I sent you from the Inhabitants on the Tensaw River in favor of Charles Wetherford who is sentenced to prison[134] and to the information I gave about the same. It has not been my purpose to minimize to the condemned the just sentence against him, for, in addition to what is mentioned in the sentence, Mr. Alexander McGillivray has informed me that the intention of the said Wetherford was to collect what goods he could get here, buy all he could on credit from Mr. Panton and obtain any others he might be able to from other sources and escape to the Americans on the Cumberland: he also has some influence over many of the traders, and is known to be obtaining goods elsewhere.

Nearly three years ago an American named Cole stole a young mulatto and his sister on the St. Johns. This Wetherford and another Englishman took them from him in the woods, brought them here and pawned them to Piti- Bautista and Mr. Jac. Since I did not want to permit them to be sold, they took advantage of my absence in Havanna two years ago to pawn to Mr. Jac. or rather to Mr. Bautista. At present he has in his possession a horse belonging to the clerk here and although he denies it, the Prisoner Story and a Spaniard named Julian testified that it is true. There are also complaints against him by another trader and by a Frenchman, a part of whose peltries he took when he passed by his house, which is a proved fact, and McGillivray says he must pay for them.[135]

Alexander became quite impatient with Charles over this episode and he was out of favor for a short time.[136] But relatives are special and by

August 1788 Alexander was again using Charles as a messenger sending him "express" with letters to Governor O'Neill.[137]

Hawkins in 1796 visited Charles at his home "on a high bluff on the left [east] bank of the Alabama one mile below the confluence of the Coosa and Tallapoosa, it is the first bluff below. Here are to be seen near his house 5 conic mounds of earth, the largest 30 yards in diameter, 17 feet high, the others are small, about 30 feet diameter and 5 feet high."[138]

Charles had developed a bad reputation and apparently deserved most of it. Timothy Barnard, a leading Lower Creek Chief, wrote on 18 January 1789 saying that Charles was a man of "many lies" and had returned to the Creek Nation with five or six Negroes he stole on the Georgia frontier. Barnard believed they could be returned if Alexander is made aware of it. He discussed others that were stealing slaves from Georgia and Alexander was determined to stop it.[139]

In 1795 Charles defended an accused horse thief, one James Stewart. "I believe Stewart is a clear of stealing the horses as you or I." But later he reversed himself and swore in a deposition that Stewart stole the horses and he had seen the evidence in the hands of Alexander McGillivray.[140] Charles did perform one good deed when he purchased a captive white woman from the Creeks. He wrote Governor O'Neill on 4 April 1793 that he is sending the woman to Pensacola and wanted O'Neill to reimburse him for his expenses.[141]

James Parton, Andrew Jackson's biographer, wrote that Charles was "a roving trader among the Creeks; married an Indian woman of the fierce Seminole tribe; accumulated property; possessed at length a plantation and negroes; became a breeder of fine horses and won prizes on the Alabama turf." He also said that his son William inherited all his property.[142] Apparently Parton never knew that Charles was married to Alexander's half-sister Sehoy III. Caleb Swan's map[143] of the Alabama River forks made in 1790 shows Charles' plantation or "place" on the east bank of the Alabama at the first bend, just below and opposite to the Coosada town, and near present day Montgomery.[144]

J. Leitch Wright writes that Charles is a "half-breed,"[145] but he is in error. James Seagrove, the Creek Indian Agent, writing to the President on 5 July 1792 said "a brother-in-law of General McGillivray is now here (a white man) of the name Charles Weatherford. . . ."[146] Pedro Olivier, the Spanish Agent, writing to Carondelet on 11 June 1793, also called Weatherford a "white man,"[147] and Woodward[148] said Charles was a white man and had come to the Creek Nation shortly after the close of the Revolution.

Perhaps the confusion comes from the statement offered by Cashin[149] and others—" Martin Weatherford was a veteran Indian trader, the father of mixed blood sons. . . ." Charles was not the son of Martin, but a contemporary. With the above accounts there is little doubt that Charles was white. Additional evidence is offered by Charles appearing on the famous loyalist list compiled by the Georgia General Assembly.

Benjamin Hawkins has unfavorable comments about Charles— "Charles W., a man of infamous character; a dealer in stolen horses."[150] Hawkins later writing in his journal on 28 May 1798 said:

> Charles Weatherford is an unworthy character and unfit to be in their land and the Chiefs had determined he should leave their land, but in consideration of his family on the Indian side, and of a promise made by Opoie Hutke of Ocheubofau, that he will in future attend to his conduct and endeavour to make him reform his conduct and behave well in the future, the Chiefs have determined to forgive the past and let him remain on his future good behaviour, and if he does misbehave again he is then to be removed without any favour or affection.[151]

Hawkins later discussed Weatherford and his debts in a letter to James Seagrove on 9 August 1799 where he commented that if Charles could get reimbursed for his losses he could pay his debts. He continued, "Charles is not now in the trade, he has lately moved down the Alabama below Sehoy's, has not much property and has been unfortunate in attempting to raise some valuable horses. The most valuable of his stock died by some unaccountable malady."[152]

Pickett writes that Weatherford lived on the first bluff on the eastern bank of the Alabama River below the junction of the Coosa and

Tallapoosa, which today is part of Montgomery. He owned the first race track in the area.[153] He also says Charles died at David Tate's in Montpelier in 1811.[154] However, he is on John Innerarity's 1812 list of traders and owed Panton Leslie Company and John Forbes Company $1110[155] Sehoy Weatherford was also still living and appeared on the same list—owing the company $1863, a sizeable sum for that day and time.

Panton Leslie Co. had always had trouble collecting debts incurred by the Indians. In 1803, the Cherokee owed the Company $2358, the Creek $113,512, the Chickasaw $11,178, and the Choctaw $16,091. The Company wanted to negotiate for a tract of land at the junction of the Alabama and Tombigbee Rivers, now Clarke County, to settle the debts. John Forbes met General Wilkinson at Little River to make his case for collecting the debts.[156]

John Weatherford, brother to Charles, came to Claiborne where he operated a ferry on the Alabama River. The U.S. Government had an agreement with him to operate the ferry as early as 1811.[157] He was still operating the ferry when Major Tatum passed down the river in 1814.[158] Under the Creek treaty of 1814, John was granted a land reserve on the southeast side of the Alabama River at T7 R5.[159] John was listed in the 1830 Clarke County Census where he owned twenty-four slaves.[160]

Charles Weatherford was a thief and renegade in the Creek Nation and only survived because of his marriage to Alexander McGillivray's half-sister Sehoy. But Charles was not above even bad mouthing Alexander. Governor O'Neill wrote to Miro on 10 September 1788 saying that Charles had just arrived in Pensacola bringing him a letter from Alexander. O'Neill said that Charles did not approve of the conduct of Alexander and assured O'Neill that several traders and the majority of Indians did not agree with Alexander.[161] Charles was also in the slave trade selling nine slaves to William Clark in Pensacola in June 1779.[162]

Sophia McGillivray, sister to Alexander, married Benjamin Durant at Little Tallasee in 1779.[163] Pickett wrote that Durant came from South Carolina to the Creek Nation as a young man. He soon met and married Sophia McGillivray. They lived on one of Lachlan's plantations on the

Savannah River with their son Lachlan Durant. When the Americans captured Savannah in 1782 and Lachlan McGillivray returned to Scotland, the Durants returned to the Creek Nation. Sophia acted as interpreter for Alexander since he spoke the Indian tongue poorly. Benjamin Durant became wealthy and owned a plantation in Durant's Bend on the Alabama River near Selma as early as 1776.[164] Sophia may have been a McGillivray family name. As far back as 1739 Dr. William McGillivray of Charleston had his daughter, Sophia, baptized in the St. Andrews Parish.[165]

Woodward wrote that Benjamin Durant, also called Peter, was a Frenchman from South Carolina. He and Sophia had three sons— Lachlan, John, and Sandy. There were four daughters—Rachel, Polly, Sophia, and Betsy, who married the leading Creek Chief Peter McQueen.[166]

Hawkins during his visit to the Creek Nation in 1796 visited Charles Weatherford near present-day Montgomery and then traveled on down the Alabama to "visit Mrs. Durant the oldest sister of Mr. McGillivray. She has had 11 children, 8 are living; I found her poor, and dirty in a small hut, less clean and comfortable than any hut I have seen belonging to any Indian however poor. She is in possession of near eighty slaves, near 40 of them capable of doing work in or out of doors. Yet from bad management they are a heavy burthen to her and to themselves, they are all idle. She told me her poverty arose from want of tools for her labourers and some misunderstanding between her and Mr. Panton. He had refused to supply her with anything. Her husband is a man of good figure, dull and stupid, a little mixed with African blood. She and her sister Mrs. Weatherford keep the command absolute of everything from their husbands. . . . The sister I am informed lives well in some taste, but expensively."[167]

As we can see this view of things is not so different from Pickett's account where he recorded that Benjamin was a tall and handsome young man when he arrived among the Creeks and soon married Sophia. "His complexion was almost as brown as that of the pretty, dark-eyed Sophia."[168]

General J.F.H. Claiborne and his Mississippi Volunteers marched up the Alabama River in late 1813 and attacked the town of Holy Ground, so sanctified by the Prophets. The Indians, led by William Weatherford, were assured of an easy victory by the Prophets, but after heavy fighting of less than an hour, most of the Indians were killed or wounded. William Weatherford, the son of Charles and Sehoy, supposedly at this time made his famous leap into the Alabama River and escaped. Claiborne's troops on entering the town square found Sophia Durant and ten other half bloods, that were friendly to the whites, tied to stakes with "piles of lightwood" around the captives.[169]

Apparently their lives were saved by the arrival of Claiborne's troops. William Weatherford, the nephew of Sophia, was seemingly going to stand by and not interfere with burning his aunt at the stake. Sam Dale said that prisoners, both whites and friendly Indians, were taken to the Holy Ground by order of the prophets and burned at the stake in the square.[170] Halbert and Ball cast doubt on Claiborne's account of Sophia about to be burned at the stake, saying the Indians did not burn their victims at the stake.[171] However, there are other accounts and indications that this practice did occur.

Sophia, earlier in 1789, had obtained the release of a captive white woman—a Mrs. Brown—held in the Creek Nation. She and her daughter were taken captive by a Creek raiding party on the Cumberland River. Sophia helped her escape from her captor and she fled to Little Tallasee for the protection of Alexander McGilivray. He ransomed Mrs. Brown and her daughter and had them returned to their relatives.[172]

Pickett and Woodward have both indicated that Benjamin Durant was a white man from South Carolina; however, the evidence indicates otherwise. Governor O'Neill wrote to Ezpeleta, the Spanish Captain General at Havanna, on 19 October 1783, saying Sophia was married to an Indian half-breed named "Duran" whose father was French. He continued by saying that they were moving down to the Escambia River with a large herd of cattle and forty slaves to settle about eighteen leagues [ca fifty miles] from Pensacola.[173] The Spanish were very class conscious and kept abreast of who had mixed blood.

The clincher comes when Benjamin Durant made a claim, along with many other Creeks, for one thousand dollars against the U.S. Government for his losses during the Creek War of 1813-14. A ledger in the National Archives dated July 1817, records a payment to Benjamin Durant of four hundred dollars made at Fort Hawkins.[174] Only members of the Creek Nation could make such claims.

Alexander wrote to Panton on 20 May 1789 mentioning "Durant's Brother Jenkins and a few other Tombigbee people seized old Walton and brought him across the River. Having left Jenkins to guard him while they went about some other matter he took the opportunity of Jenkins' falling asleep to Dispatch him with a hatchet and then fled to his home."[175]

For several years the Durants lived on the upper Escambia River which is just east of the lower Alabama River and the Tombigbee settlements.[176] Alexander wrote to O'Neill 25 July 1787 saying that Ben Durant should sell some of his negroes to pay his debts although "Mrs. Durant don't desire to part with them. Yet we advised Durant to get your leave to sell them to clear his other negroes, whatever his wife may say against the contrary."[177] Alexander had a strange way of referring to his relatives, in this case his sister. Sophia was in debt to Doctor Ruby, the Spanish physician, and she had to give up some of her cattle to settle the debt.[178]

Alexander wrote to Miro a few months later on 15 March 1788 requesting that he recover an escaped negro in New Orleans who belonged to Mrs. Durant. "They [Durants] are a poor family & have no other way at present to pay their debts but by the sale of negroes." The slave was rented out in Pensacola to Mr. Mather when he escaped. Miro replied that everything had been satisfactorily settled by paying Mrs. Durant two hundred dollars.[179]

Alexander McGillivray complained to Folch on 14 May 1789 saying one Lawrence traveling to Little Tallasee stopped off at Sophia's house on the Escambia when two men named Dyer and Johnson, who had been following Lawrence hoping to collect a reward, rushed into her house firing "across her face at Lawrence. She being at the time pregnant & near delivery, she fainted & was carried out & was with difficulty restored to life. . . ."[180] Folch caustically asked on 14 June why did Sophia faint in May when Lawrence was killed in March?[181]

A letter from "Sophiah McComb," daughter of Benjamin Durant and Sophia McGillivray, to Andrew Jackson dated 29 May 1815 and posted "Alabama River Choctaw Bluff," describes how she and her husband Dr. McComb came aboard Jackson's boat when he was going downriver. She inquired if females would be eligible for the 640 acres to be allotted to each Creek. Her husband had been absent the winter in Mobile tending the sick militia from Tennessee. White settlers had moved onto her land and taken her corn fields and cabins by force threatening her life. They had "beaten" her daughter and insulted her because of her "origin." The civil and military authorities would not give her assistance and she thought all half-breeds would be run off their lands. She appealed to Jackson for justice and begged for his help.[182] Dr. McComb was probably at Jackson's Camp Mandeville just a few miles south of Mobile. This was Jackson's staging area and many of his Tennessee Volunteers fell victim to the unhealthy and unsanitary conditions of this large encampment.[183]

Another letter written on the same day from Lachlan Durant to the Secretary of War requested redress of their grievances, claiming their property destroyed and cattle stolen. Squatters from the Mississippi Territory had moved across the Alabama River and taken possession of their "fields and houses and ordered us off at the risk of our lives." They had appealed to civil and military authorities without results. The letter was signed:

Lachlan Durant
Samuel Brashiers
Wm. Mcgirt
Rachel Walker
Sophiah McComb
Peggy Summerlin
Nancy Summerlin
Leonard McGhee

Lemi McGhee

Alex Brashiers

Harriett Linder[184]

Lachlan Durant was a brother to Sophiah McComb and son of Benjamin Durant and Sophia McGillivray. The acting Secretary of War, A. J. Dallas, wrote to Jackson about these claims and Jackson replied on 18 July 1815 saying he would make some inquiries. He had no way of knowing if the claims were legitimate.[185]

On 24 July 1815, Jackson wrote to General Gaines asking that he investigate the complaints of certain "natives" of the Creek Nation. The Secretary had written him and Gaines was to ascertain if the complaints had merit. He was also to determine if they were "really natives of the Creek Nation." If he found in the "affirmative" then Gaines was to take action to protect them "in the peacable enjoyment of the possessions secured to them by the treaty."[186]

Gaines replied to Jackson on 29 July saying he had received Jackson's letter of 15 July concerning the complaints. One was Sophia Linder-McComb, the niece of McGillivray. The others were of "little character of influence."[187] It appears that Gaines showed little interest in the matter. Jackson, an old Indian fighter, knew who these people were and that they were legitimate Creeks. No further correspondence could be found on the subject, so it appears that Jackson once again ignored Indian claims.

Another daughter of the Durants was married to Captain Dixon Bailey, a half-blooded hero of the Creek War on the lower Alabama River.[188] John Durant, son of Benjamin and Sophia, purchased a slave named Juber (Juba) from his father and then sold Juber to himself for $150 and therefore sets him free. Then on 1 January 1809, John sold Juber's wife and child to Juber. This was a compassionate act by John in setting the whole family free.[189]

Lachlan's other daughter, Jeanette, is somewhat of a mystery. We have only one firsthand account of her and the outline has to be put together from several sources. She married LeClerc Milford, the young Frenchman that arrived in the Creek Nation in 1775 and who became a close companion to her brother Alexander. Most writers spell his name "Milfort" and McCary[190] justified this based on its being spelled Milfort in his memoirs. Every person has the right to spell his name the way he "wants" it spelled. Nine letters written by Milford between 31 April 1793 and 14 April 1794 are all signed "DeMilford," and this supports the spelling as Milford herein.[191]

However, all this may be for naught as Lyon[192] writes that Milford was born at Thin-le-Moutier on 2 February 1752 and christened Jean-Antoine LeClerc. He later assumed the name Milford. He served in the Army from 1764 to 1774 when he left France for reasons unknown. He left the Creek Nation and arrived back in France in July 1795. His proposal for the recession of Louisiana to France was presented to the Committee of Public Safety where it received favorable comment. He again presented it to the Minister of Foreign Affairs on 26 February 1796. The Minister proposed giving Milford a pension and military rank. On 26 March 1796, he was appointed a Brigadier General with pay. However, when Napoleon came to power in November 1799, he took no interest in Milford nor his plan. Milford's pay and appointment were terminated on 23 September 1800.

Milford's memoirs[193] are considered by some writers as unreliable[194] and the work of a braggart; however, the dean of Creek historians, John R. Swanton, disagrees with Milford's detractors and states that his credibility is supported by other early writers such as James Adair.[195]

Milford arrived in America in 1775 from France, and made his way to the Georgia frontier where he met Alexander McGillivray at a Creek Council being held at Coweta on the Chattahoochee River. He and Alexander became quick friends and Milford took up residence at Little Tallasee. There he met and married Alexander's sister Jeanette in about 1777 or 1778. He also became a Tustunnuggee or War Chief of the Creek Nation.[196]

Major Caleb Swan left a map in 1790, from his visit to the Creek Nation, showing Milford living on the north bank of the Tallapoosa River, a short distance from its junction with the Coosa.[197] Milford had a temper that got him into trouble on occasion. Governor O'Neill complained to Alexander in 1790, and Alexander promised to keep Milford out of trouble.[198]

Governor O'Neill sent a messenger to Alexander demanding that the Creeks send him the "head" of a Creek Indian that had committed an "injustice" against a Spanish citizen. Alexander happened to be away when the messenger arrived, and Milford promptly sent a reply that he not only was sending the head, but he was sending the man also. "The bearer is the man; I have sent him to you, head and all."[199]

Carondelet wrote to Alexander on 14 September 1792 saying:

> My intention never was to employ Milfort except in expeditions which require more handiwork than headwork. He fancied that I allowed him five hundred dollars from the day of his arrival in town. In truth I promised him that sum in case he should be useful on an occasion to be indicated later, but his arrogance toward Don Pedro Olivier to whom he is by no means obedient, according to information from Governor O'Neill, though Olivier is commissioned Royal Commissary of His Majesty in the Creek Nation displeased me exceedingly and dissuaded me from employing him in the future.[200]

Pedro Olivier wrote to Governor Carondelet on 11 June 1793 saying, "These Indians do not show themselves at all disposed to advance Mr. Milford to the office or title which McGillivray held among them. I have heard that he has written to your Lordship that they had already elected him, but this never existed anywhere except in his head." Olivier says the Indians in assembly told him, "that they respected Mr. Milford as a man who had lived among them many years and who had been employed by McGillivray on some commissions with the Indians in which he merited the title or name of Tostanaky, which signifies warrior. They said that they regarded him in that light, and would allow him to remain among them as long as he wished."[201] This agrees with what Alexander wrote to Panton on 20 May 1789. "I have again given the Mareschels Staff to Milford who sett out yesterday to join a large party."[202]

The influential Creek Chief, White Lieutenant, writing to Carondelet on 14 November 1794 said, "Mr. Olivier was a very good man & his tongue was not forked, as for Milford & the man you sent last to us, they are nobody & their hearts & tongues are not straight; there is now no beloved man of yours amongst us. . . ."[203] The White Lieutenant had written earlier to Carondelet on 9 November 1793 that Milford's "heart and tongue is not straight."[204]

The above three letters are convincing evidence that the Spanish would never approve of Milford succeeding Alexander McGillivray to head the Creek Nation. As we have noted previously, Panton was well aware of this animosity toward Milford and he would never have recommended Milford to succeed Alexander.

LeClerc Milford was a person of ability to have survived for nearly twenty years wrapped in the intrigue of Spanish—English—Indian political and military confrontations. Of course, having the protection of Alexander McGillivray and being married to his sister, Jeanette, went a long way toward assuring his survival. However, time was fast running out for Milford and he was aware of this fact when he wrote in his letter to Carondelet dated 26 March 1794, "As for me I am threatened every day, and look forward to nothing except being massacred one of these days."[205] These words by Milford were not mere rhetoric and he decided it was time to return to France where he quickly generated interest in a proposal to again place the Mississippi Valley back into French hands and, of course, advance the fortunes of Milford.

The fate of Jeanette McGillivray Milford is revealed in a letter written by the Creek Chief Singer to William Panton on 28 September 1799. When Malcolm McPherson, brother to Sehoy III and half-brother to Alexander, Jeanette, and Sophia, died in 1799, the Singer was going to care for his children since his sister was their mother and married to McPherson. Due to Creek tradition, the relatives of the deceased, not the wife and children, took possession of their worldly goods. Singer wanted McPherson's oldest son to take over and manage his affairs. He previously had trouble convincing Jeanette, who had recently died, to agree but "Singer and her sister Mrs. Durant" gave her a "hard talk" and she finally agreed to let the son manage the affairs. Jeanette had been married to Ben Crook, a Creek trader at Little Tallasee, since her previous husband, Milford, deserted her in 1795 and returned to France. She died in 1799.[206] Ben Crook was the trader, along with Daniel McGillivray, to Little Tallasee in 1796. Several writers[207] say she accompanied Milford back to France, but Meek[208] says she died before Milford went back to France. All are in error.

Pickett adds a peculiar note to this episode. In 1814 Milford's home in France was attacked by a party of Russians. He defended himself with his French wife loading the guns. He was rescued by the timely arrival of French troops. Soon after this event, Milford died, but his wife lived for many more years dying in a house fire at Rheims.[209] Note that Pickett says "French wife."

Perhaps it is fitting that we close on Milford by briefly glancing at his grand proposal. The hope was that the West, and perhaps the south too, could be induced to secede from the union and form a new confederation, allied with and subservient to France. Parallel moves were the sending of Robert Fulton, a frontiersman holding a French commission as Colonel, who had just returned from consultation in the west with George Rogers Clark, to France with secret dispatches in April 1796, and "commissioning by the Directory of Jean LeClerc (better known as Milfort) for twenty years a Tustennuggee in the Creek Nation, a general of brigade, on the basis of his promise to deliver the Creek Army to the French side."[210]

A last footnote on Milford reveals a strange coincidence reported by Sam Dale, the famed "Indian fighter" and a member of the canoe battle on the Alabama River in November 1813. Dale and his party were going up the river and came upon some Indians in a canoe. The Indian leader raised his rifle, but before he could fire, Dale shot him dead. The leader was Will Milfort and Dale wrote:

> three quarters white, tall, handsome, intelligent and prepossessing and a strong attachment existed between us. He camped with me at the great Council of Took-a-batcha, and privately informed me when

Tecumseh was about to speak. By the influence of Weatherford he joined the hostiles, and was on his first warpath when he met his fate. We recognized each other in a moment; there was a mutual exclamation of surprise—a pang of regret, perhaps—but no time for parley. I dropped a tear over his body and often bewail the destiny that doomed him to fall by the hand of his best friend. Such are the dreadful necessities of war. Some time after I sought and interred his fleshless bones; they moulder on the banks of the river he loved so well.[211]

Pickett says the Chief in the other canoe recognized Dale and cried out "now for it Big Sam."[212] There is little doubt that this 'three quarters white" Indian was the son of LeClerc Milford and Jeanette McGillivray. Sutton writes that Milford and Jeanette had two children—Alexander and Polly, but gives no reference.[213]

9

Alexander McGillivray, the Creek Chief

Alexander McGillivray, son of Lachlan Lia McGillivray, became the famous Creek Indian Chief that kept the English and Spanish colonial officials at bay and contending between themselves for the loyalty of the Creeks. Later the Americans entered this arena and Alexander could only delay the rush to the frontier of the land-hungry settlers. Probably one of the best descriptions of Alexander comes from John Caughey in Bolton.[1]

McGillivray was one of the most remarkable men in the galaxy of striking figures of the old southwest. For a man to earn such a reputation in a single decade is remarkable; for a man who dies before reaching the threshold of middle age to gain such recognition is more remarkable; for a man with as many shortcomings as McGillivray to achieve such greatness is most remarkable. That he earned this praise was due to the appropriateness of his genius. There was the fortunate juxtaposition of a most perplexing problem and a leader with just the qualities necessary for its solution. A magnificent warrior would have availed the Creeks little; but the stage was set for diplomacy and intrigue, the very channels in which McGillivray was most proficient.

A description of Alexander by Allison at the turn of the century is somewhat different.

Alexander McGillivray was a noted tory during the Revolution, and had taken refuge after its close among the Creek Nation. He was a man of great courage and intelligence, entertained inveterate hostility to the whites, and had an insatiable ambition for personal promotion. He was in the Spanish pay, as agent of that government among the Indians, had usurped regal authority, and was also Chief of the Talapouches. It is said that he cherished the hope of having his nation admitted into the federal compact, although he was in the service of Spain with the rank of Colonel, and was afterward promoted to be Commissary General. This dangerous man was under the absolute control of Governor Miro in 1788.[2]

LeClerc Milford first met Alexander at a Council being held at Coweta in 1775 and they soon became fast friends. Alexander invited him to his home at Little Tallasee. Alexander, at this early date, was already a prominent figure in the Creek hierarchy. Milford said he spoke very little Creek. Alexander's house was near the Coosa River and one-half league from Fort Toulouse. He had sixty slaves that lived in separate cabins and gave his plantation the look of a small village.[3]

Major Caleb Swan, writing about Alexander in 1790, said that he returned to the Nation in 1776 leaving Georgia "in disgust." He made significant changes in the customs of the Creeks, primarily by making the lead warriors primary over the Chiefs. Alexander brought the Chiefs in line by threatening to take away their resident traders. "This at once humbles them most effectually; for they conceive the privilege of having a good white trader in their town, to be inestimable." Through an agreement with Panton and the Spanish officials in West Florida, all traders had to have a "license" from Alexander.[4]

John Stuart, the Superintendent for Indian Affairs, took notice of Alexander at an early date. Writing to Lord George Germain on 6 October 1777 and posted from Pensacola, Stuart said:

I cannot describe to your Lordship how much I was surprised, mortified and disappointed by a letter from the Assistant Commissary,

Mr. Alexander McGillivray, dated at Little Tallasee. . . . I have great hopes and expectations from Mr. McGillivray's activity and good sense, who by his mother's side is a Creek of powerful connections and consequently will be safe.[5]

A British commission for Alexander as "Commissary and Captain" for the Creek Nation was ordered by Lord Cornwallis and Sir Henry Clinton. The Commission was signed by Colonel Thomas Brown, Superintendent of Indian affairs after John Stuart died.[6]

One of the earliest extant letters by Alexander was to Stuart on 25 September 1777. He was trying to counter the influence of Galphin on the Chiefs, who wanted them to support the rebels and he had to intercede to keep the Oakfuskees from murdering Taitt, Cameron, and Moniac the interpreter. He informed Stuart that he was calling a council of all the Creeks to give them a strong talk to counter Galphin, and that Big Fellow[7] "insists I shall take all on myself, he himself is tired on this occasion and says my powerful clan will support me."[8] Emistisego, or Big Fellow, was particularly sensitive to the clan hierarchy since his mother was a captive slave and this handicapped him on occasion in dealing with the other chiefs. Alexander did not get overall power until after Emistisego was killed in the battle for Savannah in the Revolution.

Colonel Thomas Brown writing to Sir Guy Carlton on 9 October 1782, after the Revolution was over, said that "Emistisicho" led 150 warriors to Savannah and penetrated the rebel lines with virtually no loss except himself.[9] Stuart writing again to his Lordship on 2 April 1778 said that McGillivray had arrived at Pensacola with a message from the Oakfuskees. He also brought "white beads and tobaco" as symbols of friendship and that the Oakfuskees wished to be forgiven for their "raiding."[10]

David Taitt, the Creek Agent under Stuart, writes to Lord George Germain on 6 August 1779 reporting activities on the Georgia frontier. Alexander and some seventy to eighty warriors had been on the Savannah River where they encountered a force of two hundred American rebels. Six Indians and two white men were killed and three Indians and three whites taken prisoner by the McGillivray party. Taitt said that he sent Alexander and his party with "one interpreter" to join the British forces.[11] This supports Milford's statement that Alexander did not speak the "Indian tongue" well. This positive account by Taitt of Alexander's engaging the rebels runs counter to Milford's account of the incident. "From the start of the battle, McGillivray hid in the bushes where he remained until nightfall."[12] This statement by Milford seems to be for the purpose of inflating his own "bravo" image.

Alexander Cameron, the Cherokee Agent under Stuart, writing to General Augustine Prevost on 15 October 1779 from Little Tallasee, reports that Alexander and the Upper Creek Chiefs "seem to be tired of the war and would rather hunt the bear who are very numerous about them. . . ."[13]

Cameron wrote to his Lordship on 27 May 1781 reporting on the capture of Pensacola by the Spanish. He stated that Alexander and forty warriors arrived at the scene on 8 April where another Creek party joined him four days later. Cameron had the highest praise for the conduct of the Indians.[14]

Contrary to what Milford wrote about Alexander's courage, he could be assertive when the need arose. Writing to Governor O'Neill at Pensacola on 10 March 1783, Alexander demanded the release from Spanish custody one Ambrose Grizzard, a trader, whom Alexander had sent on an errand to Pensacola. He threatened trouble for the Spanish if Grizzard was not released.[15]

Governor O'Neill writing on 19 October 1783 said that Alexander had more influence in the Creek Nation than any other man. He continued by saying that he was educated in Charleston and the English named him Commissary of the "Upper Creek Nation." He had a great number of cattle and slaves in his town on the Coosa River. His sister was married to a half-breed named Durant whose father was French. He goes on to advise keeping the friendship of Alexander.[16]

Alexander did get reimbursement for some of his expenses. He submitted a bill to the British at Pensacola in the amount of 172 pounds for "presents and food" for some 420 Indians attending a council to hear a talk read from General Campbell. The Council lasted from 12 March to 31 May 1780.[17]

Lieutenant Colonel Thomas Brown, Commander of the Kings Rangers during the Revolution and the last British Indian Agent to the Creeks, advised Alexander in late 1783 to seek an agreement with the Spanish at Pensacola whereby the Creeks could obtain arms and ammunition.[18] Alexander took this advice and wrote to O'Neill on 1 January 1784 offering his service as "an agent for Indian affairs on the part of his most Catholic Majesty, in which capacity I have served his Brittanick Majesty for very near eight years past."[19] The "eight years past" converts to 1776 which confirms his position in the Creek Nation at this early date.

Alexander sent a letter to O'Neill on 3 January 1784 telling O'Neill that Panton Leslie Company of St. Augustine was planning to expand its trading business to Pensacola and Mobile. "Those Gentlemen offered me a part of it."[20] Coker[21] wrote that Alexander became a partner in 1784 and remained one until 1788.

Alexander, writing to McLatchy[22] on 4 October 1784, said "since I have taken a share in the interests of your house, I am determined to work with interest and integrity."[23] Sometime between January and October 1784, Alexander became a partner in Panton Leslie Company.

Just two months later in December Alexander accepted a partnership in Mather and Company of Mobile who had the trade with the Choctaw and Chickasaw. Alexander says Mather could not have established his business without his approval which he gave the Spaniards.[24] The charter issued to both companies exempted them from the 6% import-export tax on Indian trade goods.[25]

Alexander, writing on 25 December 1784, gives us some insight into his ambitions and what he perceives as his needs, "I have no family which obliges me to accumulate possessions; for although I have some negroes and a few dependents, since I cannot use wealth in this country and never expect to leave it, all that I want is a decent living."[26] It is strange that Alexander says he has "no family" but does have a "few dependents," when he has two wives, children, uncles, and sisters all living near him in the Creek Country. He most likely is saying he has "no white family."

Alexander's rise to power in the Creek Nation did not please everyone. Daniel McMurphy, the Georgia Creek Indian Agent, writing on 30 July 1786 to Governor Edward Telfair reported "that Alexander McGilvery, who stiles himself sovereign of the Creek Nation, has received the protection of the Spaniards. . . ." In this same letter he writes that "James McQueen a traider told me he heard McGilvery often say, that if it should be the Ruin of the whole Nation, he would drive the people off the Oconey. But McQueen said that McGilvery was much mistaken for he could never get the whole Nation to take his talk; and that he was afraid, for he had removed all his property, before he went down to Pensacola. . . ."[27]

It was about this period when Alexander was establishing his plantation on Little River in northern Baldwin County. This move was also supported by a letter from Governor O'Neill to Favrot on 1 December 1786 where he wrote, "For some time McGillivray has had a Scotchman of the same name caring for a plantation on the Alabama River.[28] to which place he had a mind to send his cattle, which according to your advice has been done, and they will certainly be safer there in case the contest betwen the Creeks and the Americans continues."[29] Alexander maintained his principal residence at Little Tallasee, a wife and home at Hickory Ground, and a wife and home on Little River in Baldwin County.[30]

At a Council between the Creeks and Americans on 21 October 1786, as reported in the *Georgia State Gazette*, one of the American Commissioners, John Habersham said, "A man by the name of half-breed McGillivray, who lives in your Nation, and calls himself King of all your Headmen, has sent us some letters." The Chiefs replied to Habersham the next day and told him, "the chief person who has been against you is Alexander McGillivrey; he is of a large family, therefore we will give him an opportunity to go away quietly. But we must remove him. If he chuses to live with the Spaniards, he may go to them, or else he must also be killed. . . ."[31]

Many of the Creeks resented Alexander and his courting the Spaniards, especially the Lower Creeks along the Chattahoochee River who were inclined to be more friendly to the Americans. This friendship and dependency goes back to earliest colonial times when the Spaniards destroyed several Lower towns and stationed a military garrison on the Chattahoochee. However, the Americans ran hot and cold in their dealings with the Indians and this gave Alexander the opportunity to solidify his hold over the Nation. He did this by reaching agreement with the Spaniards whereby the Creeks could obtain their trade goods at Pensacola only by having a requisition signed by himself. Since Panton Leslie Company moved their trading business in 1785 to Pensacola and Mobile, the Americans could not meet the competition on a regular and dependable basis. Also, the Americans from time to time, depending on their needs, threatened to cut off the trade. The Indians had long ago reached a point of no return and the trade was now essential to their survival. Alexander was a partner in Panton Leslie Company, although he received little monetary rewards from the Company, and with his control over the trade he consequently exercised control over the Nation. This fact had more to do with Alexander ascending to the leadership of the Creek Nation than any other—including his personal diplomacy and clan connections.

Alexander had continued to tighten his control over the Creeks, as observed by Governor Miro on 24 March 1787:

> He is the Commissary to the Indians, is able to manage them with absolute dominion, and is able to make them embrace the side he orders; and whether he does it for love of the Sovereign, or for his private interests, it is necessary to favor a person, who uses his powerful influence with which he rules the Indians to the greatest advantage in the present circumstance.[32]

George Whitefield had traveled in the Creek Country in 1788 and visited with Alexander. Writing to Governor Handly of Georgia on 10 July, he said "his deportment was manly and collected."[33] However, Vicente Folch, the Commandant at Mobile, wrote to Miro on 26 April

1788 and expresses his opinion of Alexander. "He had the understanding of a white man and the cruel passions of an Indian."[34]

An interesting incident occurred that shows a side of Alexander that we seldom see in the records. Governor O'Neill writing to Miro on 28 July 1788 said that a mulatto made his way into the Creek Country and arrived at Little Tallasse where Alexander gave him refuge. The owner sent two Spaniards to get him, but when they arrived at Little Tallasse, Alexander refused to give him up and "threatened to use a razor on anyone who tried to capture him, and the mulatto remained in the Nation."[35]

The relations between Alexander and the Spanish continued to deteriorate, especially between O'Neill, Folch, and Alexander. On 20 August 1788 Alexander wrote to Miro that his honor was at stake and he was resigning his Spanish Commission, making it a "blank" piece of paper.[36] O'Neill seems to have become hostile over some incidents that occurred between the Creeks and Spaniards, but especially so when he was informed that the Creeks were going to Florida to meet William Augustus Bowles and receive English presents. He expresses his animosity by calling Alexander a "half breed" and Panton a "hide merchant."[37]

O'Neill writing to Miro on 21 May 1787 says that it is best that Alexander not gain too much "authority in the Nation that he could bring about the independence of the Indians. I am sure that should he succeed in this matter he would prove more loyal to the British trade than to the Spaniards."[38]

Miro to O'Neill on 8 July 1788 severely chastised him for continually making negative statements against Alexander and William Panton without giving any evidence to back up his accusations. Miro defended Alexander and said that he had no reason to distrust him.[39] On 12 July he wrote another letter, again chastising O'Neill.[40] Miro was Governor General of all Louisiana and West Florida whereas O'Neill was the military Commandant at Pensacola and Folch commandant at Mobile. Miro certainly had his troubles in keeping the lid on O'Neill and Folch who were dealing with the Indians on a daily basis while Miro governed from afar at New Orleans. However, this would change somewhat under Carondelet who replaced Miro.

Miro wrote on 13 July 1788 saying that O'Neill wanted to try and dislodge Alexander of his influence over the Creeks, but Miro opposed such a move, claiming that he did not believe they can succeed.[41] After Bowles landed in East Florida, O'Neill was convinced of a conspiracy where the Creeks would attack Pensacola.[42] O'Neill and Folch were finally successful in raising the suspicions of Miro who wrote on 28 July 1788 that they would wait and see what Alexander would do.[43]

Folch, writing to Miro on 2 July 1789, again berates Alexander, accusing him of wanting to open a seaport in order to escape the Spanish tariffs. If he had accomplished this "he will be independent of the Spanish." He writes that "the disease of wishing to be king has possessed him as a great delirium."[44] O'Neill had become so paranoid over his suspicions of Alexander he recruited a spy, one John Maypother, in the house of Panton Leslie Company to keep him informed on Alexander's activities. Maypother made copies of Alexander's correspondence to Panton and gave them to O'Neill."[45]

Alexander complained to O'Neill on 22 August 1788 that the Indian trader Timothy Lane was spreading lies in Pensacola that he was planning an attack on Pensacola.[46] Lane was not the only informant that Alexander had trouble with. John Linder and Charles Weatherford also informed O'Neill about Bowles landing and the Creeks going to meet him to receive presents.[47]

Alexander, exasperated, wrote to his friend Panton on 12 January 1789 that he was disappointed in the Spaniards' actions against them as a result of Bowles landing and all the rumors in the Nation. "It now appears plain their talks are now both alike and we are treated as no people." The Spaniards had refused to send any ammunition to the Creeks. Alexander continued:

> Bowles is again on the Coast with a fresh quantity of Goods which no doubt will produce a fresh hubbub at Pensacola but it will be all in vain, for it is impossible to convince an Indian that it is a criminal action in him to receive a present from anyone. I, that know them so well shant

attempt it and it would be a wise measure in others if they winked at such things, if they disapprove of it, instead of raising a fruitless clamour which can only tend to create Jealouly and alarm, heat the minds of the Nation and make the name of a Spaniard so odious as at any former time. . . .[48]

O'Neill accused Alexander of forcing his wife's sister to marry a son of Colbert, in order to form an alliance with the Chickasaw.[49] It became so bad that on 29 June 1789, Governor Miro forbade Folch from ever again writing to Alexander or the Creek Nation.[50] This animosity eventually led Alexander to New York to sign a treaty with President Washington in 1790.

Things were not so friendly with the Americans either. Robert Leslie wrote Alexander on 11 December 1788 and warned him that there is an effort afoot for the Georgians to assassinate him at a coming council where there will be three hundred armed Georgians. A group of these had taken an oath "to put you to death, by some means or other."[51]

Colonel David Humphreys, former aide to General Washington, was appointed by the President to be one of the Commissioners to negotiate a peace treaty with the Creek Indians in 1789. Humphreys wrote to the President on 21 September saying, "It is also pretty well ascertained that McGillivray is desirous of peace and his word is a law to the Creeks."[52]

Humphreys reported again to President Washington on 26 September 1789:

> the next day McGillivray dined with us and although he got very much intoxicated, he seemed to retain his recollection & reason, beyond what I had ever seen in a person, when in the same condition. . . . I have not leisure to give you a description of the person & character of McGillivray. His countenance has nothing liberal and open in it. It has, however, sufficient marks of understanding. In short he appears to have the good sense of an American, the shrewdness of a Scotchman & the cunning of an Indian. I think he is much addicted to debauchery that he

will not live four years. He dresses altogether in the Indian fashion & is rather slovenly than otherwise."[53]

Humphreys did not realize how prophetic his prediction was.

The meeting failed when Alexander made excuses and suddenly departed the grounds and went home. Other leading chiefs stayed and wanted a treaty but said they could not conclude one without Alexander. Humphreys wrote at length to what he felt was treachery by Alexander and that he could not be depended on, and was obviously still in the Spanish interest.[54] The lack of a treaty brought about a split between Alexander and some of the Chiefs. He was reluctant to make the break with Panton and the Spanish. Perhaps also it was the deep resentment that he still harbored against the Georgians that continued to keep him in the Spanish interest.

On 6 March 1790, Benjamin Hawkins wrote a threatening letter to Alexander concluding that if war occurs the Creeks would be crushed. He then offered an olive branch and requested Alexander to come to New York and meet with Washington.[55]

General Washington was anxious to negotiate a treaty with the Creeks and hopefully bring peace to the Cumberland settlements and the Georgia frontier. He selected Colonel Marinus Willett to carry Hawkins's letter to Alexander and help persuade him to come to New York for negotiations. Willett left New York on 15 March 1790 and traveled to the Creek Nation where he met Alexander on 30 April, at the Hillabees in present-day Tallapoosa County. Willett recorded his first impression of Alexander—"Colonel McGillivray appears to be a man of an open, candid, generous mind, with a good judgement and very tenacious memory."[56]

On 4 May, Willett and McGillivray arrived at Hickory Ground where:

> Colonel Mcgillivray lives. In the course of the day, I went to a place called the apple grove, five miles from where Colonel McGillivray lives. This place is improved by McGillivray. It is the place of his birth, and is

situated, as well as the place where he dwells on the banks of the Coosa, a very fine river. The Apple Grove is the pleasantest place of the two. At this place I had a delicious regale of strawberries and mulberries. Under the bank of the shore I found a pleasing and delightful recess, where I spent three hours alone. After which I went up to the house, had a dinner of fish, and returned home.[57]

After a Council was held among the Chiefs, Willett, Alexander and several Chiefs and family members set off from Little Tallasse on 1 June for New York.[58]

Benjamin Rush of Philadelphia writing in his journal on July 19, 1790 said:

> this day waited on Col. McIlvery, and walked with him to Mr. Peal's museum. I invited him to breakfast with me the next day, but he told me he was going out of town early the next morning.[59] I asked him for the liberty of addressing a few questions relating to the Indians, in a letter, which he said he would endeavour to answer. He spoke with great pleasure of his prospects of civilizing the Creek Indians.

His letter to McGillivray follows:

> In consequence of your polite promise of this morning, to answer me a few questions relative to the Indians, I have taken the liberty of inserting them in this letter. I beg you will not put yourself to any immediate inconvenience in writing your answers. They will be equally acceptable whether I receive them now, or upon your return from New York.
>
> 1. What diseases are most common among your Indians?
> 2. Do the Indian women ever die in childbed?
> 3. Is there much mortality among Indian children?
> 4. Is suicide ever known among the Indians?
> 5. Do the faculties of the mind discover the same, or greater marks of decay in old people among the Indians, than among the Civilized

Americans?

6. Is the passion for the female sex as strong, and as much disposed to excess and irregularity among the Indians as among Civilized people? Is it weakened, or strengthened by the toils of war and hunting?[60]

Unfortunately we do not have the reply that McGillivray may have furnished Rush.

Arriving in New York in the middle of the summer, Alexander was wined, dined, and courted by the Americans and was induced to sign a treaty wherein the Creeks were provided an annual subsidy. It included a separate secret annuity for Alexander who was also commissioned a Brigadier General to serve as agent to the United States with an annual salary of $1200.[61]

While in New York in August 1790, Alexander related a short history of the Creeks which was found in the Knox papers. He related that the Abeika were in place when the Moscogee arrived from the northwest. They lived with the Alabama and when differences arose, the Alabama being the weaker were compelled to remove west all of their families. They moved down the Alabama River and some settled among the Tensaw on the Mobile River. When the Muscogee demanded that the Alabama be delivered up, the Tensaw refused and a war resulted causing the Tensaw to be "greatly reduced in number." At about this time the French arrived and smallpox soon reduced the Tensaw "almost to nothing."[62]

The Spaniards were so upset with Alexander going to New York that they dispatched a Spanish Agent, Carlos Howard, to New York to spy on Alexander and report back on his findings.[63]

Alexander also had a personal reason for going to New York. Writing to Panton on 10 August 1789, he said that he believed the American Commissioners will offer him the restoration of his property in Georgia worth thirty thousand pounds or $100,000.[64] Although the Georgians could use the confiscated property of Lachlan McGillivray to bargain with Alexander, it appears that Alexander never knew that he was not the legal heir to his father's property.

Alexander, reporting to Governor Miro on 26 February 1791, informed him that he tried to obtain restitution for his lands in Georgia, but was told the Congress had no authority to order the State of Georgia to do so. The United States would try to get Georgia to return the property, but they would grant him some compensation—$1200 annually. He informed Miro that he was offered a Brigadier Generalship, but would have to take an oath of loyalty to the United States which he refused to do. He assured Miro that nothing had changed and the trade would continue as before.[65] Miro probably later learned that Alexander had accepted the Commission, had taken an oath of loyalty to the United States, and that United States sovereignty would extend over the Creek lands. This would undoubtedly heighten the strained relations between the two and cause further mistrust by the Spanish authorities.

Alexander and his entourage were escorted back to the Creek Nation by Major Caleb Swan who also kept a journal of his travels. Alexander was ill before leaving New York and had to take a ship's passage to Savannah and landed at the St. Mary's River on 31 August.[66] They arrived at Little Tallasee in October 1790. Swan noted a most interesting and tragic occurrence—his journal entry on 29 October stated, "a young woman, sister to McGillivray's wife, hanged herself in a fit of violent passion, but was cut down and saved." Another entry on 20 November says "a woman related to McGillivray hanged herself at Little Tallasee and was privately buried in the Village the same evening."[67] Such events have been rarely recorded among the Indians. This sister to Alexander's wife may well have been the same one Alexander "forced" to marry a son of trader James Colbert of the Chickasaw which the Spanish accused him of doing so as to form an alliance. Her first attempt apparently failed, but the second was successful.

Swan left the Creeks in early winter and returned to Philadelphia where he wrote to the Secretary of War on 29 April 1791. In the course of his letter, he tried to justify his early return. "It is a custom of McGillivray to spend his winters on the sea coast among the Spaniards leaving his wife, servants, and horses at a plantation he has near the Tensaw, within the borders of West Florida, about 180 miles down the

Alabama River, and of returning to pass his summers in the Nation."
Swan continues that if he had remained in the Nation he would have
been exposed to the winter cold and possibly even hunger.[68]

John Pope visited the Creek Nation in 1791 and wrote in his journal
that he arrived at General McGillivray's on 1 June, where his "house was
situated on the Cousee River, about 5 miles above its Junction with the
Tallapoosee." On his arrival he was informed that McGillivray had gone
to his

> upper Plantation, on the same River, about 6 miles distant from his
> present Residence. Alexander's nephew escorted him upriver where he
> found Alexander supervising the building of a log house on the very spot
> where his father resided while a trader in the Nation. Here are some tall
> old apple trees planted by his father. He has a habitual headache. He
> possesses a liberal education, is witty and humorous. He has two
> children by his wife, Alexander and Elizabeth. They spoke the English
> tongue as well as children of a similar age usually do among us.

He had about fifty negroes with another hundred in the Spanish
West Indies, also a large stock of horses, hogs, and cattle. He had two or
three white overseers on his plantation. "He receives annual presents
from his Father in Scotland, which he modestly displays to his Friends."
Pope watched Alexander write two letters "both written in haste, and in
a circle of many chieftains, whose garrulity would have confused any
other man than McGillivray."[69]

Pope wrote:

> McGillivray who is perpetual Dictator in Time of War subdelegates
> a number of Chieftains for the Direction of all military operations and
> when the war concludes, they, in compensation for their martial
> atchievements, are invested by the Dictator with Civil authority which
> supersedes the hereditary Powers of their Demi-Kings.[70]

Pope was given a list of Creek words and their meaning by the Little

King of Broken Arrow, which included "Hippo elk meco, M'Gillivray, or the good child King."[71]

Benjamin Hawkins gives us a description of the family in 1799. Speaking of Hickory Ground he wrote:

> It is on the left bank of the Coosa two miles above the fork of the river, and one mile below the falls, on a flat of poor land, just below a small stream; the fields are on the right side of the river, on rich flat land; and this flat extends back for two miles. . . .
>
> Three and a half miles above the town are ten apple trees, planted by the late General McGillivray half a mile further up are the remains of old Talasee, formerly the residence of Lachlan McGillivray, and his son, the general. Here are ten apple trees planted by the father, and a stone chimney, the remains of a house built by the son, and these are all the improvements left by father and son.
>
> These people, are some of them, industrious. They have forty gunmen, nearly three hundred cattle, and some horses and hogs; the family of the general belong to this town; he left one son and two daughters; the son is in Scotland, with his grandfather, and the daughters with Sam Macnac, a half breed, their uncle; the property is much of it wasted. The chiefs have requested the agent for Indian affairs, to take charge of the property for the son, to prevent its being wasted by the sisters of the general, or by their children.[72]

The threats against Alexander's life, his continued health problems, and the constant need to balance the Americans off against the Spanish and vice versa, seems to have taken its toll on him. James Seagrove, the American Creek Agent, wrote to the Secretary of War on 20 February 1792, saying that there was evidence that Alexander was moving his slaves and cattle to his new residence closer to Pensacola. Also, that Alexander has his "eye" on one of Walker's daughters.[73]

Alexander went through periods of depression as expressed in a letter to Panton 20 May 1789:

I am positively Harrassed and Wearied out by the restless Life I am obliged to lead & the part I have to act with our new allies whose conduct appears so contradictory and Suspicious—with the Americans the task is no way difficult as we know them to be avowed enemies—on the other side where we ought to look for Security and Ease we find nothing but darkness and obscurity.[74]

Seagrove to the President on 5 July 1792 wrote that Captain Pedro Olivier, the Spanish Agent, had arrived at Little Tallasee earlier in the summer and Alexander had taken him around introducing him to the more important chiefs. He stressed to the Chiefs what Olivier was in a position to do for them as resident agent. Seagrove said that by July Alexander had "quit" the Creek Country and there was no doubt that Olivier was to be his successor. As soon as Alexander left, Olivier started assuming this position by telling the Chiefs what to do.[75]

The United States officially protested to the Court of Spain the stationing of a Spanish agent within the territorial limits of the United States, but the Court rejected the protest and offered a copy of the 1784 Spanish treaty with the Creeks as justification. However, the Court cautioned Las Casa and Carondelet to be "prudent" in their relations with the United States.[76]

Some writers have claimed that Alexander was "rich."[77] He did have some slaves, cattle, horses, and two "plantations," but apparently little hard cash. He was continually having visitors which he housed and fed with no complaints. There were expenses of paid messengers, interpreters, and other expenses he had to pay from his own pocket. A letter from James Innerarity to John Forbes[78] dated 22 November 1806 included excerpts from another letter, now apparently lost, written by Panton to Alexander on 2 August 1788. Alexander was a silent partner in Panton, Leslie Company until his death in 1793, but only active until 1788 when Panton became alarmed about Alexander's involvement in accepting ammunition from the English in the Bahamas. Panton feared this would cause suspicion among the Spaniards and adversely affect his trading business centered in Pensacola. He obtained Alexander's resignation in

order to protect the Company from what he foresaw as Spanish confiscation.[79] In any case, Alexander had been reduced to appealing to Panton
for spending money—his letter to Panton on 27 March 1792 ends with
this poignant sentence. "I beg you'll send me some pocket money. . . ."[80]

Alexander traveled fairly extensively in late 1792 and early 1793. He
decided to go to New Orleans to visit Governor Carondelet and on 6
June 1792 he was at Little River; in New Orleans by 6 July; back at
Mobile by 16 July; in Pensacola 3 September and back at Little Tallasee
by 28 November. He returned to Mobile by 15 January 1793 where he
informed Carondelet he was executor of John Linder's will, who lately
died.[81] He returned to Little River and then decided to visit Panton at
Pensacola where he became ill on the path.

Olivier had reported to Carondelet on 29 May 1792 that the
Americans were preparing to "force" the conclusion of the New York
treaty onto the Creeks. He was having trouble with Alexander in calling
a Council of the Creeks, Cherokee, Chickasaw, and Choctaw to conclude an alliance with Spain to defend the Indian lands. Alexander kept
putting him off and said the meeting could not come before September
because of the harvest. In his reply Carondelet deplored the "inaction
and irresolution with which McGillivray, under frivolous pretexts, like
that of a journey here, strives to hold the Creeks." He was adamant that
the Creek attack the Americans within the month.[82] Here again is
evidence that Carondelet was impatient with Alexander and hotly
questioned his motives.

Alexander had serious health problems and we first hear of his
complaints in a letter dated 12 August 1786. "The Fever has reduced me
very low & it has been succeeded by a breaking out over my body. I'm
apprehensive that I shall lose all my finger nails & tis with much
difficulty that I can take the pen in my hand to write."[83] Again in October
1786 he complains that "my being so long confined by sickness. . . ."[84] In
January 1789, he complains of having the rheumatism all summer and
was now "much troubled."[85]

An episode in the Spring of 1788 shows the humane side of his
personality. Colonel Joseph Brown brought his family down the Tennes-

see River to settle the land grants he had on the Duck and Cumberland Rivers which he received for his service during the Revolutionary War. The family was attacked by Indians at Nickajack and most of the family was killed except young Joseph, his mother, brother, and three sisters who were all captured. His 48-year-old mother and one sister were purchased by Alexander and brought into the white settlement, but he was unable to purchase the little brother or other sisters. He was ransomed some five years later from the Creeks. Young Joseph and his two sisters were exchanged about a year after their capture.[86]

Colonel John Pope, visiting Alexander at Little Tallasee in 1791, described him: "He is subject to an hibitual Head-ach and cholic, notwithstanding which his temper is placid and serene, and at intervals of Ease, quite joyous."[87] Alexander writing to Panton on 12 March 1792, complained that on his trip from Little River he was exposed to the snow and sleet, and then rain "brought on me a smart attack of the Rheumatism which yet remains in my arms."[88] In May 1792 he wrote that "my constant companion the Rheumatism has made a fresh attack upon me."[89] In November 1792 he complained that "the cursed Gout seizing me has laid me up these two months nearly. Every periodical attack grows more severe & longer in continuance, It now mounts from my feet to my knees & am still confined to the fireside. . . ."[90]

We first learn Alexander is seriously ill in a letter from Panton to Carondelet dated 16 February 1793. "It is with infinite concern that I inform your excellency that Mr. McGillivray lies dangerously ill in my house of a complication of disorders of Gout in the stomach attended with a perepneaumoney and he is so very bad as to leave scarcely any hope of his recovery."[91] Panton wrote to the Governor again on 20 February informing him that Alexander died at eleven p.m. on 17 February 1793.[92]

Panton, thinking Lachlan was dead, delayed notifying him of his son's death. Writing to him on 10 April 1794, over a year after Alexander's death, Panton described how he helped Alexander over the years and brought him into the company and by 1792 his compensation was $3500. Panton Wrote:

He died of complicated disorders of inflamed lungs & the gout on his stomach. He was taken ill on the path coming from his cowpens at Little River, where one of his wives, Joe Cornells daughter resides and died eight days after his arrival. No pain, no attention, no cost was spared to save the life of my friend but fate would have it otherwise.

Panton went on to say that Alexander's sister has seized his property and the orphan children had nothing left. Alexander had sixty-six slaves, three hundred head of cattle, and a large stock of horses. He had been a partner in Panton, Leslie Company from 1785-1788. Panton continued saying that he had pushed Alexander to greatness and the Company had followed and reached a height unattainable except for Alexander. He said:

> Aleck[93] is old enough to be sent home to school, which I mean to do next year, and you will see him. What I intended to do for the father, I will do for his children. This ought not to operate against your making that ample provision for your grandson and his two sisters which you have it in your power to make.
>
> They have lately lost their mother, so that they have no friends, poor things, but you and me. My heart bleeds for them, and what I can I will do. The boy, Aleck is old enough to be sent to Scotland to school, which I intend to do next year, and then you will see him.[94]

Their mother, Alexander's wife, died in 1794 and Panton vented his frustration on Lachlan. "Your daughters conduct is unjust and cruel in the extreme but I impute a great part of the business to the Villany of Durant & Weatherford who are their husbands." Panton asked that Lachlan write "Sophy and Jenny & Sehoy" a letter asking them to at least give up the slaves for the children.[95] The sisters had seized all his property, according to Creek custom, and had paid no attention to Alexander's will which left everything to his children. The girls lived with their mother's sister after she died, and later we find them living with their uncle, Sam

Moniac, who was probably married to the sister of Alexander's wife.

There is no evidence that Lachlan ever showed any interest in his grandson nor contributed one farthing for his upkeep and schooling for the four years he was in Scotland. John Innerarity Sr. first acted as his guardian and when he became ill, John Leslie took over those duties. Although Lachlan died in 1799 knowing his grandson was at Banff he made no provision in his will for supporting the boy. If Aleck was present and accepted by Lachlan as a member of the McGillivray family, he could have laid claim to Lachlan's estate. However, if the boy was off in another part of the country and kept invisible, no one would ever know the difference and Lachlan could, and did, leave his estate to his beloved young cousin, John Lachlan McGillivray, the 10th Chief. Furthermore, there is no evidence that Lachlan ever recognized nor offered help to his two granddaughters who were orphans living with their uncle, Sam Moniac. The Indian family ties were strong and they supported their relatives in need.

Arthur Whitaker,[96] an earlier writer on Alexander, was unduly harsh with his condemnation of Panton after Alexander died. Whitaker falsely accused him and wrote "there is no indication that he ever gave the children anything more than the coffee and sugar that Sister Durant promptly appropriated." Panton did send Alexander Junior to Scotland to be educated and paid for all his expenses while there for several years. He also tried to get custody of the daughters.

When Alexander died, he owed Panton $5824. Panton gave Lachlan McGillivray a breakdown of Alexander's debts—$5824 to Panton; $700 to Sophia; $1000 to Sehoy and his estate incurred a debt of $1531 after his death, making a total of $9055. Apparently Lachlan Lia never made good on his son's debts and Panton and the others had to "write it off."[97]

Pickett writes that Alexander was buried in Panton's "splendid" garden with Masonic honors. He goes on to give a detailed description of him.

> General McGillivray was six feet high, spare made, and remarkably
> erect in person and carriage. His eyes were large, dark and piercing. His

forehead was so peculiarly shaped, that the old Indian countrymen often spoke of it: It commenced expanding at his eyes and widened considerably at the top of his head. It was a bold and lofty forehead. His fingers were long and tapering, and he wielded a pen with the greatest rapidity. His face was handsome, and indicative of quick thought and much sagacity. Unless interested in conversation he was disposed to be taciturn, but even then, was polite and respectful. When a British Colonel, he dressed in the British uniform, and when in the Spanish service, he wore the military dress of that country. When Washington appointed him a brigadier general, he sometimes wore the uniform of the American Army, but never when in the presence of the Spaniards. His usual dress was a mixture of the Indian and American garb. He always traveled with two servants, David Francis, a half-breed, and Paro, a negro, who saved the lives of over a hundred royalists, in 1781. He had good houses at the Hickory Ground and at Little Tallase, where he entertained, free of charge, distinguished government agents, and persons travelling through his extensive dominions. Like all other men, he had his faults. He was ambitious, crafty, and rather unscrupulous; yet he possessed a good heart, and was polite and hospitable. For ability and sagacity, the reader will admit that he had few superiors. We have called him the Talleyrand of Alabama.[98]

Pickett obtained much of his information from interviews with many of the "Old Timers" of the Nation who were still living in 1850. He interviewed the old trader Abram Mordicai, who was ninety-two years old at the time, and had been in the Nation for sixty years. He told Pickett that Alexander was born at Hickory Ground, was slim in stature, 5'10" tall and died at Pensacola of poison.[99]

Over the years Alexander's health had continued to deteriorate and Governor Carondelet writing to him on 14 December 1792 said:

> I am infinitely sorry that you are tormented so frequently with Rheumatism. I have some famous powder invented by one Olivenza, to whom the King granted the exclusive privilege of selling it during his

life. The powder is a specific against galico, venerian complaint, without being disagreeable and without requiring a tedious regimen. Should you desire to try it, I shall send you some with the prescription or a translation thereof, on the understanding that it be not displayed to any physician.[100]

Panton writes on the death of Alexander, "he died on 17 February 1793, of complicted disorders—of inflamed lungs and the gout on his stomach. He was taken ill on the Path coming from his cowpens on Little River. . . ."[101]

It appears that Alexander's health had been deteriorating for several years and became more serious during the last year before his death. He frequently complained of symptoms related to syphilis and based on Carondelet's offer of the "powder," it is possible that he was cursed with that disease. However, these same symptoms may also be the results of Reiters disease. Also poisoning was rumored at the time of his death. In any case it is worth examining whether this rumor had a basis in fact.

The letter from Carondelet offering the "powder" for his "rheuma-tism" raises legitimate questions as to his intent and motive in wanting it kept secret. This powder was quaiacum, or quaiac, which came from tree bark in the West Indies. The wood is lignum vitae and comes from the guayacum trees (Guaiacum offinale) of Cuba, Haiti, Yucatan, and Dominican Republic, and other scattered regions of tropical America. Other species called by this name, but not true lignum vitae, are found in the Philippines, Argentina, Colombia, Venezuela, and Central America. The wood is very hard, heavy, and tough. The grain is very fine and twisted, having a greasy feel. The weight is from 72-88 pounds per cubic foot. The wood is commercially used today for pulley blocks, ship's propeller bearings, rollers, and mallet heads. In bearings it withstands pressure up to four thousand pounds per square inch. Guaiacum oil distilled from the wood is used in medicine as a stimulant and laxative, and in soaps and perfumes. The odor is a combination of tea leaves and roses. The wood yields 5-6% oil and it becomes solid at temperatures below forty-five degrees centigrade.[102]

It was originally used by native Americans to treat skin eruptions and since it seemed to help the natives, Europeans thought it may be the answer to the syphilis epidemic that swept Europe and it quickly became a very popular "cure." Mercury had also been used for a long time to treat skin problems, but for some reason guaiacum was more acceptable to the Roman Catholic Church than was mercury. It soon became known as "holywood" because of its use by priests in Rome. Importers of the tree bark became wealthy because syphilis was the primary medical problem for the first half of the 16th century. On some patients it seemed effective due to the sometimes latent symptoms of syphilis, but it never quite gained the reputation of mercury as a cure for this venereal disease.[103]

Dr. Milligen came to America in 1748 as surgeon's mate in General Oglethorpe's Georgia Regiment. He remained in America after his military service and became a prominent physician in South Carolina. In 1768 he was commissioned Surgeon to all the royal forces in South Carolina. He was a staunch loyalist which later drew the wrath of the rebels. Milligen left South Carolina in late 1775 or early 1776 and sailed for England, never to return, leaving behind his wife and children. He prescribed the "Jesuits' Bark" for "Intermitting Fevers" and in large quantities, all the "stomach will bear."[104]

The "inventor" of this powder is credited to one "Olivenza' by Governor Carondelet. His name was Oviedo y Valdes, Don Goncalo Fernandez De, who lived from 1478 to 1557. He was sent as a young man to the Court of Castile where he served as a page. He entered the service of the King in 1497 and was sent to America in 1513. He made several trips to and from America and spent much of his life in the New World. In about 1525 he published his *History of the West Indies*, and about ten years later his *General History of America*. He became known for his writings on medicinal plants of the New World, and wrote extensively on syphilis and its treatment. He was recalled in 1545, and became the official historian to the King of Spain. Oviedo "does not hesitate to ascribe the disease to native Americans and to affirm that the Spaniards contracted it during their intercourse with the women of that nation."[105] Carondelet also mentions the powder "is a specific against galico." Gallico was the author of a book on syphilis in 1532.[106]

The famous physician, John Hunter, writing in 1786, stated that he had tried using "guaiacum and sarsaparilla' in the treatment of syphilis. He found guaiacum had some effect but needed further study and that sarsaparilla had no effect at all.[107] Vogel[108] writes that guaiacum wood was also found in Florida and even though its use was a hoax it was used for nearly three hundred years in the treatment of syphilis.

The first outbreak of syphilis occurred in either France, Spain, or Italy in 1493-4. Some historians insist it was Italy although it was called the French Pox and later just the Pox. When the French Army invaded Italy in 1494, syphilis broke out among the French troops, and when they withdrew the following year, they spread the disease throughout Europe causing an epidemic. Early physicians and historians thought it was a new disease and some were convinced it was brought back from America by Columbus's sailors.[109]

Two creditable theories exist concerning the origin of the disease—one is that the disease existed under various names throughout human history and due to some factor such as social disorders, which increased sexual contact, or a transformation of the organism, it caused an explosive epidemic in Europe coincidental to Columbus's return from America. The other is that the sailors of Columbus brought it back from America where it became epidemic due to the lack of natural resistance of the European population. The Columbian theory first appeared in 1539 and received powerful backing from the contemporary historians, Oviedo and las Casas. Studies of old world bones over a five thousand year period found no substantive evidence of syphilis before 1493. On the contrary, bones studied from America for five hundred years before 1493 show apparent syphilitic lesions. Interestingly a search of European medical records before 1493 reveals no positive identification of the disease; whereas, after 1493 the medical literature abounds in the description of syphilis.[110]

Perez also offers evidence that syphilis was carried back to Europe by Columbus's sailors. He writes that "there is one of the rarest of books that describes how it came from the New World with Columbus' crew, the clinical picture of the disease, and its treatment, that solves the question of the origin." The book *Tractado Contra el mal serpentino* written by Ruy Diaz de Isla (1469-1562), a Spanish surgeon practicing at the Hospital de Todos os Santos, at Lisbonne, describes the three stages of syphilis and also gives the clinical picture of yaws and gonorrhoea found in Columbus' sailors.[111]

The origin and early treatment of syphilis remains to this day controversial. Some students of Chinese medicine claim that skin eruptions were recognized as early as the 7th Century and were treated with mercury. Others claimed the Crusaders returned to Europe with what was called leprosy and were successfully treated with mercury.[112]

The word syphilis first appears in the poem "De Morbo Gallico" published in 1530 by Hieronymus Fracastorius. Syphilis was a shepherd in the poem and was stricken ill because of his irreverence toward the Sun. Ilceus was also stricken for killing a sacred deer. The former was cured with guaiac, the latter with quicksilver or mercury.[113]

The symptoms of syphilis may come and go and lay dormant for months or even years only to suddenly erupt in the patient. The skin eruptions may vary from a rash to ulcerating sores. In later stages it can damage the heart and the nervous system.[114] Another description by Griggs[115] says the disease flares up and may be accompanied by "racking pains in the bones and joints." It may recede only to reappear months or years later striking the heart or brains, or nervous system, and results in paralysis and finally death.

John Hunter writes that with syphilis you "commonly find fever, restlessness or want of sleep, and often headach. It also gave the patient a "sallow look."[116]

"Rheumatism in many of its symptoms, in some constitutions, resembles the lues venerea; the nocturnal pains, swelling of the tendons, ligaments, and periosteum, and pain in those swellings are symptoms both of rheumatism and veneral disease when it attacks these parts."[117]

Jean Bernard Bossu, a French naval officer, traveled extensively in the lower Mississippi Valley, including part of present-day Alabama, in the years 1751 to 1762. He writes that the island of "Santo Domingo has become famous as the origin of the disease of Naples, or syphilis." However, "the Indian wife of a Castilian discovered a certain wood called guaiacum which can cure the disease."[118]

Reiters disease as a possible source of Alexander's problems needs to be reviewed also. Dr. Charles G. Roland, professor of the History of Medicine at McMasters University, Hamilton, Ontario, and Dr. W. Watson Buchanan, rheumatologist with the Sir William Osler Health Institute, Hamilton, Ontario, were consulted for their opinions on the illness of Alexander. Dr. Buchanan suggests[119] that the breaking out over his body and loss of his fingernails results from psoriasis. His recurring rheumatism could be Reiters disease especially of venereal origin. Other symptoms suggest infections consistent with Reiters disease.

Reiters disease is recognized in two forms—sexually transmitted and dysenteric, and commonly occurs in men age twenty to forty. Joint pain generally occurs in the large joints of the lower extremities; ulcers are common on the tongue and lips and the penis, with skin lesions of the palms and soles and around the fingernails. Arthritis may be mild or severe, internal infections may occur affecting the urinary tract and stomach. The symptoms may occur for several years.[120] Reiters also may invoke fever, malaise, weakness, urinary infections, arthritis affecting the knees and ankles, inflamation of tendons, genital lesions, nail shedding may occur, heart problems occur after several years, and the disease is found in younger men.[121]

Consulting Dr. James H. Halsey Jr.[122] as to the many health problems of Alexander resulted in his study of the limited information available. He consulted colleagues who were expert in infectious diseases, arthritis, and diseases of the skin and nails. He wrote:

> The best concensus that I can find is that Alexander probably suffered a chronic rheumatic disease causing arthritis which would have been the source of his pain. It is uncertain if his fevers were an essential part of his illness or represented simple intercurrent infections which must have been common in those days in the face of primitive levels of sanitation. Indeed, recurring infections could have been one underlying

cause of the arthritis producing the clinical entity known as Reiter's syndrome which can be a painful arthritis source of other bodily pains, particularly a sequel to recurring diarrhea and dysentery. Other disease possibilities in this general constellation would include rheumatoid arthritis, psoriasis (a skin disease often associated with rheumatoid-like arthritis and with special propensity to cause disease of the fingernails) and lupus erythematosus, a cousin of rheumatoid arthritis which has a greater propensity to attacking young women but certainly can occur in men, with lesser frequency than psoriasis, it can attack the fingernails, incidentally.

All of these considerations would seem to be independent of the primary question you were interested in, whether he was poisoned as the cause of his death. There is really no information about his final illness to support or contradict this hypothesis, as far as I can tell.

As you have indicated and we have discussed, some forms of mercury poisoning can cause acute or chronic smoldering lung infections.[123]

Mercury had been used for a long time to treat skin eruptions, and for this reason it was applied to patients during the European epidemic starting in 1493. It proved effective although its misuse caused untold suffering and death.[124]

Hunter wrote in 1786 that:

Mercury is administered orally or through the skin although sometimes it does not work through the skin, when then it must be administered by mouth. If one method does not work the other must be used until satisfaction is obtained.

Mercury may affect the intestines and stomach, but may kill if taken by the stomach. Many courses of Mercury which are absolutely necessary, would kill the patient if taken by the stomach, proving hurtful to the stomach and intestines, even when given in any form, and joined with the greatest correctors: on the other hand, the way of life will often not allow it to be applied externally. It is not every one that can find convenience to rub mercury, therefore they must take it by the mouth if possible.

The visible effects of mercury are of two kinds, the one on the constitution, the other on some parts capable of secretion. In the first it appears to produce universal irritability, making it more susceptible of all impressions; it quickens the pulse, also increases its hardness, producing a kind of temporary fever; but in many consitutions it exceeds this, acting as it were as a poison. In some it produces a kind of hectic fever, that is, a small quick pulse, loss of appetite, restlessness, want of sleep, and a sallow complexion.[125]

Hunter described a case history of mercury poisoning where the patient came down with loss of appetite, sallow complexion, loss of sleep, swollen legs, and painful joints. It may cause sores of the mouth and affects the intestines. Mercury often produces headaches and affects the mouth and gums, or the cheeks which become thick and ulcerate. The tongue, cheeks, and gums swell and the teeth become loose all in proportion to the amount of mercury given. The breath also becomes bad.[126]

Medical opposition to the use of mercury for the treatment of syphilis arose as early as 1496. Many physicians felt that quicksilver in any form was too toxic.[127] Mercury vapor inhalations were being used for syphilis as early as the first decade of the 16th century. If too much of the vaporized mercury is breathed into the lungs, an acute case of pneumonia will result—often in death in a few days.[128]

Dr. Milligen, of South Carolina, describes his prescription of "mercurial medicines" for venereal disease. It should be taken for two or three months. Some patients pass the mercury without any benefit and he had learned to use it with "Salt of Wormwood, or any of the fixed alcaline salts, with every Dose of Mercury." When the patient shows improvement he gives them "for eight or ten days a Decoction ought to be taken in large quantities, even until the Patient appears bloated with it, who is then to be put into a Sweating-Box once or twice every Day, if the Patient can bear it. . . ."[129]

In 1796 mercury was used for syphilitic herpes treatment on Spanish troops at Pensacola. Medicines were in short supply for the Spanish troops and sometimes they just ran out and had to await the next supply ship which may be months in arriving.[130]

From the foregoing we can see that syphilis, Reiters disease, and mercury poisoning had many common symptoms. Alexander McGillivray complained of rheumatism, but also several other symptoms such as fever, rash over his body, loss of finger nails, gout in his feet and knees, headaches, and almost a constant "misery" of pain and fever, especially during the last two or three years of his life.

John Hennen, M.D. a medical officer in the British Army, wrote in 1829 that American Indians often applied to Europeans for mercury to treat their disease.[131] Brady[132] gives a good short outline of mercury. "mercury is a metallic element and is the only metal that is a liquid at ordinary temperatures. Black mercurous oxide is used in skin ointments. Mercuric chloride, a white crystalline powder soluble in water and alcohol, is extremely poisonous."

Panton wrote twice describing Alexander's death by complicated disorders, inflamed lungs and gout on the stomach. Writing to Governor Carondelet he said that Alexander lay dangerously ill with "a complicction of disorders of gout in the stomach attended with a perepneaumony."[133]

This description is sketchy and draped in 18th century medical terms; however, these symptoms may indicate mercury poisoning. No doubt Alexander had gout and rheumatism at varying levels, but Panton's description of inflamed lungs and peripneumony leans toward mercury poisoning. Peripneumony does not appear in modern medical dictionaries, but Dunglison's Medical Dictionary of 1846[134] defines it. "Latent peripneumony is that whose symptoms are so obscure as to be recognized with difficulty. Known as false or Bastard Peripneumony. It resembles pneumonia."

Even if Panton knew or suspected that Alexander had been poisoned, he was not in a position to challenge the Spanish authorites. They of course would have brushed aside such charges. Also, his trading business was dependent on Spanish goodwill and he would have difficulty in proving such a charge.

Panton said that he spared no cost in trying to save Alexander. No doubt with his position and influence, he would have had the best physicians in Pensacola attending Alexander, including the Spanish medical officers. When he uses the word peripneumony, this seems to imply that Alexander's "inflamed lungs" were caused by some malady other than pneumonia. Mercury could have caused the "false pneumonia." Rumors were widespread in the Creek Nation that Alexander had been poisoned by the Spanish. These rumors may have been well founded since trouble had developed between Alexander and the Spanish authorities, especially before and after his trip to New York to sign a treaty with the Americans. The Spanish became distrustful and thought Alexander was slipping from their grasp and they could replace him with their Commissary, Pedro Olivier, whom they sent to live at Little Tallasee. He arrived in April 1791.[135]

Further evidence of the distrust the Spanish had of Alexander comes from a letter written by Las Casas to Floridablanca on 21 April 1792:

> A long time ago, I made known my lack of confidence in this leader of Indians, recognizing in the treaty which he made with the Confederated States on the 7th of August 1790, the manifest infraction of the one he made with us in Pensacola on the first of June 1784. I am also firmly persuaded that he is interested with the house of Panton in the Indian commerce. There is evidence that he was one of those involved in the Company of South Carolina for the projected settlements which McGillivray himself offered to oppose with all his forces. This makes me suspect McGillivray to be one of those men who have no other object than their own interests.[136]

Carondelet replaced Miro in December 1791 as Governor of Louisiana. Caughey[137] said that he was a most unlikely personality to deal with the Indians. He did not understand the border problems, was tempermental, impetuous, and took rash actions that threatened Spain's position with the Americans and Indians.

Carondelet to Alexander 6 February 1792 said that he was sending Lt. Pedro Olivier to reside among the Creeks and he was "particularly charged to promote & support the credit & authority you acquired among the Creeks, as well as to endeavour to oppose Bowles. . . ."[138] However, Carondelet really sent Olivier to spy on Alexander and his dealings, if any, with Bowles. Writing to Las Casas 22 March 1792, Carondelet made a powerful statement, "and finally to prepare for the Commissioner of his Majesty, Pedro Olivier, the means to win the confidence of the Creek Nation in such a way that the government can in the future get along without the support of McGillivray and be promptly informed of all that should occur among those Indians, at present more powerful and civilized than any other savage nation."[139] The only way Carondelet could accomplish this was to get rid of Alexander which he may have done in less than a year.

Carondelet had induced Bowles to come to New Orleans to negotiate and had promised him safe passage and a safe return to St. Marks. When Bowles arrived at New Orleans and talks did not go as Carondelet wanted, he clamped Bowles in prison and later shipped him off to Havana.[140] Bowles eventually escaped and returned to Georgia, but this reveals the unscrupulous personality of Carondelet where the ends justified the means.

Carondelet, sounding desperate, wrote a long threatening and almost insulting letter to Panton ordering him to do everything in his power to cause his friend Alexander to break with the Americans and the New York treaty. If necessary the Spanish would use Bowles to disrupt Alexander and the Creek Nation and also cut off his pension.[141]

The old Indian trader Abram Mordicai who knew Alexander and had lived in the Creek Country for over sixty years told Pickett that Alexander died of poison in Pensacola. Pickett traveled to Talladega, where Mordicai lived nearby, to get a personal interview and information from the old trader.[142] Milford, writing to Carondelet on 26 May 1793, said that he feared for Olivier's life since the "McGillivray family are circulating the rumor that he was poisoned."[143]

It seems unreal that the Spanish would have gone to such extreme measures; however, it is very significant that Carondelet tells Alexander not to show his prescription of the "powder" to any physician. Reflecting on this, it seems a strange request for the Governor of Louisiana to make. In his position of power he could have nothing to fear from its revelation—unless the prescription was an overdose of mercury, which any physician reading the prescription would readily detect. This "powder" Carondelet writes about may have been the white powder Mercuric Chloride which is easily dissolved in water. If it had been guaiacum, as Carondelet claimed, why would it need to be kept secret and not to be shown to any physician, when physicians in Europe had been widely using it for over two hundred years?

Another hypothesis of what may have happened is that Alexander had been using mercury for several years and as his condition grew worse on the trail, he increased the dosage to gain relief from his pain and suffering. His death has the elements of mercury poisoning from inhaling Mercury Chloride vapors. In any case, whether Carondelet prescribed the overdose or Alexander unintentionally took one, it so inflamed his lungs he could not recover, especially with his delicate and deteriorating health condition.

In fairness to Carondelet, he wrote to Las Casas on 9 March 1793 saying Alexander's death "could not have come at a more inopportune time, and will perhaps be the cause of the Separation of that Nation from the Spanish Alliance, and a war between it and the Chickasaw Nation, of which the Americans will take advantage to carry out their plans for settlements at Chickasaw Bluffs, Muscle Shoals, and on the Yazoo."[144]

This letter indicates Carondelet's quickness to cover himself by blaming his loss of control over the Creeks on Alexander's death. The Spanish had to look on almost helplessly as the Americans aggressively settled around and on the Spanish borderlands. The deterioration of relations between the Creeks and Spanish had been developing for several years, but the responsibility would fall on Carondelet's watch. No doubt he would be anxious to direct the blame in other directions other than himself.

Two very significant points are to be made—one is a letter from

Arthur O'Neill, the Commandant at Pensacola, to Governor Carondelet dated 5 February 1793. O'Neill wrote, "They are now free from McGillivray's policies." McGillivray died on 17 February, but O'Neill refers to him in the past tense on 5 February. How else could this be unless O'Neill knew that by the time Carondelet received the letter McGillivray would be dead? When O'Neill wrote the letter, Alexander had not yet taken ill on the trail, which he did on the 8th of February.[145] The other point is at a meeting held in Tennessee on 6 February 1793 between Governor Blount of the Southwest Territory and the Cherokee Chief John Watts. Blount asked Watts if he had heard from McGillivray and Watts replied, "he has heard lately that Alexander McGillivray had sickened and died at his own house."[146] Both of these events take place prior to Alexander's death!

This lengthy review of Alexander's illness and death results in several possibilities. He may indeed have had syphilis as other writers and historians have accepted, but the case is weak and Dr. Buchanan[147] believes he did not have this disease. Reiters disease is a more likely candidate as all the symptoms Alexander complained of can be found in this disease—especially losing the fingernails. However, mercury poisoning cannot be ruled out, even though both Dr. Roland and Dr. Buchanan expressed a negative opinion. The circumstantial evidence, outside the medical opinions, is strong, especially O'Neill's letter of 5 February 1793 declaring that the Spanish are "now free from McGillivray's policies," some three days before Alexander became ill on the trail. His death was from some form of "false pneumonia" and this well may have been induced by mercury vapor poisoning.

10

The Final Days

Greenslade writes that it appeared there was an "understanding" that Alexander's remains would be sent to Scotland to his father; however, it is the belief of Mrs. Emma Hulse Taylor, great grandniece of Panton and granddaughter of John Interrarity, that Mrs. Durant, his sister, had him removed to Alabama. It is very doubtful that Lachlan ever considered having Alexander's body shipped to Scotland, and Greenslade offers no supporting source for the claim.[1]

A letter from Milford to Carondelet dated 26 May 1793, in which he wrote that he and Pedro Olivier were not getting along and Olivier was now very cool and aloof to him. He also said "McGillivray and I feared one another, I was afraid of him because of what I knew of his disposition and the perfidy of his family, and he feared me because he knew what a considerable influence I have in general of the Nation, always ready to march at their head when ever necessary." He said the Chiefs required him to live at Tuckabatchee. He fears something will happen to Olivier since he lives so far away at Little Tallasee and "McGillivray's family is circulating the rumor that he was poisoned."[2]

Olivier also wrote to Carondelet on 11 June 1793 that it was rumored in the Nation that Alexander was poisoned by the Spaniards.[3] Charles Weatherford, writing to Governor O'Neill at Pensacola on 4 April, said after the death of Alexander "there is much confusion in the Nation at present."[4]

Captain Pedro Olivier on 14 June 1793 wrote to Carondelet that the Creek Indians were not about to give Milford the title that Alexander had held. Also, he reported again that rumors were circulating that the Spaniards poisoned Alexander at Pensacola.[5]

Milford, writing to Colonel Enrique White on 19 October 1793, said that a meeting took place at Tuckabatchee which he could not attend due to illness, but he sent his "spy" and was informed that Joseph Cornells spoke to the Chiefs and stated the Creeks had been friends to the Spanish only through the "treachery of McGillivray." They now saw clearly and they could not trust the Spaniards. The other Chiefs laughed at him and the White Lieutenant of Oakfuskee was the only Chief to approve of his speech.[6] The spy in this case was probably Alexander Cornells, nephew of Joseph Cornell.

Governor Carondelet queried Panton about papers that Alexander may have had in his possession when he died at Pensacola. Panton answered on 21 March 1793 saying, "He had no papers here saving a letter from his father and another from a friend in England. . . ."[7] This may have been true, but we know that in 1789 Alexander kept some of his papers with Panton. Pickett said that a copy of the 1790 treaty was written on parchment and was among the McGillivray papers that came into possession of William Panton when McGillivray died.[8]

Georgia took little notice of Alexander's death and the account of his death that appeared in the *Georgia Gazette*[9] was very brief. "Mr. McGillivray died about two months ago in Pensacola." His death received much more attention in Europe where *Gentlemans Magazine*[10] reported that, "In the latter part of his life he composed, with great care, the history of several classes of the original inhabitants of America; and this he intended to present to Professor Robertson for publication in the next edition of his history."[11] No evidence exists to indicate Alexander ever wrote this history of the Indians; however, if such a document could be found, a valuable addition would be made to the history of the American Indian.

Scots Magazine[12] reported:

At Pensacola, Mr. Macgillivray, the Creek Chief. There happened to be at that time at Pensacola a numerous band of Creeks, who watched his illness with the most marked anxiety, and when his death was announced to them, and while they followed him to the grave, it is impossible for words to describe the loud screams of real woes which they vented in their unaffected grief. He was, by his fathers side, a Scotchman, of the respectable family of Dunmaglass, in Inverness-shire. The vigour of his mind overcame the disadvantage of an education had in the wilds of America, and he was well acquainted with all the most useful European sciences. In the latter part of his life he composed, with great care, the history of several classes of the original inhabitants of America, and this he intended to present to Principal Robertson, for publication in the next edition of his History. The mss, it is feared, have perished, for the Indians adhere to their custom of destroying whatever inanimate objects a dead friend most delighted in. It is only since Mr. Macgillivray had influence amongst them, that they have suffered the slaves of a deceased master to live.

After the takeover of Pensacola by the Spanish in 1781, Alexander bought lots 17 and 18 from Antonio Balona. Lot 18 had formerly belonged to Henry Stuart, brother to John Stuart, the Superintendent of Indian Affairs. On these lots was a group of buildings including a house, kitchen, and store.[13] Alexander had purchased the lots to hold for William Panton who moved his trade from East Florida to Pensacola. Panton could not purchase property until he had taken an oath of allegiance to the Spanish Crown which he did in order to gain a monopoly license for the Indian trade. Panton lived in the house on the north half of lot 17. Alexander died at the house on lot 17 in 1793. Panton built his mansion in 1796 on lot 16.[14] Some forty years later, John Forbes Company was still trying to obtain a clear title to lot 16. It was originally granted by Governor White to Panton in 1781 and was 80 by 170 feet.[15]

One of his close neighbors was Dr. Juan Ruby, a black physician attached to the Spanish Army. Ruby grazed large cattle herds on the open

range between the Perdido and Mobile Rivers. He also owned a brick-
yard and other large tracts of land.[16] Lot 18 and one-half of lot 17 was
purchased in 1819 by Salvador Ruby—no doubt a relative to Dr. Juan
Ruby.[17]

Lot number 17, belonging to Alexander, was probably where Panton
buried his body in order to leave his own property "unencumbered."
When the new Santa Rosa County Courthouse was constructed on this
property, extensive archaeological work took place and no burial remains
were found that could have been the grave of Alexander.[18]

Sophia, the strong-willed sister to Alexander McGillivray, had his
body removed from Pensacola to Choctaw Bluff in Clarke County on
the Alabama River opposite the mouth of Little River where Alexander
had his plantation. It is believed that Alexander was reburied next to his
wife at Choctaw Bluff who died within a year of his death.[19]

Edward Forrester, a half-blooded trader among the Lower Creeks
and probably the son of trader John Forrester, wrote to Quesada, the East
Florida Governor at St. Augustine, on 28 March 1793, informing him of
McGillivray's death and saying that he was buried in Panton's "backyard
and garden."[20]

William Panton had built his brick mansion in about 1796. The
three story house was 34' x 102'. Panton had arrived in Pensacola from
East Florida in April 1785 and established his trade. Without the help of
Alexander McGillivray he never would have obtained a monopoly on the
Creek trade. In 1789 he expanded his business out of Mobile to the
Choctaw and Chickasaw. After Alexander died in 1793 his fortunes
began to slip. The Creeks had accepted the United States factory system
in 1795, creating competition for the first time. Panton became ill but
could not obtain proper care from the Spanish so he sailed for Nassau,
but died at sea on 26 February 1801. In 1806 one of the surviving
partners, John Innerarity, moved into the house and lived there until
1848 when it was destroyed by fire along with most of Pensacola. He had
the large warehouse, which was adjacent to the mansion converted into
a home almost as lavish as the original. The walls were brick and three feet
thick at the base and it had three stories. The converted warehouse

survived until 1915 when it too was destroyed by fire.[21]

Dr. James S. Herron, reminiscing in the Pensacola newspaper *The Evening News* in December 1908, wrote:

> To all students of Pensacola early history I strongly recommend as a valuable book *Colonial Florida* which would have been invaluable had the author given more dates and extracts from his authorities instead of ideas and deductions. He asks 'why Panton did not lament over the grave of his friend the celebrated Indian Chief Alexander McGillivray, quarter French and quarter Indian and half Scotch.
>
> Some years ago that question was answered to me by a grand niece of William Panton[22] who said the Chief's sister had recovered the remains to Choctaw Bluff, Alabama. General Haldimand, the friend and heir of General Bouquet, may have removed his body; but if he lies in an unmarked grave General Haldimand is responsible and not Pensacola's old residents.[23]

General Henry Bouquet was the new Commander of the Southern District and arrived in Pensacola in 1765 where he died shortly after arrival.[24] General Frederick Haldimand was appointed to succeed Bouquet and arrived in Pensacola in March 1767. He had been promoted to Brigadier on 12 December 1765. He arrived in Pensacola just in time to preside over the court martial of Major Robert Farmer, the Commandant at Mobile. In 1773 he was ordered to New York as Governor of that Colony and to temporarily replace General Gage as North American Commander while Gage took leave and returned to England. Haldimand had been promoted to Major General in 1772. He was promoted to Lieutenant General and was Governor General of Canada from 1778 to 1784. Both Bouquet and Haldimand were Swiss and were naturally drawn to each other and had developed a lasting friendship. They had entered into land investments and speculation as partners, and when Bouquet died without heirs, he willed his entire estate to Haldimand.[25]

Some of their land speculation was in West Florida and Haldimand resided in Pensacola for some time after his retirement. Between 1772 and 1777 he was granted seven thousand acres in seven different grants.[26]

Dr. James Herron became the owner of the original Panton property on 1 January 1873. He also inquired of Melanie Hulse, the daughter of John Innerarity who was the last surviving partner of Panton Leslie Co., where the grave of Alexander McGillivray was located, and she told him that Sophia had it removed to Choctaw Bluff many years before.[27]

After Alexander's death, Panton traveled to the Creek Country to settle Alexander's affairs and during one of these trips he had a marker erected at the burial site on Choctaw Bluff. The tracings from this monument for Alexander are very complimentary and the wording was probably Panton's own. It seems to express a sincere friendship between Panton and Alexander. This tracing was donated to the Pensacola Historical Museum in 1959 by Ms. Leslie Leigh of Mobile, a granddaughter of John Forbes Innerarity. The epitaph reads:

> *Here are deposited*
> *the Remains of*
> *Alexander McGillivray,*
> *Chief of the Creek Nation:*
> *A Dignity not derived from his ancestors*
> *but conferred by the suffrages of his Countrymen,*
> *as the Reward of exalted merit;*
> *and dictated by a confidence,*
> *(which, during an active administration of nine*
> *years, he never disappointed)*
> *in his zeal and ability to promote their Interests.*
> *His mind,*
> *though fettered in early life by the Prejudices*
> *attached to the ruder Stages of Society,*
> *was wrong, expanded, liberal, and well-informed*
> *He afforded*
> *the rare Example of an aboriginal American*
> *acquainted with the Learning of Ancient and Modern*
> *Europe,*

and eager in the Attainment of Knowledge,

In Private Life,

Hospitable, Generous, Kind, and Benevolent;

he was beloved by his Friends,

respected and esteemed by his acquaintances.

In his Public Character,

influenced by no other Views than those suggested by

the purest and most disinterested Patriotism,

he was revered by his own People,

and held in the highest Estimation by Foreign Powers,

Reader!

whosoever thou art

disdain not to mingle thy tears with those of the

untutored natives of these wilds;

but pay thy sad tribute

to the Memory of

an Honest Man, and Patriot Chief.

This Monument

was erected at the Desire of the Creek Nation

and in Testimony of a Friendship, which terminated

but with the Life of their beloved Chief,

By William Panton, Esy.

1794[28]

No evidence of the grave can be found today at Choctaw Bluff. Time has erased all traces or it may have washed into the river.

Timothy Barnard, a Chief of the Lower Creeks, wrote to James Seagrove on 26 March 1793 adding one small but significant footnote to Alexander's death. "He was interred in Mr. Panton's garden, as the Dons would not admit of his being laid in their burying ground."[29] Spanish officials had used Alexander relentlessly for their own purposes, but he was not good enough—a mestizo—to be buried in "their" cemetery.

Alexander's will, which was quickly written and witnessed at his death bed, left his property to his children in equal parts. His wives should receive "but little." His will was taken on 16 February and he asked that Panton and Forbes be the executors. Dr. Thomas Blair was the attending physician.[30]

Some highly romanticized descriptions of Alexander have been written which bear little truth of the man. One of these is *Alexander McGillivray, Emperor of the Creeks* by Carolyn Thomas Foreman[31] using Pickett plus her own embellishments. Others, writing more recently, are unusually harsh in their description. Florette Henri writes, "Here was the Creek Chief, cadaverous, sickly, nervous, depressed, indolent, and hating trouble or violence; very rich, capable and powerful, but aloof and lonely; an armchair general who did not inspire loyalty among the troops; an educated half-Indian living in two worlds and fitting neither of them"[32] It would be difficult to come up with more negatives than that about anyone, and many of these Alexander did not deserve.

Alexander had three children by his wife that lived at Little Tallasee. He later had another wife who lived at his home on Little River in Baldwin County. There were no known children from this union.

William Eustis had inquired of Benjamin Hawkins of Alexander's children, and Hawkins replied on 27 August 1809,

> The family of the late General Alexander McGillivray are no longer in a situation to be benefited by your friendly inquiries. The youngest of the two daughters is fourteen or fifteen years old[33] and has an Indian husband. On my arrival in this agency[34] I made inquiry after these children. I found the General had left three only, one boy and two girls, which he had by a well informed and well disposed half breed woman of the name of Mcrae, who died not long after the General. The children were left in the care of Sam Manawa[35] a very wealthy half breed, their uncle. Mr. Panton of Pensacola of the house of Panton, Leslie & Co. sent the boy to Scotland to be educated where he died. I intended to bring up the daughters under my own roof, to fit them for acts of usefulness, and particularly to fit them to be instrumental in civilizing their brethren, but their family did not accord with the idea and the

custom of the Nation forced it otherwise.

The General left behind him a considerable property in negroes, horses and cattle, little of which went to his children. According to the custom of this nation a man's children have no claim to his property, it belonging to his relations on the maternal line, and they seize upon it, as was the case in this instance. Mrs. Durand and Mrs. Weatherford, the first a sister and the other a maternal sister only, took possession of the greatest part of the property and have destroyed the stock of horses and cattle. The former or her sons have made way with all the negroes they possessed themselves of. Mr. David Tate, a son of the maternal sister, has possession of his mother. He was educated in Scotland, he lives on the Alabama within this agency, is careful and conducts himself well.[36]

Lizzy and Peggy, daughters of Alexander, may not have wanted to live with Hawkins. Sometime after 1801, John Forbes had sent some goods and presents to the girls being delivered by Daniel McGillivray. Daniel wrote[37] to Forbes that "they do not thank you for your kindness."

Daniel McGillivray had a different opinion of Tate. Writing to Panton on 28 September 1799 and again on 27 July 1800, he said the "Wind family" had taken all the cattle and were now taking the negroes. He thought Mrs. Durant had sent her relatives and "Mr. David Tate I have no manner of confidence in him, he is like the rest a grasping what he can."[38] Daniel at times was the overseer of Alexander's "cowpens" on the lower Alabama at Little River in Baldwin County.

David Tate writing to David Moniac on 23 April 1822, said that he was making arrangements for his homecoming from West Point and mentioned Moniac's uncles William and John Weatherford. Tate addressed the letter as "Dear Nephew."[39] Moniac was the first Indian graduate from West Point. Hawkins is our only source for the name of Alexander's wife who lived at Little Tallasee and Hickory Ground. She was a half-blooded woman named "Mcrae." In 1796 he wrote that the two daughters, Margaret (Peggy) and Elizabeth (Lizzy), were living with Sam Mac-nac, a half-blooded uncle.[40]

Hawkins repeatedly had trouble with the correct name—Moniac—

substituting "Macnac" or "Mcrae" and even "Menawa." Writing to
William Eustis on 21 April 1810 and again on 6 April 1812, he
mentioned "Sam Macrae as a wealthy half-breed" who had a tavern on
the post road at "Kettoma Creek."[41]

Hawkins had written earlier to Eustis on 27 August 1809 and
discussed the condition he found Alexander's daughters—"which he had
by a well informed and well disposed half breed woman of the name
Macrae, who died not long after the General. The children were left in
care of Sam Menawa, a very wealthy half-breed, their uncle."[42] In all these
errors, Hawkins obviously meant Moniac. The "Macrae" woman was
Sam Moniac's sister who was married to Alexander. Menawa was
another Creek Chief unrelated to Moniac. The historian Halbert discussing the descendants of Sehoy mentions "Moniac or MacNae".[43]

Sehoy III, the daughter of Lachlan McGillivray's Indian wife, Sehoy
II, was raised in the home of Jacob Moniac, Alexander McGillivray's
trusted friend and interpreter for many years. Woodward wrote that
"Moniac was a Hollander and the father of Sam Moniac" and that Sehoy
III was "brought up in her early days by the father of Sam Moniac."[44]

We first hear of Jacob Moniac when David Taitt, the Creek Agent,
visited the Upper Creeks in the spring of 1772 and used "Jacob Monthack"
as an interpreter.[45] The Georgia Council in 1774 records that "Moniack
the Indian interpreter" had agreed to return to the Creek Country and
continue there in order to collect information on the Indians and send it
to the Council from time to time, for which the Governor had promised
him fifty pounds.[46] Jacob could not write and signed his name with the
customary mark.

Jacob Moniac's daughter, we do not know her name, was married to
Alexander McGillivray making Jacob his father-in-law[47] and Sam his
brother-in-law. This relationship could well have been the reason Sehoy
III was raised in their home. The uncle in the family had substantial
responsibility for his nieces and nephews especially in the early years.
Jacob, the uncle, had taken in Sehoy to be raised in his household. We see
this again when Hawkins wrote that Alexander's two daughters, Peggy
and Lizzy, were living with their uncle Sam Moniac in 1799.[48]

It is some ten years later in 1784 before we hear of Jacob again when Alexander sends him as a messenger to McLatchey, a partner in Panton Leslie Co.[49] Alexander on 4 April 1787 informed O'Neill that "Moniac his interpreter is dead of a dry bellyache. He was a just & faithful man in his place. I shall never have such another again."[50] Alexander could not speak nor understand the Muscogee language and required a reliable interpreter which he apparently had found in Jacob Moniac.

Alexander, writing to O'Neill in 1788, mentions "Young Moniac"[51] obviously referring to Sam. Sam accompanied Alexander to New York in 1790 and signed the treaty with his mark as "Totkeshajou or Samoniac."[52] In 1799 Hawkins wrote that Sam lived at Tuskegee[53] where he had a large number of cattle and calves. He noted that the Tuskegee had lost their language and speak Muscogee.[54] The 1832 Creek census[55] lists "Samuel Manack" of Tuskegee Town with two males, one female and no slaves in his household. Tuskegee town removed after the Fort Jackson treaty in 1814 to Macon County near its present namesake.

In 1803 William August Bowles had become such a threat to the Spaniards that they offered 4500 pesos for his capture. At a Council held at Tukabatchee, Bowles was seized by the Alibama Chief Topalco, Sam Moniac, and Chief Nonenthe Mathla and a small party of warriors. Bowles was taken downriver to Mobile and on to New Orleans. The record indicates only 1500 pesos were ever paid, with 1200 going to the three chiefs and the remaining 300 divided among the warriors. In the fall of 1803 Opayo Micco, Speaker of the Creeks, went to Pensacola and complained that the other chiefs who had helped capture, confine and deliver Bowles had never received any pay. Governor Folch claimed ignorance and Opayo Micco became upset and Folch promised to do everything possible to get the reward. Despite the promise, no record could be found where the Spaniards lived up to their word.[56]

A deposition by Moniac on 2 August 1813 says the Prophet Francis is his brother-in-law and that the peaceful Indians were being forced by High Headed Jim to join the hostiles. His houses on Little River had been burned and his cattle stolen. The "two daughters of the late Gen. McGillivray had been induced to join them to save their property."[57]

Hawkins writing to John Armstrong on 28 June 1813 recounts some of the ravages of the war and says Sam's "brother, his brother in marriage and his son actually burnt his houses and destroyed much of his property."[58] The brother was John Moniac and the brother-in-law was Josiah Francis the Prophet.[59]

Brannon writes that his way station was on Pinchona Creek (near present Montgomery) and was the first licensed stopping place out of the State of Georgia in present Alabama at that time. He was forced to give up his property in 1814 after the treaty of Fort Jackson.[60]

Southerland writes that Sam's tavern was located on Pinchony Creek, a branch of Pintlala Creek which flows into the Alabama River about 12 miles below Montgomery. It was the first licensed tavern in Alabama and he operated it from 1803 until 1816 when he was forced to abandon the property and move down the Alabama to Little River, there to join his many relatives.[61] Tatum on his trip downriver on the Alabama in 1814 just below Choctaw Bluff writes "Improvements of Samual Manack a friendly half breed on both sides" of the river.[62]

On 27 April 1816 "an Act for the Relief of Samuel Manac" was passed by the House to compensate him for losses to the hostile Creeks during the war of 1813-14. His petition to Congress says he is a half blood and had for many years resided near the Federal road from Fort Stoddart to Georgia, and due to his hard work had amassed a "considerable property." He was the first to convey to the United States authorities the hostile intentions of the Creeks and consequently was marked for death and had to flee with his family to Mobile. He was assured by General Wilkinson that he would be protected and his losses compensated. His plantation near Little River was laid to waste, his houses and mills destroyed, his slaves killed or stolen, his cattle killed or driven away, and other property burned or stolen. He claimed a loss of $12,595.25.

Captain John S. Wirt witnessed the petition and stated that Moniac had served on two expeditions against the Hostiles—one against the towns on the Alabama and the other on the Indians on the Escambia. Both times he led a party of friendly Indians. Colonel Gilbert C. Russell, previously serving in the United States Army, witnessed that "Manac" did convey the intentions of the hostile Creeks to Judge Henry Toulmin, and he was an honorable man who suffered great loss during the war. He was noted for "integrity, truth and honesty." Lt. Colonel George Gibson witnessed that while he was commander at Mobile, Moniac came in with his family and remained there on rations from the Army as they were destitute. Sam could not write so he signed his mark to an authorization appointing Colonel Russell to act as his agent concerning the claim. His claim was granted in full and he signed the receipt on 4 May 1816.[63]

When Chief William McIntosh was assassinated in 1825, there was considerable consternation among government officials. McIntosh was the principal chief to sign the removal treaty and officials were afraid the treaty might "come apart." Sam signed a deposition, along with twenty-nine other Chiefs, on 25 May 1825 stating that they, the Chiefs, in session at the National Council, had determined to execute William McIntosh and that no one else, including the Creek Agent John Crowell, had anything to do with it.[64]

A letter from John Crowell, the Creek Agent, to the Secretary of War dated 20 November 1830, said that Samuel Manack held a section of land in Alabama as a reservation resulting from the treaty of Fort Jackson. Manack also claimed to have commanded a company of friendly Creeks during the Creek War of 1813-14 and was never paid for his services. He now wanted his pay.[65]

Sam Moniac is last heard from in a report by Major John M. Huger to Governor C. C. Clay of Alabama dated 11 July 1836. He reports on the activities of the hostile Creeks and that Lieutenant Moniac had led a scouting party along the Chattahoochee River.[66] Faust writes that Moniac is a derivative from "Manague, a French spelling of the Dutch word." It often appears in later times as Manac.[67]

Tarvin wrote that Sam was the son of Polly Colbert and William Moniac. Sam married Elizabeth Weatherford, sister of William Weatherford, and William married Sam's sister Polly Moniac.[68] Tarvin and Driesbach are our sources for William Moniac being Sam's father. No William Moniac appears in the contemporary records of the time; whereas Jacob Moniac was very close to Alexander McGillivray and

Alexander being married to his daughter also helped strengthen that relationship. She died in 1794 soon after Alexander. Thompson[69] also follows Tarvin on William being the father of Sam, although she did write that William "looked after Alexander McGillivray's business while he was away." However, as indicated earlier, this description fits the role that Jacob Moniac had with Alexander.

In support of this closing argument, John Linder, a wealthy settler on the Tensaw River and well acquainted with Alexander McGillivray, wrote to Favrot, the interim commander at Mobile, in 1786 that "Jacob Magnaque was father-in-law to Mr. Alexander McGillivray."[70]

Pickett said John Linder was a native of Switzerland and resided many years in Charleston as a British engineer and surveyor. It was there that Alexander McGillivray became acquainted with him, and during the Revolution assisted him and his family, including many slaves, in relocating on the Tensaw River. Pickett referred to him as Captain John Linder.[71] Halbert and Ball also repeat this event.[72] Governor O'Neill informed Miro on 15 August 1788 that he would have the Commandant at Mobile secretly watch Tarvin and the two Linders (father and son) "who correspond with Mr. McGillivray."[73]

Disagreements often arise between friends, and Alexander chastized Linder in 1788 for bringing suit against his overseer Walker over a mulatto slave that Alexander had purchased. He sternly rebuked Linder to behave.[74] Alexander had a bill of sale for the slave that had earlier been validated by the Creek Agent David Taitt.[75] In 1789 Linder was killed along with three companions camped at Murder Creek in Escambia County, Alabama.[76] John Catt, leader of the Creek party that killed Linder, was ordered executed by Alexander McGillivray. Linder in 1788 had been the unofficial mayor of Tensaw where he served as a Justice of the Peace.[77] Alexander, writing to Carondelet from Mobile on 15 January 1793, said that John Linder was dead and he was in that city acting as executor for Linder.[78]

John Linder Jr. was a courier of letters for Alexander, often to the Spanish authorities in Pensacola, and was referred to as "young Linder" in 1789.[79] A letter undated but written soon after Linder Jr's death, from

Daniel McGillivray to John Forbes states that John Linder Jr. was an uncle to David Tate.[80] The daughter of Sophia McGillivray Durant was identified in an 1801 Washington County deed as Sophia Linder McComb, but we are unable to unravel the Linder connection.[81]

Hawkins wrote that Alexander had three children—Alexander Junior (Aleck), Margaret (Peggy), and Elizabeth (Lizzy).[82] William Panton, writing to Lachlan McGillivray on 10 April 1794,[83] said "Alexander's daughters are too young to be moved and at the present time live with their mother's sister." When they were of school age, he decided to have them removed and placed in a school.

Margaret married Charles Cornell whose Indian name was Oche Finceco.[84] Charles was the son of Alexander Cornell, a half-blood, who was an interpreter and assistant to Hawkins and other officials for many years in the Creek Nation.

After William McIntosh signed the Creek Removal Treaty of 12 February 1825, he was assassinated by the Creeks on 1 May. A Creek delegation consisting of a large number of Chiefs traveled to Washington to protest the Removal Treaty. They were paid large sums of money totaling $153,500 plus $30,000 paid to their Cherokee secretaries, John Ridge and David Vann. Of this amount, Charles Cornell was paid $10,000 along with several other chiefs receiving the same amount.[85] The list of recipients was dated 25 April 1826 and signed by Thomas L. McKenney, the Indian Superintendent. Apparently the delegation was in Washington several months as the Niles Register noted their arrival in November 1825.[86]

McKenney noted that after Cornell was paid his $10,000 he fell in with some "blacklegs" and lost all his money gambling. He was so distraught he "went to his loft and hung himself." McKenney, in 1827, traveled through the Creek Country and noted how the people still mourned "Oche Finceco." They faithfully tended his grave and at the time some warriors were building a roof of split shingles over the grave. McKenney said he was "a man held in much esteem by his people."[87] Woodward said that Peggy McGillivray had died "long" before Charles hung himself.[88]

Peggy McGillivray Cornells died sometime after 1816 and before 1826 since she appears as head of household in the 1816 census of Monroe County, and Woodward said she was dead before Cornells hung himself in 1826.[89] She apparently died in early 1822 as Henry Goldwaite was approved as the administrator of the "estate of Peggy McGillivray deceased."[90]

Elizabeth had lived many years near General Woodward. He purchased the land of her and her son which was located in Macon County near present day Tuskegee. She was married to Captain Sam Isaacs, a Coosada Chief of some note.[91] Owen, using Pickett, wrote that Isaacs was born around 1765. He participated in the raids on the Cumberland settlements around present day Nashville. On one such raid 21 August 1793 his party murdered a widow Baker and all her family except a daughter named Elizabeth. She was taken to Coosada Town just across the Alabama River from present-day Montgomery. Charles Weatherford lived opposite Coosada and he ransomed the girl and later returned her to the settlements. Isaacs was the only Chief present to reject Tecumseh's talk at the Great Council held at Tuckabatchee in 1811. It is disappointing how bare the records are concerning Alexander's three children. Very little is reported and we do not know the ultimate fate of the two daughters . . .

Owen also reported that Captain Isaacs, his nephew, and three warriors were killed by the Red Sticks in June 1813.[92] However, this is apparently in error as "Nomatlee Emantla, or Captain Isaacs, of Cousondee" [Coosada] signed the peace treaty of Fort Jackson on 9 August 1814.[93]

Alexander's wife, who lived at Little River on the lower Alabama River, was Vicey Cornell, the daughter of Joseph Cornell. Joseph was married to a half-blooded Tuckabatchee woman and had five children— sons George, Alexander, and James, daughters Lucy and Vicey.[94]

Joseph was a white trader as early as 1753 and seemed to reside at Tallassee on the lower Tallapoosa River opposite to Tuckabatchee. Lachlan McGillivray mentions him as an Upper Creek packhorseman in 1756.[95] He became an accomplished interpreter and as early as 1772 he was referred to as the "Kings Interpreter" by John Stuart, the Indian Superintendent.[96]

Alexander McGillivray had a high regard for Cornell and used him as an interpreter after his trusted friend and interpreter Jacob Moniac died in 1787. Cornell traveled to New York with Alexander in 1790 and was the official interpreter to President Washington and other government officials.[97]

Joseph Cornell became the only interpreter the Creek Nation would use in their Councils with the Spanish. They had been confused at a Council in 1792 at Pensacola where the interpreter Antonio Garcon mistranslated directions from Governor O'Neill which resulted in some serious problems in the Creek Nation. However, Pedro Olivier, the Spanish Agent among the Creeks, had great respect for Cornell and complimented him in his correspondence to Carondelet. Olivier also reported that Cornell in 1793 lived at the Tensaw settlements on the lower Alabama River where he had his house and family.[98] Cornell was living at Little River as early as 1788 where O'Neill describes him as a "herdsman and trader."[99]

An entry on 15 December 1796 in Hawkins journal of his trip through the Creek Country recorded:

> Mrs. Cornell has four children and 4 grandchildren, she is a widow,
> the wife of Joseph Cornell, deceased, formerly interpreter. George, her
> oldest son is a trader, James is a lad at school. Lucy, her oldest daughter
> is a widow, her husband John Cane died at Tensaw. She has 3 children,
> Vica, the youngest, has one little girl.

Mrs. Cornell was a half blood.[100] "Widow Cornels" was listed in the 1832 census as living at Cubahatchee Town on the lower Tallapoosa and had in her family one male, one female, and ten slaves.[101]

It is reported that Vicey Cornell McGillivray married Zachariah McGirth in 1794, soon after Alexander McGillivray died in 1793. From Hawkins's description in 1796, it appears that Vica and Vicey are the same person. Vicey and McGirth had five daughters and one son. The son was killed at Fort Mims. Vicey was alive in 1813 but apparently did not live long thereafter.[102]

Joseph Cornell apparently was a just and capable man. Although he could not write,[103] he was the Creek interpreter to President Washington, the King's interpreter to Great Britain, and interpreter to the Spanish officials of West Florida. He obviously was very fluent in Creek, Spanish, and English.

Years before the Fort Mims massacre, a lonely small Indian boy, an orphan named Sanota, stopped at the house of Vicey McGirth. She fed and clothed him and adopted him into her family. When war came, she and her eight children were at Fort Mims while her husband Zachariah was in Mobile. Sanota had left to join the Red Sticks. During the slaughter of the people at Fort Mims, Sanota recognized Vicey and hid her and her children and later proclaimed them his prisoners and slaves. He took them to his home and sheltered them. He left to fight Jackson at the Horseshoe where he was killed. Vicey made her way to Mobile to join her husband.[104]

John Forbes, a partner and successor to Panton Leslie Company, was granted a large tract of land in West Florida by the Spanish government as compensation for his losses in the War of 1812. Heirs of Panton, John Leslie, Thomas Forbes, and Alexander McGillivray, tried to get John Forbes to settle accounts that they believed were due them. Alexander's heirs, his two daughters Elizabeth and Margaret, entered a lawsuit trying to recover what they felt was Alexander's interest in the company. However, they sold their claim to one Daniel Johnson of Savannah and George Edwards of Charleston for $18,000. Johnson and Edwards brought suit in Charleston but were unsuccessful. They then sued in Mobile, but again without success. They then brought suit in New Orleans where the court ruled against them. In 1830 they appealed to the Louisiana Supreme Court, but the Court ruled that only Panton Leslie Company owed anything to the heirs and their successor, John Forbes, could not be held liable. Alexander had been a partner in only Panton Leslie Company.[105]

The saga continued with A. A. McWhorter applying for administrator of Alexander McGillivray's Estate on 17 January 1820. On this same date R. P. Johnson also applied for administrator to the estate, but they both lost out to Harrison Young who was appointed administrator by the Montgomery Orphans' Court on 27 December 1820.[106]

Alexander Junior, or Aleck, was sent to Scotland by Panton to be educated probably sometime in 1797 or 1798. Panton paid his expenses and tuition for several years along with his companion and cousin, David Tate. David, nephew to Alexander, and son of Adam Tate and Sehoy III, seems to have been well educated. He had accompanied Alexander to New York in 1790 where he had been left behind with General Knox to further his education. He was 10-12 years old at the time and spoke "English well."[107] Knox reported in May 1792 that David was doing well and learning very well. His "morals are irreproachable."[108] It is not known when he returned to the Creek Country, but by 1798 he was in Scotland with young Alexander Junior.

Some writers would have us believe that Lachlan welcomed his grandson with open arms and spent many happy hours with him during his visits to Dunmaglass.[109] There is no evidence to support this and it is really unknown if Lachlan ever met his grandson while he was in Scotland. The sparse records indicate otherwise. We know that William Panton paid for Aleck's expenses and school tuition while in Scotland. Panton wrote to Lachlan in April 1794 saying, "What I intended to do for the father [Alexander], I will do for his children. This ought not to operate against your making that ample provision for your grandson and his two sisters which you have it in your power to make."[110] Lachlan apparently did nothing monetarily to assist either Aleck or his two granddaughters left adrift in the Creek Nation. Lachlan was at this time an "old man," comfortable among his family members looking after the estates and "mothering" and doting on his young cousin John Lachlan, the 10th Chief of the Clan, living at Dunmaglass. He was the senior member of the family and carried considerable influence and prestige in the community. For Aleck, a part blood "savage" from the woodlands of America, to appear on the doorstep of Dunmaglass would likely have proven an embarrassment hard to explain to his neighbors. It is doubtful Lachlan ever saw his grandson, even though he was only seventy miles away.

Aleck entered school at Banff, located on the eastern coast of Scotland just north of Aberdeen. This area was the homeplace of William Panton and his family. Panton would have been well acquainted with the school and a natural choice for him to make in sending Aleck there. If Lachlan was really interested in Aleck he would have arranged to send him to the same school in Inverness that his young cousin John Lachlan was attending.

John Innerarity Jr, son of one of the Panton Leslie Co. partners, may have been in school at Banff at the same time as Aleck.[111] This arrangement would have been reassuring to Panton by having someone to look after young Aleck who was indeed in "a strange world."

A grammar school was established at Banff by 1544 or probably earlier. In 1585 Bishop Cunningham signed a charter for the school and appointed a Rector to preside. By 1792 it became Banff Academy and John Cruickshank was appointed Rector after serving many years as assistant. He was Rector for over forty years, dying in 1830. Cruickshank increased attendance to 180 students and the school had to be enlarged. James Imlach writing about Banff in 1868 said of Cruickshank:

> Who within our recollection sent so many talented men into the world to fight the battle of life, with the sinews of high education and firm discipline to guide them through its devious ways, the brilliant result of which some of us have lived to see, in the successful and honourable career of many of his pupils holding high places in the Army and Navy, Church and State, and in the humbler walks of civilian life.

Charles Dickens and Robert Burns had a connection to the school.[112]

David Tate, Aleck's cousin, was sent to Banff with Aleck as his companion. John Innerarity Sr., living in London, acted as their guardian while they were in Scotland. He handled the expense payments for Aleck and received instructions and funds from Panton for their care. Innerarity wrote to Panton on 24 September 1798 that he was sending David home because he could do nothing with him. He had left Banff and suddenly appeared in London at Innerarity's home.[113]

Innerarity writes to Edwin Gairdner on 25 September 1798 and asks him to care for David and send him on to Charleston. Apparently he had engaged Gairdner earlier because he complained of the high expenses and would never have committed David to their care had he known of the high costs. Gairdner & Co. was located in Charleston with offices in London.[114]

Innerarity wrote Panton that he was removing Aleck from Mr. Robertson's care and would board him with Mr. Cruickshank, if he would take him. If not, he would bring him to London and find a suitable school for him.[115]

William Panton became seriously ill in Pensacola and wanted to go to Havanna for medical treatment, but Spanish red tape delayed the papers needed by Panton. Panton sailed for Havanna anyway and the authorities there refused to allow him to even land without proper papers. He had already been delayed by bad weather so he decided to go to Nassau. He died enroute on 26 February 1801 and was buried in the Bahamas at Great Harbour on Berry Island.[116]

John Innerarity Sr. had become ill in London and John Leslie, a senior partner of the Company, had taken overseeing of Aleck's education and well being. He wrote to John Forbes on 15 July 1802 that Aleck had come down with "consumption" known today as tuberculosis. Mr. Cruickshank had sent Aleck to London where Leslie took him into his home and placed him under the care of Dr. Wells, a London physician. Wells suggested Aleck be sent to the Surrey Hills south of London and Leslie said that is where he was at this time. It was hoped that the country air would help him recover.[117]

"Dr. Wells" was the famous physician-scientist of London, William Charles Wells. He was born in Charleston in 1757 to Robert and Mary Wells. His parents had emigrated to South Carolina from Scotland in 1753 where Robert tried his hand at being a merchant, but ended in failure. He became a bookseller, binder, and printer of a newspaper in Charleston. His father was a staunch loyalist and deeply instilled this loyalty into his sons.[118] Wells, at age eleven, was sent to Dumfries school, located in the south of Scotland, in 1768 where he completed his work in two and one-half years. In 1770 he went to Edinburgh University but returned to Charleston in 1771 and there placed himself as an apprentice to the leading physician, Dr. Alexander Garden.[119] He studied under Garden for three years and when war broke out in 1775 he refused to sign a rebel loyalty oath and prepared to leave Charleston. His father had already left and Wells arrived in England in the fall of 1775. His mother, brothers, and sisters remained in Charleston, but later followed the father to England.[120]

In the winter of 1775, he re-entered Edinburgh University to begin the study of medicine where he took his trials for a degree in 1778, but failed to graduate. He soon moved to London and studied under the prominent physician, Dr. William Hunter.[121]

In 1779 he enlisted in a Scotch regiment as surgeon and served in Holland. He soon found himself in trouble with his commanding officer who had him confined in the stockade for several months. Disillusioned, he resigned his commission. In the fall of 1780, he returned to Edinburgh and resumed his studies, receiving his degree in medicine.[122]

When the loyalists again occupied Charleston in 1780, his father asked him to return and straighten out the affairs of business that his brother Robert had mismanaged. His brother was the only family member to remain in South Carolina during the rebel occupation. Wells arrived in early 1781 where he found his father's property in ruins. Wells now became the printer, bookseller, and newspaper publisher in order to make ends meet.[123]

When the British evacuated Charleston in 1782 for the last time, Wells emigrated to St. Augustine with thousands of other Tories and arrived there in December. He had his press disassembled for shipment which arrived safely along with his other property and supplies. He set up a print shop and began publishing a newspaper under his brother's name. He soon became a captain of militia and manager of a theatrical group acting in some of the roles himself.[124]

Since the war had come to a close, his father again requested him to go to Charleston to look after his property. Wells obtained a pass from

Governor Tonyn of East Florida and embarked in the summer. Although the Americans honored the pass which gave him immunity from public arrest, it did not protect him from private suits. He was soon arrested over his brother's business affairs, but on principle he refused bail and remained in prison some three months. At one time a mob gathered to lynch him and at other times he was robbed and abused in prison.[125] Wells appealed for help to Governor Tonyn who sent Captain Wyllie aboard a vessel to demand his release. He was released and returned with Wyllie who misjudged the wind and tide, causing them to run aground off St. Augustine. With the ship breaking up, Wells lashed himself to a broken mast and hoped for the best since he could not swim. He floated for several hours and when the tide changed, he drifted ashore where he was soon rescued.[126]

His brother returned to Charleston to look after their business affairs and Wells embarked for England in May of 1784.[127] In 1785 he hung out his shingle in London, but his private practice was unsuccessful. After several years he received an appointment as physician to the Finsbury Dispensary in 1789 at the meager salary of fifty pounds yearly. His income had never exceeded 250 pounds and by 1795 he was in considerable debt, mostly to his friends, in the amount of six hundred pounds.[128] He remained at Finsbury until 1799. In 1793 he was elected to the Royal Society of Physicians of London, and in 1795 elected assistant physician to St. Thomas Hospital, becoming physician in 1800. In 1814 he was elected to the Royal Society of Physicians in Edinburgh.[129]

Around the turn of the century Wells became ill and suffered almost continuously until his death. He died on 18 September 1817[130] and was buried at St. Bride's Church on Fleet Street in downtown London.[131]

Wells is best known for his research on the formation of dew. He lived in a small house at Serjeants' Inn on Fleet Street near the heart of London. His research on dew was carried out in the garden of Mr. James Dunsmore, a merchant friend of Wells, who lived in Surrey about three miles south of Blackfriar's Bridge over the Thames. Wells walked to the garden late in the afternoon and returned early in the morning to his work at St. Thomas Hospital. When his illness progressed to where he could no longer go to Surrey, he continued his study closer by at Lincolns In Fields which is only about one-quarter mile from Fleet Street.[132] His study proved that dew formed from condensation. His theory, published in 1813, was not generally accepted until confirmed by John Aitkin in 1885.[133]

Another significant contribution by Wells was his early theory on natural selection which he published in 1818. Charles Darwin recognized and credited Wells with this principle some fifty years later.[134] Darwin wrote that "he [Wells] distinctly recognizes the principle of natural selection, and this is the first recognition which has been indicated."[135]

Wells was described as:

> an isolated figure, a sensitive man with unalterable convictions of duty, devotion, fairplay, and ethics, a scientist of unusual originality and attainments, and an able, observing level-headed practitioner who made many outstanding contributions to clinical medicine. Wells was poor and his medical practice was never lucrative. He was irritable, hypersensitive, introspective, and unwilling and unable to flatter. He was courageously outspoken in matters of injustice, and thereby, offended those in medical power. Wells was responsible, more than any other person, for the reforms and investigations into conditions of medical education and the restricting practices of the Royal College of Physicians.[136]

The Rev. W. Henshall in October 1799 criticized Wells and undertook "to expose the malignity, Jacobinism, and slander of one Dr. William Charles Wells."[137]

Wells was a cranky but outstanding physician-scientist of his day who conducted studies on dew, natural selection, color of blood, vision and optics, rheumatic heart disease, proteinuria, hematuria, edema due to scarlet fever, and scarlatina.[138] Apparently Wells practiced medicine only to the extent of making enough money to meet his basic needs which were few. He spent his time and effort on his first love—scientific study.

Since Wells was born in Charleston and spent many years there, William Panton, John Leslie and John Innerarity would have been well acquainted with him and his parents.[139] It is only natural that Innerarity and Leslie would have called on their fellow Scotsman to evaluate young Alexander McGillivray Jr. Wells may have seen young Aleck at his house on Fleet Street or at the St. Thomas Hospital. He sent Alexander to the nearby Surrey Hills, where he conducted his research on dew, just south of the Thames.

Wells gave Aleck only about three months to live. Leslie, in July 1802, was considering sending him to Nassau by "Captain Hyndman" on the ship *Mary* where the sun and sea breeze might give "him a chance."[140]

The *Mary* was owned by Panton Leslie Company. At the peak of their business they employed fifteen sloops and schooners carrying goods to and from England which also plied the waters of the West Indies.[141] Hyndman came over in September and brought John Innerarity, Jr. to America. There is no mention of Aleck.[142]

Certification of death did not start in Scotland until 1855. It did start earlier in England—about 1837—where Aleck died. Parish records are not consistent as some kept death records and others did not. The term Surrey Hills can be applied almost to the whole county and it was considered a resort area for Londoners to escape to.[143] A search was made of the Caterham Burial Registers and the Lambeth Burial Registers for Stockwell, but no record of young Aleck was found.[144]

Hoping that some record might exist that Alexander Jr. was admitted to St. Thomas Hospital where Wells was physician in 1802, a search of patient admission and discharge records failed to uncover such a record.[145] A search was also made to see if he left a will, but none was found.[146]

However, on site research by Mr. John Dagger of Tonbridge turned up the records on Alexander Jr. Although brief, they are revealing. An entry in the Chipstead Parish burial records simply states "25 July 1802, Alexander McGillivray from London."[147] He was buried in the St. Margaret's Churchyard (Anglican) and a search of the Chipstead Gravestone inscriptions at the Society of Genealogists found no mention of Alexander Jr.[148]

John Innerarity Sr. lived at Stockwell which was in the same neighborhood that Dr. Wells carried out his research on dew, just south of the Thames. Chipstead is just a few miles south on a ridge of hills (Surrey Hills) rising some five hundred to six hundred feet above sea level providing a sea breeze from which Alexander Jr. would derive some benefit. He lies buried in the Churchyard, lost in an unmarked grave, far away from his native land.

EPILOGUE

Alexander McGillivray was a giant among his people and for a decade outmaneuvered and held at bay the great powers of the New World—the British, the Spanish, and the Americans; however, he was slowly losing his country, not to great armies nor brilliant generals, but to the common man—the forest clearing farmer and settler that was relentlessly pushing the Georgia frontier to the west. The thirst for land would not abate until it reached the Pacific Ocean.

Contemporaries and later writers have described Alexander in all terms from a villain to a saviour, but it is best left to one of his contemporaries, the Cherokee Chief Turkey, writing to William Panton on 24 July 1793, where he expressed how sad he was over McGillivray's death and how he looked to McGillivray for advice and was always treated kindly by him. He had "tears" in his eyes as he wrote the letter.[149]

NOTES

Chapter 1

[1]Montcreiffe, 1982: 60.

[2]CCJ, 1993, Vol. 9:253.

[3]NLS, MSS 9854. McGillivray of Dunmaglass.

This is called the Farr manuscript and is part of the vast collection of Charles Fraser-Mackintosh who was a prominent historian of the Highlands in the 19th century. Part of his collection also resides in the Scottish Record Office at Edinburgh and in the Public Library at Inverness. It was the same Mackintosh family that handled much of the McGillivray family legal affairs in the late 18th century.

[4]The Gaelic Society, 1894, Vol. 20:29-31.

[5]McIan, 1845:110.

[6]CCJ, 1985, Vol. 8:154-7.

[7]CCJ, 1993, Vol. 9:282; McIan, 1845:110.

[8]Gaelic Society, 1894, Vol. 20:35.

[9]Tommashangan is about three miles northwest of Gask, one of the McGillivray estates, and some 12 miles from Dunmaglass, at a place known as Daviot. The Fairy's hill is also known as Dun Daviot or Fort of Daviot. (HRRS report 15 December 1990).

[10]Gaelic Society, 1894, Vol. 20:37-8.

[11]HRRS report, 22 August 1991.

[12]Gask is some nine miles north of Dunmaglass about halfway to Inverness.

[13]NLS, McGillivray of Dunmaglass. MSS 9854; Macgillivray 1973:23.

[14]NLS, McGillivray of Dunmaglass. MSS 9854; SRO, Papers Relating to McGillivrays of Dunmaglass. GD/128/26/6.

[15]McGillivray Testaments, SRO, HRRS Report 14 June 1990. Edward J. Cashin, Lachlan's biographer, writes (1992:269) that Lachlan's mother, Janet McIntosh, died in 1770; however, this is doubtful. A document written in 1743 and filed with the McGillivray testaments in the SRO indicates an effort to cease payments to Janet McIntosh, or her heirs, and recover sums granted her on her marriage to Captain Ban. This type action is usually not taken until the person is dead which indicates that Janet probably died in 1743 or earlier.

[16]HRRS report 15 December 1990.

[17]Macgillivray, 1973: 43-5.

[18]Moncreiffe, 1982:30.

[19]Ibid:33-4.

[20]Smith, 1970:29.

[21]Braden, 1958, Vol. 17:223; Dodson, 1990, Vol. 9:6-7.

[22]Macgillivray, 1973:113.

[23]Headlam, 1930:167.

[24]Filby, 1981, Vol. 2:1371-2.

[25]Ibid.

[26]Goose Creek was a settlement located a few miles upriver from Charleston. Most of the traders resided and maintained their warehouses here prior to and sometime after the settlement of New Windsor and Augusta on the Savannah River.

[27]Langley, 1983: 375.

[28]Salley, 1919:22-3.

[29]*South Carolina Gazette*, 18-25 May 1734.

[30]Ibid, 27 March - 3 April 1736.

[31]SCA, Legislative Journal 1721-23; PRO CO 5/425. Microfilm BMP D487.

[32]CCC, Willbooks, Vol. 3:283-4.

[33]SCHGM, 1922, Vol. 23: 132.

[34]McDowell, 1955: 248.

[35]Ibid.:283.

[36]CCC, Willbooks, Vol. 5:18.

[37]McDowell, 1955:6.

[38]GSA, Journal of the Board of Commissioners for Indian Affairs in the Province of South Carolina, 1753-1765. Microfilm. DR70, Box 12.

[39]HRRS report 22 August 1991; Macgillivray, 1973:113.

[40]HRRS report 22 August 1991.

[41]Filby, 1981, Vol. 2:1371-2; Coulter, 1949:83-4.

[42]Cashin, 1992:42-3, 323.

Cashin, the biographer of Lachlan Lia McGillivray, confuses the two Archibald McGillivrays as one and the same person. Archilbald of Daviot could not have arrived in Georgia in 1716 since his parents, John McGillivray and Janet McIntosh, were not married until 1719. This makes Archibald of Daviot the candidate for arrival in 1736 at age 15. Cashin also writes that he may have been a brother to Lachlan Lia and that nothing further is known of him. In fact he was a second cousin to Lachlan Lia and was married to Lucy McIntosh. He returned to Scotland and obtained the lands of Daviot. The other Archibald was older and a successful trader by 1735—a year before young Archibald of Daviot arrived in 1736 at age 15.

[43]HRRS report 28 March 1990.

[44]HRRS report 22 August 1991; SRO, Daviots Wadset 1751, GD 176/810; CCJ, 1993. Vol. 9:306; CCJ, 1982,

Vol. 7:325-7.

[45]Crane, 1929:125-7.

[46]Reese, 1974:259.

[47]*South Carolina Gazette*, 19 August 1732.

[48]Ibid, 23 December 1732.

[49]Easterby, 1951:117.

[50]*South Carolina Gazette*, 5-12 January 1737.

[51]Reese, 1974:265.

[52]Moore, 1964:32.

[53]*South Carolina Gazette*, 18-25 April 1739; 1-8 September 1739.

[54]Ibid, 13-20 November 1740; 4-11 December 1740.

[55]Ibid, 5-12 September 1741; 12-19 September 1741.

[56]Ibid, 19-26 September 1741.

[57]White, 1855:600.

[58]Braund, 1986:38-40.

[59]*South Carolina Gazette*, 15 August 1743.

[60]Ibid, 27 August 1744.

[61]Ibid., 19 October 1747.

[62]Ibid, 22 September 1746.

[63]Ibid, 23 July 1744.

[64]Ibid., 31 December 1744.

[65]Easterby, 1955:60, 306, 309.

[66]Pringle, 1972:808 9.

[67]Warren, 1977:86-7.

Chapter 2

[1]PRO. Georgia Loyalist Claims, Bundle 36, Reel 936. GSA. Microfilm DR 40, Box 46.

[2]Scottish Ancestral Research Society. Report B/53257, 1985; HRRS report 22 January 1990.

[3]Cashin, Lachlan's biographer (1992:6-7) states that Lachlan was born and raised at Dunmaglass, but there is no direct evidence to support this. Cashin bases his statement on Farquhar, the 6th Chief, bestowing "free and life rent" to Captain Ban, Lachlan's father. How-

ever, this does not mean residence on the estate, but means rents coming from the estate; so what Farquhar was bestowing was only the rent from Dunmaglass.

[4] HRRS report, 11 July 1992.

[5] Transactions of the Gaelic Society, 1894. Vol. 20:35-7; HRRS report 15 December 1990.

[6] Scottish History Society, 1915. ed. William McKay. Letterbook of Baille John Stewart of Inverness.

[7] HRRS report 5 December 1991.

[8] Owens, 1930, Vol. 1:113-5.

[9] Pickett, 1962: 342-6; Tarvin, 1893; Caughey, 1959:9-16; Macgillivray, 1973:49; Braund, 1986:40-1.

[10] Filby, 1981, Vol. 2:1371-2; Coulter, 1949, Vol. 2:83.

[11] Salley, 1945:79.

[12] Ibid.:41.

[13] Easterby, 1951:120.

[14] CCC, Willbooks, Vol. 3:98.

[15] SCHGM, 1931, Vol. 32:30.

[16] Shaftbury Papers, 1897, Vol. 5:190-2.

[17] Bolton, 1925:121.

[18] Moore, 1988:50; Lanning, 1935:180-1.

[19] CCC, Willbooks, Vol. 1:3.

[20] Coe Papers, Folder 11/569/2. South Carolina Address to the Lords Commissioners for Trade...., 29 January 1719, SCHS.

[21] Headlam, 1908, Vol. 17:524.

[22] Sainsbury, 1896, Vol. 10:60.

[23] French, 1875:13.

[24] Williams, 1928:17.

[25] Coe Papers, Folder 11/509/2. Letter from James Sutherland to Lord Granville, n.d., ca 1729, SCHS.

[26] Kingsbury, 1906, Vol. 1:499.

[27] SCHGM, 1931, Vol. 32:92.

[28] Brannon, 1935:52.

[29] Neeley, 1974, Vol. 36:6-7, 14.

[30] Cashin, 1992:13.

[31] MacLean, 1900:149-50.

[32] South Carolina Gazette, 24-31 January 1736.

[33] Ibid., 21-28 February 1736.

[34] MacLean, 1900:151-2; South Carolina Gazette, 24-31 January 1736.

[35] MacLean, 1900:160; Coulter, 1973:56.

[36] Easterby, 1953:355.

[37] Ibid.:324, 419.

[38] Ibid.:343.

[39] Cashin, 1992:17, 31-6.

[40] Lanning, 1935:194. Lanning writes that it takes three to four years of frequent usage to learn to speak a different language fluently.

[41] McPherson, 1962:351.

[42] Coulter, 1949:83-4.

[43] South Carolina Gazette, 5 October 1738.

[44] McPherson, 1962:184; PRO A013/36:564.

[45] Lyttelton Papers, Reel 2, WLCL.

[46] GSA, Journal of the Board of Commissioners for Indian Affairs. Microfilm DR 70, Box 12.

[47] Alden, 1966:99.

[48] Cashin, 1992:186.

[49] Coleman, 1978, Vol. 28:266.

[50] Candler, 1907, Vol. 8:523.

[51] Hamer, 1972, Vol. 3:550-1.

[52] Howard, 1965:97.

[53] HRRS report 22 August 1991.

[54] Coldham, 1980. Vol. 1:312-3.

[55] Coker, 1982:178-9.

[56] PRO, Lachlan McGillivray's Affidavit 21 May 1784. AO 13/36/560-1.

[57] PRO, John McGillivray's Affidavit 18 October 1783. AO 12/4/11-2.

[58] PRO, William McGillivray's Claim for Compensation, AO 12/4/10.

[59] PRO, William McGillivray's memorial. AO 13/36/583.

[60] PRO, William McGillivray's Will 25

January 1784. B 11/1112/303.

[61] PRO, John McGillivray's Will 25 February 1788. B 11/1162/286.

[62] SRO, Inventory of Miscellaneous Deeds and Papers. GD 128/23/4, item 1.

[63] HRRS report 22 August 1991.

[64] Easterby, 1962:201.

[65] Candler, 1907, Vol. 6:294

[66] Easterby, 1962:417.

[67] Olsberg, 1974:79.

[68] McDowell, 1958a:388.

[69] Ibid.:216.

[70] Lyttelton Papers, Reel 1, WLCL.

[71] McDowell, 1958b:7.

[72] Ibid., 1958a:518.

[73] McPherson, 1962:194.

[74] Spalding, 1989:101-4.

[75] Cashin, 1986:36.

[76] DeVorsey, 1982:58.

[77] Britt, ed., 1973, Vol. 57:139 GHQ.

[78] Lyttelton Papers, Reel 1, WLCL.

[79] McDowell, 1958b:7.

[80] Ibid.:103-4.

[81] Lyttelton Papers, Reel 1, WLCL.

[82] Hamer, 1982:44-5.

[83] Hamer, 1970, Vol. 2:266.

[84] GSA, Journal of the Board of Commissioners for Indian Affairs. Microfilm DR 70, Box 12.

[85] Ibid.

[86] McDowell, 1958b:56-71.

[87] Ibid.:38-9.

[88] Ibid.:72-3.

[89] Hamer, 1968, Vol. 1:284-5.

[90] Ibid:285.

[91] Lyttelton Papers, Reel 1, WLCL.

[92] Ibid., Reel 2, WLCL.

[93] Ibid.

[94] Ibid.

[95] Ibid.

[96] Ibid.

[97] Ibid.

[98] Ibid.

[99] Pringle, Letterbooks, Vol. 2:488.

[100] Lyttelton Papers, Reel 2, WLCL.

[101] Ibid.

[102] Ibid.

[103] NLS, MSS 9854.

[104] Moore, 1969:228.

[105] South Carolina Gazette, 7 October 1745.

[106] SCHM, 1964, Vol. 65:212.

[107] SCHM, 1973, Vol. 74:198.

[108] Jones, 1988:22, 55.

[109] Jerney, 1906:167.

[110] CCC, Willbooks, Vol. 9:403.

[111] Hamer, 1970, Vol. 2:25; Cashin, 1992:211.

[112] Cashin, Lachlan Lia's biographer, uses a manuscript in the Archives of the South Carolina Historical Society titled "A Sketch of the McGillivrays of Charleston and Connections," Folder 30-4. This manuscript was written in about 1930 by Hugh Swinton McGillivray, a descendant of Alexander McGillivray, the ship captain that died in 1763. Cashin uses this sketch to support his position that Alexander and Lachlan Lia were brothers. The author provides no primary source other than the will of Alexander and it cannot be definitively determined from this will that the Lachlan mentioned therein is in fact Lachlan Lia. Otherwise the sketch is based on secondary sources and contains several historical errors. It should be used with caution.

[113] Langley, 1983, Vol. 1:179, 182.

[114] Ibid.,:257.

[115] Moore, 1964:3.

[116] Holcomb, 1980:159.

[117] CCC, Willbooks, Vol. 8:3-4.

[118] Moore, 1964:220; Moore, 1969:304.

[119] Clark, 1981, Vol. 1:174; Vol 3:431-2.

[120] SCHGM, 1917, Vol. 18:85.

[121] Lyttelton Papers, Reel 2, WLCL.

[122]Ibid.

[123]Ibid, Reel 3, WLCL.

[124]Ibid.

[125]Ibid.

[126]Alden, 1966:99; Cashin, 1992:186.

Cashin writes that John McGillivray intervened to save Atkin and cites Atkin's letter on the incident, and the deposition by John Reed, when in fact there is no mention of John McGillivray in these documents or others relating to the incident.

[127]Lyttelton Papers, Reel 3, WLCL.

[128]Ibid.

[129]Ibid, Reel 3, WLCL.

[130]The Creeks were noted for their haughty independent nature. John Stuart writing to his counterpart, Sir William Johnson, of the Northern department on 30 March 1766, says that the Creeks have 4000 gunmen and are "the most insolent and ungovernable" in his Southern Department. (Johnson Papers, RC 1222, Vol. 7, PAC.)

[131]Lyttelton Papers, Reel 3, WLCL. Atkins earlier statement that "Estates have been got in succession for a great number of years in two births...," would appear to refer to two people—William and John or Archibald and Alexander McGillivray.

[132]Lyttelton Papers, Reel 3, WLCL.

[133]Coe Papers, Address to the Lords Commissioners for Trade, 29 January 1719. Folder 11/569/2, SCHS.

[134]Lyttelton Papers, Reel 3, WLCL.

[135]Ibid.

[136]Ibid.

[137]Ibid.

[138]Ibid.

[139]Ibid.

[140]Ibid.

[141]Ibid.

[142]Ibid.

[143]Ibid.

[144]Ibid.

[145]Ibid.

[146]Ibid.

[147]Ibid.

[148]Ibid.

[149]Ibid.

[150]Ibid.

[151]Fisher, 1990:344.

[152]Williams, 1930:299, 393.

Chapter 3

[1]Reese, 1974:259.

[2]Hamer, 1982:15.

[3]Easterby, 1953:419.

[4]Candler, 1916, Vol. 26:152-5.

[5]Braund, 1986:38-40.

[6]Fort Toulouse was located in the forks of the Alabama River at the junction of the Coosa and Tallapoosa Rivers.

[7]Candler, 1937, Vol. 36:295.

[8]*South Carolina Gazette*, 15 June 1747.

[9]McDowell, 1958a:129.

[10]Beckemeyer, 1975:54-5.

[11]Lipscomb, 1974:155.

[12]Braund, 1986:41-2.

[13]Ibid.:43-4.

[14]Olsberg, 1974:504.

[15]Moore, 1964:196; SCHS, 1755 Will of Patrick Brown, MSS File, Folder 35; CCC, Willbook, Vol. 7:364-5.

[16]Hamer, 1982:16; Stephens, 1742, Vol. 2:188.

[17]Bartram, 1942, Vol. 33:28.

[18]Easterby, 1962:304.

[19]McDowell, 1958a:129

[20]Cashin, 1986:104.

[21]Lyttelton Papers, Reel 2, WLCL.

[22]Candler, 1907, Vol. 8:522-4.

[23]Cashin, 1986:85.

[24]Davies, 1972, Vol. 12:72.

[25]Ibid.:78.

26Dumont, 1971:123.

27Ibid.:10.

28Mereness, 1916; 545-6.

29O'Donnell, 1973:37-8.

30Candler, 1937, Vol. 38:18.

31GSA, Court of ordinary wills. Microfilm DR 17, Box 24; Dumont, 1971:120.

32Candler, 1907, Vol. 8:315.

33McDowell, 1958a:326.

34Ibid.:342.

35Olsberg, 1974: 134-5.

36McDowell, 1958a:365.

37Cashin, 1986:103-4.

38Dumont, 1971:8.

39Easterby, 1953:419.

40McDowell, 1958a:128.

41Ibid.:326.

42Cashin, 1986:103.

43Easterby, 1951:121-3.

44White, 1855:600.

45Easterby, 1962:193-4.

46McDowell, 1958a:310, 518.

47White, 1855:600.

48McDowell, 1958a:129.

49Candler, 1907, Vol. 6:341.

50McDowell, 1958a:37.

51Moore, 1964:228.

52Starr, 1976:18.

53Braund, 1986:46.

54Rea, 1979:xiii, xxiv, 4, 71.

55Haldimand Papers, Reel 614, PAC.

56Ibid., Reel 612, PAC.

57DeVille, 1986:8-11, 14.

58McBee, 1953:155, 402.

59Ibid.:402, 432.

60Ibid.:460.

61Hamer, 1982:14.

62White, 1855:600.

63Hamer, 1982:47.

64Ibid.:62, 106-7.

65Pickett Papers, Folder 25, Sect. 7, ASA.

66Candler, 1936, Vol. 36:320-1.

67GSA, Journals of the Board of Commissioners for Indian Affairs, Microfilm DR 70, Box 12.

68Candler, 1907, Vol. 8:522.

69Romans, 1775:91.

70Bartram, 1942:25, 29.

71Rogers, 1979, Vol. 7:210. Laurens was a United States Peace Commissioner and was taken prisoner late in the war. It was proposed that he be exchanged for Lord Cornwallis, but the war had ended. (Smith, 1992, Vol. 19:293).

72Rowland, 1925, Vol. 5:125.

73Hamer, 1982:134.

74White, 1855:246-50.

75O'Donnell, 1973:27-8.

76Davies, 1972, Vol. 12:78.

77Ibid., Vol. 17:181.

78Cashin, 1989:106.

79White, 1855:98-103.

80Hays, 1939a, Vol. 1:108. Creek Indian Letters.

81Hamer, 1982:122.

82Georgia Gazette, 5 November 1795.

83Ibid., 1 March 1764.

84White, 1855:600.

85McDowell, 1958a:3, 338.

86Alden, 1966:55.

87Candler, 1907, Vol. 7:39.

88GSA, Conveyance Book U. Microfilm DR 40, Box 21.

89Candler, 1907, Vol. 8:187-8.

90Ibid.:226-7.

91Alden, 1966:98.

92Candler, 1907, Vol. 8:308-9.

93McDowell, 1958a:129.

94Alden, 1966:180.

95Zubley, 1989:31.

96Carlton Papers, M 356:5108, PAC.

97Ibid., M 357:5936, PAC.

98Rogers, 1978, Vol. 6:222.

99GSA, Conveyance Book U. Microfilm DR 40, Box 21; Langley, 1984, Vol.

4:127.

Chapter 4

[1]Candler, 1907, Vol. 8:522-4.

[2]IPL, FMC, 3429, Doc. 1, Sect. 18.

[3]Candler, 1907, Vol. 13:419.

[4]Granger, 1947:456-7; Coldham, 1980, Vol. 1:312.

[5]Ibid.:455-6.

[6]DeVorsey, 1982:106-7, 114-5.

[7]Ibid:62.

[8]Britt, 1973, Vol. 57:102 GHQ.

[9]Cashin, 1989:14, 20; Norwood, 1975:5-8, 13-4.

[10]Hoffman, 1985:266.

[11]Candler, 1907, Vol. 8:777.

[12]Granger, 1947:455-6.

[13]Hamer, 1973, Vol. 3:132.

[14]Savannah Gazette, 19 May 1763.

[15]This table was compiled from: Fortson, 1973; Candler 1907, Vol. 6, 7, 8, 9, 11; Coleman, 1978, Vol. 28; Hemperly, 1974:123-5.

[16]Savannah Gazette, 6 October and 13 October 1763.

[17]Ibid., 27 October 1763.

[18]GSA, Conveyance Books C1 and C2. Microfilm DR 40, Box 19.

[19]Ibid.

[20]Savannah Gazette, 23 February 1764.

[21]Georgia Gazette, 1 March 1764.

[22]Ibid., 27 September 1764.

[23]Rogers, 1974, Vol. 4:119-20.

[24]Ibid:144.

[25]Rogers, 1976, Vol. 5:271; Gregorie, 1950:531, 554.

[26]GSA, Conveyance Books C1 and C2. Microfilm DR 40, Box 19.

[27]Green, 1960, Vol. 17:183-94.

[28]Savannah Gazette, 14 February 1765.

[29]Ibid., 29 August 1765.

[30]Ibid., 10 October 1765.

[31]Ibid., 28 May 1766.

[32]GSA, Conveyance Book S. Microfilm DR 40, Box 20:76.

[33]Ibid.:111.

[34]Ibid.:413.

[35]Braund, 1986:38.

[36]Cashin, 1992:256. Cashin, Lachlan's biographer, mentions this episode but fails to mention who the mother was or the fact that Abigal was an indentured servant.

[37]Dumont, 1971:8.

[38]Ibid.:29.

[39]Ibid.:32.

[40]LaFar, 1963:109.

[41]Alden, 1966:293.

[42]Savannah Gazette, 17 June 1767.

[43]Ibid., 24 June 1767.

[44]Daniel, 1935, Vol. 19:1-16 GHQ.

[45]Savannah Gazette, 16 March 1768.

[46]IPL, FMC, 3429, Doc. 1, Sect. 16. Wills of John and Lachlan McGillivray, 1767.

[47]Ibid.

[48]Savannah Gazette, 8 July 1767.

[49]Hamer, 1976, Vol. 5:546.

[50]Savannah Gazette, 24 February 1768.

[51]Ibid., 25 May 1768.

[52]Candler, 1907, Vol. 10:566.

[53]Rogers, 1976, Vol. 5:690.

[54]Rogers, 1978, Vol. 6:222.

[55]Savannah Gazette, 14 December 1768.

[56]Georgia Gazette, 1 March 1769.

[57]Savannah Gazette, 3 May 1769.

[58]Georgia Gazette, 31 May 1769.

[59]GSA, Conveyance Book U. Microfilm DR 40, Box 21:144.

[60]Savannah Gazette, 12 July 1769.

[61]Langley, 1984, Vol. 4:127.

[62]Georgia Gazette, 4 October 1769.

[63]Savannah Gazette, 6 December 1769.

[64]IPL, FMC, 3429. Doc. 1, Sect. 18; McCrary and McGowan, 1972. History of St. Andrews Society of Savannah, Georgia.

[65]*Savannah Gazette*, 14 February 1770.

[66]Ibid., 21 February 1770.

[67]Ibid., 25 April 1770.

[68]Candler, 1937, Vol. 37:458-9.

[69]Davies, 1972, Vol. 3:119-20.

[70]GSA, Conveyance Books X1 and X2. Microfilm DR 40, Box 22:244, 300.

[71]Ibid.:853.

[72]Rogers, 1980, Vol. 8:349.

[73]Ibid.:477.

[74]"Roy" means red-haired, from Gaelic "Ruadh." (HRRS report 22 January 1990).

[75]SRO, Inverness Sheriff Court, SRO/SC29/44/14.

[76]SRO, Papers Relating to McGillivrays of Dunmaglass. SRO GD/128/23/5.

[77]HRRS report 30 March 1990; SRO, GD 128/23/4 Inventory of John Lachlan McGillivray Papers.

[78]IPL, FMC, 3429. Doc. 1, Sect. 18.

[79]SRO, Papers Relating to McGillivrays of Dunmaglass. SRO GD/128/23/5.

[80]GSA, Conveyance Books X1 and X2. Microfilm DR 40, Box 22:853.

[81]HRRS report 22 January 1990. Lachlan's biographer (Cashin 1992:256, 270) is misinformed on the meaning of "Dunie." He writes that Dunie was Duncan McGillivray, sister Jean's oldest son and that he accompanied Lachlan Lia back to Georgia in 1772. It was traditional to call the laird of the estate after the name of his home, in this case Dunmaglass—hence, "Dunie." Captain William McGillivray was Chief of the Clan and laird of Dunmaglass, and fondly referred to as "Dunie." It was William who accompanied Lachlan Lia back to Georgia. Also, it was Duncan McGillivray she was married to. Her son was Lachlan Jr.

[82]PRO, A013/36/583.

[83]GSA, Conveyance Books X1 and X2. Microfilm DR 70, Box 22:954.

[84]Dalrymple, 1978:155.

[85]Macgillivray, 1973: 43-5.

[86]IPL, FMC, 3429, Doc. 1, Sect. 18.

[87]Macgillivray, 1973:43-5.

[88]NLS, MSS 9854.

[89]Dalrymple, 1978:160.

[90]MPC, 1937, Vol. 1:32; Vol. 2:440

[91]*Georgia Gazette*, 5 January 1774.

[92]Ibid., 26 January, 23 February, 1 March 1774.

[93]Ibid., 2 November 1774.

[94]Ibid., 2 March 1774.

[95]Stokes, 1982:128-32; Collections GHS, 1901, Vol 5:1.

[96]Lyttelton Papers, Reel 2, WLCL.

[97]Hoffman, 1985:279.

[98]*Savannah Gazette*, 7 September 1774.

[99]Ibid., 19 April 1775.

[100]Ibid., 15 November 1775.

[101]Ibid., 25 January 1775.

[102]Candler, 1937, Vol. 38, Part 1:558.

[103]*Savannah Gazette*, 29 November 1775.

[104]Collections GHS, 1913, Vol. 5:21, 23.

[105]*Savannah Gazette*, 6 December 1775.

[106]*Georgia Gazette*, 24 May 1775.

[107]Granger, 1947:458-9.

[108]Candler, 1937, Vol. 38, part 2:19-20.

[109]Collections GHS, 1873, Vol. 3:219.

[110]Coleman, 1958:68-70.

[111]Chesnutt, 1988, Vol 11:140.

[112]Candler, 1937, Vol 38, part 2:78-80.

[113]Ward, 1952, Vol. 2:679.

[114]Granger, 1947:458-9; Collections GHS, 1913, Vol. 8:142.

[115]Coleman, 1958:119-145.

[116]Collections GHS, 1901, Vol. 5, part 1:138.

[117]Jones, 1874:19.

[118]Collections GHS, 1873, Vol. 3:253.

[119]SRO, Papers Relating to the McGillivrays of Dunmaglass. GD 128/23/6, item 23.

[120]Ibid.

[121]Dumont, 1971:32; Candler, 1909, Vol. 15:590-1.

[122]Hoffman, 1985:266.

[123]Coleman, 1958:65.

[124]Candler, 1909, Vol. 15:590-1.

[125]White, 1855:98-103.

[126]Carlton Papers, M341:135, PAC.

[127]Davis, 1979:5.

[128]*Royal Georgia Gazette*, 1 May 1781.

[129]Ibid., 24 January 1782.

[130]GSA, Creek Indians. RG 37-8.

[131]Ward, 1952, Vol. 2:837-40.

[132]Carlton Papers, M356:5104, PAC; Mitchell, 1984, Vol. 68:238.

[133]PRO, AO12/4/17; HRRS report 28 March 1990.

[134]Carlton Papers, M359:6475, PAC.

[135]SRO, GD 128/23/6, item 26.

[136]Ward, 1952:842.

Chapter 5

[1]Coker, 1982:179. (Wright in Coker) Wright indicates that Lachlan was a partner.

[2]Rea, 1990:42.

[3]Gage Papers, John McGillivray to Governor Johnstone, December 1764. WLCL.

[4]Rea, 1979:xxiv, 272.

[5]Ibid.:xxiv, 35, 38.

[6]Hamilton, 1952:296.

[7]MPC, 1937, Vol. 1:7.

[8]Haldimand Papers, Reel A613, PAC.

[9]Gage Papers, James Hewitt to McGillivray & Struthers, 27 November 1767, WLCL.

[10]Dalrymple, 1978:179.

[11]Ibid.:112.

[12]Ibid.:126.

[13]Ibid.:174.

[14]Ibid.:38. The Spanish Reale was comparable to the American Dollar.

[15]Ibid.:47.

[16]Ibid.:71.

[17]Ibid.:46, 90, 93, 164.

[18]Coker, 1982:30.

[19]MPC, 1937, Vol. 1:8, 32.

[20]Rowland, 1925, Vol. 5:113.

[21]Dalrymple, 1978:100, 119.

[22]Romans, 1775:332.

[23]An arpent is about .85 acre.

[24]MPC, 1937, Vol. 1:440.

[25]Ibid.:145.

[26]Hahn, 1983:4, 7, 39, 64; MPC, 1937, Vol. 2:440; Alabama Secretary of State, BFS records.

[27]Alabama Secretary of State, BFS records, :39.

[28]MPC, 1937. Vol. 1:145.

[29]Arrowpoints, 1924, Vol. 8, no. 3:48-9.

[30]Ibid., no. 5:66-8.

[31]Alabama Secretary of State, BFS records,: 64-5.

[32]U.S. Geological Survey, Maps NH16-1 Hattiesburg and NH16-2 Andalusia; U.S. Corps of Engineers, Mobile District, Tombigbee River Navigation Chart #18; Alabama Highway Department, map of Washington County, 1991.

[33]Hamilton, 1952:247, 330.

[34]MPC, 1937, Vol. 1:48.

[35]ASP, 1832, Public Lands, Vol. 1:730.

[36]DeVille, 1986:5-6, 15, 32.

[37]ASP, 1832, Public Lands, Vol. 1:594-5.

[38]Fabel, 1988:46.

[39]Ibid.:218, 223.

[40]Ibid:229.

[41]Ibid.:236.

[42]Ibid.:221.

[43]Carlton Papers, M350:2615, PAC.

[44]Ibid.:2665, PAC.

[45]Dalrymple, 1978:160, 167.

[46]Coker, 1982:177-191.

[47]McDowell, 1958a:152.

[48]Coleman, 1978, Vol. 28:266.

[49]JCTP, 1936, Vol. 12:69.

[50]Candler, 1937, Vol. 37:487.

[51]Mereness, 1916:550.

[52]Candler, 1908, Vol. 12:316.

[53]Davies, 1972, Vol. 12:160.

[54]Corbitt, 1938, Vol. 22:75 GHQ.

[55]Grant, 1980, Vol. 2:656.

[56]ASP, 1832, Public Lands, Vol. 3:36.

[57]DeVille, 1986:14, 16.

[58]Vidrine, 1985:367.

[59]Carlton Papers, M350:2933, PAC.

[60]Dalrymple, 1978:396.

[61]ASP, 1832, Public Lands, Vol. 1:594.

[62]Haldimand Papers, Reel A612, PAC.

[63]Dalrymple, 1978:170-3.

[64]IPL, FMC, 3429, Doc. 1, Sect. 16, Will of John McGillivray.

[65]Dalrymple, 1978:220, 224.

[66]Bartram, 1928:324, 341.

[67]This was the Shawnee town in Talladega County, Alabama, known today as Sylacauga.

[68]McDowell, 1958a:90.

[69]Candler, 1907, Vol. 8:539-46.

[70]Candler, 1907, Vol. 8:523.

[71]Coleman, 1978, Vol. 28, part 2:39.

[72]Rowland, 1911:516.

[73]Alden, 1966:213.

[74]Rea, 1979:xxiv.

[75]Starr, 1976:55-6; Collections GHS, 1901, Vol. 5, part 1:4.

[76]Dalrymple, 1978:302.

[77]Dalrymple, 1978:393; Clark, 1981, Vol. 1:561.

[78]Coldham, 1980, Vol. 1:20.

[79]Coker, 1982:47.

[80]Davies, 1972, Vol. 15:96

[81]HRRS report, 22 August 1991.

[82]Howard, 1965:97.

[83]Ibid.:110-1

[84]Ibid.:35, 45, 91.

[85]Ibid.:97.

[86]HRRS report, 22 August 1991.

[87]Dalrymple, 1978:190.

[88]Ibid.:176-7.

[89]Ibid.:397.

[90]IPL, FMC, 3429, Doc. 1, Sect. 16. Will of John McGillivray.

[91]Clark, 1981, Vol. 1:531.

[92]HRRS report, 22 January 1993.

[93]Hamilton, 1952:306.

[94]Vedrine, 1985:377.

[95]Rea, 1990:142.

[96]DeVille, 1986:868.

[97]McBee, 1953:24, 257-8.

[98]Carlton Papers, M350:2665, 2827, PAC.

[99]Hays, 1939b:59. Timothy Barnard to Governor Telfair, 14 August 1786.

[100]Caughey, 1959:239.

[101]Warren, 1968:70.

[102]Ibid.; ASP, 1832, Public Lands, Vol. 1:594-5.

[103]ASA, Halbert Papers, Folder 6. The treaty provided one section of land for each head of household, 1/2 section for each child over 10, and 1/4 section for each child under 10. They had to make their claims within six months of the treaty ratification date. In 1832 the lands were surveyed and a land agent sent to locate the claimants. Of the 1500 families on record, the agents claimed they could locate only 70.

[104]ASP, 1832, Public Lands, Vol. 7:33.

[105]Ibid.:25.

[106]Ibid.:7.

[107]Alabama Secretary of State, 1834, Land Survey - Pickens County.

[108]ASP, 1832, Public Lands, Vol. 7:73, 651.

[109]Ibid.:133.

[110]U.S. Land Sales, Noxubee County, Book 1.

[111]Noxubee County, Deed Book 128:605-628.

[112]U.S. Land Tract Books, Mississippi (N

& E), Vol. C-7:135.

[113]Noxubee County, Deed Book A:766, 830.

[114]U.S. Land Tract Books, Mississippi (N & E), Vol. C-6:137.

[115]Ibid., Vol. C-7:137.

[116]Noxubee County, Deed Book A:766, 830; ASP, Public Lands, 1860, Vol. 7:650-1.

[117]U.S. Land Grants, Pickens County, Book of U.S. Land Grants.

[118]U.S. Land Sales, Noxubee County, Book 1:104.

[119]U.S. Land Tract Books, Mississippi (N & E), Vol. C-6:137.

[120]Noxubee County, Deed Book A:832.

[121]Alabama Secretary of State, Alabama State Tract Book, Pickens County.

[122]U.S. Land Sales, Noxubee County, Book 1:116.

[123]U.S. Land Tract Books, Mississippi (N & E), Vol. C-7:137.

[124]Noxubee County, Superior Chancery Court, Book 1:280, 283, 316, 331, 420.

[125]NA, Armstrong Roll, 1831, RG 75, Roll A39; ASP, 1860, Public Lands, Vol. 7:73.

[126]Carlton Papers, M341:73, M349:2508, PAC; Dalrymple, 1978:338.

[127]LaFar, 1963:164. Willbook B.

[128]Carlton Papers, M349:2532, PAC.

[129]NA, Letters Received by the Secretary of War, Indian Affairs, M271, Roll 1.

[130]Rea, 1979:272.

[131]Filby, 1981, Vol. 2:1371-2; Macgillivray 1973:64-5; HRRS report, 22 August 1991.

[132]MacLean, 1900:166.

[133]Warren, 1977:86.

[134]IPL, FMC, 3429, Doc. 1, Sect. 16, Will of John McGillivray.

[135]Alabama Secretary of State, BFS records:12.

[136]Whyte, 1986, Vol. 2:89-90.

[137]IPL, FMC, 3429, Doc. 1, Sect. 18, Letters as to Dunmaglass Succession. William McGillivray to Lachlan McGillivray, 23 August 1769.

[138]Cashin, 1992:36, 267.

[139]SCHS, McGillivray Family Papers, Misc. folder 30-4. Cashin (1992:267) writes that Farquhar died in August 1770; however, as noted, he was alive and well in West Florida helping his brother John in the Indian trade.

[140]Hamilton, 1952:287, 323; MPC, 1937, Vol. 1:145.

[141]ASP, 1832, Public Lands, Vol. 1:730.

[142]Carlton Papers, M350:3793, PAC.

[143]McBee, 1953 :472.

[144]Dalrymple, 1978:184.

[145]ASA, Daniel McGillivray Papers, 1779.

[146]McBee, 1953:472; ASP, 1832, Public Lands, Vol. 1:874.

[147]Caughey, 1959:84.

[148]Georgia State Gazette or Independent Register, 15 September 1787.

[149]Pickett, 1851:388.

[150]Corbitt, 1949, Vol. 21:151 ETHS.

[151]Georgia Gazette, 19 February 1795.

[152]GHQ, 1940, Vol. 24:260-1. Indians to be invited to Pensacola.

[153]McBee, 1953 :288.

[154]Grant Foreman Papers, Panton Leslie & Co. Papers, Folder 4. Thomas Gilcrease Institute.

[155]Grant, 1980, Vol. 1:25-6.

[156]Ibid.:46-7.

[157]Forbes Papers, Reel 1, Daniel McGillivray to Panton Leslie & Co., 28 September 1799, MPA.

[158]GHQ, 1941, Vol. 25:169, William Panton to Governor Gayoso, 24 July 1800.

[159]ASA, Daniel McGillivray Papers, 1800.

[160]NA, Letters Received by the Secretary of War - Indian Affairs, M271, Roll 1.

[161]Grant, 1980, Vol. 2:432.

[162]McBee, 1953: 472.

[163]ASA, Pickett Papers, Folder 25, Sect. 8.

[164]Brannon, 1935:34.

[165]Woodward, 1859:109-10; Stiggins, 1989, Wyman notes.

[166]Grant, 1980, Vol. 1:30; Cashin, 1992:42, 74.

[167]HRRS report, 22 August 1991.

[168]NA, George Stiggins MSS; Brown, 1989:129, 164.

[169]Niles Register, 4 December 1824:223-4.

[170]NA, Letters Received by the Office of Indian Affairs, Creek Agency, M234, Roll 220:Frame 222. List signed by Thomas L. McKinney, 25 April 1826.

[171]Kappler, 1904, Vol. 2:341-3.

[172]NA, Creek Census 1832, T275, Roll 1.

[173]NA, Letters Received by the Office of Indian Affairs, Creek Agency, M 234, Roll 223. Names of Chiefs of the Creek Nation and the township and range in which each town in located, 1833.

[174]Waselkov, 1982:43.

[175]Bartram, 1928:355.

[176]U.S. Senate, 1835, Doc. 512, Vol. 4:24.

[177]House of Representatives, 1836, Doc. 278:313.

[178]Foreman, 1966:162-3.

[179]Corbitt, 1938, Vol. 24:471 GHQ.

[180]IPL, FMC, 3429, Doc. 1, Sect. 16, Will of John McGillivray; Kinniard, 1946, Vol. 3:28-9.

[181]IPL, FMC, 3429, Doc. 1, Sect. 16, Will of John McGillivray.

[182]NA, Letters Received by the Secretary of War., 1814-1815, M 221, Roll 63:6447.

[183]Carter, 1952, Vol. 18:11.

[184]Braden, 1958, Vol. 17:246.

[185]Moser, 1994, Vol. 4:79-80.

[186]Hall, 1904:20-1.

[187]Winston, 1927:43-4.

[188]MH, 1829, Vol. 25:386.

[189]U.S. Senate, 1835, Doc. 512, Vol. 2:244.

[190]Williams, 1930:288-9.

[191]Cashin, 1992:155. Referring to John McGillivray's will of 1767, in which John tacitly recognized his two Chickasaw sons, Cashin writes that nothing further is known of his sons Samuel and William.

[192]NA, Muster Rolls of the Chickasaw 1837 & 1839, RG 75, Roll A36; Hitchcock, 1930:169, 199.

[193]NA, Creek Census, 1832, T275, Roll 1.

[194]NA, Chickasaw Census, 1847, RG 75, Roll A36.

[195]Haynes, 1976:56-73; Carlton Papers, M341:214 PAC; Caruso, 1963:252; Bolton, 1932:228; Caughey, 1932:5-36.

[196]Haynes, 1976:98-9.

[197]Carlton Papers, M341:214, PAC.

[198]Ibid.:160.

[199]Kinniard, 1949, Vol. 2:291-3.

[200]Ibid.:301-2.

[201]Caughey, 1932:5-36; Caruso, 1963:252; Bolton, 1932:228.

[202]Kinniard, 1949, Vol. 2:306-7.

[203]Ibid,:308-9.

[204]Rea, 1979:312.

[205]Ibid.:314-5.

[206]Kinniard, 1949, Vol. 2:355-7.

[207]Ibid.:358, 364.

[208]Rea, 1979:314-5.

[209]Dalrymple, 1978:393.

[210]Clark, 1981, Vol. 1:559-61.

[211]Caughey, 1959:130.

[212]Ibid.

Chapter 6

[1]HRRS report, 1 January 1993.

[2]Coulter, 1949:83-4.

[3]IPL, FMC No. 3429, Doc. 1, Sect. 16, Will of Lachlan McGillivray; HRRS

report, 1 January 1993.

[4]Cockran, 1967:76.

[5]Rea, 1979:xxiv-xxv.

[6]Dalrymple, 1978:58.

[7]Rea, 1979:353.

[8]Dalrymple, 1978:76.

[9]Dalrymple, 1978:398; Fabel, 1988:232.

[10]Dalrymple, 1978:58, 84; Fabel, 1988:221.

[11]Davies, 1972, Vol. 2:105-6.

[12]Williams, 1930:xviii.

[13]Dalrymple, 1978:88, 94; Fabel, 1988:221.

[14]Ibid.:142, 152.

[15]DeVille, 1986:5, 14, 20, 24; ASP 1832, Public Lands Vol. 1:755, 862, 882; McBee, 1953 :472.

[16]Vidrine, 1985:359.

[17]Fabel, 1988:46.

[18]Dalrymple, 1978:148.

[19]Ibid.:169, 173-4.

[20]Ibid.:240.

[21]Claiborne, 1964:119-20.

[22]Haynes, 1976:62-4.

[23]Ibid.:88.

[24]McBee, 1953:321.

[25]Haynes, 1976:135-6.

[26]McBee, 1953:1-2.

[27]Ibid.:235.

[28]Ibid.:398.

[29]Ibid.:237.

[30]Ibid.:3.

[31]Ibid.:17. Bingaman's daughter was married to a prominent Spanish citizen of American descent, Stephen Minor, who for 20 years played an important role in Spanish-American affairs along the lower Mississippi River (Journal of Mississippi History, 1980, Vol. 42:26).

[32]Ibid.:21.

[33]Ibid.:471.

[34]IPL, FMC, No. 3429, Doc. 1, Sect. 16, Will of Lachlan McGillivray.

[35]HRRS report, 22 January 1993.

[36]McBee, 1953:34.

[37]ASP , 1832, Public Lands Vol. 1:422, 868, 879.

[38]MPC, 1937, Vol. 1:48; Hahn, 1983:6.

[39]MPC, 1937, Vol. 1:33, 50.

[40]Hamilton, 1952:285.

[41]McBee, 1953:204.

[42]Ibid,402-3, 547, 588.

[43]Ibid.:402-3.

[44]Ibid.:71.

[45]Ibid.:151.

[46]NA, Letters Received by the Secretary of War Relating to Indian Affairs, M271, Roll 1, Atlanta Branch.

[47]Ibid.

[48]Ibid.

[49]Dalrymple, 1978:131.

[50]Ibid.

[51]NA, Armstrong Roll - 1831, Choctaw Census, Microfilm RG 75, Roll A39.

Chapter 7

[1]Collections GHS, Letters of Joseph Clay, Vol. 8:174-5.

[2]Granger, 1947:458-9.

[3]Ibid.:460-70.

[4]GSA, Confiscated Property, RG 1-6.

[5]PRO, Commissioners of Confiscated Estates (sale of Lachlan McGillivray's property) AO 13/36/568-9.

[6]Macgillivray, 1973:43-5.

[7]Ibid.:49.

[8]PRO, Will of Captain William McGillivray, PROB 11/1112/303.

[9]Calhoon, 1973:500-1; Mitchell, 1984, Vol. 68: 235-6; Bull, 1991:304.

[10]Hutchinson's Island is a large island in the Savannah River opposite Savannah.

[11]PRO, Evidence on the claim of William McGillivray, AO 12/4/10.

[12]PRO, Affidavit of John McGillivray, AO 12/4/11-2.

[13]PRO, Memorial of Captain William McGillivray, AO 13/36/587.

[14]PRO, Deposition by William McGillivray, AO 13/36:583.

[15]PRO, Commissioners Decision on William McGillivray's claim, AO 12/109.

[16]Coldham, 1980, Vol. 1:216; PRO, Deposition by Lachlan McGillivray for William Harding, AO 13/35/302-4.

[17]PRO, Deposition by John McGillivray for William Harding, AO 13/35/306.

[18]PRO, Deposition by John and Lachlan McGillivray on the price of rice, AO 13/5/17.

[19]SRO, Papers Relating to McGillivray of Dunmaglass, GD 128/23/6, item 26.

[20]PRO, Affidavit of Lachlan McGillivray, AO 13/36/589.

[21]PRO, Affidavit of Lachlan McGillivray Jr, AO 13/36/564. St. Martin-in-the-field was located just off Trafalgar Square in the heart of London.

[22]HRRS report, 22 August 1991.

[23]PRO, Memorial by John McGillivray, AO 13/36/553-6. The actual sum of the list is a little less than the claim.

[24]PRO, Commissioners Decision on William McGillivray's Claim, AO 12/109.

[25]It has been explained that John and Lachlan Lia were first cousins. John was not the nephew of Lachlan Lia.

[26]PRO, Affidavit by Lachlan McGillivray on his gifts to John McGillivray, AO 13/36/560-1.

[27]PRO, Amounts paid to John McGillivray by Lachlan McGillivray, AO 13/36/581.

[28]GSA, Georgia Loyalist Claims, Microfilm DR 40, Box 46; PRO; Reel 936, Bundle 36.

[29]Gazette State of Georgia, 30 June 1785.

[30]Georgia Gazette, 7 June 1792.

[31]SRO, Papers Relating to McGillivray of Dunmaglass, GD 128/23/6, item 4.

[32]PRO, An accounting by Charles Graham on annuity payments, AO 13/128/566.

[33]SRO, Papers Relating to McGillivray of Dunmaglass, GD 128/23/6, item 6.

[34]Hunter, 1788: 13, 14, 18, 23, 70, 78, 80.

[35]HRRS report, 22 August 1991.

[36]SRO, Papers Relating to McGillivray of Dunmaglass, GD 128/23/6, item 5.

[37]Ibid.

[38]Ibid.

[39]JA, Crop report 1B/11/4/45, folio 157.

[40]JA, Baptisms 1B/11/8/14/, folio 1.

[41]JA, Inventory 1B/11/3/128, folio 51.

[42]JA, Inventory 1B/11/3/50, folio 65.

[43]JA, Inventory 1B/11/3/148, folio 121.

[44]PRO, the 1786 will of John McGillivray, PROB 11/1162/286.

[45]PRO. The 1786 will of John McGillivray, PROB 11/1162/286. For some reason John McGillivray felt very strongly that the annuity to his cousin Lachlan Lia be paid on a timely basis. He was saying that if current cash receipts from the estate was not enough to pay the annuity, then some part of the estate was to be sold for that purpose.

[46]SRO, Accounting of John McGillivray's will, GD 128/23/5.

[47]Inverness Archives, Burgh of Inverness, Register of Deeds, Document dated 19 October 1789.

[48]Ibid., Document dated 3 February 1789.

[49]SRO, Papers Relating to McGillivray of Dunmaglass, GD 128/23/5.

[50]Ibid.

[51]Inverness Archives, Burgh of Inverness, Register of Deeds, Document dated 3 February 1791.

[52]SRO, Papers Relating to McGillivray of Dunmaglass, GD 128/23/5.

[53]Ibid.

[54]McGillivray, 1985, CCJ, Vol. 8:154-7.

[55]Miss Marjorie was the daughter of his sister Jean Roy (HRRS report, 30 March 1990).

[56]SRO, Inventory of Miscellaneous Deeds

and Papers, GD 128/23/4, item 1.

[57]NLS, MSS 9854:264-5.

[58]HRRS report, 5 December 1991.

[59]*Edinburgh Advertiser* 26-29 November 1799; HRRS report, 5 December 1991.

[60]HRRS report, 22 August 1991.

[61]Warren, 1968:70; GHS, 1993, Early Deaths in Savannah, Georgia 1763-1803. *The Georgia Gazette Columbian Museum and Savannah Advertiser*, 21 August 1800.

[62]Macgillivray, 1973:113.

[63]Lachlan Lia's great grandfather.

[64]Legal guardian.

[65]Lachlan Lia's grandfather.

[66]Lachlan Lia's father.

[67]IPL, FMC, Court of Sessions Cases, Inverness-Shire 1855, Vol. 772; Court of Sessions Papers, SRO/CS 237/MC 23/37; Chancery Court, Service of Heirs Records, SRO, C 28/49/Folios 70-74.

[68]CCJ, 1992, Vol. 9:206-9.

Chapter 8

[1]Pickett, 1962:366-7.

[2] IPL, FMC, No. 3429, Doc. 1, Sect. 16, Will of Lachlan McGillivray.

[3]Candler, 1907, Vol. 8:123-4; Land Grants were based on how many children, slaves and indentured servants one had to work the land. It was an opportunity for Lachlan to obtain another 100 acres.

[4]Alabama Digest, 1956, Vol. 12:158.

[5]Fortson, 1973:134.

[6]Pope, 1792:46-52.

[7]Pickett, 1962:345.

[8]Caughey, 1959:13.

[9]Coker, 1986:24.

[10]IPL, FMC, No. 3429, Doc. 1, Sect. 16, Will of Lachlan McGillivray.

[11]Rowland, 1925, Vol. 5:89. Edward Mease was in the land speculation business with David Taitt the Creek Agent

(DeVille, 1986:15).

[12]Pickett, 1962:342-5.

[13]O'Donnell, 1965, Vol. 59:172-4; Caughey, 1959:9, 15; Coker, 1986:53.

[14]Moore, 1964:164.

[15]Moore, 1969:86.

[16]Jones, 1887:38.

[17]ASA, Pickett Papers, folder 25, Section 7.

[18]Milfort, 1959:158.

[19]Driesbach, 1874.

[20]Woodward, 1939:59; Kinniard, 1946, Vol. 3:108.

[21]Caughey, 1959:62; Corbitt, 1957, Vol. 29:62 ETHS

[22]Caughey, 1959:185.

[23]Corbitt, 1943, Vol. 15:97; South Carolina Gazzetter, 4 January, 1738.

[24]Caughey, 1959:66.

[25]Thompson, 1991:7.

[26]ASP, 1832, Public Lands, Vol. 4:385.

[27]Stiggins, 1989:31.

[28]Corbitt, 1949, Vol. 21:143 ETHS.

[29]*South Carolina Gazette*, 4 January 1739.

[30]Williams, 1930:317, 335-6.

[31]*Journal of Mississippi History*, 1953. Vol. 15:256-7, Lieutenant Minor's Trip over the Natchez Trace 1792. Edited by Hunter Ross.

[32]Holmes, 1964, Vol. 1:337.

[33]Brannon, 1974, Vol. 1:86-7.

[34]Neeley, 1974, Vol. 36:7-8.

[35]Rowland, 1932, Vol. 3:400, 475.

[36]Galloway, 1984, Vol. 4:124-5.

[37]Waselkov, 1982:48-9.

[38]Rowland, 1932, Vol. 3:316-7.

[39]Cashin, 1990:72.

[40]Vidrine, 1985:47, 57.

[41]Andrews, 1987:16.

[42]Brannon, 1957:153-4.

[43]*Baldwin County Historical Quarterly*, 1974, Vol. 1:96-9. David Tate was the son of Sehoy III.

[44]Tarvin, 1893:1-20.

45Meek, 1857:263-5.

46Meagher, M.D., McGillivray Family, Creek file, Folder 40, Thomas Gilcrease Institute.

47Milfort, 1959:198-202.

48Pickett, 1962:345.

49Grant, 1980, Vol. 2:556.

50ASA, Pickett Papers, folder 25, Section 7.

51Blue, M.P., 1937, ASA. Blue lived from 1824-1884. Alabama Town was founded in 1818 on the river bluff just below and joining present Montgomery. At an earlier date the Indian town was located in the forks of the Alabama River.

52Woodward, 1939:89.

53Panton Leslie Papers, John C. Pace Library. Letter from Olivier to Carondelet 14 June 1793.

54Caughey, 1959:220.

55Corbitt, 1943, Vol. 15:102 ETHS.

56Caughey, 1959:198-9.

57Ibid.:211.

58Ibid.:215-8.

59Ibid.:241-2. Alexander, for some reason, had revoked the trading license of Lane in 1787, and Lane became incensed and threatened Alexander. Lane fled to Pensacola under the protection of the Spanish authorities.

60Grant, 1980, Vol. 1:169.

61Brannon, 1935:35.

62Reese, 1974:263.

63Dobson, 1989:229; Filby, 1981, Vol. 2:1413.

64Davies, 1972, Vol. 18:124.

65Carlton Papers, M 341:278, PAC.

66DeVille, 1986:21, 23.

67McLean, 1900:153.

68South Carolina Gazette, 7 March 1743.

69Brannon, 1935:34-5.

70Hawkins, 1982:41-4.

71Salley, A.S. Jr., 1973:702-3.

72Kappler, 1904:28-9.

73ASA, Pickett Papers, Folder 25, Section 15.

74Panton Leslie Papers, 1937, Vol. 15:173-4; Panton Leslie Papers, Microfilm Reel 12, Samford University.

75Panton Leslie Papers, Microfilm Reel 8, Samford University; Caughey, 1959:359.

76GHQ, 1940, Vol. 24:82.

77Stiggins, ca. 1831.

78Cockran, 1967:315.

79Caughey, 1959:356.

80Kinniard, 1946, Vol. 4:170.

81Panton Leslie Papers, Microfilm Reel 13, Samford University.

82Owen, 1951, Vol. 13:35.

83Tarvin, 1893:1-20

84Andrews, 1974:67.

85Tarvin, 1893:1-20.

86Driesbach, 1874.

87Tarvin, 1893:1-20.

88ASP, 1832, Public Lands, Vol. 4:860.

89Alabama Trace books, Vol. 1, Clarke County, Alabama Secretary of State.

90Brannon, 1925, Vol. 2.26, 33.

91Andrews, 1974:70.

92AHQ, 1951, Vol. 13:151; Brannon, 1974, Vol. 1:86-7.

93Cashin, 1990:77.

94Cotterill, 1963:41.

95Cashin, 1989:114; Woodward, 1939:59.

96Mathews, 1977:115.

97Davies, 1972, Vol. 5:35.

98Mereness, 1916:496. Taitt kept a detailed journal of his trip to the Creek Country.

99Candler, 1908, Vol. 12:334, 363.

100Davies, 1972, Vol. 15:33.

101Ibid., Vol. 12:109.

102Ibid., Vol. 15:96.

103Carlton Papers, M 344, PAC; Davies, 1972, Vol. 17:178-83.

[104]Davies, 1972, Vol. 15:188.

[105]Searcy, 1985:165; Davies, 1972, Vol. 18:118.

[106]Carlton Papers, M 347:1656, PAC.

[107]Ibid., M348:2022, PAC.

[108]Ibid.:2080, PAC.

[109]Coker, 1982:86.

[110]Alden, 1966:297; Coldham, 1980, Vol. 1:473.

[111]PRO, Georgia Loyalist Claims, Bundle 37; Coldham, 1980, Vol. 1:473; PRO, A 013/37:182-92.

[112]ASP, 1832, Public Lands, Vol. 4:382.

[113]Ibid., Vol. 1:594-5.

[114]Fabel, 1988:33-4, 71.

[115]Woodward, 1939:59.

[116]Brannon, 1974, Vol. 1:86, *Baldwin County Historical Society Quarterly*.

[117]Brannon, 1925. Bulletin, Alabama State Department of Archives and History, Vol. 2, no. 1.

[118]Driesbach, 1874.

[119]Davies, 1972, Vol. 15:33.

[120]Ibid.:188.

[121]Caughey, 1959:212.

[122]PRO, War Office 65/3-65/8; Raikes, 1910:11.

[123]PRO, War Office 10/117-10/133.

[124]Candler, 1908, Vol. 2:229-30.

[125]Driesbach, 1922, Vol. 4:112.

[126]Nuzum, 1978, Vol. 5:80.

[127]Faust, 1973:18.

[128]Driesbach, 1874.

[129]ASA, Pickett Papers, Folder 26.

[130]Driesbach, 1884, Vol. 2:2-3.

[131]Lyttelton Papers, Reel 2, WLCL.

[132]GSA, Creek Indians, RG 37-8.

[133]Carlton Papers, M344:677, PAC.

[134]Charles was probably in prison for refusing to take the Spanish oath of allegiance.

[135]Corbett, 1939, Vol. 11:67, ETHS.

[136]Caughey, 1959: 158.

[137]Ibid.:167.

[138]Grant, 1980, Vol. 1:22.

[139]Hays, 1939:133, Barnard letters.

[140]McBee, 1953:288.

[141]Kinniard, 1946, Vol. 4:145.

[142]Parton, 1863:173.

[143]Major Caleb Swan escorted Alexander McGillivray back to the Creek Nation from New York after he signed the 1790 treaty with President Washington. He remained about six months in the Creek Country.

[144]Schoolcraft, 1851-57, Vol. 5:254.

[145]Wright, 1967:166.

[146]ASP, 1832, Public Lands, Vol. 4:305.

[147]Kinniard, 1946, Vol. 4:168.

[148]Woodward, 1939:88.

[149]Cashin, 1989:14; Thompson, 1991:872.

[150]Hawkins, 1916:170.

[151]Grant, 1980, Vol. 1:187-8.

[152]Ibid.:256.

[153]Pickett, 1851:421.

[154]ASA, Pickett Papers, folder 26.

[155]Brannon, 1935:34.

[156]NA, Letters Received by the Secretary of War, Indian Affairs, M271, Roll 1.

[157]Wyman, 1957, Vol. 19:280.

[158]Tatum, 1898, Vol. 2:159.

[159]DeVille, 1986, Vol. 4:860.

[160]U.S. Census, 1830, Clarke County, Alabama.

[161]Corbitt, 1943, Vol. 15:101, ETHS.

[162]Fabel, 1988:236.

[163]Tarvin, 1893.

[164]Pickett, 1851:418-9.

[165]SCHGM, 1912, Vol. 13:217.

[166]Woodward, 1939:113-4.

[167]Grant, 1980, Vol. 1:23-4.

[168]Pickett, 1851:418-9.

[169]Claiborne, 1964:330.

[170]Claiborne, 1976:37.

[171]Halbert and Ball, 1962:264.

[172]Ramsey, 1967:516.

[173]Caughey, 1959:62.

[174]NA, Letters Received by Office of Indian Affairs, M234, Roll 220.

[175]Corbitt, 1937, Vol. 21:285 GHQ.

[176]Caughey, 1959:168.

[177]Ibid.:159.

[178]Corbitt, 1939, Vol. 11:71 ETHS.

[179]Caughey, 1959:172.

[180]Ibid.:231.

[181]Ibid.:237.

[182]Moser, 1991, Vol. 3:359-60.

[183]Arrowpoints, 1924, Vol. 8, no. 3:48-9.

[184]NA, Letters Received by Secretary of War, Indian Affairs, M271, Roll 1.

[185]NA, Letters Received by Secretary of War, M221, Roll 63.

[186]NA, Jackson Papers, Roll 62.

[187]NA, Jackson Papers, Roll 75.

[188]Halbert and Ball, 1962:164.

[189]*National Genealogical Society Quarterly*, 1995, Vol. 83:137, Macon County Orphans Book 1:33-4.

[190]Milfort, 1959:vii.

[191]Kinniard, 1946, Vol. 4:154-266.

[192]Lyon, 1938, Vol. 4:72-6.

[193]Milfort, 1959.

[194]Caughey, 1959:219.

[195]Swanton, 1970:429.

[196]Milfort, 1959:10, 18-24, 202.

[197]Schoolcraft, 1851-7, Vol. 5:255.

[198]Caughey, 1959:286.

[199]Grant, 1980, Vol. 1:138.

[200]Caughey, 1959:338.

[201]Kinniard, 1946, Vol. 4:170-1.

[202]Corbitt, 1937, Vol. 21:287 GHQ.

[203]Kinniard, 1946, Vol. 4:377.

[204]Caughey, 1959:361.

[205]Kinniard, 1946, Vol. 4:262.

[206]Panton Leslie Papers, Microfilm Reel 12, Samford University. Letter from Mucklesaopay, the Singer, to William Panton, 28 September 1799; Panton Leslie Papers, 1937, Vol. 15:173-4;

Hawkins, 1938:34.

[207]Driesbach, 1874; Tarvin, 1893.

[208]Meek, 1975:264.

[209]Pickett, 1851:75.

[210]Echeverria, 1952, Vol. 9, No. 4.

[211]Claiborne, 1976:120-1; Austill, ND, Canoe Battle, SPR 55, ASA.

[212]Pickett, 1851:565.

[213]Sutton, 1991:104.

Chapter 9

[1]Bolton, 1969:266-8.

[2]Allison, 1971:91-2.

[3]Milfort, 1959:19-22.

[4]Schoolcraft, 1851-7, Vol. 5:280-1.

[5]Davies, 1972, Vol. 14:194.

[6]Clark, 1981, Vol. 3:388.

[7]Emistisego, the principal Upper Creek Chief.

[8]Carlton Papers, M344. PAC.

[9]Ibid., M341, M357.

[10]Davies, 1972, Vol. 15:33.

[11]Ibid., Vol. 17:180.

[12]Milfort, 1959:86.

[13]Davies, 1972, Vol. 17:233.

[14]Ibid., Vol. 20:150.

[15]Bolton, 1969:270.

[16]Caughey, 1959:62.

[17]Carlton Papers, M350, PAC.

[18]Cashin, 1989:166.

[19]Caughey, 1959:66.

[20]Ibid.:67.

[21]Coker, 1986:363.

[22]An early partner in Panton Leslie Company.

[23]Caughey, 1959:82.

[24]Ibid.:85-6.

[25]Corbitt, 1941, Vol. 25:93, 167 GHQ.

[26]Caughey, 1959:86.

[27]Hays, 1939a, Vol. 1:129-32.

[28]This was his cousin Daniel McGillivray, the son of Farquhar McGillivray.

[29]Corbitt, 1938, Vol. 10:155 ETHS.

[30]Brannon, 1982:36; Caughey, 1959:320.

[31]*Georgia State Gazette or Independent Register*, 4 November 1786.

[32]Corbitt, 1939, Vol. 11:70 ETHS

[33]*Georgia Gazette*, 2 October 1788.

[34]White, 1981:8.

[35]Corbitt, 1943, Vol. 15:96 ETHS.

[36]Caughey, 1959:195.

[37]Ibid.:197-8.

[38]Ibid.:153.

[39]Ibid.:186.

[40]Ibid.:189.

[41]Corbitt, 1943, Vol. 15:94 ETHS.

[42]Caughey, 1959:197.

[43]Ibid.:191.

[44]Caughey, 1959:242; White, 1975, Vol. 28:265-274.

[45]Corbitt, 1943, Vol. 15:96 ETHS.

[46]Caughey, 1959:196.

[47]Ibid.:212.

[48]Ibid.:214.

[49]Ibid.:212.

[50]Ibid.:241.

[51]Corbitt, 1937, Vol. 21:282 GHQ.

[52]Humphreys, 1917, Vol. 1:5.

[53]Ibid.:6, 8.

[54]Ibid.:9-12.

[55]Caughey, 1959:256-8.

[56]Willett, 1831:101; Pickett Manuscript, 1930, Vol. 1:129.

[57]Willett, 1831:103-4.

[58]Willett, 1831:110; Pickett Manuscript, 1930, Vol. 1:129.

[59]McGillivray on his way to New York for negotiations had paused a few days in Philadelphia where he met Rush.

[60]Rush, 1970:188-9.

[61]ASP, 1834, Indian Affairs, Vol. 1:127; Pickett Manuscript, 1930, Vol. 1:137.

[62]Knox Papers, Vol. 27:163-5. Massachusetts Historical Society.

[63]Caughey, 1959:281, 283.

[64]Caughey, 1959:248; IPL, FMC, No. 3429, Doc. 1, Sect. 16, Will of Lachlan McGillivray.

[65]Caughey, 1959:288-91.

[66]Ibid.:281.

[67]Schoolcraft, 1851-7, Vol. 5:254.

[68]Ibid.:252.

[69]Pope, 1979:46-52.

[70]Ibid.:65.

[71]Ibid.

[72]Grant, 1982, Vol. 1:39-40.

[73]ASP, 1834, Indian Affairs, Vol. 1:250.

[74]Corbitt, 1937, Vol. 21:287-8 GHQ.

[75]ASP, 1834, Indian Affairs, Vol. 1:304.

[76]Caughey, 1959:324.

[77]Henri, 1986:75.

[78]The successor to Panton Leslie Company.

[79]Panton Leslie Papers, John C. Pace Library.

[80]Corbitt, 1938, Vol. 22:189 GHQ.

[81]Caughey, 1959:327-32, 351.

[82]Ibid.:326-7.

[83]Ibid.:128.

[84]Corbitt, 1938, Vol. 10:153 GHQ.

[85]Hays, 1939a, Vol. 1:193.

[86]Brown, 1988:11, 25.

[87]Pope, 1979:48.

[88]Corbitt, 1938, Vol. 22:189 GHQ.

[89]Caughey, 1959:322.

[90]Ibid.:348.

[91]Ibid.:353.

[92]Ibid.:354.

[93]Alexander Jr. was called Aleck.

[94]Panton Leslie Papers, John C. Pace Library. Letter from Panton to Lachlan McGillivray 10 April 1794. This same letter appears in Caughey, 1959:362-3, but in an altered and abbreviated form. Also for the complete text, see Pickett Manuscript in AHQ, 1930, Vol. 1.

[95]Pickett Manuscript, 1930, Vol. 1:146-7.

[96]Whitaker, 1928, Vol. 5:307.

[97]Pickett Manuscript, 1930, Vol. 1:146.

[98]Pickett, 1851:431-2.

[99]Pickett Papers, Folder 25:57, ASA.

[100]Caughey, 1959:350.

[101]Greenslade, 1935, Vol. 14:114-5.

[102]Brady, 1947:379-80.

[103]Goldwater, 1972:215-21.

[104]Milling, 1951:165-7.

[105]Cabanis, 1828:25-6; Nevil, 1991.

[106]Nevil, 1991.

[107]Hunter, 1786:367.

[108]Vogel, 1970:211.

[109]McGrew, 1985:330-1.

[110]Ibid.:332-3.

[111]Perez, 1994:169.

[112]Goldwater, 1972:216.

[113]Ibid.:219.

[114]McGrew, 1985:330.

[115]Griggs, 1982:33.

[116]Hunter, 1786:300-1, 329.

[117]Ibid.:381.

[118]Bossu, 1962:13-4.

[119]Roland, 19 December 1995.

[120]Merck Manual, 1992:1337-8.

[121]Rothe and Kerdel, 1991, Vol. 30:173-8.

[122]Dr. Halsey was formerly head of the Department of Neurology, University of Alabama Medical School at Birmingham.

[123]Halsey, 1991.

[124]McGrew, 1985:333-4.

[125]Hunter, 1786:335-9.

[126]Ibid.:340-3.

[127]Goldwater, 1972:225.

[128]Ibid.:151-61.

[129]Milling, 1951:179-81.

[130]Holmes, 1964, Vol. 1:333.

[131]Henner, 1829:516.

[132]Brady, 1947:421.

[133]Caughey, 1959:353, 363.

[134]Dunglison, 1846:566.

[135]Caughey, 1959:320. Letter Olivier to Carondelet, 10 April 1792.

[136]Kinniard, 1946, Vol. 4:28-9.

[137]Caughey, 1959:295.

[138]Ibid.:307.

[139]Ibid.:313.

[140]Ibid.:50, 312.

[141]Ibid.:317.

[142]Pickett Papers, Folder 25, Section 7, ASA.

[143]Caughey, 1959:359.

[144]Corbitt, 1959, Vol. 31:67 ETHS.

[145]Panton Leslie Papers, Samford University, Microfilm Reel 8.

[146]ASP 1832, Indian Affairs, Vol. 4:447.

[147]Roland, 1996.

Chapter 10

[1]Greenslade, 1935, Vol. 14:115-6.

[2]Kinniard, 1946, Vol. 4:160-2.

[3]Ibid.:172.

[4]Ibid.:145.

[5]Panton Leslie Papers, Samford University, Microfilm Reel 8.

[6]Kinniard, 1946, Vol. 4:221-2.

[7]Caughey, 1959:356.

[8]Ibid.:216; Pickett Manuscript, 1930, Vol. 1:137.

[9]*Georgia Gazette*, 18 April 1793.

[10]*Gentlemens Magazine*, August 1793, Vol. 63, Part 2:767.

[11]A History of the Discovery and Settlement of America. By William Robertson, New York, 1937, a revised 1777 edition that was published in Scotland. Book 4 (Chapter) spends some 74 pages on the American Indian and their many qualities and social organization. Supposedly it was in Chapter 4 that Alexander would have made his contribution.

[12]*Scots Magazine*, August 1793.

[13]Sutton, 1991:19.

[14]Sutton, 1976:9.

[15]ASP, 1832, Public Lands, Vol. 4:189.

[16]Sutton Papers; Sutton, 1991:19.

[17]Sutton, 1991:38.

[18]Greenslade, 1935, Vol. 14:116.

[19]Sutton Papers; Sutton, 1991:30.

[20]Panton Leslie Papers, Samford University, Microfilm Reel 8.

[21]Watson, 1981, Vol. 60:42-6; Sutton, 1976:48; Campbell, 1892:102.

[22]Emma Hulse Taylor.

[23]Herron, James, *Pensacola Evening News*, December 1908.

[24]Rea, 1976, Vol. 54:512-3; *Georgia Gazette*, 3 October 1765.

[25]Campbell, 1975:75-7; Rea, 1976, Vol. 54:513-29.

[26]DeVille, 1986:15, 22-3.

[27]Sutton, 1991:87.

[28]Sutton Papers. A copy was retained in the Company papers by James Innerarity at Mobile. Sutton 1991:30; another copy is also with the Pensacola Historical Society.

[29]ASP, 1834, Indian Affairs, Vol. 1:447.

[30]Panton Leslie Papers, John C. Pace Library; Pickett Manuscript, 1930, Vol. 1:147-8.

[31]Foreman, Carolyn Thomas, 1929, Vol. 7:106-20.

[32]Henri, 1986:75.

[33]Surely Hawkins is in error. She would have been born in 1794-95 to be 14 or 15 years old in 1809. Her father died in 1793. Pope writes in 1791 that Alexander had 2 children, making the youngest daughter born in 1792. She then would be 17 in 1809.

[34]He arrived in 1796.

[35]Hawkins is in error. Their uncle was Sam Moniac who was married to the sister of Alexander's wife. Menawa was a Creek Chief of Oakfuskee Town. He welcomed Tecumseh to the Creek Nation and became the war chief for the Creeks during the Creek War of 1813-14.

[36]Grant, 1980, Vol. 2:556.

[37]Daniel McGillivray Papers, ASA.

[38]Panton Leslie Papers, Samford University, Microfilm Reel 13. Letter from Daniel McGillivray to Panton 28 September 1799 and 27 July 1800.

[39]David Moniac file, SPR 357. ASA.

[40]Hawkins, 1982:40.

[41]Grant 1980, Vol. 2:567, 605.

[42]Ibid.:556.

[43]Halbert and Ball, 1969:165.

[44]Woodward, 1959:77, 89.

[45]Mereness, 1916; 536.

[46]Hawes, 1950, Vol. 34:208; *Savannah Gazette*, 2 November 1774.

[47]Corbitt, 1938, Vol. 10:149 ETHS. Letter from O'Neill to Galvez, 11 October 1786.

[48]Grant, 1980, Vol. 1:39-40.

[49]Caughey, 1959:82.

[50]Ibid.:148.

[51]Ibid.:191.

[52]Kappler, 1904:28.

[53]Tuskegee up until the 1814 Treaty of Fort Jackson was located in the forks of the Alabama River adjacent to old Fort Toulouse.

[54]Grant, 1980, Vol. 1:298.

[55]NA, 1832, T 275, Roll 1, Creek Census.

[56]White, 1981:66-7.

[57]Alabama Historical Reporter 1880, Vol. 1:2-3; Halbert and Ball, 1969:91-3.

[58]Grant, 1980, Vol. 2:643.

[59]Ibid.:652.

[60]Brannon, 1925, Vol. 2:63-4.

[61]Southerland, 1989:94-5.

[62]Tatum, 1898, Vol. 2:164.

[63]U.S. Congress, HR document 200, 1828:3-15.

[64]NA, Office of Indian Affairs, M234, Roll 219.

[65]Ibid., Roll 220.

[66] Papers of Governor C. C. Clay, Creek War of 1836, N.D. 421, ASA.

[67] Faust, 1973:21.

[68] Tarvin, 1893, folder 40:1-20, The Muscogees or Creek Indians, Thomas Gilcrease Institute.

[69] Thompson, 1991:873, 921.

[70] Caughey, 1959:137; Kinniard, 1946, Vol. 3:189.

[71] Pickett, 1851:416-7.

[72] Halbert and Ball, 1969:29.

[73] Corbitt, 1943, Vol. 15:100 ETHS

[74] Caughey, 1959:212-3.

[75] Ibid.:212.

[76] Hawkins, 1916:79.

[77] Corbitt, 1943, Vol. 15:97 ETHS.

[78] Caughey, 1959:351.

[79] Ibid.:231.

[80] Daniel McGillivray Papers, ASA.

[81] NA, Jackson Papers, Reel 75; Deed Book I:23-4, Washington County. Copy courtesy of Dr. Woodrow W. Wallace.

[82] Grant, 1980, Vol. 2:556.

[83] Pickett Manuscript, 1930, Vol. 1:147.

[84] Horan, 1972:128; Woodward, 1939:65.

[85] NA, Office of Indian Affairs, M234, Roll 220.

[86] Niles Register, 3 December 1825.

[87] Horan, 1972:128.

[88] Woodward, 1939:113.

[89] McMillian, n.d., Alabama Early Settlers, 1816 Census.

[90] Orphans Court Records, 1817-1822, LGM 82, Reel 12, Montgomery County, ASA.

[91] Woodward, 1939:37, 65.

[92] Owen, 1951, Vol. 13:27-8; Pickett, 1851:425.

[93] Kappler, 1904, Vol. 2:107.

[94] Woodward, 1939:111-2; Meek, 1975:274.

[95] McDowell, 1958:103; Hays, 1939a, Vol. 1:321; Kinniard, 1946, Vol. 4:168.

[96] Mereness, 1916: 495.

[97] Kappler, 1904, Vol. 2:29.

[98] Kinniard, 1946, Vol. 4:172; Panton Leslie Papers, John C. Pace Library.

[99] Corbitt, 1943, Vol. 15:101 ETHS.

[100] Hemperley, 1969, Vol. 31:212, 216.

[101] NA, Creek Census, 1832, M275, Roll 1.

[102] Woodward, 1939:112-3; Alabama Historical Reporter, 1880, Vol. 1:3.

[103] Davies, 1972, Vol. 3:228.

[104] Halbert and Ball, 1969:158-9; Pickett, 1851:541.

[105] Coker, 1986:350, 359.

[106] Orphans Court Records, 1817-1822, LGM 82, Reel 12, Montgomery County, ASA.

[107] Caughey, 1959:283.

[108] Ibid.:323.

[109] Cashin, 1992:308.

[110] Panton Leslie Papers, John C. Pace Library, Letter from Panton to Lachlan McGillivray, 10 April 1794.

[111] Greenslade, 1935, Vol. 14:116.

[112] Barclay, 1925;12-7.

[113] Panton Leslie Papers, Microfilm reel 11, Samford University; Greenslade, 1935, Vol. 14:117-9.

[114] Panton Leslie Papers, Microfilm reel 11, Samford University.

[115] Ibid.

[116] Coker, 1986:235; Greenslade, 1935, Vol. 14:125-7.

[117] Greenslade, 1935, Vol. 14:118-9.

[118] Wells' Memoirs, 1818, Microfilm reel 77-37, item 4:vii-viii, National Library of Medicine.

[119] Ibid.:ix.

[120] Ibid.:x-xii; Munk, 1878, Vol. 2:279-83.

[121] Ibid.:xiii.

[122] Ibid.:xv, xvii.

[123] Ibid.:xvii-xviii.

[124] Ibid.:xx-xxi.

[125] Ibid.:xiii, xv.

[126]Ibid.:xxvi-xxvii.

[127]Ibid.:xxviii.

[128]Ibid.:xxx-xxxi.

[129]Ibid.:xl.

[130]Ibid.:xxxii-xli.

[131]Behrman, 1976, Vol. 60:183.

[132]Barlett, 1849:25; Pleadwell, 1934, Vol. 4:136.

[133]Block, 1983, Vol. 83:253.

[134]Keil, 1936, Vol. 4:803.

[135]Wells, 1973, Vol. 64:215; Keil, 1936, Vol. 4:803.

[136]Kiel, 1936, Vol. 4:789-90.

[137]Montluzin, 1988:108.

[138]Dictionary of Scientific Biography, 1976, Vol. 14:253-4.

[139]The name is more commonly spelled Inverarity in Scotland—HRRS Report, 22 August 1991. The will of John Innerarity Sr. does not mention Alexander Jr. PRO/PROB6/1805/Vol. 181/Folio 69.

[140]Greenslade, 1935, Vol. 14:115-9.

[141]Claiborne, 1964:132.

[142]Panton Leslie Papers, Samford University, Microfilm Reel 14; Corbitt, 1941, Vol. 25:167 GHQ.

[143]HRRS Report 15 December 1990.

[144]Caterham Baptisms and Burials, 1759-1812, Microfilm 2+, Surrey Record Office; Lambeth Burial Records, 1802-5, p. 85/MRY/349, Greater London Record Office.

[145]St. Thomas Hospital Archives, H.I./ST, 1796-1802:B4/3, Greater London Record Office.

[146]Indexes to the Archdeaconry Court of Surrey, the Commissary and Peculiar Courts of Canterbury, Greater London Record Office.

[147]Chipstead Baptismal, Marriage and Burial Records, 1656-1812, Surrey Record Office, Dagger Report 8 March 1996.

[148]Dagger Report, 11 April 1996.

[149]Panton Leslie Papers, Samford University, Microfilm Reel 8.

Bibliography

Primary Sources

Alabama Department of Archives and History, Montgomery.

H. S. Halbert Papers. Historical Ingatherings from Pickett's Manuscript.

Daniel McGillivray Papers.

Orphans Court Records, Montgomery County 1817-1822. Microfilm LGM 82, Reel 12.

Albert J. Pickett Papers, Folder 25 and 26.

U.S. Census, Clarke County, Alabama, 1830.

The Canoe Battle. N.D. By Jeremiah Austill, Typescript SPR 55.

David Moniac File, SPR 55.

Papers of Governor C. C. Clay, Creek War of 1836.

Alabama Secretary of State, Lands Division, Montgomery.

Transcribed British, French and Spanish Records Relative to Land Claims in Alabama. Copy in Alabama Department of Archives and History

Alabama State Trace Books, Pickens County; Clarke County.

Land Survey of Pickens County, 1834.

Bureau of Land Management, Springfield, Virginia.

U.S. Land Tract Books, Mississippi (N&E) Vol. C-6 and 7.

Charleston County Courthouse, Charleston.

Probate Office Willbooks 1-9, 1670-1840.

William L. Clements Library, Ann Arbor

Gage Papers, American Series.

Lyttelton Papers, Microfilm Reels 1-3.

Georgia Department of Archives and History, Atlanta.

Court of Ordinary Wills, Chatham County, Georgia, Vol. A, 1775-1801; Vol. B., 1777-1787.

Conveyance Books C1, C2, 1750-1766; S, 1766-1769; U, 1768-1769; V, 1769-1771; XI, 1771-1774; CC-1, CC-2, 1774-1784.

Journals of the Board of Commissioners for Indian Affairs in the Province of South Carolina, 1753-1765. Book of Indian Affairs, 1753-1755.

Creek Indian Letters, talks and Treaties, 1705-1839. Part 1. Typescript. Edited by Mrs. J. E. Hays, 1939a.

Unpublished Letters of Timothy Barnard, 1784-1820. Typescript. Edited by Louise F.

Hays, 1939b.

Creek Indians, RG 37-8.

Georgia Loyalist Claims, Microfilm DR 40, Box 46.

Confiscated Property, Record Group 1-6.

Creek Indian Letter Books, Record Group 37-8.

Thomas Gilcrease Institute of American History and Art, Tulsa.

Grant Foreman Papers, Panton Leslie Papers, Folder 4.

The Muscogees or Creek Indians from 1519 to 1893; also an Account of the McGillivray Family and others in Alabama, 1893. By Marion E. Tarvin. Creek File, Folder 40.

McGillivray Family, N.D. Creek File, Folder 40. By Thomas F. Meagher, Jr.

Greater London Record Office, London.

Lambeth Burial Records, 1802-5.

St. Thomas Hospital Archives, H.I./ST, 1796-1802.

Index to the Archdeaconry Court of Surrey.

Index to the Commissary and Peculiar Courts of Canterbury.

Inverness Public Library Archives, Inverness.

Fraser-Mackintosh Collection, #3429.

Copies of Various Deeds, Document #1, Section 16 (Lachlan McGillivray's and John McGillivray's Will of 1767).

Letters as to Dunmaglass Succession, Document #1, Section 18.

1855 Court of Session Cases, Inverness-shire, Vol. 772.

Burgh of Inverness Register of Deeds, Documents dating 1789-1791.

Jamaica Archives, Spanish Town.

Archives Report #12/1, 17 September 1993.

Inventory 1B/11/3/148, folio 121, 16 July 1837 (John McGillivray Estate).

Inventory 1B/11/3/128, folio 51, 12 September 1816 (Lachlan McGillivray Estate).

Baptisms 1B/11/8/14, folio 1, 10 June 1797 (Lachlan McGillivray Plantation).

Crop Reports 1B/11/4/45, folio 157, 25 March 1813 (Lachlan McGillivray Plantation).

Inventory 1B/11/3/50, folio 65, 11 January 1770 (John McGillivray Estate).

Massachusetts Historical Society, Boston.

Papers of Henry Knox, Vol. 27. Minutes Taken from Gen'l. McGillivray Affecting the Creeks, August 1790.

Mobile Municipal Archives, Mobile.

Forbes Papers, Microfilm Reel 1.

Mobile Probate Court, 1937. Interesting Transcripts of the British, French and Spanish Records of the City and District of Mobile, State of Alabama, found in Probate Court in two volumes in the City of

Mobile 1715 to 1812, Vol. 1 and 2.

National Archives, Atlanta.

George Stiggins Manuscript. A Historical Narration of the Genealogy, Traditions and Downfall of the Ispacoga or Creek Tribes of Indians written by one of the Tribe, ca. 1830.

Lyman C. Draper Papers, Driesbach to Draper, July 1874.

National Archives, Washington

Letters Received by the Office of Indian Affairs 1824-81. Creek Agency 1826. M 234, Roll 219, 220, 223.

Letters Received by the Secretary of War 1801-1860. May 1814 - December 1850. M 221, Roll 63.

Letters Received by the Secretary of War Relating to Indian Affairs 1800-1824. M 271, Roll 1.

Bureau of Indian Affairs, Armstrong Roll, 1831 Choctaw Census. RG75 E 258, Roll A39.

Bureau of Indian Affairs, Removal Records, Chickasaw Muster Rolls 1837 and 1839; Chickasaw Census Records 1847, Indian Territory. RG 75, Roll A36.

1832 Census of the Creek Indians. T 275, Roll 1.

Cherokee Indian Agency in Tennessee 1801-35. Correspondence & Misc. Records 1801-2. RG 75, M 208, Roll 1.

Andrew Jackson Papers, RG 75, Roll 62.

National Library of Medicine, London.

Memoir of William Charles Wells, 1818.

National Library of Scotland, Edinburgh.

Commissariat of Inverness. Testaments prior to 1800.

Fraser Macintosh Collection. McGillivray of Dunmaglass (Farr Manuscript) MS 9854.

Parochial Registers for Counties of Inverness and Moray.

Noxubee County Courthouse, Macon, Mississippi.

Superior Chancery Court, 4th Chancery District 1841-49, Book 1.

Deed Record Book A and 128.

U.S. Land Sales, Book 1.

John C. Pace Library, Pensacola.

Special Collections, Panton Leslie Papers, various correspondence.

Pickens County Courthouse, Carrolton, Alabama.

Probate Office, Book of U.S. Land Grants.

Public Archives of Canada, Ottawa.

Sir Guy Carlton Papers, February 1777 - October 1783. Microfilm M 341 - M 361.

Sir Guy Carlton Papers, Index, February 1777 - October 1783. Microfilm M 341 - M 345.

Sir Frederick Haldimand Papers. Microfilm A 612 - A 618.

Sir William Johnson Papers. RC 1222, Vol. 7.

Public Record Office, Kew.

Audit Office A 012, A 013.

Probate Records, 11/1112/303; 11/1162/286; 6/1805/Vol. 181, folio 69.

Georgia Loyalist Claims. Bundle 36, 37, Unbundled, Georgia Department of Archives and History, Microfilm Drawer 40, Box 46, 47, 49.

War Office 10/117-10/133.

War Office 65/3-65/8.

Samford University Library, Birmingham.

Special Collections. Panton Leslie Papers. Microfilm Reel 8, 11-14.

Scottish Public Record Office, Edinburgh.

McGillivray Testaments (wills).

Daviots Wadset 1751. GD 176/810.

Inventory of Miscellaneous Deeds and Papers. GD 128/23/4, item 1.

Accounting of John McGillivray's Will. GD 128/23/5.

Papers Relating to McGillivray's of Dunmaglass. GD 128/23/5; GD 128/23/6.

Court of Sessions Papers. SRO/CS 237/MC 23/37.

Chancery Court, Service of Heirs. SRO/C 28/49/folios 70-74.

Inverness Sheriff Court Commissary Records. SRO/SC 29/44/14.

South Carolina Department of Archives and History, Columbia.

Legislative Journal 1721-23.

PRO Colonial Office 5/425. Microfilm BMP D 487.

Central Manuscript Index, Miscellaneous Records and Bills of Sale 1729-1824, Vol. 4.

South Carolina Historical Society, Charleston.

Will of Patrick Brown, 15 August 1755. Manuscript File, Folder 35.

Coe Papers 11/569/2. South Carolina, Address of the Lord Commissioners for Trade and the Assemblys Answer to their Lordships Queries, 29 January 1719; Letter from James Sutherland to Lord Granville.

McGillivray Family Papers. South Carolina Court of Ordinary Journal 1764-1771. Misc. Folder 30-04.

A Sketch of the McGillivrays of Charleston and Connections. By Hugh S. McGillivray, ca. 1930. Manuscript File, Folder 30-04.

List of Grants made in South Carolina, 1674-1773. Microfilm B, PRO, Reels 45-84.

Surrey Record Office, County Hall, Kingston upon Thames.

Caterham Baptisms and Burials 1759-1812. Microfiche 2+.

Chipstead Baptismal, Marriage and Burial Records, 1656-1812. Alexander McGillivray Jr., 25 July 1802.

Newspapers

Gazette State of Georgia. 1785.

Georgia Gazette. 1764-1795.

*Georgia State Gazette or Independent Register.*1786-1787.

Gentlemen's Magazine. 1793.

Edinburgh Advertiser. 1799.

Niles Register. 1824-1825.

Pensacola Evening News. 1908.

Royal Georgia Gazette. 1781-1782.

Savannah Gazette. 1763-1775.

Scots Magazine. 1793.

South Carolina Gazette. 1732-1747.

References Cited

Alabama Digest, 1956. Indians - Insurance, covering cases from State and Federal Courts. Vol. 12. St. Paul.

Alabama Historical Reporter. 1880. Alabama Historical Society Vol. 1.

Alden, John R. 1966. *John Stuart and the Southern Colonial Frontier.* New York

Allison, John, 1897. *Dropped Stitches in Tennessee History.* Nashville. Reprint, Nashville 1971.

American State Papers, 1832-1860. Public Lands. 9 Vols. Washington, DC.

_____, 1832-1834. Indian Affairs. Vols. 1-4, Washington, DC.

Andrews, Johnnie Jr. 1987. *Fort Toulouse Colonials, A Compendium of the Colonial Families of Central Alabama, 1717-1823.* Prichard, AL.

_____, 1974. *Creole Mobile, A Compendium of the Colonial Families of the Central Gulf Coast 1702-1813.* Bienville Historical Society, Prichard, AL.

Baldwin County Historical Quarterly.

1976. James Denny Driesbach. Vol. 3.

Barclay, William, 1925. *The Schools and Schoolmasters of Banffshire.* Banff, Scotland.

Bartlett, Elisha. 1849. "Brief Sketch of the Life, Character and Writings of William Charles Wells, M.D." F.R.S. Philadelphia. An address delivered before the Louisville Medical Society, December 7, 1849.

Bartram, John. 1942. "Diary of a Journey through the Carolinas, Georgia, and Florida, from July 1, 1765 to April 10, 1766." *Transactions of the American Philosophical Society.* M.S. 33, Part 1. Philadelphia.

Bartram, William. 1928. *Travels of William Bartram.* Ed. Mark Van Doren. New York.

Beckemeyer, Frances H. Comp. 1975. *Abstracts of Georgia Colonial Conveyance Book C-1, 1750-1761.* Atlanta.

Behrman, Simon. 1976. "William Charles Wells 1757-1817, Eye Physician." *British Journal of Ophthalmology.* Vol. 60.

Bloch, Harry. 1983. "William Charles Wells, M.D.,F.R.S., 1757-1817, An American Physician-Scientist America Almost Forgot." *New York State Journal of Medicine.* Vol. 83.

Blue, M.P. 1937. *A Brief History of Montgomery.* Birmingham. Manuscript in the Alabama Department of Archives and History.

Bolton, Herbert E. 1925. "Spanish Resistance to the Carolina Traders in Western Georgia." *Georgia Historical Quarterly.* Vol. 9..

_____. 1932. *New Spain and the Anglo-American West.* Reprint, New York 1969.

Bond, Lula Sams. 1963. "The Sams Family of South Carolina. *South Carolina Historical Magazine.* Vol. 64.

Bossu, Jean Bernard. 1962. *Travels in the Interior of North America 1751-1762.* Trans. and edited by Seymour Feiler. Norman.

Boyer, Carl 3rd. 1979. *Ship Passenger Lists, The South (1538-1825).* Newhall, CA.

Braden, Guy B. 1958. "The Colberts and the Chickasaw Nation." *Tennessee Historical Quarterly.* Vol. 17.

Brady, George S. 1947. *Materials Handbook.* New York.

Brannon, Peter A. 1925. "Montgomery and Its Interesting Vicinity." *Bulletin of the Alabama State Department of Archives and History.* Vols. 2 and 3.

_____. 1935. *The Southern Indian Trade.* Montgomery.

_____. 1957. "The Coosa River Crossing of British Refugees, 1781." *Alabama Historical Quarterly,* Vol. 19.

_____, 1974. "Through the Years, John Tate, the British Colonel." *Baldwin County Historical Society Quarterly.* Vol. 1.

Braund, Kathryn E. H. 1986. *Mutual Convenience - Mutual Dependence: the Creeks, Augusta, and the Deerskin Trade 1733-1783.* Ph.D. Dissertation, Florida State University.

Britt, Albert S. Jr. and Lilla M. Hawes,

eds. 1973. "The Mackenzie Papers," *The Georgia Historical Quarterly.* Vol. 57.

Brown, Colonel Joseph. 1853. *Indian Battles, Murders, Sieges and Forays in the Southwest, the Narrative of Colonel Joseph Brown.* Reprint, Franklin TN 1988.

Brown, Virginia Pounds, ed. 1989. *Creek Indian History.* Birmingham.

Bull, Kinloch Jr. 1991. *The Oligarchs in Colonial and Revolutionary Charleston, Lieutenant Governor William Bull 2nd and his Family.* Columbia.

Cabanis, P.J.G. 1828. *An Essay on the Certainty of Medicine.* Trans. by R. LaRoche, M.D. Philadelphia.

Calhoon, Robert M. 1973. *The Loyalists in Revolutionary America 1760-1781.* New York.

Campbell, Richard L. 1892. *Historical Sketches of Colonial Florida.* Reprint, Gainesville 1975.

Candler, Allen D. 1904-1916. *The Colonial Records of the State of Georgia.* 26 vols. Atlanta.

_____. 1908. *The Revolutionary Records of the State of Georgia.* 3 vols. Atlanta.

_____. 1937. *The Colonial Records of the State of Georgia.* Vols. 29-39. Typescript. Georgia State Department of Archives and History.

Carter, Clarence E. 1952. *The Territorial Papers of the United States. Territory of Alabama 1817-1819.* Vol. 18. Washington DC.

Caruso, John A. 1963. *The Southern*

Frontier. Indianapolis.

Cashin, Edward J. 1986. *Colonial Augusta, Key to the Indian Country*. Macon, GA.

_____. 1989. *The King's Ranger, Thomas Brown and the American Revolution on the Southern Frontier*. Athens, GA.

_____. 1992. *Lachlan McGillivray, Indian Trader*. Athens, GA.

Caughey, John W. 1932. "Willings Expedition Down the Mississippi, 1778." *Louisiana Historical Quarterly*. Vol. 15.

_____. 1959. *McGillivray of the Creeks*. Norman.

Chesnutt, Daniel R. 1988. *The Papers of Henry Laurens*. Vol. 11. Columbia.

Claiborne, J.F.H. 1880. *Mississippi as a Province, Territory and State*. Reprint, Baton Rouge, 1964.

_____. 1860. *Life and Times of General Sam Dale*. Reprint, Spartanburg, 1976.

Clan Chattan Journal. 1992. Nairnside School, Vol. 9.

_____. 1993. Peace Treaty That Brought Clan Factions Together. Vol. 9.

Clark, Murtie J. 1981. *Loyalists in the Southern Campaign of the Revolutionary War*. Vols. 1-3. Baltimore.

Coker, William S. 1982. *Anglo-Spanish Confrontation on the Gulf Coast During the American Revolution*. Pensacola.

_____. 1986. *Indian Traders of the Southeastern Spanish Borderlands*.

Panton Leslie & Co. and John Forbes & Co. 1783-1847. Gainesville.

Coldham, Peter W. 1980. American Loyalist Claims. National Genealogical Society. Vol. 1. Washington, DC..

Coleman, Kenneth. 1958. *The American Revolution in Georgia 1763-1789*. Athens, GA.

_____, ed. 1978. *Colonial Records of the State of Georgia*. Vols. 27 and 28. Athens, GA.

Corbin, Harriet T. P. 1967. *A History and Genealogy of Chief William McIntosh Jr. and his known Descendants*. Long Beach, CA.

Corbitt, D.C. 1930-1962. Papers from the Spanish Archives Relating to Tennessee and the Old Southwest. *East Tennessee Historical Society Publications*. Vol. 2-34.

_____. 1937-1941. "Papers Relating to the Georgia-Florida Frontier 1784-1800." *Georgia Historical Quarterly*. Vol. 21-25.

_____. 1938. "James Colbert and the Spanish Claims to the East Bank of the Mississippi. *Mississippi Valley Historical Review*. Vol. 24.

Corkran, David H. 1967. *The Creek Frontier*. Norman.

Cotterill, R.S. 1963. *The Southern Indians*. Norman.

Coulter, E. Merton. 1949. *A List of Early Settlers in Georgia*. Athens, GA.

_____. 1973. *Georgia, a Short History*. Chapel Hill.

Crane, Verner W. 1929. *The Southern Frontier 1670-1732*. Ann Arbor.

Dalrymple, Margaret F. 1978. *The Merchant of Manchac, the Letterbooks of John Fitzpatrick, 1768-1790*. Baton Rouge.

Daniel, Marjorie. 1935. "John Joachim Zubley—Georgia Pamphleteer of the Revolution." *Georgia Historical Quarterly*. Vol. 19.

Daughters of the American Revolution. 1962. *Abstracts of Colonial Wills of the State of Georgia, 1733-1777*. Atlanta.

Davies, K. G., ed. 1972. *Documents of the American Revolution 1770-1783*. Vols. 1-20. Shannon, Ireland.

Davis, Robert S. Jr. 1979. *The Wilkes County Papers 1773-1833*. Easley, SC.

DeVille, Winston. 1986. *English Land Grants in West Florida, A Register for the States of Alabama, Mississippi, and parts of Florida and Louisiana 1766-1776*. Ville Platte, LA.

DeVorsey, Louis Jr. 1982. *The Georgia-South Carolina Boundary*. Athens, GA.

Dictionary of Scientific Biography. 1976. "William Charles Wells," Vol. 14. New York.

Dobson, David. 1984. *Directory of Scottish Settlers in North America 1625-1825*. Vol. 1. Baltimore.

_____. 1989. *The Original Scots Colonists of Early America 1612-1783*. Baltimore.

_____. 1990. "Highland Emigration to Colonial America 1640-1785." *Journal of Highland Family History Society*. Vol. 9.

Driesbach, C. H. 1922. "William Weatherford." *Arrowpoints,* Vol 4:No. 6.

Driesbach, James D. 1884. "Weatherford the Red Eagle." *Alabama Historical Reporter*. Vols. 2, 3, 5.

Dumont, William H. 1971. *Colonial Georgia Genealogical Data 1748-1783*. National Genealogical Society. Arlington, VA.

Dunglison, Robley. 1846. *Dictionary of Medical Science*. Philadelphia.

Easterby, J. H. ed. 1951-1962. *The Journal of the Commons House of Assembly. Colonial Records of South Carolina*. 9 vols. Columbia.

Echeverria, Durand. 1952. "General Collot's Plan for a Reconnaissance of the Ohio and Mississippi Valleys." *William and Mary Quarterly*. Vol. 9.

Fabel, Robin F.A. 1988. *The Economy of British West Florida 1763-1783*. Tuscaloosa.

Faust, Richard H. 1973. *William Weatherford: A Case Study of a Man Dominated by Historical Events in the Creek Nation, 1780-1824*. M.S. Thesis, University of Southern Mississippi.

Filby, P. William. 1981. *Passenger and Immigration Lists*. Index 2. Detroit.

Fisher, Doris B. 1990. *Mary Musgrove, Creek Englishwoman*. Ph.D. Dissertation, Emory University.

Foreman, Carolyn Thomas. 1929. "Alexander McGillivray, Emperor of the Creeks." *Chronicles of Oklahoma*, Vol. 7.

Foreman, Grant. 1966. *Indian Re-

moval. Norman.

Fortson, Ben W. Jr. 1973. *English Crown Grants in the Parishes of St. David, St. Patrick, St. Thomas, and St. Mary in Georgia, 1755-1775.* Atlanta.

French, B.F. 1875. *Historical Collection of Louisiana and Florida,* 2d.series. New York

Gaelic Society of Inverness, 1894. *Transactions of the Gaelic Society of Inverness.* Vol. 20.

Galloway, Patricia Kay, ed. 1984. *Mississippi Provinical Archives, French Dominion, 1729-1748.* Vol. 4. Baton Rouge.

Georgia Historical Quarterly. 1940. "List of Indians to be Invited to Pensacola." Vol. 24.

_____. 1941. "Letter from Panton to Gayoso, 24 July 1800." Vol. 25.

Gerstner, Herbert B. 1977. "Clinical Toxicology of Mercury." *Journal of Toxicology and Environmental Health.* Vol. 2.

Goldwater, Leonard J. 1972. *Mercury, a History of Quicksilver.* Baltimore.

Granger, Mary, ed. 1947. *Savannah River Plantations.* Savannah.

Grant, C. L. 1980. *Letters, Journals and Writings of Benjamin Hawkins.* 2 Vols. Savannah.

Grant, Neil. 1987. *Scottish Clans and Tartans.* New York.

Green, E.R.R. 1960. "Queensborough Township: Scotch-Irish Emigration and the Expansion of Georgia, 1763-1776." *William and Mary Quarterly.* 3d series Vol. 17.

Greenslade, Marie T. 1930. "John Innerarity 1783-1854." *Florida Historical Quarterly.* Vol. 9.

_____. 1935. "William Panton." *Florida Historical Quarterly.* Vol. 14.

Gregorie, Anne King, ed. 1950. "Records of the Court of Chancery of South Carolina 1671-1779." *American Legal Records.* Vol. 6. The American Historical Association. Washington, DC.

Griggs, Barbara. 1982. *Green Pharmacy, A History of Herbal Medicine.* New York.

Hahn, Marilyn D. 1983. *Old St. Stephens Land Office Records and American State Papers, Public Lands, 1768-1888.* Vol. 1. Birmingham.

Halbert, H.S. and Ball, T.H. 1969. *The Creek War of 1813 and 1814.* Edited by Frank L. Owsley Jr. Tuscaloosa.

Hall, James II.B. 1904. "The History of the Cumberland Church in Alabama Prior to 1826." *Historical Contributions* No. 1, Alabama Synod, Cumberland Presbyterian Church. Montgomery.

Halsey, James H. Jr., M.D. Letter to the author, 30 August 1991. Author's collection.

Hamer, Friedrich P. 1982. *Indian Traders, Land and Power, Comparative Study of George Galphin on the Southern Frontier and Three Northern Traders.* MS. Thesis, University of South Carolina.

Hamer, Phillip M. ed. 1968-1972. *The Papers of Henry Laurens.* Vols. 1-3. Columbia.

Hamilton, Peter J. 1952. *Colonial Mobile*. Mobile.

Hawes, Lilla M. 1950. "Georgia Council Minutes, 1774." *Georgia Historical Quarterly*. Vol. 34.

_____. 1952. *The Proceedings and Minutes of the Governor and Council of Georgia, October 4, 1774 through November 7, 1775, and September 6, 1779 through September 20, 1780*. Collections of the Georgia Historical Society Vol. 10. Savannah.

_____. 1952. "Proceedings of the President and Assistants in Council of Georgia, 1749-1751." *Georgia Historical Quarterly*. Vol. 36.

Hawkins, Benjamin. 1848. *A Sketch of the Creek Country in the Years 1798 and 1799*. Reprint, Spartanburg 1982.

_____. 1916. *Letters of Benjamin Hawkins 1796-1806*. Collections of the Georgia Historical Society. Vol. 9. Savannah.

Haynes, Robert V. 1976. *The Natchez District and the American Revolution*. Jackson, MS.

Headlam, Cecil. 1908-1930. *Calendar of State Papers, Colonial Series, America and the West Indies*. Vols. 17-29. London. Reprint, Vadiz 1964.

Hemperley, Marion R. 1969. "Benjamin Hawkins Trip Through Alabama, 1796." *Alabama Historical Quarterly*. Vol. 31.

_____. 1974. *English Crown Grants in St. Paul Parish in Georgia 1755-1775*. Atlanta.

Henner, John, M.D. 1829. *Principles of Military Surgery*. London.

Henri, Florette. 1986. *The Southern Indians and Benjamin Hawkins 1796-1816*. Norman.

Herron, James S., M.D. 1908. Article in the *Pensacola Evening News*. Christmas Edition.

Highland Family History Society Journal. 1991. Vol. 9. Inverness, Scotland.

Highland Roots Research Service. Various reports by Graeme Mackenzie. Author's collection.

Hitchcock, Ethan Allen. 1930. *A Traveler in Indian Territory, The Journal of Ethan Allen Hitchcock*. Edited by Grant Foreman. Reprint Norman 1996.

Hoffman, Ronald. 1985. *An Uncivil War, the Southern Backcountry during the American Revolution*. Charlottesville, VA.

Holcomb, Brent H. 1980. *South Carolina Marriages 1688-1799*. Baltimore.

Holmes, Jack D.L. 1964. "Medical Practice in the Lower Mississippi Valley During the Spanish Period, 1769-1803." *Alabama Journal of Medical Science*. Vol. 1.

Horan, James D. 1972. *The McKenney-Hall Portrait Gallery of American Indians*. New York.

Howard, Milo B. Jr. and Robert R. Rea, Trans. 1965. *The Memoire Justificatif*. University, AL.

Humphreys, Frank L. 1917. *Life and Times of David Humphreys, Soldier-Statesman-Poet*. Vols. 1-2. New

York.

Hunter, John, M.D. 1786. *A treatise on the Venereal Disease.* London.

_____. 1788. *Observations on the diseases of the Army in Jamaica; and on the best means of preserving the health of Europeans in that climate.* London.

Innerarity, John. 1930. "The Creek Nation, Debtor to John Forbes & Company, Successor to Panton Leslie Company. A Journal of John Innerarity, 1812." *Florida Historical Quarterly.* Vol. 9.

James, Marquis. 1938. *The Life of Andrew Jackson.* Camden, NJ.

Jerney, Clare. 1906. *Inscriptions on the Tablets and Gravestones in St. Michaels Church and Churchyard.* Columbia.

Jones, Charles C. Jr. 1874. *The Siege of Savannah in 1779.* Albany, NY.

_____. N.p., n.d. *Memorial History of Augusta, Georgia.* Reprint, Spartanburg, 1980.

_____. 1887. *The Life and Services of the Honorable Maj. Gen. Samuel Elbert of Georgia.* Georgia Historical Society.

Jones, Jack M. 1988. *South Carolina Immigrants 1760 to 1770.* Danielsville, GA.

Journal of the Commissioners for Trade and Plantations from January 1764 to December 1767. 1930. Vol. 12. London.

Kappler, Charles J. 1904. *Indian Affairs, Laws and Treaties,* Vol. 2. Washington, DC.

Keel, Harry M. 1936. "Dr. William Charles Wells and His Contribution to the Study of Rheumatic Fever." *Bulletin of the Institute of the History of Medicine.* Johns Hopkins University. Vol. 4.

Kingsbury, Susan M. 1906. *The Records of the Virginia Company of London.* 4 vols. Washington, DC.

Kinniard, Lawrence. 1931. "The Significance of William Augustus Bowles Seizure of Panton's Apalachee Store in 1792." *Florida Historical Quarterly.* Vol. 9.

_____. 1946. "Spain in the Mississippi Valley 1765-81." *Annual Report of the American Historical Association for 1945.* Vol. 2, 3, and 4. Washington, DC.

LaFar, Mabel F. 1963. *Abstracts of Wills, Chatham County, Georgia 1773-1817.* National Genealogical Society. Washington, DC.

Langley, Clara A. 1983-4. *South Carolina Deed Abstracts 1719-1772.* Vols 1 and 4. Easley, SC.

Lanning, John T. 1935. *The Spanish Missions of Georgia.* Chapel Hill.

Lipscomb, Terry W. ed. 1974. *The Journal of the Commons House of Assembly, November 14, 1751 - October 7, 1752.* Colonial Records of South Carolina. Columbia.

Lyon, E. Wilson. 1938. "Milfort's Plan for a Franco-Creek Alliance and the Retrocession of Louisiana." *The Journal of Southern History.* Vol. 4.

MacDowell, Alexander R. 1936. "The Settlement of the Scotch Highlanders at Darian." *Georgia Historical Quarterly.* Vol. 20.

Macgillivray, Robert and George. 1973. *A History of the Clan Macgillivray*. Ontario.

MacLean, John P. 1900. *An Historical Account of the Settlements of Scotch Highlanders in America*. Cleveland.

"Macon County Orphans Book 1." 1995. *National Genealogical Society Quarterly*. Vol. 83.

Mathews, Hazel C. 1977. *British West Florida and Illinois Country*. Nova Scotia.

McBee, May W. 1953. *The Natchez Court Records, 1767-1805. Abstracts of Early Records*. Ann Arbor.

McCrary, Royce C. Jr. and John F. McGowan. 1972. *History of St. Andrews Society of Savannah, Georgia*. Savannah.

McDowell, William L. Jr. ed. 1955. *Journals of the Commissioners of the Indian Trade 1710-1718. Colonial Records of South Carolina*. Columbia.

_____. 1958a. ed. *Documents Relating to Indian Affairs, May 21, 1750 - August 7, 1754. Colonial Records of South Carolina*, Columbia.

_____. 1958b, ed. *Documents Relating to Indian Affairs 1754-1765. Colonial Records of South Carolina*. Columbia.

McGillivray, Robert. 1982. "The Officers of the Mackintosh Regiment 1746." *Clan Chattan Journal*. Vol. 7.

_____. 1985. "Dunmaglass." *Clan Chattan Journal*. Vol. 8.

McGrew, Roderick E. 1985. *Encyclopedia of Medical History*. New York.

McIan, R. R. 1845. *The Clans of Scottish Highlands*. Reprint, New York, 1986.

McMillian, William. n.d. *Alabama Early Settlers, 1816 Census - Alabama Counties (Mississippi Territory)*. Washington County, AL.

McPherson, Robert G. ed. 1962. *The Journal of the Earl of Egmont 1732-1738*. Athens, GA.

Meek, A. B. 1857. *Romantic Passages in Southwestern History*. Reprint, Spartanburg, 1975.

Merck Manual of Diagnosis and Therapy. 1992. 16th Edition. Rahway, NJ. Edited by Robert Berkow, M.D.

Mereness, Newton D. 1916. *Travels in the American Colonies*. New York. Journal of David Taitt's Travels from Pensacola, West Florida, to and through the Country of the Upper and Lower Creeks.

Meserves, John B. 1932. "The MacIntoshes." *Chronicles of Oklahoma*. Vol. 10.

Milfort, LeClerc, 1959. *Memoirs or a Quick Glance at My Various Travels and My Sojourn in the Creek Nation*. Kennesaw, GA. Edited by Ben C. McCary.

Milling, Chapman J. ed. 1951. *Colonial South Carolina, Two Contemporary Descriptions*. Columbia. Dr. Milligan-Johnston's Addition to his Pamphlet on the use of the Jesuit Bark and use of Mercury to treat syphilis.

Missionary Herald. 1829. American

Board of Commissioners for Foreign Missions. Vol. 25. Boston.

Mitchell, Robert G. 1984. "The Losses and Compensation of Georgia Loyalists." *Georgia Historical Quarterly*. Vol. 68.

Moncreiffe, Sir Iain. 1982. *The Highland Clans*. New York.

Montluzin, Emily L. 1988. *The Anti-Jacobins, 1798-1800*. New York.

Mooney, James. 1972. *Myths of the Cherokees*. Nashville.

Moore, Alexander. 1988. *Nairnes Muskhogan Journal, the 1708 Expedition to the Mississippi River*. Jackson, MS.

Moore, Caroline T. 1964. *Abstracts of the Wills of the State of South Carolina 1740-1760*. Columbia.

Moore, W.O. Jr. 1973. "The Largest Exporters of Deerskins from Charleston, 1735-1775." *The South Carolina Historical Magazine*. Vol. 74.

Moser, Harold D., ed. 1991-1994. *The Papers of Andrew Jackson*. Vols. 3 and 4. Knoxville.

_____. 1969. *Abstracts of the Wills of the State of South Carolina 1760-1784*. Columbia.

Munk, William. 1878. *Roll of the Royal College of Physicians, 1701-1800*. Vol. 2. London College, London.

Neeley, Mary A. 1974. "Lachlan McGillivray: A Scot on the Alabama Frontier." *Alabama Historical Quarterly*. Vol. 36.

Nevil, Elizabeth. 1991. Letter dated 5 April 1991. Report on Syphilis. Reynolds History Library. Birmingham, Author's collection.

Norwood, Martha F. 1975. *A History of the White House Tract, Richmond County, Georgia*. Atlanta.

Nuzum, Kay. 1978. "Red Eagle's Grave Site is Deeded to Baldwin County." *Baldwin County Historical Quarterly*. Vol. 5.

O'Donnell, J. H. 1965. "Alexander McGillivray: Training for Leadership, 1777-1783." *Georgia Historical Quarterly*. Vol. 49.

O'Donnell, James H. 3d, 1973. *Southern Indians in the American Revolution*. Knoxville.

Olsberg, R. Nicholas, ed. 1974. *Journal of the Commons House of Assembly, 23 April 1750 - 31 August 1751. The Colonial Records of South Carolina*. Columbia.

Owen, Marie B. 1930. "Albert James Pickett, Alabama's First Historian." *Alabama Historical Quarterly*. Vol. 1.

Owen, Thomas M. 1951. "Indian Chiefs." *Alabama Historical Quarterly*. Vol. 13.

Panton Leslie Papers. 1937. *Florida Historical Quarterly*. Vol. 15.

Parton, James. 1863. *Life of Andrew Jackson*. 3 vols. New York.

Perez, Francisco G. 1994. "Calendar of the Introduction of Infectious Diseases in the New World after 1492." *Actas del 33 Congreso Internacional de Historia de la Medicina, Grenada - Sevilla: 1-6 Septiembre 1992*. Sevilla.

Pickett, Albert J. 1851. *History of Alabama and Incidentally of Georgia and Mississippi.* Reprint, Birmingham, 1962.

_____. 1930. "Pickett Manuscript." *Alabama Historical Quarterly.* Vol. 1.

Pleadwell, Frank Lester. 1934. "That Remarkable Philospher and Physician, Wells of Charleston." *Annals of Medical History.* Vol. 4.

Pope, John. 1792. *A Tour Through the Southern and Western Territories of the United States of North America.* Reprint, Gainesville 1979.

Pringle, Robert. 1972. *The Letterbook of Robert Pringle.* 2 vols. Columbia. Edited by Walter B. Edgar.

Raikes, G. A. 1910. *Roll of Officers of the 84th Yorks and Lancer Regiment.* London.

Ramsey, J.G.M. 1853. *The Annals of Tennessee.* Reprint, Knoxville 1967.

Rea, Robert R. 1976. "Brigadier Frederick Haldimand - The Florida Years." *Florida Historical Quarterly.* Vol. 54.

_____. 1979. *The Minutes, Journals, and Acts of the General Assembly of British West Florida.* Universty, AL.

_____. 1990. *Major Robert Farmer of Mobile.* Tuscaloosa.

Reese, Trevor R. 1974. *Our First Visit in America. Early Reports from the Colony of Georgia 1732-1740.* Savannah.

Robertson, William. 1837. *A History of the Discovery and Settlement of America.* New York.

Rogers, George C., Jr., ed. 1974-1980. *The Papers of Henry Laurens.* Vols.

4-8. Columbia.

Roland, Charles G. M.D. 1996. Letter from Dr. Buchanan to Dr. Roland 19 December 1995, enclosed in letter from Dr. Roland to the author 4 January 1996. Author's collection.

Romans, Bernard. 1775. *A concise Natural History of East and West Florida.* Reprint, Gainesville 1962.

Ross, Hunter, ed. 1953. "A Journey over the Natchez Trace in 1792: A Document from the Archives of Spain." *Journal of Mississippi History.* Vol. 15.

Rothe, Marti J., M.D. and Francisco A. Kerdel, M.D. 1991. "Reiter Syndrome." *International Journal of Dermatology.* Vol. 30.

Rowland, Dunbar. 1929, 1932. *Mississippi Provincial Archives, French Dominion.* Vols. 2 and 3. Jackson, MS.

_____. 1911. *Mississippi Provincial Archives, English Dominion.* Nashville.

Rowland, Mrs. Dunbar. 1925. "Peter Chester, Third Governor of the Province of West Florida under British Dominion, 1770-1781." *Publications of the Mississippi Historical Society.* Vol. 5.

Rush, Benjamin. 1970. *The Autobiography of Benjamin Rush, His Travels through Life Together with his Commonplace Book for 1789-1813.* Westport, CT. Edited by George W. Corner.

Sabine, Lorenzo. 1979. *Biographical Sketches of Loyalists of the American Revolution.* 2 vols. Baltimore.

Sainsbury, W. Noel. 1896. *Calendar of State Papers, Colonial Series, America and West Indies*. Vol. 10. London.

Salley, A. S. Jr. 1919. *Minutes of the Vestry of St. Helena's Parish, South Carolina, 1726-1812*. Columbia.

_____. 1973. *Warrants for Lands in South Carolina 1672-1711*. Columbia.

Salley, A. S. 1945. *Journal of the Commons House of Assembly of South Carolina 1724-1725; 1725-1726*. Columbia.

Schoolcraft, Henry R. 1851-7. *Historical and Statistical Information Respecting the History, Conditions, and Prospects of the Indian Tribes of the United States*. 6 vols. Philadelphia. The Caleb Swan Report 1790.

Scots Magazine. 1793. Death Obituary of Alexander McGillivray, Creek Chief. August issue. Edinburgh.

Scottish Ancestral Research Society Report. 1985.B/53257. Edinburgh. Author's collection.

Scottish History Society. 1915. *Letterbook of Baille John Stewart of Inverness*. Edinburgh. Edited by William McKay.

Searcy, Martha C. 1985. *The Georgia-Florida Contest in the American Revolution 1776-1778*. University, AL.

Shaftbury Papers. 1897. Collections of the South Carolina Historical Society. Vol. 5. Charleston.

Smith, Paul H., ed. 1992. *Letters of Delegates to Congress 1774-1789*. Vol. 19. Washington, DC.

Smith, Warren B. 1970. *White Servitude in Colonial South Carolina*. Columbia.

South Carolina Historical and Genealogical Magazine. 1912. "Christenings" 13; 1915. "Death Notices 16; 1916. "Death Notices" 17; 1917. "Marriage and Death Notices" 18; 1920. "Marriage and Death Notices" 21; 1922. "St. Helena Parish Register" 23; 1926. "Marriage and Death Notices" 27; 1931. "Letters from John Stewart to William Dunlop" 32. South Carolina Historical Society. Charleston.

South Carolina Historical Magazine. 1964, 1973. "Charles Town Merchants in the Negro Trade." Vols. 65 and 74. South Carolina Historical Society. Charleston.

Southerland, Henry D. Jr. 1989. *The Federal Road Through Georgia, the Creek Nation, and Alabama, 1806-1836*. Tuscaloosa.

Spalding, Phinizy. 1989. *Oglethorpe in Perspective*. Tuscaloosa.

Starr, J. Barton. 1976. *Tories, Dons, and Rebels, the American Revolution in British West Florida*. Gainesville.

Stephens, William. 1742. *A Journal of the Proceedings in Georgia*. Vols. 1 and 2. Reprint, New York 1966.

Stokes, Thomas L. 1982. *The Savannah*. Athens, GA.

Sutton, Leora M. ca. 1965. *Women in Pensacola 1765-1965*. Pensacola.

_____. ca. 1976. *Archaeological Investigations, Blocks 3 and 11, Old City Plat of Pensacola*. Pensacola.

_____. 1991. *Success Beyond Expectations, Panton Leslie Co. of Pensacola*. Pensacola.

_____. Personal Collection, Archivist for Santa Rosa County, Pensacola.

Swanton, John R. "Social Organization and Social Usages of the Indians of the Creek Confederacy." *BAE Annual Report*. Vol. 42. Reprint, New York 1970.

Tanner, Helen H. 1989. *Zespedes in East Florida 1784-1790*. Jacksonville, FL.

Tatum, Major Howell. 1898. "Topographical Notes and Observations on the Alabama River, August 1814." *Alabama Historical Society Transactions 1897-98*. Vol. 2.

Thompson, Lynn H. 1991. *William Weatherford, His Country and His People*. Bay Minette, AL.

Thompson, Theodora J. 1963. *Journals of the House of Representatives 1783-1784. The State Records of South Carolina*. Columbia.

U.S. Army Corps of Engineers. 1972. Mobile District. Tombigbee River Navigation Chart No. 18.

U.S. Congress. House. An Act for the Relief of Samuel Menac. 15 March 1828. 20th Cong. 1st sess. 1828. H. Doc. 200. Washington, DC.

U.S. Congress. House. Documents in Relation to Hostilities of Creek Indians. 6 June 1836. 24th Cong. 1st sess. 1836. H. Doc. 276. Washington, DC.

U.S. Congress. Senate. Correspondence on the Subject of the Emigration of Indians Between 30 November 1831 and 27 December 1833. Doc. 512, Vols. 2, 4 and 5. Washington, DC.

U.S. Geological Survey. Maps NH 16-2 Andalusia, 1953 revised 1965; NH 16-1 Hattiesburg 1953 revised 1970.

Vidrine, Jacqueline O. 1985. *Love's Legacy. The Mobile Marriages Recorded in French, Transcribed with Annotated Abstracts in English 1724-1786*. Lafayette, LA.

Ward, Christopher. 1952. *The War of the Revolution*. Vol. 2. New York.

Warren, Mary B. 1968. *Marriages and Deaths, 1763 to 1830*. Danielsville, GA.

_____. 1977. *South Carolina Jury Lists 1718 through 1783*. Danielsville, GA.

Waselkov, Gregory A. 1982. *Colonization and Conquest: The 1980 Archaeological Excavations at Fort Toulouse and Fort Jackson, Alabama*. Auburn University Archaelogical Monograph No. 4. Auburn University at Montgomery.

Washington County, AL. *Deed Book 1*. Copy courtesy of Dr. Woodrow W. Wallace.

Watson, Thomas D. 1981. "A Lost Landmark Revisited: The Panton House of Pensacola." *Florida Historical Quarterly*. Vol. 60.

Wells, Kentwood D. 1973. "William Charles Wells and the Races of Man." *ISIS*. Vol. 64.

Wells, William Charles. 1818. *Two Essays: Upon Single Vision with Two Eyes; The Other on Dew; With a Memoir of his Life*. National Library of Medicine, Microfilm reel 77-37, item 4. London.

Whitaker, Arthur P. 1928. "Alexander McGillivray 1783-1789." *North Carolina Historical Review*. Vol. 5.

White, David H. 1975. "The Indian Policy of Juan Vicente Folch, Governor of Spanish Mobile, 1787-1792." *Alabama Review*. Vol. 28.

_____. 1981. *Vicente Folch, Governor in Spanish Florida, 1787-1811*. Washington, DC.

White, George. 1835. *Mary Musgrove and Thomas Bosomworth. Historical Collections of Georgia*. New York.

_____. 1855. *The George Galphin Claim. Historical Collections of Georgia*. New York.

Whyte, Donald. 1972-1986. *A Dictionary of Scottish Emigrants to the USA*. Vols. 1 and 2. Baltimore.

Willett, William M. 1831. *A Narrative of the Military Actions of Colonel Marinus Willett, taken Chiefly from his own Manuscript*. New York.

Williams, Samuel Cole, ed. 1928. *Early Travels in the Tennessee Country*. Johnson City, TN. Reprint, New York 1972.

_____, ed. 1930. *Adairs History of the American Indians*. Reprint, New York n.d.

Winston, E. T. 1927. *Father Stuart and the Monroe Mission*. Meridian, MS.

Woodward, Thomas S. 1859. *Woodward's Reminiscences*. Reprint, Birmingham, 1939.

Wright, J. Leitch Jr. 1967. *William Augustus Bowles: Director General of the Creek Nation*. Athens, GA.

Wyman, Justus. 1957. "Fort Claiborne." *Alabama Historical Quarterly*. Vol. 19.

Zubley, John Joachim. 1989. *Journal of John Joachim Zubley*. Edited by Lilla Mills Hawes. Savannah.

Index

AMOS J. WRIGHT (1926–2003) served in the U.S. Navy and graduated from Auburn University with a degree in industrial management. He retired from Redstone Arsenal (U.S. Army Missile Command) in Huntsville, Alabama. A long-time avocational archaeologist, he was a member of the Alabama Historical Society (winning the Award of Merit and the Distinguished Service Award), the Alabama Archaeological Society (winning the Outstanding Member Award, and holding the offices of President, Chairman of the Archives Committee, and a member of the Board of Directors), and the Alabama DeSoto Commission (1985–1990). He published articles in numerous journals, including the *Journal of Alabama Arhaeology*, and the *Tennessee Archaeologist*. *The McGillivray and McIntosh Traders* (2000) was his first book. In 2003, he also published *Historic Indian Towns in Alabama, 1540-1838* (University of Alabama Press). He and his wife, Carolyn Shores Wright, had two sons.